I0813308

GAMBLE
IN THE
CORAL SEA

GAMBLE IN THE CORAL SEA

JAPAN'S OFFENSIVE, THE CARRIER BATTLE, AND THE ROAD TO MIDWAY

MICHAŁ A. PIEGZIK

Naval Institute Press
Annapolis, Maryland

Naval Institute Press
291 Wood Road
Annapolis, MD 21402

ISBN: 978-1-68247-996-4 (hardcover)
ISBN: 978-1-68247-997-1 (eBook)

Library of Congress Cataloging-in-Publication Data is available.

♾ Print editions meet the requirements of ANSI/NISO z39.48-1992 (Permanence of Paper).
Printed in the United States of America.

33 32 31 30 29 28 27 26 25 9 8 7 6 5 4 3 2 1
First printing

All maps created by the author unless otherwise noted.

Contents

Abbreviations

†	killed in action
#	seriously wounded in action
NDL	National Diet Library (Japan)
ABDA	American-British-Dutch-Australian
ANZAC	Australian and New Zealand Army Corps
CAP	Combat Air Patrol
CINCPAC	Commander in Chief, Pacific Fleet
COMINCH	Commander in Chief, United States Fleet
HYPO	Station HYPO, Hawaii
IFF	Identification Friend or Foe
SNLF	Special Naval Lading Force
TBS	talk between ships
USAAF	United States Army Air Force
USS	United States Ship
BB	battleship
CA	heavy cruiser
CL	light cruiser
CV	aircraft
DD	destroyer
VB	bomber squadron
VF	fighter squadron
VS	scouting squadron
VT	torpedo squadron
F4F	Grumman F4F Wildcat
PBY	Consolidated PBY Catalina
SBD	Douglas SBD Dauntless
TBD	Douglas TBD Devastator

(B)	*buntaichō* (division / group leader)
(C)	*chūtaichō* (flight leader)
(F)	flagship
(H)	*hikōtaichō* (carrier / striking group leader)
(S)	*shōtaichō* (section leader)

Capt.	captain
Cdr.	commander
Lt. Cdr.	lieutenant commander
Ens.	ensign
Lt.	lieutenant
Sub. Lt.	sub-lieutenant

AM1c	aviation mechanic second class
AM2c	aviation mechanic second class
AM3c	aviation mechanic third class
PO1c	petty officer first class
PO2c	petty officer second class
PO3c	petty officer third class
Sea1c	seaman first class
Sea2c	seaman second class
Sea3c	seaman third class
WO	warrant officer

Japanese Units

Sentai = Squadron

e.g., 5th Sentai = 5th Squadron

Kōkū Sentai = Air Flotilla or Carrier Squadron

e.g., 25th Kōkū Sentai = 25th Air Flotilla, 5th Carrier Squadron

Suirai Sentai = Torpedo Squadron

e.g., 6th Suirai Sentai = 6th Torpedo Squadron, also known as "DestroyerSquadron" in West

Kū = Kaigun Kōkūtai = Navy Air Group

e.g., Tainan Kū = Tainan Air Group

Illustrations

Maps

Photos

Figures

INTRODUCTION

Summer 2024 marked fifteen years of my immersion in Pacific War research. My teenage interest in this conflict, which involved galloping through many books, probably with an excited look on my face, quickly evolved into something more profound—a drive to contribute to global scholarship. Despite having read many works, however, I was always disappointed by one-sided narratives, which were primarily written by the victors. This disenchantment resonated even more strongly in my Polish mind, because my home country was scarred by World War II and had been condemned to Soviet domination for forty-five years. For some time in Poland, talking about history could be perilous, and the academic studies about the war were subjugated to historical politics steered from Moscow. The collapse of the Iron Curtain opened up a broad spectrum of options in Poland, including reading a massive influx of Western books. As for the Pacific War, Polish researchers en masse were finally able to get acquainted with the groundbreaking works of American or British historiography. Despite the undeniable introduction of freedom of speech, the liberalization of society wasn't followed by the diversification of research in many fields. Many years later, in 2013, when I had my first book—which is about the Guadalcanal campaign—published in Poland, I witnessed the same problem in my field. The American perspective overmatched the Pacific War research, and the sparse Japanese memoirs could not make up for this knowledge gap in the historiography.

After critically reflecting on my first publication, I made a decision that dramatically changed my life. I started learning Japanese to become a better historian and author. It was a challenging task during my intense legal studies. Luckily, however, I crossed paths with Professor Leonard Górnicki, my longtime academic adviser, who encouraged me to pursue my research career in law and history by applying my passion for the Japanese language. I published my monograph on the Battle of the Coral Sea in 2016, and at that stage I had basic experience in reading Japanese books and primary sources in their original versions. Nonetheless, it was the first attempt to cover, at least to some extent, the Japanese views of this landmark carrier clash. The book was well received and garnered several positive scholarly reviews.

In response to this demonstration of my achievements and skills, the Japanese Ministry of Education, Culture, Sports, Science and Technology (MEXT) sponsored my PhD exchange program during the 2016–2017 academic year. Once I had conducted my initial research in Tokyo, I quickly realized that my academic career, particularly completing my PhD thesis on Japanese private law, depended on a more extended stay in Japan. Between 2020 and 2022 I received another MEXT scholarship, which resulted in obtaining my doctoral degree. While studying legal matters, I mastered language skills and acquired additional documents that were needed for the second edition of my Pacific War books. The Battle of the Coral Sea remained my central interest due to the battle's impact on the collapse of the Japanese strategy for resolving the war within the first year of the conflict.

Once I had drafted a comprehensive plan for the second edition of the monograph, which was designed as extensive research on the Japanese perspective on the first carrier clash, I discussed my ideas with Steve Catalano from the Naval Institute Press. It's hard to overestimate his support in convincing the editorial team that the book should be released quickly, by one of the most respected U.S. publishers dealing with naval topics, to enrich the scholarship on the Battle of the Coral Sea.

I launched this project with a strong awareness of the existing works representing the world-class level of American research. Notably, I started my journey fifteen years ago with superb John B. Lundstrom monographs. They were one of my main motivations for investigating the primary sources and testimonies. In recent years, Robert C. Stern has produced an even more detailed account, which is still, in 2024, the most important study of the American archival documents. However, Lundstrom and Stern didn't function in a vacuum. To a certain extent they profited from the earlier works of Samuel E. Morison, Robert Bates, Bernard Millot, Edwin P. Hoyt, Hedley P. Willmott, and others.

Before examining the archival documents produced by both sides on the Battle of the Coral Sea, I thoroughly investigated the Japanese secondary sources. Undeniably, there are two fundamental monographs on the battle. The first is volume 49 of the official history of the so-called Greater East Asian War (Daitōa Sensō), edited by the National Institute for Defense Studies (Bōei Kenkyūsho). Most people know this series of 102 volumes under the name of *Senshi Sōsho*. Some Western historians have tried to use the commissioned translations of it to a limited extent. It is essential to note, though, that volume 49 was published in 1971, when the primary sources were still insufficiently cataloged in Japan. Thus, I believe the best Japanese work on this topic is Shirō Mori's monograph, released in 2004 (the second edition in 2009); the book is an expanded edition of the work from the 1970s about the navy fighter groups. Written like a novel, the book, embedded with meticulous research, refutes multiple Japanese command and mentality myths in Western historiography. Testimonies and quotations collected by Mori during his interviews with the surviving crews were a valuable part of my study. I also tried to find every Japanese publication that touched on the Battle of the Coral Sea. Readers can assess my efforts by studying the bibliography.

This book's main objective is to present my research on Japanese primary materials. The bulk of these primary sources is accessible in the National Archives of Japan, the Japan Center for Asian Historical Records (Kokuritsu Kōbunshokan: Ajia Rekishi Shiryō Sentaa), the National Institute for Defense Studies (Bōei Kenkyūsho), and the National Diet Library (Kokuritsu Kokkai Toshokan). I also identified some unique supplementary documents, mainly private diaries and notes, in the Yūshūkan Museum and in personal collections. Unfortunately, despite all my efforts, I haven't received formal permission to use these supplementary documents in my publication. To respect the decision of this museum and the wishes of the relevant families, I focus on shedding light on the Japanese perspective by analyzing public sources. In my opinion, the available materials are extensive enough to produce a comprehensive monograph. Moreover, due to the sheer number of reports made, I decided to narrow the wide scope of the research to the main actors of the battle—the Japanese Fourth Fleet, the MO Kidō Butai (the part of the Japanese carrier strike force, Kidō Butai, assigned to the Port Moresby operation, MO), and the crews of the Japanese carriers.

Regarding American sources, I primarily used the documents stored by the National Archives and Records Administration. I'm indebted to Robert Stern, who helped me acquire extra files. Because I was trying to find more English-language materials, I also made enquiries at the National Australian Archives and the Australian War Memorial. It's important to note, though, that the book doesn't aspire to exhaust the topic or substantially revise the narrative of the Allied side.

The natural consequence of my focus on the Japanese perspective is the raising of questions, at some points research questions, to reexamine the battle. First, I want to reassess the Fourth Fleet's plan to seize Port Moresby, the largest city of Papua New Guinea, in early May 1942 by engaging the MO Kidō Butai in the first South Pacific campaign. Second, I intend to find the most critical mistakes made by the Japanese, which led to the unfavorable outcome of the carrier battle and Operation MO. Finally, I will consider the lessons the Nippon Kaigun—the Imperial Japanese Navy—could have learned before the decisive clash at Midway in June 1942, including points noticed by the Japanese themselves.

The Japanese primary and secondary sources opened up for me entirely unknown aspects of the Battle of the Coral Sea. I felt genuine human emotions related to the first carrier clash, the dilemmas of commanders and pilots, and the untold stories that unveil many mysteries on the Japanese side. Despite a widespread belief the Nippon Kaigun was a highly hierarchical institution with no room for any arguments or disobedience, I found dialogues and discussions that might seem peculiar even to Western readers. Most importantly, I revised the existing narrative about the theoretical participation of the carrier *Zuikaku* in the Battle of Midway by showing the concrete numbers of the Japanese losses. Finally, I have included tables presenting all the Japanese aircrews and their contributions to the battle in order to humanize them beyond what anyone else has done.

The book consists of an introduction, eighteen chapters in four parts, a bibliography, and six appendices. Part 1 outlines Operation MO, the Japanese plan that envisaged overcoming the strategic stalemate in the New Guinea campaign and seizing Port Moresby to cut off the supply lines between the United States and Australia. It also focuses on the American intelligence efforts to intercept enemy communications to prepare the defense of Port Moresby against the landing operation, the Japanese invasion of Tulagi, the *Yorktown*'s air raid on the island, and both sides' search for the enemy carrier task force. Part 2 presents in detail the first day of the carrier battle, 7 May, which ended with the sinking of the *Shōhō* on the Japanese side and the *Neosho* and the *Sims* on the American side. It also sheds light on the other critical events of that day, including the failed 25th Kōkū Sentai (land-based combat aviation unit) strike against Rear Adm. John Crace's group and the disastrous MO Kidō Butai dusk attack. Part 3 focuses on the main carrier battle on 8 May, which resulted in the sinking of the *Lexington* and severe damage being inflicted on the *Shōkaku*. Finally, part 4 summarizes the battle and reflects on the questions asked in the introduction.

Because I had chosen to write about a topic related to the Pacific War, I needed to systematize the Japanese terminology throughout the book. For the spelling of names, places, given names, and surnames in Japanese, I use the old Hebon-Shiki rōmaji—the traditional version of the Hepburn transcription system—which allows kanji, hiragana, and katakana characters to be written in the Latin alphabet with specific diacritics characterizing Japanese pronunciation. The exceptions are geographical names and terms that appear in English in a commonly recognized changed form. For practical reasons, I adopt the method of referencing people by providing first names followed by surnames, deliberately departing from the usual rule of East Asian languages in this respect. I also include some words or fragments of statements in Japanese in the main text to promote new terms in Western scholarship.

The battle depicted in the book took place in a vast area of the Coral Sea. In many cases, the time difference between the events in the battle was three hours (between Fiji and Tokyo time). For this reason, I use dates and times in local time (UTC+11:00), with minor exceptions explicitly noted in the text. As far as possible, I adopt the metric system for describing the Japanese part of the narrative and the imperial system for that of the Allies. The distances specified in miles are nautical miles (1 NM = 1,852 meters) and the speed of vessels is universally expressed in knots.

Finally, I would like to thank my first benevolent readers, Michał Kopacz and Grzegorz Jeziorny, passionate Pacific War researchers whose detailed comments caused me to reflect on my work and my new research problems differently.

My acknowledgments could not leave out my dear wife, Ola, who persuaded me to submit a book proposal to the Naval Institute Press. Her confidence in me helps me to fulfill my biggest dreams.

PART 1

SEPTEMBER 1941–6 MAY 1942

Chapter 1

JAPANESE NAVY PLANNING FOR OPERATION MO

It is challenging to unequivocally identify the precise moment when the Nippon Kaigun, the Imperial Japanese Navy, realized that the Coral Sea might become the site for a major carrier battle that affected the entire course of the Pacific War. The clash between two carrier task forces in early May 1942, notably the first one in history, undoubtedly resulted from the Japanese plan to seize Port Moresby, an important city located on the southwestern coast of the Papuan Peninsula of New Guinea, then an Australian mandate. But why did the military planners think they needed to control this remote place? The answer is straightforward: to achieve air superiority in the South Pacific area and cut off the critical supply lines between Australia and the United States, both mortal enemies to the Japanese war plan.

In the late summer of 1941, when the outbreak of the conflict between the Empire of Japan and the Allied powers in East Asia was still pending political decisions, the Nippon Kaigun had, naturally, elaborated a detailed strategy to defeat more potent enemies. Japanese chances of success were meager, but it was thought that a comprehensive and brilliant war plan, backed up by a steadfast determination to win, contrasted with the feeble will of Western nations, could improve the odds. Surprising the U.S. Pacific Fleet in Pearl Harbor and significantly reducing its combat potential for the following months was considered essential, but this was merely an opening move. The actual game was about to start with Nampō Sakusen, the so-called Southern Operation, allowing the Japanese to secure a vast area of Southeast Asia to acquire strategic natural resources for the mobilized economy. Tokyo had openly declared that "Asia for Asians," governed and defended by the Japanese, needed to withhold the anticipated Allied, primarily American, counterattack from all possible directions. At this point, the idea of the defensive perimeter was born. If the Nippon Kaigun extended the controlled area far into the north, central, and south Pacific areas, any U.S. Navy advance would result in its tragic defeat in the *kantai kessen* (the decisive battle), and colossal losses in a series of other operations, which would ultimately convince the Americans to agree to peace on Japan's terms.

Notwithstanding some critical voices, this plan sounded rational at first glance. But it needed to be meticulously drawn up, particularly regarding the envisaged borders of the controlled area. Establishing the boundaries of the defensive perimeter in positions that were too advanced could strain the navy's supply capacities, and locating frontal bases too close to the crucial areas, like the Dutch East Indies, would threaten the Japanese war machine, which was strongly dependent on raw materials extracted from the conquered colonies. The Rengō Kantai, better known as the Combined Fleet, also considered the areas that it was pivotal to secure in the South Pacific. In September and October 1941 the high command organized several war games on the battleship *Nagato* to consider possible developments of the future conflict. Among its key participants, who are also the main actors in this book, were officers of the Fourth Fleet, alternatively named in operational jargon Nanyō Butai, the South Seas Force. Subordinated directly to the Combined Fleet since October 1940, the Fourth Fleet had its headquarters in Truk and was responsible for shielding the Caroline Islands, the Marshall Islands, and Palau, the "soft underbelly" of the home islands.

Despite the vast area that the Nanyō Butai had to protect against its enemies, it always struggled to secure enough resources to feel confident while performing its assigned tasks. Even worse, in the first half of 1941, there were rumors suggesting that it would be reduced in size to benefit other fleets.[1] This threat never materialized, yet the struggle to prevent any warships, planes, or men from being removed away from the unit would become an inherent part of its existence. One might think that the unfortunate position of the Fourth Fleet was due to the person in charge. This was not the case: the *shireichōkan* (commander in chief) since August 1941, Vice Adm. Shigeyoshi Inoue, was Adm. Isoroku Yamamoto's close associate and among his most trusted men. Together with Adm. Mitsumasa Yonai, the former prime minister and minister of the navy, they created *saha no torio* (the left-wing trio) of the Nippon Kaigun, which adamantly opposed the Tripartite Pact and wanted to avoid a clash with the United States.[2] Perverse fate made Yamamoto the leading originator of the naval war strategy, Inoue one of his admirals on the critical section of the front, and Yonai a member of the cabinet who advocated for and later approved the unconditional surrender in 1945.

Inoue was born in 1889 in Sendai, the capital city of Miyagi Prefecture, the eleventh son of a vineyard owner. His father was a former samurai retainer from the Sendai clan. However, the Meiji Restoration, which Inoue's ancestors had tried to oppose as loyal vassals of the Tokugawa family, fundamentally reorganized Japanese society, and the legendary warriors were forced to rebrand themselves, becoming, among other things, entrepreneurs, politicians, public servants, or soldiers of the reformed armed forces. As a pupil, Inoue demonstrated exceptional intellectual potential, especially in math and English, yet his destiny was to return to a military career.[3] Graduating from the renowned Naval Academy in 1911, he was ranked second in his class, behind only Manichirō Kobayashi, who died in his thirties. This meant that Inoue was always considered the elite of the elite. Like others, he progressed up the military career ladder, but the episode that left a mark on his life and command style was joining the Kaigun Hōjutsu Gakkō, the Gunnery School, in 1912, where he was taught by Lt. Isoroku Yamamoto, a *senpai* (senior) who was six years older. He was also enrolled in the Kaigun Suirai Gakkō, the Torpedo School, in the second half of the year. Both specializations were inextricably linked to cutting-edge naval warfare and had a significant effect on the development of the outstanding reputation of the Nippon Kaigun at the time. When the Great War broke out, Inoue performed patrol duties in the East China Sea for one month but didn't see any combat action. More importantly, in 1917 he graduated from the Kaigun Daigakkō, the Naval War

College. The next twenty years of his military career were filled with many national and overseas assignments, which earned him the rank of vice admiral in November 1939 while he was serving as the China Area Fleet's chief of staff.

Inoue's position in the Nippon Kaigun was significantly enhanced after September 1940, when he openly opposed the Japanese alliance with Nazi Germany and Fascist Italy and spoke against the advance to French Northern Indochina.[4] The prolonged "Chinese incident" opened his eyes to the reality of war and allowed him to understand the evolution of the battlefield. The emergence of increasingly advanced aircraft reversed his vision of what a dominant force looked like. By as early as October 1940 he had been appointed head of the Kaigun Kōkū Hombu, the Navy Aviation Bureau, and from this position he criticized the Maru 5 Plan in January 1941, which envisaged the expansion of the Nippon Kaigun by prioritizing the construction of capital warships at the expense of the aircraft carriers. Inoue dared to speak frankly, saying that the doctrine regarding the decisive battle with the U.S. Navy, understood traditionally as an artillery and torpedo duel, was outdated and that participating in the race to have more battleships and cruisers was consuming most of the limited resources. He also suggested scattering army forces among fortresses on Pacific islands instead of concentrating them on the mainland, because on the mainland they could easily starve to death as a result of the American blockade. Above all, he emphasized defending the shipping lines and paying special attention to submarine warfare.[5] His suggestions were generally proved to be correct in the following years. However, no matter how good his ideas were, they directly opposed those of the navy minister, Adm. Koshirō Oikawa. Some Japanese historians say this is why Inoue was later disregarded for appointments in the navy leadership. Notably, though, he didn't give up quickly. He spent the next six months persuading Oikawa and other central figures that the war against the United States would be suicide and that if there was any hope of having an equal fight, the Nippon Kaigun had to invest in naval aviation. His battle was lost in July 1941 when the army entered French Southern Indochina, which triggered the Allied oil embargo policy and the rapid Japanese preparations toward a military resolution rather than diplomacy. Inoue, one of the few who had read *Mein*

Kampf carefully in its original and grasped Hitler's idea of using Japan as a tool, knew that the armed conflict with the Americans would end in disaster.

There was no consensus on Inoue's next assignment, but he was eventually appointed commander in chief of the Fourth Fleet in August 1941. He was subject to Yamamoto's orders, and the close bond between the two admirals could have yielded positive results. However, the Combined Fleet's commander remained neutral regarding Inoue's struggle for peace and distanced himself from the case. According to Rear Adm. Yoshio Yamamoto, who collaborated with our leading actor in the China Area Fleet, Inoue's nickname, "Kamisori" (the Razor), might have given the impression that he was a cold person, but open-minded people could perceive his kind and peace-loving heart. It was known that geishas adored Inoue, and this connection with Japanese societal norms explained a lot about his personality.[6] But what kind of field commander was he? His intellect and accurate observations didn't automatically translate into tactical or operational successes. In the first days of the Pacific War, Inoue supervised the invasion of Guam and Wake. While the first landing operation ended with a sweeping Japanese victory in three days, the second revealed hidden weaknesses of the Nippon Kaigun. It took Inoue more than two weeks to conquer Wake, but the other great triumphs resulting from the Nampō Sakusen made the Combined Fleet forget about this incidental setback. The Fourth Fleet couldn't dwell on one faltering step either, because the next month was to bring a crucial invasion of Rabaul, in New Britain. However, a watchful eye would already have noticed that Inoue was not made for major offensive operations. The most accurate description of him has probably been provided by Masataka Chihaya, a Japanese veteran and famous historian, who said he was a "unique military politician in the Nippon Kaigun and educator."[7] Undoubtedly, he was a great personality, yet his nature didn't fulfill the definition of an inspirational chieftain leading his men to glorious victories.

Returning to the Japanese war games taking place on the *Nagato* on 10 September 1941, during the debrief the Fourth Fleet noticed that if it was supposed to seize Rabaul, the adjacent positions in Lae and Salamaua should also be secured. The opinion was that "[t]aking only Rabaul won't bring any

PHOTO 1 ■ Vice Adm. Shigeyoshi Inoue, commander in chief of the Fourth Fleet
NDL

profits," emphasizing that airfields in Lae and Salamaua were only 240 miles from Rabaul so they couldn't be ignored.[8]

At this point, the navy planners had already projected that the navy should extend its air bases to Java, New Guinea, the Solomon Islands, and the Gilbert Islands to wage a smart war of attrition. However, before the cabinet and military command approved the strategic outline, the Gunreibu, the Navy General Staff, agreed to "Gōshū no Beiei kara no ridatsu o hakaru hōshin," that is, to "prepare a plan to separate Australia from the British and the United States." The Combined Fleet was equally concerned about the future role of Australia because it could become a route through which the American forces could rebuild the Allied potential and launch a counterattack against Japan from the bases on Australia's northern coast.[9]

There are no written materials left from the war games. And no two volumes of the *Senshi Sōshō* are consistent in this matter. They agree that the navy had noticed the need to extend its control beyond Rabaul, but only volume 80 mentions establishing the frontline in Tulagi and Port Moresby, and it does so without noting any specific strategy.[10]

However, the debate between the Navy General Staff and the Combined Fleet was reflected in Secret Operation Plan No. 1 issued by Yamamoto on 5 November 1941. The document divided the initial Japanese strategy into two major phases. The first, Dai Ichi Dan, focused on conquering the Malayan Peninsula, Singapore, the Philippines, and the Dutch East Indies. The second, Dai Ni Dan, provided for seizing or annihilating the enemy forces in four distinct areas:[11]

1. the eastern part of New Guinea, New Britain, Fiji, and Samoa;
2. the Aleutian Islands and Midway;
3. the Andaman Islands; and
4. Australia.

Although the plan would be slightly modified during the first phase, the Nippon Kaigun set up explicit priorities to run from April to July 1942, when Dai Ni Dan was projected to be executed. The Fourth Fleet intended to shield its primary base in Truk from direct enemy counterattacks by seizing vital

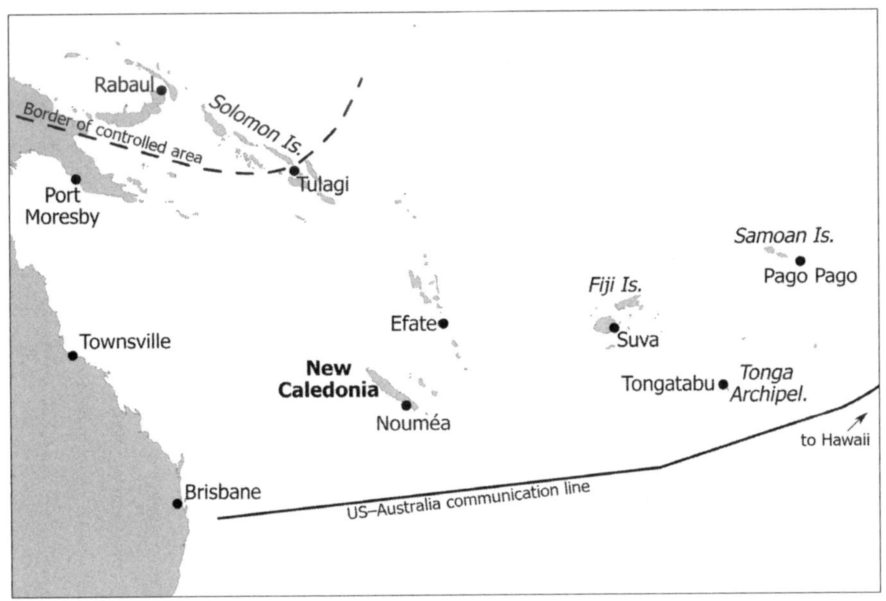

MAP 1 ■ Line of communication between the United States and Australia in the first half of 1942

positions in the area encompassing New Britain, New Guinea, and the Solomon Islands. Once the war broke out and the invasion of the Philippines was progressing according to the schedule, the Fourth Fleet successfully occupied Kavieng and Rabaul between 22 and 24 January, forcing the Australian garrison to withdraw to the interior of New Britain, where many of the soldiers were captured or secretly evacuated from in the following weeks.

The rapid developments in the South Pacific encouraged the Nippon Kaigun and the Nippon Rikugun, the Imperial Japanese Army, to initiate a discussion about the invasion of Australia. This topic became a bone of contention even within the navy and the army, arousing extreme emotions from both supporters and opponents. In the end, the large-scale operation leading to the occupation of some of the Australian cities on the northern coast was perceived as something unreal but led to another substantial agreement. In the last week of January 1942, the military command agreed that the shipping lines between Australia and the United States must be cut off, and to achieve this, the Japanese should advance to the eastern part of New Guinea and the southern part of the Solomon Islands.[12] Inoue was informed about this by the Combined Fleet on 27 January.[13]

The internal discussion was reflected in Navy General Staff Order No. 47, issued on 29 January 1942.[14] The commander of the Combined Fleet was instructed to prepare and execute the operation, which was aimed against the "British part of the New Guinea and the Solomon Islands." According to the agreement between the army and the navy, Yamamoto was to seize the most critical positions in the eastern part of New Guinea and the Solomon Islands to isolate Gōshū hondo (the Australian mainland) and achieve supremacy over the sea area adjacent to the northern coast of Australia. The navy was supposed to occupy Lae and Salamaua first in collaboration with the army as soon as possible and to seek the opportunity to take control of Tulagi independently to establish a seaplane base. Having secured Lae and Salamaua, the army and the navy would then be ordered to seize Port Moresby. The units designated to implement the operation were the main part of the Fourth Fleet and Nankai Shitai, the South Seas Detachment. Once these bases had been secured, the navy would be responsible for garrisons in Lae, Salamaua, and Tulagi, while the army would be responsible for those in Port Moresby. On 30 January the

Combined Fleet acknowledged receipt of Navy General Staff Order No. 47 and instructed the Fourth Fleet to execute it.[15]

The army and navy planners agreed that besides taking control of Tulagi and Port Moresby, the isolation of Australia must be accomplished by seizing the major enemy bases in the South Pacific, including New Caledonia, Fiji, and Samoa. They were all added to the objectives of the second phase, yet only the general concept was discussed at the time.[16]

The essential part of the Japanese plans in the South Pacific was the smooth cooperation between the Fourth Fleet and the South Seas Detachment. The latter unit was a brigade-size force that had been formed by the Nippon Rikugun on 4 October 1941. It was drawn from the 55th Division and was commanded by Maj. Gen. Tomitarō Horii. The unit initially consisted of the 144th Infantry Regiment, the 1st Battalion of the 55th Mountain Artillery Regiment, the 3rd Squadron of the 55th Cavalry Regiment, the 3rd Company of the 55th Engineer Regiment, the 2nd Company of the 55th Transportation Regiment, and other detachments. Its strength varied depending on the period, but it mostly oscillated at around five thousand men, one thousand horses, and one hundred vehicles. The South Seas Detachment was formally under the control of the Army General Staff, which had its headquarters in Tokyo, but operationally it was connected to the Fourth Fleet. The unit was designated to seize Guam and Rabaul in the first weeks of the Pacific War. After completing those two tasks by the end of January, its next objectives were Lae, Salamaua, and Port Moresby.

The first military action aimed against the Allied positions in New Guinea was given the code name "SR." The execution of SR Sakusen, Operation SR, was based on a separate agreement signed by the navy and the army on 16 February. Three days later the Kidō Butai, consisting of four carriers, raided Darwin and inflicted considerable damage. Satisfied with the results of this strike, on 20 February the Fourth Fleet issued detailed orders relating to Operation SR. However, the detection of the *Lexington* near Bougainville and the unsuccessful air attack on the enemy carrier from the land bases forced the Japanese to postpone Operation SR. On 25 February, when the threat of American intervention significantly diminished, the Fourth Fleet issued Operational Order No. 109, aiming to vigilantly return to the preparations for the invasion of Lae and Salamaua.[17] The navy remained cautious about a possible raid by the enemy carrier task force and conducted additional war games between 26 and 28 February before the screening forces set off from Truk and headed for Rabaul.[18]

On 27 February the Navy General Staff issued Operational Order No. 59, which added to the Fourth Fleet's goals regarding taking control of Nauru and Ocean for the upcoming months. This operation was given the code name "RY" and was to be executed immediately after securing Port Moresby.[19]

On 8 March the South Seas Detachment, transported and screened by part of the Fourth Fleet, successfully landed in Lae and Salamaua. At the end of the following day it was announced that Operation SR had been completed when the nearby villages had been mopped up. The construction units immediately began building new airfields to progress with the next steps of the South Pacific campaign. Apart from minor setbacks the Japanese war plan went according to the schedule at this stage. When the Dutch forces capitulated on Java on 8 March, the first phase was heading to its end. The projected beginning of the second phase and the invasions of Tulagi and Port Moresby were initially scheduled to be completed by 10 April.

Even before the Japanese advance to New Guinea materialized, the Allies were aware of it. The Americans had knowledge of the plan in early March, and Australian politicians and military interpreted the capture of Lae and Salamaua, especially after the Kidō Butai's strike on Darwin in February, as evidence of the long-term strategy of bold amphibious operations threatening the northern coast. Canberra felt Port Moresby could be lost in late March, followed by Darwin in early April. The Americans, relying on their intelligence reports, added Townsville to the list of possible targets. Thus, to slow down the enemy's potentially victorious march southward, the *Lexington* and the *Yorktown* attacked the newly established Japanese positions in Lae and Salamaua on 10 March. This unexpected raid was a severe blow to the Fourth Fleet, which lost four transport ships, while nine other warships were damaged to varying extents. The details in the Japanese reports are not consistent, but it is very likely that 130 men were killed and 245 wounded.[20]

Despite the quickly organized reprisal bombing missions against Port Moresby, the Fourth Fleet lost a significant proportion of the ships it needed for the next amphibious operation. The Navy General Staff, aware of this issue, was forced to postpone the beginning of the second phase by one month. In the meantime, the Fourth Fleet was supposed to strengthen its positions in Rabaul by establishing auxiliary bases in the vicinity. Several places were studied, and the Japanese eventually agreed to set up additional airfields in Bougainville, New Ireland, and the other end of New Britain. Notably, in Buka and Kieta, both in Bougainville, provisional airstrips had already been built by the Australians, but they needed to be secured. Shortland Island also seemed to be a perfect spot for a new seaplane base because of its favorable location. The Japanese assessment was that it would be easier to seize Tulagi once they set foot in those locations.[21]

The other consequence of the American raid on Lae and Salamaua was calling into question the effectiveness of the screening force and air support that came from Rabaul, because the enemy lost only one aircraft on 10 March. Horii started to doubt whether the Fourth Fleet's cruisers and destroyers would manage to protect his men on the long route to Port Moresby. Horii conveyed his feelings in the cable sent to the Army General Staff on 20 March: "Based on experience gained in Operation SR, I believe it was challenging for our land-based aircraft to cover the landing spots and the convoy at the same time against the enemy surface task force built around the carriers." He continued, saying, "By the time of the next operation, I hope the high command will jointly consider strengthening the land-based air force and engaging aircraft carriers. I think that the carrier *Shōhō*, already belonging to the Fourth Fleet, should be enough." He openly suggested this solution, yet it was the Combined Fleet that allocated additional carriers independently.[22]

The light carrier *Shōhō*, converted from the submarine tender *Tsurugizaki* and commissioned on 30 November 1941, was the Japanese answer to increasing the combat potential of the Nippon Kaigun on the eve of the Pacific War. She was designed to have an air group made up of thirty aircraft in two groups—fighter and torpedo bombers. She had close to this number only once, in January 1942. She was initially assigned to the 4th Kōkū Sentai—the 4th Carrier Squadron—but did not see combat action in the first weeks of the conflict. The carrier was mostly used to ferry aircraft between mainland Japan and the bases in the Pacific. On 1 February the Navy General Staff assigned the *Shōhō* to the Fourth Fleet. She departed from Yokosuka on 4 February, arrived at Truk five days later, and performed antisubmarine patrols around the base.[23] She wasn't engaged in the invasion of Lae and Salamaua, though, and continued to ferry fighters from Truk to Rabaul due to different priorities in the South Pacific campaign. If she participated in the Port Moresby landing operation, as suggested by Horii, it would mean a significant change for the Fourth Fleet and the *Shōhō* crew.

Early April saw landmark decisions relating to the Nippon Kaigun's strategy for defeating the U.S. Navy in the Pacific. While the Japanese were using an operational gap between the first and second phases to dispatch the Kidō Butai to the Indian Ocean to annihilate the Eastern Fleet and the Fourth Fleet was preparing its invasion of Port Moresby, the Combined Fleet investigated the plan to seize Midway and shifted its attention to a major carrier battle in the Central Pacific. After a heated debate with Yamamoto's delegates about the second phase, on 5 April the Navy General Staff officially authorized MI Sakusen, Operation MI, after receiving a promise from the Combined Fleet that the western part of the Aleutian Islands would be secured at the same time.[24] The process of formulating Operation MI is not studied in this book, yet it became a pivotal point in Yamamoto's head around which he shaped his vision of the months of the Pacific War that were to follow. According to what we know based on the memories of his staff members, the Combined Fleet presented the following schedule: early May, Port Moresby; early June, Midway (and Aleutians); early July, Fiji and Samoa; and in October, preparations to invade Hawaii.[25]

What is interesting from the Fourth Fleet's perspective is that on 13 April, Lt. Cdr. Akira Sasaki, the Combined Fleet's staff air officer, went to Tokyo to convey the operational timetable regarding the South Pacific to the Navy General Staff. He assumed that taking control of Port Moresby, Midway, Nauru, and Ocean was a formality. After Operation MI, the Japanese forces would be gathered in Truk by 18 June. The Kidō Butai would set off on 1 July, followed by the invasion of New Caledonia on 8 July. Fiji would be secured by 18 July and Samoa by 21 July. Notwithstanding the reality of this plan, the Combined Fleet leadership believed that by conquering these islands the Nippon Kaigun would firmly cut Australia off from American support.[26]

On 5 April at 0730 hours the Combined Fleet issued Secret Order No. 694, which announced *heiryoku busho* (a major reorganization of its forces). The projected change was to be effective from 10 April—the day when the second phase would commence officially. Points 4–6 of the order concerned the Fourth Fleet. The invasion of Port Moresby was to be supported by the Sixth Fleet and its submarines would be instructed to provide data on the enemy shipping and bases. The Eleventh Air Fleet, operating from five main airfields, was responsible for air cover in the North and South Pacific and the execution of Operation K. The Fourth Fleet was to control the 5th Sentai (minus the *Nachi*), the 6th Sentai, the 18th Sentai, the carriers *Kaga* and *Shōhō*, the seaplane tender *Mizuho*, the 7th Destroyer Division, the 21st Destroyer Division, and the 3rd Kure Special Naval Landing Force. Port Moresby, called RZP in the Japanese documents, was to be secured by 10 May. The Combined Fleet's order also set up a code name for the upcoming operation, designated from this point as "MO."[27]

The reason for allocating the *Kaga* to Operation MO was the Combined Fleet's fear about the possible intervention of the American carriers and land-based bombers. The *Shōhō* alone couldn't single-handedly provide the air cover for the convoy heading toward Port Moresby, so Yamamoto decided to deploy one of his four most valuable carriers. Notably, the *Kaga* ran aground on a reef near Palau on 9 February. After some provisional repairs, she participated in the raid on Darwin and mop-up operations off the southwest Java coast in early March. However, the carrier was not in perfect condition, so when the rest of the Kidō Butai was preparing for the Indian Ocean operation, she headed toward Japan for permanent hull repairs. She entered Sasebo Naval Yard on 22 March, and it was expected that this maintenance would be completed within three weeks.

On learning about the new organization of naval forces, Inoue and his staff were highly unsatisfied with allocating the *Kaga* to Operation MO. Despite her excellent reputation, it was confirmed on 8 April that she would need to remain in dry dock for another three to four weeks. Undeniably, the Fourth Fleet was looking at raw numbers, and one carrier was not enough for it to achieve air superiority during the landing operation. Inoue's diary doesn't mention the negotiations with the Combined Fleet, yet we know from the other sources the circumstances surrounding exchanging the *Kaga* for the entire carrier squadron. Initially, Inoue requested the 2nd Kōkū Sentai, namely the *Sōryū* and the *Hiryū*. The Combined Fleet agreed to deploy more carriers to the South Pacific but needed the 2nd Kōkū Sentai to return to the mainland to prepare for Operation MI. Instead, Yamamoto offered the 5th Kōkū Sentai, which consisted of two relatively new carriers, the *Zuikaku* and the *Shōkaku*. This decision was strongly dictated by the idea of giving the 5th Kōkū Sentai an additional chance to gain combat experience.[28] It wasn't precisely what Inoue had opted for, but nobody doubted it was a far better arrangement for the Fourth Fleet than having only the *Kaga*. The deal was done. Combined Fleet Secret Order No. 724, issued on 10 April, officially confirmed the replacement and the new organization.[29]

Many readers and scholars may not agree that it was the best possible solution. Of the three Japanese first-line carrier squadrons from the Kidō Butai that attacked Pearl Harbor, the 5th Kōkū Sentai was considered the most inferior. Despite it having the most recently built carriers, commissioned before the war, this unfavorable assessment stemmed from its unseasoned crews, who underwent a lot less training and had significantly less combat experience than crews from other carrier squadrons. Improving the skills of the aircrew was always a long process, and during the first operations, the *Shōkaku* and the *Zuikaku* were mainly focused on integrating into two effective carriers and one deadly squadron, like the *Akagi* and the *Kaga* or the *Sōryū* and the *Hiryū*. Still, the internal inferiority complex of the 5th Kōkū Sentai when it compared itself to the 1st and the 2nd Kōkū Sentai didn't change the fact that the 5th Kōkū Sentai had been the Combined Fleet's primary offensive force. This was particularly the case after the Kidō Butai's raid on Ceylon, where the *Shōkaku*'s and the *Zuikaku*'s dive bombers contributed the most to the sinking of the British carrier *Hermes*.[30] The 5th Kōkū Sentai completed the Indian Ocean operation on 9 April and then headed toward its next assignment.

The 5th Kōkū Sentai's participation in Operation MO required close cooperation with the Fourth Fleet. The 5th Kōkū Sentai's commander was Rear Adm. Chūichi Hara; he was born in 1889 in Matsue, Shimane Prefecture. Behind his back he was called "King-Kong" because he was very tall and had a massive silhouette, but to close friends he was just "Chū," as the first kanji of his name stands for loyalty. At first glance, Hara was Inoue's peer. However, not only did he graduate from the Naval Academy two years later, in 1909, but he was also ranked only 85th in his class. In 1914 and 1915 he graduated from the Torpedo and Gunnery Schools respectively, mastering the second specialization by attending additional courses in the following years. In 1926, already lieutenant commander, he graduated from the Naval War College but was ranked sixteenth out of twenty students in his class. He began working with the fleet's staff and made a round trip to the United States and Europe as captain during 1933 and 1934. Hara's assignments to torpedo squadrons, torpedo schools, and arsenal torpedo departments made him an expert on this weapon, which resulted in a position at the Navy Technical Department in 1937. However, he always felt that his destiny was to be a military leader on the battlefield rather than an "office admiral," so as rear admiral he was appointed chief of staff of the 2nd China Expeditionary Fleet in November 1939. In August 1941 he was transferred to the 1st Air Fleet's command, but shortly afterward, on 1 September, he was appointed the commander of the 5th Kōkū Sentai.

As evidenced by his military career, Hara didn't have much experience of or professional knowledge about carrier tactics. His competencies were acquired mainly during private study and a short appointment with the 1st Air Fleet. The attack on Pearl Harbor was his first contact with naval air warfare, but he fulfilled all his duties seamlessly. This operation, however, revealed his true nature as a carrier commander. Hara was highly cautious and focused on carrying out tasks. During and after the war, he said many times that the third strike on Pearl Harbor, analyzed as a purely alternative scenario at the time, was unnecessary. And when he had a conversation about the possible moves with Cdr. Kyōzō Ōhashi, his chief of staff at the time, Ōhashi was scolded for being too reckless. "We can't take the eye off the objective. Going with the flow is dangerous!" Hara had said, and some witnesses remembered those words.[31]

One might think that the tactical command in the 5th Kōkū Sentai depended only on Hara, but that wasn't the case. His staff, accommodated in the flagship *Zuikaku*, included several other officers. In January 1942 Ōhashi was replaced by Cdr. Mineo Yamaoka, known for his stubborn and persuasive personality.

PHOTO 2 ■ Rear Adm. Chūichi Hara, commander of the 5th Kōkū Sentai *NDL*

Yamaoka's primary educational background was his attendance at the Torpedo School, yet he had stayed in purely naval aviation posts since 1926. Before being transferred to the 5th Kōkū Sentai, his most recent position had been as the *Hiryū*'s executive officer. Hara's second most important associate was Lt. Cdr. Takeshi Mieno, his flight officer. Mieno had a reputation as a cool-headed officer of the younger generation; he graduated in 1925. His specialization and military career were always bound up with naval aviation, so he was judged to be an excellent aide for Hara. The 5th Kōkū Sentai's staff also included the Communications Officer, Lt. Cdr. Tōnosuke Ōtani, the Chief Engineer, Lt. Cdr. Tsuyoshi Yoshida, and the Main Cryptologist, WO Shinobu Kinoshita.[32]

On 12 April the Combined Fleet issued Secret Order No. 752 and confirmed that the 5th Sentai, the 5th Kōkū Sentai, the *Shōhō*, and the 7th and 27th Destroyer Divisions would be under the control of the Fourth Fleet from 18

April. Additionally, the 27th Destroyer Division was instructed to head to the navy base at Makō, Taiwan, to arrange a rendezvous with the 5th Kōkū Sentai. The next day the Fourth Fleet also confirmed that the MO Kidō Butai, a new task force built around the *Shōkaku* and the *Zuikaku* and screened by the 5th Sentai (minus the *Nachi*) and the 7th and 27th Destroyer Divisions, should be concentrated in Truk by 25 April.[33]

Since the MO Kidō Butai was to consist of the 5th Kōkū Sentai under Rear Adm. Chūichi Hara (as the core striking force) and the 5th Sentai under Rear Adm. Takeo Takagi (as the screening force), the latter was given the command over the MO Kidō Butai due to his higher rank.[34] Takagi was born in 1892 in a small village called Ōmura, in Fukushima Prefecture. He graduated from the Naval Academy in 1911 and was ranked seventeenth in his class. He was a diligent young officer and was quickly promoted to sub-lieutenant in 1914. In 1919 he graduated from the Torpedo School and, two years later, from the Submarine School. He was already considered a prospective commander, and he entered the Naval War College in 1923. Having held various posts on warships, in military schools, and the staff, he had the occasion to work under Rear Adm. Zengo Yoshida, who became the minister of the navy a few years later. Takagi was a skipper of the heavy cruiser *Takao* and the battleship *Mutsu*, which helped him with his promotion to rear admiral in November 1938. During the period when Inoue was criticizing the Nippon Kaigun's preparations for the potential war with the United States, Takagi was working on the detailed mobilization plan as one of the central figures of the Planning Department of the Navy General Staff. In December 1941, as the commander of the 5th Sentai made up of the *Myōkō*, *Nachi*, and *Haguro*, he returned to service on the frontline. Takagi was mostly famous in the Nippon Kaigun for the decisive victory in the Battle of the Java Sea, where he destroyed the ABDA (American-British-Dutch-Australian) task force commanded by Rear Adm. Karel Doorman. Despite the successful landing on Java and the unquestionable accomplishment of the relevant tasks, the Combined Fleet's command noticed a fly in the ointment. They felt that Takagi's stance was too cautious in that he kept a considerable distance from the enemy's formation and didn't try to annihilate Doorman's group completely. Nevertheless, Takagi had a favorable reputation, and he was promoted to vice admiral, effective on 1 May.[35] Also, his tactical command over

PHOTO 3 ■ Rear Adm. Takeo Takagi, commander of the MO Kidō Butai *NDL*

the MO Kidō Butai wasn't designed to stir up the decision-making process, because the air operations remained Hara's responsibility. Theoretically, Takagi could always discuss his opinion on particular moves with Hara, but he didn't interfere with Hara's assessment of the carrier warfare.

Neither of the two admirals responsible for the tactical command in the most critical section of Operation MO used an aggressive command style. Nor had they experienced making tough, independent decisions under pressure in operations involving the carriers. Takagi and Hara made nothing more than decent choices when executing the Fourth Fleet's plan step by step. They both understood the importance of destroying the enemy carrier task force to protect the convoy heading toward Port Moresby. But they weren't very good at taking risks that could prove beneficial or developing original solutions. It is essential to underline that Inoue didn't have staffing alternatives, so his Operation MO plan had to be mastered to the maximum extent to mitigate the risk of negative surprises. This way of thinking, also typical of the Combined Fleet command, became a severe shortcoming after the first phase of the Pacific War, which, ironically, bolstered the Japanese conviction that complex operational planning in the face of the American industrial power was an advantage in the long run.

According to the orders of the Combined Fleet and the Fourth Fleet, the 5th Kōkū Sentai was on its way from the Indian Ocean to Truk to participate in Operation MO. The raid on Ceylon was evaluated as successful and rich in new experiences for the crews, albeit not without losses. The *Shōkaku* and the *Zuikaku* departed for Operation C with fifty-six and fifty-five aircraft, respectively. During the strike on Colombo and Trincomalee, the *Shōkaku* lost one Val and one Zero, while the *Zuikaku* lost five Vals and two Zeros, including the fighter group's *buntaichō*, Lieutenant Makino.[36] This brought both air groups to 102 aircraft—too few to feel comfortable participating in Operation MO as the primary striking force. Thus, at 0800 hours on 14 April, when the Kidō Butai had already passed the Malaka Strait and entered the South China Sea, the Kidō Butai executed Vice Adm. Chūichi Nagumo's order, issued at noon on 11 April, to transfer planes to the *Shōkaku* and the *Zuikaku* from other carriers. According to the initial idea, the *Shōkaku* was supposed to receive one Zero from the *Akagi*, one from the *Sōryū*, and one from the *Hiryū*, and one Val from the *Akagi*. The *Zuikaku* was supposed to receive one Kate from the *Akagi*, three Vals from the *Akagi*, two Vals from the *Sōryū*, four Vals from the *Hiryū*, and five Zeros from the *Hiryū*. In return, the *Zuikaku* would transfer two repaired Zeros and two repaired Vals to the *Akagi*.[37]

However, the number of planes exchanged on 14 April slightly differed for unknown reasons. The 5th Kōkū Sentai received two Zeros, four Vals, and one Kate from the *Akagi* and eight Zeros and six Vals from the 2nd Kōkū Sentai. In return, the 5th Kōkū Sentai transferred three Zeros and two Vals to the *Akagi* and two Zeros to the *Sōryū*.[38] After the transfers, the number of planes in the 5th Kōkū Sentai rose to 116, but the planes given to the *Shōkaku* and the *Zuikaku* required additional maintenance. However, according to the reports of the *Shōkaku* and the *Zuikaku* about the Battle of the Coral Sea, we know that both carriers had only 112 crew members when they left Truk. The 5th Kōkū Sentai's detailed roster is shown in appendix 3.

TABLE 1 **Number of Planes in the 5th Kōkū Sentai, Late April 1942**

Carrier	Date	Kates	Vals	Zeros	Total
Zuikaku	1 April	18	19	18	55
	10 April	18	14	16	48
	14 April (planned)	19	21	19	59
	14 April (executed)	19	21	19	59
	30 April (crews)	19/20*	18	19	56
Shōkaku	1 April	19	19	18	56
	10 April	19	18	17	54
	14 April (planned)	19	19	20	58
	14 April (executed)	19	19	19	57
	30 April (crews)	19	19	18	56

* *Zuikaku's* torpedo bomber group had nineteen full crews and one crew with two of three required men.

Having secured the carrier task force and captured the Admiralty Islands, Inoue could begin Operation MO's detailed planning phase. He had to confer with Horii to find the safest way to transport the South Seas Detachment to Port Moresby. Geography was their main adversary. The land route, theoretically the most compelling one, was immediately discarded. Although the Japanese could have landed in Buna and advanced one hundred miles in the southwestern direction, the route that had been voted for, which went through the wild Owen Stanley Range, was extremely bad.[39] The solution for the navy wasn't much better. The shortest sea route from Rabaul to Port Moresby was only 670 miles, but as John B. Lundstrom vividly describes, "It passed through a maze of reefs, fast currents and narrow straits in the form of the D'Entrecasteaux and Louisiades archipelagos, jutting out far into the Coral Sea from the of eastern New Guinea."[40] The safest route was 950 miles—too long, considering that there was an Allied air force in Port Moresby and on Australian bases that would harass the convoy on its way, exploiting the limited potential of the Japanese land-based forces in Rabaul and New Guinea. Eventually, the 840-mile route through the Louisiades was found to be the best solution out of the three equally far-from-perfect alternatives. The Fourth Fleet's decision also took into account the South Seas Detachment's remarks. The army was worried about the unpredictable weather, the need to gather many transport ships and landing craft, and the threat from the enemy land-based bombers and seaplanes, particularly during the last two days of the final leg of the route in the Coral Sea. Overall, the army and navy planners had to address five main issues:

1. The enemy's relative air superiority in New Guinea and the Coral Sea. This stemmed from the reduced number of Japanese land-based planes from early April, which meant that the Allied bombers from Townsville could easily harass the convoy. The partial answer to this problem was the 5th Kōkū Sentai.
2. The enemy's seaplane activity. The Japanese fighters from Lae could not arrive in convoy fast enough. By setting up convenient seaplane bases in Tulagi and Deboyne and using the available resources in Rabaul, the Fourth Fleet could extend its reconnaissance patrol range and provide direct support.
3. The lack of precise maps of New Guinea's southern coast and the nearby coral reefs. The charts they had were pretty old, and their credibility was questionable. The Japanese wanted to solve this issue by dispatching planes and submarines, particularly to the Port Moresby entrance, to prepare better maps and guide the convoy.
4. The convoy's slow advance toward Port Moresby. The geographical and technical constraints limited the convoy's speed to only eight knots, putting it in a vulnerable position. Although the Fourth Fleet and the South Seas Detachment requested fast transport ships, they received only one, the *Asakasan Maru*.
5. The supply of the friendly garrison after seizing Port Moresby. The successful completion of Operation MO didn't change the fact that the Fourth Fleet needed to secure a stable supply line, which would still be under the threat of the Allied bombers from the Australian bases. The inland route through the Owen Stanley Range was rejected as too ineffective. The Japanese planned to solve this issue by establishing a halfway post on Samarai Island (near Milne Bay) and using smaller craft on the last section of the route to Port Moresby.[41]

The last of these problems was the most difficult to overcome during the war games between the Fourth Fleet and the South Seas Detachment staff, which took place on the training vessel *Kashima* on 16 and 17 April. Although we don't have a detailed description of this meeting, we know from other testimonies that Inoue reassured the participants that if the area controlled by the Japanese was pushed southward to the Timor–New Guinea–Solomons line and sealed by new airfields with many planes, these issues should fade away.[42]

Parallel to the operational planning, the Japanese tried to predict the American response to their swing against Port Moresby. The military command received an intelligence report that the enemy knew about the Combined Fleet's plan to seize Port Moresby, Guadalcanal, and possibly the Northern

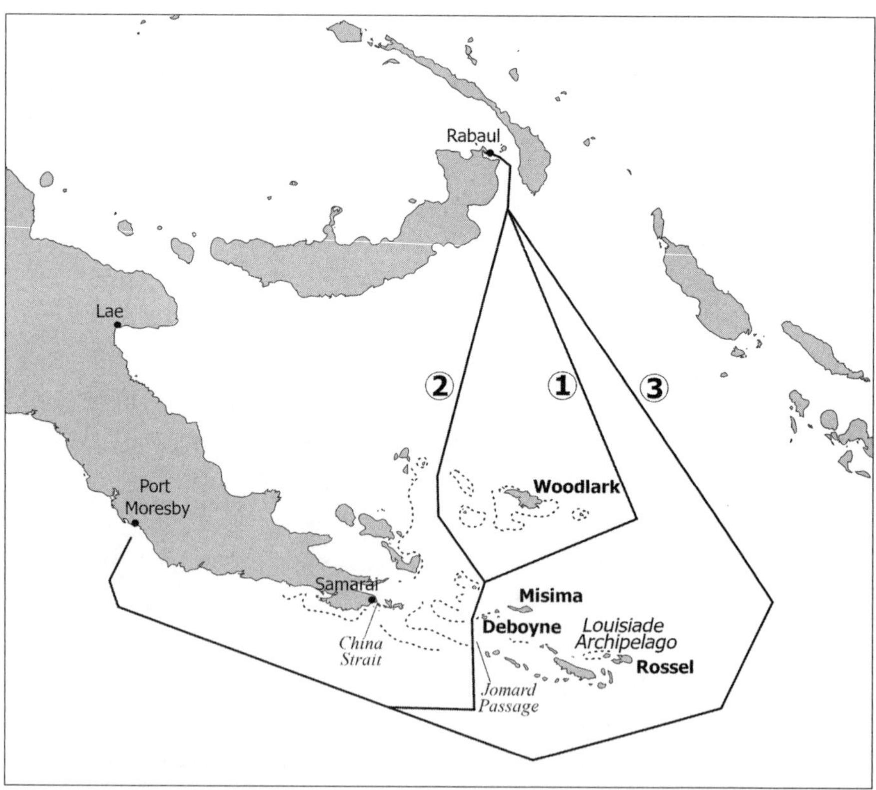

MAP 2 ■ Alternative sea routes of the Port Moresby Invasion Force. The Japanese selected option number 1.

Australian bases. This information, sent on the night of 4 February through a radio facility in Salt Lake City, was intercepted by Japanese spies and communicated to Tokyo.[43] The U.S. Navy's activity in defense of New Guinea in March also raised a natural question: How many carriers would the enemy deploy to halt Operation MO? Although historians tend to focus on the American ability to read the Japanese intentions, the Nippon Kaigun's intelligence system was also based on gathering data on enemy moves, particularly those of its carriers. When the U.S. Navy carriers set off from the bases, the Japanese could expect an air raid on one of their newly established positions. This pattern was repeated in early April. On the eve of the Indian Ocean raid, two American carriers disappeared from Pearl Harbor. They finally struck Tokyo on 18 April. The Combined Fleet immediately recognized that the *Enterprise* and the *Hornet* were the main actors of this bold initiative, called the Doolittle Raid. Consequently, they could not reach the South Pacific in early May, which hindered the MO Kidō Butai. The uncertainty was reduced to whether there were two carriers or only one. The Japanese believed their submarine had sunk the *Lexington* in early January, so they anticipated that only one carrier was defending Port Moresby—the *Saratoga*. The confusion about the presence of a second American carrier and the correct distinction between the *Saratoga* and the *Lexington* is visible throughout the entire Battle of the Coral Sea.[44]

The war games on the *Kashima* resulted in the signing of the agreement between the Fourth Fleet and the South Seas Detachment, which were joined by the 25th Kōkū Sentai as the naval air unit responsible for supporting Operation MO. The agreement became the basis for Fourth Fleet Secret Operational Order No. 13, issued on 23 April. First, Inoue mentioned an estimated two hundred American aircraft gathered in Townsville and Darwin. He confirmed that while there was no strong American carrier task force in the area, the Allied navy force was reinforced by the British group consisting of one battleship, two or three big cruisers, and some light cruisers and destroyers. The presence of the U.S. Navy was noted, but it was described as a "light force" that operated nearby. Inoue knew about one or two enemy submarines patrolling the Rabaul area. However, his concern was primarily Allied aircraft, which would try to spot and attack the convoy.

The Japanese estimated that seventy Australian soldiers were in Tulagi and thirty in Gavutu. They constituted a small communication detachment with several machine guns. The garrison also had one to three flying boats. As for Port Moresby, the Fourth Fleet identified two fully operational airfields (Kila Kila Airfield and Jackson Airfield) and a seaplane base, which could be turned into an advanced position for the Japanese in the following months. The five-thousand-man garrison disposed of ten antiaircraft guns and many high-caliber machine guns and searchlights. No vessels were reported to be in the harbor. The Japanese identified some military facilities in Samarai but no enemy presence in Nauru and Ocean.[45]

The Fourth Fleet order provided detailed instructions to the MO Kidō Butai and the MO Invasion Force. The former was to set off from Truk on day X-10, with X set as 10 May, the day of the planned landing in Port Moresby. The Japanese carrier task force was to pass the Solomon Islands from the east and support the invasion of Tulagi. On day X-5 Takagi was to enter the Coral Sea and take advantage of the air reconnaissance from Tulagi to operate in the area and support the MO Invasion Force. Inoue specified five steps:

1. If a strong enemy surface force was encountered, it should be destroyed.
2. If a strong enemy surface force was not encountered, the Townsville airfield should be raided immediately.
3. After bombing Townsville, the MO Kidō Butai was to move toward Cooktown and Port Moresby and bomb the local airfields.
4. After securing Port Moresby, the MO Kidō Butai was to remain in the Coral Sea within the range of the enemy air bases until day X+5 and be prepared for the arrival of a strong enemy force. Then, the MO Kidō Butai should support the invasion of the northern part of the Gilbert Islands and return to Truk.
5. The MO Kidō Butai should closely cooperate with the friendly invasion force, land-based air force, and submarines. If a strong enemy surface force was encountered, the MO Kidō Butai should merge with the nearby friendly surface force.[46]

The MO Invasion Force was to screen the Tulagi Invasion Force and partially support it until day X-5. In the meantime, it was to screen the Port Moresby Invasion Force, which would depart from Rabaul on day X-6. After seizing Port Moresby, the MO Invasion Force was to support the setting up of the air bases, particularly for fighters. It was also to seize Samarai to secure the shipping line. On the way to Port Moresby the MO Invasion Force was to establish the seaplane base in Deboyne and the southeastern tip of New Guinea by day X-6 and X-2, respectively. After the completion of Operation MO, the surface force and the transport ships were to return to Rabaul quickly. On day X+20 the Fourth Fleet planned to send a bigger convoy to Port Moresby.[47]

From the strategic point of view, Operation MO's schedule looked as follows:

1. 25 April: concentration of forces in Truk and the 25th Kōkū Sentai air attack on Port Moresby
2. 1 May: departure of the MO Kidō Butai from Truk
3. 3 May: invasion of Tulagi and setting up the seaplane base
4. 4 May: the departure of the Port Moresby Invasion Force from Rabaul
5. 6 May: setting up the seaplane base in Deboyne
6. 7 May: crossing the Jomard Passage
7. 8 May: setting up the seaplane base on the southeastern tip of New Guinea
8. 10 May: invasion of Port Moresby and immediately transferring the 25th Kōkū Sentai's aircraft to the secured airfields
9. 12 May: invasion of Samarai and setting up the halfway point of the supply line.
10. 15 May: invasion of Nauru and Ocean

In the second half of April the Fourth Fleet effectively gathered its forces for Operation MO. After a short stay in Makō on 18 April the 5th Kōkū Sentai headed toward Truk the following day, arriving in the planned location on 25 May. The 5th Sentai and part of the 7th Destroyer Division joined it two days later.[48] The last Japanese carrier, the *Shōhō*, set sail from Yokosuka on 24 April and arrived in Truk on 29 April. Fourth Fleet Secret Operational

Order No. 13 meant that Hara was on the last section of the route to Truk. He was highly dissatisfied that his carriers would be used against Townsville and Cooktown. This was not how he had imagined Operation MO. He knew the enemy could deploy at least one carrier. In his eyes, Townsville was too far south to clash with the enemy and suppress the land bases until the Port Moresby Invasion Force had crossed the Jomard Passage on 7 May. Additionally, the Nippon Kaigun intelligence estimated that by early April the Americans had shipped about two hundred long-range bombers to Australia that could easily be swapped between several bases on the northeastern coast. Inoue felt that reducing the Allied air potential in that area was necessary and pressed for it once he learned about the plans to get reinforcements to the *Kaga*. According to Lt. Cdr. Kazuo Dohi, the navigation officer in the Fourth Fleet's staff, Inoue even insisted that he lead the warships against the Australian bases. Notwithstanding his genuine concern about the convoy's safety, two carriers could not risk dispersing their attention toward multiple targets in the Coral Sea. Hara understood that perfectly. Thus, on his arrival at Truk, he intended to officially raise his concerns and ask Inoue to revise the order written by the Fourth Fleet's staff, which he approved.[49]

On 26 April Capt. Iwao Kawai, talking on behalf of the Fourth Fleet's staff, conferred with the 5th Kōkū Sentai delegates, Yamaoka and Mieno. Having invited these guests to the *Kashima*, Kawai explained the basic assumptions of Operation MO: "If you don't find the enemy task force, you will attack the Townsville airfield." His words were enough to provoke a heated discussion. "I can't agree with this plan," Yamaoka protested firmly. He considered getting close to the bases packed with the enemy's B-17s too hazardous. The 5th Kōkū Sentai had just returned from the Indian Ocean raid, where the British bombers from Trincomalee had dared to attack the *Akagi* and only missed by a narrow margin on 9 April. Considering the number and type of bombers in northern Australia, Yamaoka thought counting on another stroke of luck was foolish. Kawai acknowledged this. Yet he repeated the expectation that the 5th Kōkū Sentai must destroy the Allied bombers in Townsville and Cooktown. S. Mori presents a valuable insight regarding Inoue's determination to strike the Australian bases. In early April Inoue discussed with Rear Adm. Sadayoshi Yamada, the commander of the 25th Kōkū Sentai, the details of

Operation MO and heard complaints about the limited air potential of the land-based units. To gain Yamada's support regarding the convoy heading to Port Moresby, he agreed to use the carriers to bomb Townsville and Cooktown. However, Yamaoka and Mieno remained adamantly opposed to this idea. Unexpectedly, they were supported by the Fourth Fleet's chief of staff, Capt. Shikazō Yano. He knew Hara's opinion and couldn't simply ignore it. Yano exchanged views with Inoue, and they agreed to modify the original order to make it less difficult for the 5th Kōkū Sentai.[50]

By the time Takagi arrived in Truk on 27 April on his flagship, the *Myōkō*, he had missed a significant part of the discussion. Still, he knew that Hara and his staff officers remained dissatisfied even with the revised plan. He couldn't change much, though. On the morning of 29 April he issued MO Kidō Butai's Operational Order No. 1 to summarize the negotiations. He confirmed that the Japanese carriers would carry out a surprise attack on Townsville if they did not encounter the enemy surface task force. However, the subsequent raids on Cooktown and Port Moresby were to be made only if the circumstances allowed.

Notably, Takagi's order also included an estimate of the enemy's strength. He mentioned two surface task forces. The British one consisted of one battleship, two heavy cruisers, four light cruisers, ten destroyers, and a few submarines in an unknown position. The American one featured one carrier, three heavy cruisers, two light cruisers, and nine destroyers operating close to New Zealand along the eastern coast of Australia. Takagi also set up the operational schedule of the MO Kidō Butai:

1. 1 May, 0600 hours: departure from Truk
2. 3 May: support for the invasion of Tulagi
3. 4 May, morning: refueling the 5th Sentai and the destroyers from the tanker *Tohō Maru* east of the Solomon Islands
4. 4 May, evening: after refueling, entering the Coral Sea and heading westward
5. 7 May, 0800 hours: raid on Townsville and withdraw northward at twenty-four to thirty knots while recovering the planes
6. 8 May, 1000 hours: the second refueling of the 5th Sentai and the destroyers

7. From 9 May: support for the Port Moresby Invasion Force and withdrawal toward Truk to support Operation RY[51]

Soon after this, the 5th Kōkū Sentai's officers again raised their objections about the raids on Australian bases. This time, however, the response of Inoue's staff was less rigid. In the next few hours the Fourth Fleet issued Secret Operational Order No. 7. The raid on Townsville was suspended and the strikes against Cooktown and Port Moresby depended on the 5th Kōkū Sentai's command assessment.[52] Hara probably may have felt partially relieved but had to pay the price for it. At 1720 hours the Fourth Fleet issued Operational Order No. 92 and gave him additional tasks. On the route toward Tulagi, the 5th Kōkū Sentai was supposed to deliver nine Zeros for the Tainan Kū (the Tainan Naval Air Group) in Rabaul.[53] Since Inoue strongly relied on Yamada's air support for the convoy and had broken the promise to use both carriers to strike Townsville, Cooktown, and Port Moresby, he could only compensate by helping to replenish his fighter group, which suffered high losses in the last days of April.

Inoue's decision to modify the order wasn't a coincidence. Besides the 5th Kōkū Sentai's objection, there were other circumstances he needed to consider. Once Yamamoto got the Navy General Staff's approval to proceed with Operation MI, his chief of staff, Rear Adm. Matome Ugaki, "watched over the Japanese carriers." The *Shōkaku* and the *Zuikaku* were to rejoin the Kidō Butai in the last week of May, so Ugaki expected they would return from the Coral Sea intact. Inoue, still believing in the necessity of harassing the American land-based bombers, could not openly oppose this and quietly departed from the hazardous attack on the Australian bases. However, the Combined Fleet wanted to ensure he would take no foolish risks.[54] Thus, at 2220 hours Ugaki sent Combined Fleet Secret Order No. 907 and canceled the strikes against the Australian bases. At 1520 hours on 30 April the Fourth Fleet confirmed the new disposition for the MO Kidō Butai and officially removed the attacks on Townsville, Cooktown, and Port Moresby from Operation MO. As a natural consequence of this, the MO Kidō Butai needed to revise its plans. At 2030 hours Takagi issued 5th Sentai Secret Order No. 838 and set up a new operational schedule. The main differences from the previous plan included passing south of Rennell Island and operating about three hundred

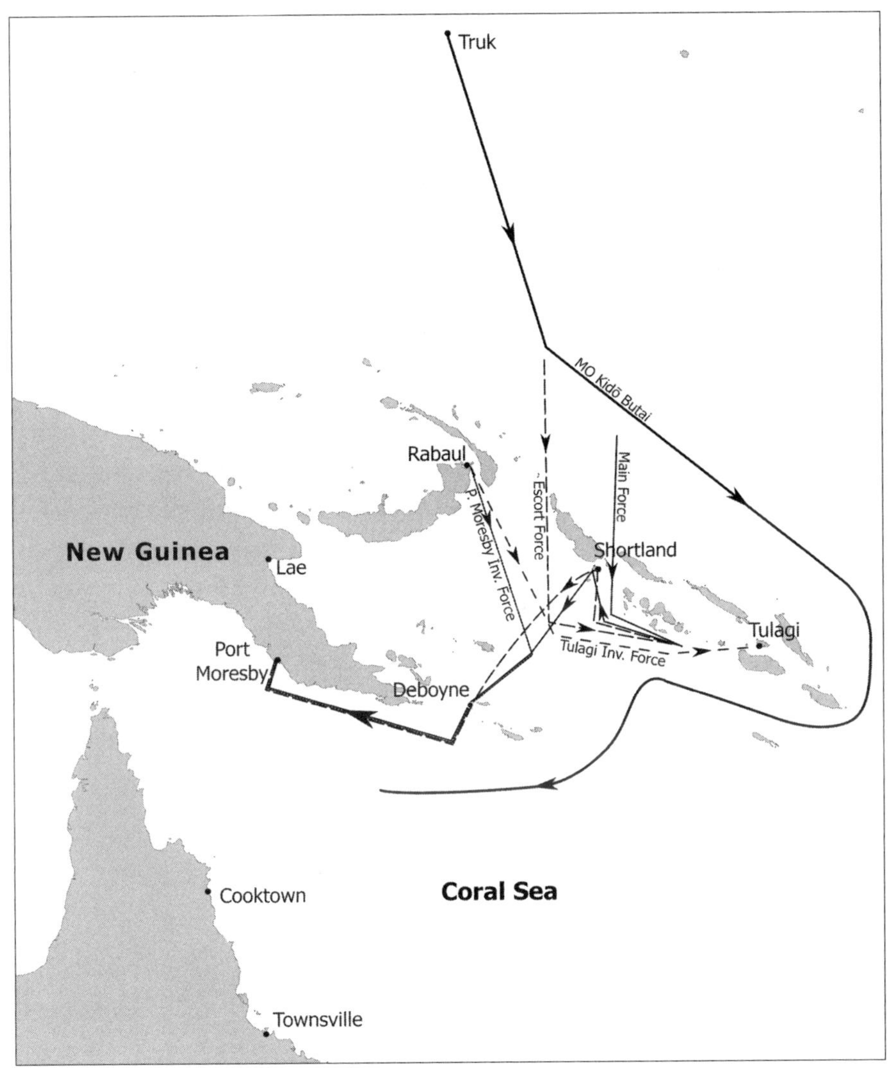

MAP 3 ■ Operation MO plan after the revision

miles southwest of Tulagi to find and destroy the enemy carrier task force on 7 May. The second refueling was to be carried out on the morning of 8 May. After that, Takagi planned to operate southwest of Deboyne to support the landing on Port Moresby. Finally, the MO Kidō Butai would pass between Buka Island and New Ireland on 14 May to cover the invasion of the Gilbert Islands and would return to Japan via Truk.[55]

The modified Operation MO plan was more reasonable for the 5th Kōkū Sentai because it didn't bind the unit with the raids on the Australian bases and left a lot of space for a potential clash with the enemy carrier task force between 5 and 8 May. On the other hand, Hara was saddled with another responsibility on the route toward the Solomon Islands. In theory, transferring nine fighters for the Tainan Kū wouldn't significantly slow his march southward. This part of the plan was essential for Inoue, who considered reinforcements for the 25th Kōkū Sentai a crucial step before passing the Jomard Passage and landing at Port Moresby.

The air campaign in New Guinea, particularly over Port Moresby, is not the topic of this book, but the preparations of the 25th Kōkū Sentai (also known in the Japanese sources as Dai 5 Kūshū Butai, the 5th Raiding Force) for Operation MO cannot be overlooked. When the Japanese seized Lae and Salamaua in early March and transferred the fighters and bombers to the captured airfields, their aircraft immediately became a severe threat to Port Moresby. The Japanese advance, however, soon turned out to be a double-edged sword. Southeastern New Guinea was the first place in the Pacific where the Nippon Kaigun tasted the air war of attrition. The Americans and Australians not only defended their positions but also used bombers and fighters to harass Lae and Rabaul. Their principal opponent was the 25th Kōkū Sentai.

Established on 20 March and officially activated on 1 April, the 25th Kōkū Sentai, commanded by Rear Adm. Sadayoshi Yamada, was a land-based air flotilla subordinated to the Eleventh Fleet. Its primary task was supporting the Fourth Fleet in New Guinea and the South Pacific campaign.[56] However, in the first ten days of April, even before issuing detailed orders for Operation MO, the 25th Kōkū Sentai suffered losses that made it impossible to secure air superiority over eastern New Guinea. This problem mainly concerned the fighter wing, which had more pilots than aircraft. On 7 and 12 April the Eleventh Fleet replenished the Tainan Kū with twelve and twenty-four Zeros respectively, but the number of fighters in the unit was still far from desirable. The situation was not much better in the bomber wing. Due to the flotilla's mediocre strength on the eve of Operation MO, it was decided that the Genzan Kū would be assigned to the 25th Kōkū Sentai on 12 April.[57] Although the Genzan Kū's first nine bombers arrived in Rabaul on 20 April, the remaining eighteen aircraft did not reach the base until 1 May.[58]

Once Operation MO's objectives and schedule were apparent, the 25th Kōkū Sentai's command, based on an agreement with Inoue and Horii, issued separate orders to determine the scope of air support for the Fourth Fleet and the South Seas Detachment.[59] A summary of the 25th Kōkū Sentai's units and their bases and tasks during Operation MO is shown in table 2.

Inoue assigned Hara the additional task of transferring nine Zero fighters to Rabaul because of the diminished strength of the Tainan Kū in late April. Like the 25th Kōkū Sentai's bomber units, the Tainan Kū had suffered high losses in the air campaign over New Guinea. Thus, the unit desperately needed additional aircraft to provide air cover for the convoy in early May, especially considering the number of available pilots. As seen in table 3, nine

TABLE 2 **Organization of the 25th Kōkū Sentai and Its Bases and Tasks during Operation MO**

Unit	Bases	Tasks
Tainan Kū	Rabaul (Lakunai), Lae (Port Moresby, Kila Kila—after Operation MO)	Destroy enemy air forces in New Guinea and NE Australia, cover the convoy, patrol the area
4th Kū	Rabaul (Vunakanau), Lae (Port Moresby—after Operation MO)	As above, plus attack the enemy surface ships, support the landing
Genzan Kū	Rabaul (Vunakanau)	Patrol the area, attack the enemy surface ships, destroy the enemy air forces in New Guinea and NE Australia
Yokohama Kū	Tulagi, Shortland, Deboyne (during Operation MO)	Patrol the area, do reconnaissance, attack the enemy surface ships
Mogamigawa Maru		Transport the supply

TABLE 3 **Number of Aircraft and Crews in the 25th Kōkū Sentai, April–May 1942**

Date	Fighters	Fighter crews	Bombers	Bomber crews	Flying boats	Flying boat crews
1 April	18	31	17	23	11	9
5 April	13	?	13	?	13	13
10 April	12	26	7	18	13	13
15 April	8	37	9	14	12	13
20 April	31	49	25	30	14	13
25 April	29	44	20	35	14	13
1 May	23	38	42	40	13	13

Source: *Senshi Sōshō*, 49:205–6.

extra Zeros for the Tainan Kū would help to reinforce the unit and positively affect Operation MO.

The last element of the preparations for Operation MO included mutual confirmation of the internal agreement between the Fourth Fleet and the South Seas Detachment. Since the memorable American strike on Lae and Salamaua, Horii had been worried about the safety of his men during the route to Port Moresby. Inoue's response to his calls was allocating the *Shōhō* to cover the convoy. However, his diplomatic decision wasn't universally accepted. The critics of this solution included the officers from the *Shōhō*. The light carrier's skipper, Capt. Ishinosuke Izawa, had an Artillery School educational background and, with his mild personality, usually accepted all assignments without asking too many questions. This time, however, he sensed that protecting the transport ships with his mediocre air group looked like a suicidal mission. His concerns were shared by the *Shōhō*'s flight officer, Lt. Cdr. Toshikatsu Sugiyama, who had graduated from the Aviation School. Despite his young age, Sugiyama had one of the brightest minds in the Nippon Kaigun and was earmarked to take over a post on a fleet carrier at some point in the future.

Izawa and Sugiyama were terrified when they saw their new objective. They arrived in Truk on 29 April and were expected to depart the next day without any rest or additional training. Sugiyama used the precious hours on the atoll to participate in a heated discussion between the 5th Kōkū Sentai and the Fourth

Fleet. On that memorable day, Yamaoka and Mieno fought to cancel the raids on the Australian bases. Apart from this topic, which was successfully resolved for them, they also raised the subject of the *Shōhō* in the upcoming operation. "If the *Shōhō* encountered the enemy fleet carrier, she probably wouldn't be able to fight alone," Mieno said. He suggested another modification to Operation MO: "Instead, it would be more effective to put her under our command, next to the *Shōkaku* and the *Zuikaku*, and concentrate our carrier forces." Kawai's response left little room for negotiations: "We can't do that. The South Seas Detachment can't be deserted, and the convoy needs air support on its way." But Sugiyama dared to speak up to follow-up on Mieno's point. "Assigning the *Shōhō* to cover the convoy comprising eleven transport ships is futile. If we scatter our forces in this way, it doesn't make sense, doesn't it?" he said, seeing a unique chance to alter the orders. However, Kawai was unfazed. He had strict instructions from Inoue, who promised Horii direct air support. Kawai did not seem to be persuaded by Mieno's and Sugiyama's arguments, either. If the *Shōhō* was attached to the MO Kidō Butai, she would play a secondary role in Operation MO as the carrier whose only responsibility was CAP (Combat Air Patrol) and antisubmarine missions. Since her torpedo bomber group consisted of only six Kates, she couldn't contribute much to the strikes of the *Shōkaku* or the *Zuikaku* on the enemy task force. According to Kawai and Inoue, the *Shōhō* could contribute to Operation MO more than as an extra.[60]

Having set the stage for the new offensive in the South Pacific, Inoue had a panoramic view of the particular steps that should take place in the upcoming days. Because of the dangerous sea route toward Port Moresby and the possible presence of the Allied surface force, the Fourth Fleet's plan encompassed engaging several forces, some of which had more than one task. The detailed Japanese order of the battle is covered in appendix 1. Flawless coordination and mutual support were paramount factors for the success of Operation MO. One altered element could severely affect the sequence of events and lead to the failure of the final goal—the capture of Port Moresby. The Japanese anticipated the American opposition to their advance but were ready for the confrontation. They certainly didn't expect their meticulous plan to start going wrong in less than two days from the departure of the MO Kidō Butai from Truk.

Chapter 2

INTERCEPTING JAPANESE NAVAL MESSAGES AND RESPONSES TO OPERATION MO

The beginning of 1942 marked the continuation of the disastrous Allied defeats in the war with Japan. The collapse of the British defense in Malaya and Singapore, the American withdrawal to Bataan in the Philippines, and the enemy's conquest of the Dutch East Indies left the Australians in a very challenging situation. After losing advanced positions in New Britain and New Ireland, the Australian mainland became the Allied stronghold in the South Pacific, and it came under enormous pressure from the Nippon Kaigun, as shown by the Kidō Butai's raid on Darwin. On 5 March, while the Dutch forces were still fiercely defending Java, the American intelligence in Australia warned that the Japanese had gathered land-based planes, two or three carriers, and one infantry division in Rabaul ready to attack Port Moresby.[1]

Allied expectations regarding the enemy's imminent advance to New Guinea came true when the enemy captured Lae and Salamaua. However, after the U.S. Navy carrier raids on 10 March, the Fourth Fleet refrained from further large-scale operations and focused on securing the seized areas.

The problem of the Japanese push southward returned at the beginning of April, when CINCPAC noted on 3 April that the enemy was ready to attack Tulagi and Port Moresby simultaneously and could land one infantry division.[2] The potential threat to Port Moresby wasn't a novelty. The first alarm had already been raised on 27 January when the Japanese seized Rabaul. And on 20 February a cable had warned about the enemy's upcoming invasion of Port Darwin and Port Moresby.[3] The South Pacific was one of the places where the enemy could surprise the U.S. Navy. The Kidō Butai could have been planning to strike Pearl Harbor again, as well as the stations at Midway, Johnston, and Palmyra, as mentioned by COMINCH in the message to CINCPAC on 10 March and then passed as a direct warning from Hawaii.[4]

At this stage of the war, American actions against the Japanese were limited to slowing their advance and waiting for them to make a major mistake. It was hoped that the latter could be achieved by predicting or ascertaining the enemy's intentions. This opportunity suddenly became real in April 1942. Between 5 and 7 April the 14th Naval District radio station in Hawaii reported increased radio traffic between the Combined Fleet headquarters and the Fourth Fleet. Incomplete and encrypted Japanese dispatches were sent to Station HYPO (referred to as Hypo later), which was led by Lt. Cdr. Joseph Rochefort.[5] On 8 April he realized that the intercepted messages concerned unusual communications between the *Kaga* and the Fourth Fleet. He and Lt. Cdr. Edwin Layton found out that "the *Kaga* would head to New Britain at the end of April" and that "the *Kaga* was scheduled for RZP." The location "RZP" had now appeared in the Allied analysis for the second time. On 25 March cryptanalysts in Melbourne and Pearl Harbor decrypted Inoue's message; he had ordered his force to assist in the "RZP campaign."[6] Rochefort had an epiphany. He immediately informed King, Nimitz, and the U.S. Navy intelligence in Washington that RZP was Port Moresby. But King and Nimitz couldn't simply take his reasoning as an undeniable fact. The U.S. Navy had been working on deciphering Japanese abbreviations that stood for specific bases. For example, they already suspected on 11 March that AF was Midway, AG was Johnston Island, OH was Oahu, and AK was Pearl Harbor. Additionally, thanks to Station Cast on Corregidor, the Americans discovered that the enemy used R for targets in New Guinea and the Solomon Islands. It didn't take much time for Hypo to learn that RR was Rabaul, RXS was Noumea, and RZM was Lae. However, RZP remained a mystery. Nimitz and King anticipated a major Japanese offensive, but RZP could be the Solomon Islands or the Gilbert and Ellice Islands.[7]

Even though the U.S. Navy broke the enemy code, it did not enjoy real-time knowledge about its intentions. The American cryptanalysts could only read 10 to 15 percent of the intercepted messages. Eighty percent of the messages remained blank and had different levels of complexity and interdependence. Lundstrom notes that "even in May, the Americans copied only about 60 percent of Japanese naval transmissions, and of these, only about 40 percent could be analyzed because of the lack of time and qualified personnel."[8] This fact demonstrates that depending on intelligence without understanding the fog of war could become a most critical mistake.

Because King had responsibility for the strategic planning, he had to consider three possible directions—the central, south, and, to a lesser extent, north Pacific. He could not commit most of the U.S. Navy forces to defending one flank, because the Nippon Kaigun could strike anywhere else. He and Nimitz knew that Yamamoto was famous for his big gambles and wouldn't hesitate to hit Pearl Harbor again if he had the opportunity. Besides defense, the American vision of the war included carrier raids on the Japanese positions. The strike on Lae and Salamaua revealed this strategy's effectiveness. However, it could also be dangerous for any carrier to be discovered while approaching the enemy's base, as the *Lexington*'s story off Bougainville demonstrated.

At the beginning of April 1942 the only American carrier left in the South Pacific was the *Yorktown* in Task Force 17 (TF 17), which was under the command of Rear Adm. Frank Fletcher. The second available carrier, the *Lexington* in TF 11, under the command Rear Adm. Wilson Brown, arrived at Pearl Harbor on 26 March and was docked for maintenance. On 2 April Nimitz considered deploying TF 11 to the South Pacific or asking Brown to train with TF 1 south of Hawaii. Hesitant about strengthening TF 17, CINCPAC decided to keep the *Lexington* in the Central Pacific. One day later Rear Adm. Aubrey W. Fitch replaced Brown as the commander of TF 11.

The Kidō Butai's attack on the British bases in Ceylon wasn't a complete surprise. Still, the enemy made an opening move later than the Allies had initially expected. Six aircraft carriers in the Bay of Bengal were a significant threat to the Eastern Fleet, but it was doubted that the Japanese army would launch an offensive toward the Indian border or dare to land in Ceylon. The presence of the Kidō Butai in the Indian Ocean also precluded the enemy's offensive in the South Pacific in the following weeks. Although Nimitz wasn't happy to see the *Enterprise* and the *Hornet* going into the belly of the beast, King felt that mid-April would be the perfect moment for Doolittle to bomb Tokyo. Hone assesses this bold initiative as "a strategic necessity" despite some practical concerns.[9]

When Vice Adm. William "Bull" Halsey was steaming toward Japan and the Kidō Butai had set its return course from the Indian Ocean, Fitch was ordered to leave Hawaii on 15 April and go for additional training with TF 1 westward of Palmyra, which would last until 4 May. Then he was supposed to return to Pearl Harbor.[10] CINCPAC was preparing to repel the Japanese offensive in New Guinea and the Solomon Islands but didn't have enough information to elaborate a concrete plan. On 14 April Nimitz ordered Fletcher to head to Tongatabu. TF 17 was to arrive there on 19 or 20 April and the *Yorktown* was to undergo refurbishment. On 27 April Fletcher would leave Tongatabu and return to the Coral Sea to defend Allied bases against Japanese carriers.[11]

Nimitz's plan was short-lived. On 15 April CINCPAC received a warning from Washington that the Japanese had probably deployed two additional carriers for operations in the South Pacific. The warning was based on the intercepted and deciphered message the 5th Kōkū Sentai's commander sent on 13 April; he informed the Fourth Fleet that he would arrive at Truk on 28 April. For most of the time, CINCPAC believed that the Japanese had only two carriers available for the offensive in the South Pacific, the *Kaga* and the *Shōhō*, the latter erroneously identified as the *Ryūkaku*,[12] but it suddenly faced a vision of the concentration of the enemy's forces for an offensive in the Southwest Pacific that was "shaping up."[13]

On 17 April Nimitz convened a meeting with his staff to discuss the Nippon Kaigun's intentions in the upcoming weeks. Rochefort's claims were taken as a foundation for further arrangements. According to Hypo, the 5th Kōkū Sentai would join the forces in Truk and go to Rabaul to support large-scale operations in the south. Rochefort believed that as many as four carriers screened by cruisers, destroyers, and land-based air forces in the Rabaul area would launch the offensive in the closing days of April. Nimitz suggested to King that to halt the enemy the U.S. Navy should deploy TF 11 and TF 17 under Fletcher as the most senior officer. King supported this proposal but disagreed regarding the date of the potential Japanese air strike and amphibious operation at Port Moresby. He was more convinced about the scenario of the enemy attacking in the first week of May.[14] When deciding to commit two carriers to the South Pacific, Nimitz and King agreed that Fletcher would have to fight against a larger enemy force by adopting the strategic initiative. But the Americans were still unsure about the place and date of the enemy's attack despite Hypo's effort to decipher as many details as possible.

The situation of the U.S. Navy in the South Pacific in April 1942 wasn't as unfavorable as it might have seemed. Hypo made an error when decoding Japanese messages regarding the number of carriers participating in the upcoming offensive. The *Shōkaku* and the *Zuikaku* were only intended to replace the *Kaga*, not join her. The Fourth Fleet's advantage over Fletcher was even smaller since the *Shōhō* didn't have her regular air group and was assigned to provide air cover for the convoy. The MO Kidō Butai wasn't necessarily more potent than the combined TF 11 and TF 17, especially when counting the number of available aircraft and crews.

The Doolittle Raid became an excellent opportunity for American cryptanalysts to continue reading enemy messages. The strike on Tokyo provoked a massive exchange of cables between Japanese units. Still, Hypo couldn't fully profit from this situation due to staff shortages and time limitations. According to the latest information acquired from the Fourth Fleet's order, the *Shōhō* and the 5th Sentai were scheduled to arrive at Truk on 25 April, so the Eleventh Air Fleet commenced the preparations for the South Pacific campaign. It was discovered that the Fourth Fleet had committed part of its forces to pursuing the *Enterprise* and the *Hornet*. Thus, despite Nimitz's critical opinion of this initiative in general, the Doolittle Raid also gave CINCPAC a few extra days to prepare for the defense of Port Moresby.[15]

On 19 April Nimitz ordered TF 11 to head southward. A day later he instructed Fitch to prepare for operations in the South Pacific. At the same time, another meeting was held at the CINPAC headquarters to elaborate a defense plan. Relying on the messages deciphered by Hypo, which again mentioned the "RZP campaign" and the "concentration of carrier forces," the Americans incorrectly concluded that the Fourth Fleet had more carriers than previously assumed. This mistake is particularly visible in the strategic situation estimate dated 22 April. CINCPAC rightly indicated that the Japanese offensive would be directed against New Guinea, New Britain, and the Solomon Islands, beginning on 3 May. On the other hand, the Americans believed that the MO Kidō Butai would consist of five aircraft carriers: the *Shōkaku*, *Zuikaku*, *Kaga*, *Kasuga Maru*, and *Ryūkaku*.[16] The screening force was estimated to be one battleship, at least four heavy cruisers, at least four light cruisers, and twelve destroyers What's more, CINPAC was aware that Nagumo could support the MO Kidō Butai by joining the campaign with the *Akagi* and two battleships.[17]

King was informed about the possible disproportion of forces in the upcoming campaign. He asked Nimitz to prepare an alternative plan to avoid fighting two U.S. carriers against five enemy carriers. CINCPAC initially intended to send one of Halsey's carriers to the South Pacific, but the staff soon realized that leaving one carrier near Hawaii would be a waste. Nimitz eventually convinced himself to use all four available carriers to defend Port Moresby: the *Yorktown*, *Lexington*, *Enterprise*, and *Hornet*.

Fletcher's task, once he had the *Yorktown* and the *Lexington* under his command by 30 April, was to repel the first Japanese attack on Port Moresby. Nimitz assumed that TF 16 would return to Pearl Harbor on 25 April. By the end of the month the *Enterprise* and the *Hornet* would be prepared to dash south. Depending on the situation in the South Pacific, all four carriers would be put under Halsey's command between 14 and 16 May. With about three hundred planes at his disposal, he could have a decisive battle with the Kidō Butai, which was to consist of up to six carriers, according to American estimates. CINCPAC took the possibility of a decisive battle in the South Pacific seriously and deployed seven tankers to supply Halsey. However, Nimitz warned they could remain in the Coral Sea until 1 June because they had to return to Fiji and Samoa.[18]

By sending twelve PBYs to Noumea, Nimitz also planned to reinforce local patrol forces. His strategy was based on a calculated risk—waiting for a Japanese offensive on Port Moresby and the Solomon Islands, which could also develop into an advance toward Fiji and New Caledonia. The enemy, cruising through dangerous waters famous for treacherous coral reefs, was to be tracked by flying boats and submarines and unexpectedly attacked by Halsey in favorable conditions for the U.S. Navy.[19]

On 24 April one of Rochefort's linguists, Joe Finnegan, deciphered Inoue's message, which informed him that seven Japanese forces had been deployed for the offensive in the South Pacific: the MO Fleet, two MO Invasion Forces, the MO Kidō Butai, the RZP Invasion Force, the RXB Invasion Force, and the RY Invasion Force. Hypo didn't doubt that RXB stood for Tulagi. However, the appearance of "MO" four times with "RZP" in the message caused a lot of confusion. Previous assumptions, which had designated RZP as Port Moresby, may not have been possible if the Japanese had just used MO. The identification of RY, which cryptanalysts guessed stood for the Gilbert Islands, also remained a mystery.[20]

On the day that Finnegan identified seven enemy task forces, Nimitz informed Fletcher that he had assigned TF 44 to be under his command. TF 44 consisted of two heavy cruisers, the light cruiser, and two destroyers and was commanded by Rear Adm. John G. Crace of the Royal Navy.[21]

Feeling increasingly uncertain about the enemy's plans for Hawaii, Nimitz told Fletcher that TF 17 would likely be withdrawn to Pearl Harbor on 15 May. Despite concerns about the situation in the Central Pacific, CINPAC had already decided to halt the Japanese offensive against Port Moresby, and Nimitz considered keeping TF 17 in the South Pacific if necessary for the following weeks.[22]

On 25 April, the same day the *Enterprise* and the *Hornet* returned to Pearl Harbor from the Doolittle Raid, Nimitz met with King in San Francisco to discuss the details of the strategy to defend Port Moresby. They agreed to deploy four carriers to the South Pacific, supported by nine heavy cruisers and twenty-one destroyers. King, who saw a chance to attack the Japanese if they made any mistakes, ordered Nimitz to keep at least two carriers with screening vessels in the area. The most critical period for the U.S. Navy would be in early May, before the planned concentration of the American carriers in the South Pacific.[23] Fortunately for Nimitz, he received news that the *Saratoga* was scheduled to return to service in the first half of June, so she could help to close the gap to the Nippon Kaigun.

Besides appointing Vice Adm. Robert Ghormley as the commander in chief of the South Pacific Area, Nimitz and King discussed other personnel-related matters. They were worried about Fletcher's command style, particularly his lack of aggressiveness. He was responsible for checking the enemy's offensive, which required initiative and a good sense of naval tactics. Until Halsey arrived in the South Pacific with TF 16, Nimitz and King planned to observe Fletcher and his decisions.[24]

The meeting in San Francisco ended on 27 April. King returned to Washington, and Nimitz went to Pearl Harbor. On the same day, Hypo reported that the Japanese appeared ready to change their codes and ship call signs. This usually meant a larger offensive operation was planned. To the surprise of the Americans, the Japanese retained their old codes, which allowed Hypo to continue reading the most critical enemy messages for about a month.[25]

After returning to Pearl Harbor, Nimitz and his staff prepared concrete orders for the next two days. On 29 April CINCPAC issued Operational Plan No. 23–42, which was mainly based on 22 April estimations and the most recent intelligence findings. Nimitz assumed that the Japanese offensive would begin in early May and be directed primarily against Port Moresby and some positions in the Solomon Islands and the Gilbert Islands. The next phase would include the invasion of Ocean and Nauru and the carrier raids on New Caledonia and Fiji. The Japanese advance in the South Pacific was to be opposed by TF 11 and TF 17, which awaited the arrival of TF 16. Depending on the situation, Nimitz planned to withdraw TF 17 around 15 May and TF 11 in early June. The *Yorktown* and the *Lexington* were to return to Hawaii to shield the Central Pacific area from an enemy raid or a potential invasion of Midway.[26]

Halsey, who got an order to leave Pearl Harbor on 30 April, was to join the defense of Port Moresby in the second phase of the campaign. Nimitz also assigned the heavy cruiser *Pensacola* and one destroyer to TF 16. They were to depart from Pearl Harbor as soon as possible. On the route south, the *Enterprise* and the *Hornet* would ferry a squadron of fighters to the Efate air base. Halsey was supposed to conduct reconnaissance missions over Howland Island and Baker Island. Whenever the opportunity arose, TF 16 was to raid enemy positions in the area encompassing the Gilbert Islands, Nauru, and Ocean.[27]

Increased communication traffic between Japanese units in the last days of April allowed Hypo to decipher other critical messages before the start of Operation MO. On 30 April Rochefort alerted King and Nimitz that the enemy had RZP Occupation Force Operation Order No. 1 stating that two transport ships would set sail from Rabaul on day X-7 and would rendezvous at Deboyne with the "Saipan Force," which would arrive there on day X-5. On the basis of this message, the Americans deduced that the departure from Rabaul was scheduled for 3 May, the rendezvous with the "Saipan Force" for 5 May, and the invasion of Port Moresby for 10 May. Hypo also determined that the Tulagi Invasion Force would be used to seize Nauru and Ocean on 15 May.[28]

By 1 May Hypo had found out that the Fourth Fleet intended to engage the 5th Kōkū Sentai, the 5th Sentai, the 25th Kōkū Sentai, the 18th Sentai, the 6th Suirai Sentai, the 8th Gunboat Division, and several auxiliary vessels in the offensive in the South Pacific. In Rochefort's assessment, a direct attack on Australia was unlikely. The Japanese were expected to pay much more attention to raids on Palmyra, Samoa, Canton Island, and the Central Pacific area, including Hawaii. The Americans were also not ruling out that the Aleutian Islands could soon be the target for the enemy carriers. The forces assigned to attack the North Pacific were the *Kaga* and the *Sōryū*, and the 1st, 2nd, 4th, and 6th Sentai were already gathered in Japan and were awaiting the Combined Fleet's orders.

The last American memo regarding enemy intentions in the South Pacific before the Japanese launched Operation MO was recorded in the CINCPAC diary on 1 May. The *Graybook* indicated that the enemy's offensive would be directed against New Guinea and the Solomon Islands, with air raids on Northeastern Australia and probable strikes on Efate, Noumea, Fiji, and Samoa. The Americans also mentioned that the Central and North Pacific areas were at risk, although they had no concrete evidence of the Japanese plans.[29]

■ ■ ■

Having assumed command of the reconnaissance wing at Noumea, Fletcher had the seaplane tender *Tangier* and six PBYs at his disposal, which could search the area within seven hundred miles of New Caledonia. Another six flying boats were scheduled to arrive on the island on 3 May. According to

Fletcher's orders, they were to scout north and northwest of New Caledonia and the New Hebrides to the boundary of the SoWePac Area and then north to the boundary of the SoWePac and SoPac Areas, as well as the Santa Cruz Islands, which are located about 350 miles to the southeast of Tulagi. Due to the limited number of PBYs, he reassigned them from the reconnaissance missions in the sectors east of the Solomon Islands.[30]

On 26 April Fletcher received the CINCPAC order with a refueling schedule. The *Tippecanoe* and the *Neosho*, assigned to TF 11 and TF 17, carried 153,000 barrels of oil between them. The *Neosho* could begin refueling TF 17 as early as late April. The *Tippecanoe*, which was supposed to deliver 14,000 barrels to the convoy heading toward Efate, could start refueling TF 11 on 1 May. By steaming at 15 knots, TF 11 and TF 17 consumed about 11,400 barrels daily. Thus, both tankers could supply Fletcher until 10 May, provided his forces didn't use more fuel on the approach to the Coral Sea. If the speed was increased to the maximum, the Americans expected to use an additional 30,000 barrels. In such a scenario, the *Neosho* and the *Tippecanoe* would run out of fuel on the evening of 7 May. These estimations did not include TF 44, supplied by Australian tankers, which could also help American vessels if necessary.

Although CINCPAC's plans envisaged TF 17's return to Pearl Harbor on 15 May, Fletcher was in a very difficult position. Even with the Australian tankers, he did not have enough fuel to conduct operations against the enemy in the Coral Sea by steaming for too long at a speed exceeding fifteen knots. An additional problem related to protecting the vulnerable tankers. Fletcher couldn't afford to lose a single tanker. To minimize the risk of the *Neosho* being sunk, she was to wait between Point Corn and Point Rye after each refueling to be about 180 miles distant from TF 17.[31]

On 27 April, TF 17 departed Tongatabu and had a rendezvous the next day with the *Neosho* and the *McCall* about three hundred miles southwest. On 30 April Fletcher received a message from Hawaii that warned him that the enemy's main objective was Port Moresby and that Deboyne was a possible concentration point of the Japanese forces before the decisive phase of Operation MO.

Just after dawn on 1 May, TF 17 and TF 11 made contact 250 miles southwest of Espiritu Santo. Fletcher took command of the combined forces and issued

Operational Order No. 2–42 to set up a new organization and tasks. However, before implementing this order, Fletcher used the advantage he had because of a few extra hours that had not been envisaged in the original plans and sent TF 11 to refuel at Butternut Point, about three hundred miles northwest of New Caledonia. This is where TF 11 would rendezvous with the *Chicago*, *Perkins*, and *Tippecanoe*. TF 17 would join TF 11 at dawn on 2 May, immediately after completing refueling via the *Neosho*.[32]

Bad weather delayed the refueling of TF 17, which was completed late in the evening. Rough seas and strong winds injured several sailors on the *Neosho*. Fletcher moved away from Butternut Point while waiting for the weather to improve. Around noon, TF 11 sighted the *Tippecanoe*, *Chicago*, and *Perkins*. Fitch still didn't have Fletcher's permission to refuel so awaited his arrival. Just after sunrise on 2 May, TF 17, TF 11, and the *Tippecanoe* group merged. Two hours later both tankers began refueling Fletcher's forces, which was to continue until the afternoon of 3 May. Soon after, the *Tippecanoe* returned to Efate. Due to logistical problems, Fletcher preferred to keep the faster *Neosho* with TF 17 to supply his ships anytime.[33]

On the afternoon of 2 May Fletcher learned from Leary's report about "a ship sighted on the afternoon of 1 May" and air raids on Tulagi, which were probably carried out by "aircraft from a cruiser or a seaplane tender." The commander of TF 17 was particularly worried about two vessels of an unspecified type located by the Australian flying boat thirty-five miles southwest of Gizo, New Georgia. The Catalina planned to shadow the enemy ships throughout the night but lost track of them. Leary also advised that sectors east of New Guinea to Bougainville and east of the Solomon Islands, where the Japanese intended to enter the Coral Sea, were not scouted on 1 May.

Fletcher was unaware that the Australian PBYs had stumbled on not only two ships but the Support Force, made up of five other transport ships. One of the flying boats shadowed the Japanese vessels for the following five hours, reporting one 2,500-ton ship and several armed fishing vessels. This sighting occurred in the section that Leary had previously indicated had not been searched by friendly aircraft.

TF 17 made the first contact with the enemy vessel on the afternoon of 2 May, when two SBDs located a Japanese submarine nearby. The enemy sighted the American planes and decided to submerge. The dive bombers couldn't attack the submarine and returned to the *Yorktown* by 1543 hours to report their discovery. In less than twenty minutes, three TBDs led by Lt. Thomas Ellison took off to destroy the submarine. Each torpedo bomber was armed with two depth charges.

Devastators found the Japanese submarine at 1615 hours, about three miles from the original contact. They dropped the bombs and most of them fell near the target. Ellison was convinced that the submarine was severely damaged, although he saw no debris or oil slick on the surface. He soon landed on the carrier to report on the attack. The remaining two TBDs circled over the area to ensure that the enemy didn't get away. Fletcher took the threat seriously and sent eleven SBDs. He also detached the *Anderson* and the *Sims* to hunt down the submarine and rejoin TF 17 at dawn the next day.

But the Americans failed to locate the intruder. The SBDs had returned to the carrier by 1825 hours. According to Japanese documents, the spotted submarine was *I-21*, which was on a reconnaissance patrol near Noumea. She avoided any damage and continued her mission. Although Fletcher believed that the submarine reported his position, her crew didn't realize they had been attacked by carrier-borne planes, because they felt they were close to the enemy base in New Caledonia.[34]

Although Fletcher learned that the Japanese had bombed Tulagi again, he received no new intelligence about enemy movements on the afternoon of 2 May. Having no reason to change the original plans, he headed west. Before dawn on 3 May Leary confirmed that the RAAF was evacuating the Tulagi garrison. The *Anderson* and the *Sims* rejoined TF 17, which was about one hundred miles west of TF 11 at the time. By 1530 hours, TF 17 had completed the refueling and was heading toward TF 11 to link up the following morning. In the meantime, Fitch also finished refueling and sent the *Tippecanoe* to Efate with the *Worden*.[35] Thus, at sunset on 3 May, TF 11 and TF 17 were refueled and ready to challenge the MO Kidō Butai. Fletcher, Fitch, and Crace just needed to join their forces and fight against the Japanese. In the following minutes, however, Fletcher would receive some breaking news that forced him to change the plans and make the first American move in the Battle of the Coral Sea.

Chapter 3

THE INVASION OF TULAGI

First Japanese Move under Operation MO

The Japanese made their first opening move of Operation MO on 26 April. The gunboat *Nikkai Maru*, carrying about 120 construction workers, left Rabaul to set up a seaplane base at Shortland for the Yokohama Kū. The vessel arrived on the island on the morning of 28 April and hastily unloaded the men and materials in the following hours.[1] On the same day, the submarines *I-21* and *I-27* set off from Truk for patrol missions. *I-21* headed for Noumea to investigate the situation around New Caledonia, while *I-27* took the course to the Australian East Coast, particularly Brisbane, to check on the local shipping. Both submarines were equipped with one Type 0 two-seat reconnaissance seaplane, better known by the Allies as Yokosuka E14Y or by the code name "Glen." Finally, at 1600 hours, the 18th Sentai (the light cruisers *Tenryū* and *Tatsuta*) and the seaplane tender *Kamikawa Maru*, reinforced by part of the *Kiyokawa Maru* air group, set sail from Truk. Rear Adm. Kuninori Marumo's Covering Force was to take position in the Queen Carola anchorage near Kieta, Bougainville, and provide air support against Allied aircraft and submarines over the Tulagi area and survey the enemy's movements.[2]

The preparations of the Tulagi Invasion Force were completed by the early morning of 28 April when the soldiers, guns, equipment, and supplies had been loaded onto the *Azumasan Maru* in Rabaul.[3] The core of the RXB Landing

Force was built around the freshly formed 3rd Kure Special Naval Landing Force, taken to New Britain via the Caroline Islands by the same transport ship in March. Ens. Junta Maruyama, the commander of the 2nd Company, was in charge of the 430-man detachment assigned to the landing operation. The RXB Landing Force also consisted of the 54-man antiaircraft Mitsuwa Unit under Ens. Toshichi Mitsuwa and 132 men from the civilian 7th Construction Unit, alternatively called the Hashimoto Unit because Shin'ya Hashimoto, a civilian engineer assigned to the Nippon Kaigun, was commanding it.[4]

The first event on 29 April was the Yokohama Kū's reconnaissance missions over Shortland. Three flying boats, which took off from Rabaul, did not track any presence of the enemy and returned safely. Later during the day, five Mavises were deployed to the newly established base to extend the range of the patrol sectors into the Solomon Islands and the Coral Sea.[5] The subchaser *Toshi Maru No 3*, screened by the gunboat *Keijō Maru*, left Rabaul to set up a seaplane base at Thousand Ships Bay, located on the south coast of Santa Isabel Island.[6]

The situation in the Solomon Islands was developing according to the Japanese plans. Before sunset on 30 April the Yokohama Kū sent three flying boats from Shortland, each armed with two 250-kg and six 60-kg bombs. Led by Lieutenant Commander Tashiro, the group was ordered to attack the Allied aircraft stationed at Gavutu. The Mavises arrived there at about 0700 hours and dropped their bombs on two Catalinas they spotted, reporting both destroyed. They encountered no resistance and returned safely to the base by 1000 hours.[7] The attacked Catalinas belonged to No. 20 RAAF Squadron, which was still in the process of forming and had been ordered from Canada. Australian records admitted that the Japanese scored near hits on two flying boats. One was only slightly damaged, but the second turned out to be unserviceable. The following night, she was towed to Aola village on the north coast of Guadalcanal.[8]

Besides harassing the enemy positions at Tulagi, at 0705 hours the Yokohama Kū launched two Mavises from Shortland. Both flying boats, commanded by WO Hamano and PO1c Fujimori, went for a long patrol in the southeastern sectors. They didn't spot anything and returned to the base by 1710 hours.[9]

At the same time, the *Kamikawa Maru* arrived in the Queen Carola anchorage and, at 0900 hours, sent three Daves from the *Kiyokawa Maru* air group on patrol over Shortland. Two and a half hours later she sent two Petes in the same direction and finally one more Dave. None of the seaplanes found the enemy, but they informed the group about the weather conditions in the area.[10] The *Kamikawa Maru*'s three Petes had been circling the Queen Carola anchorage since 1500 hours without encountering enemy surface vessels, submarines, or planes.[11]

Achieving domination in the air, at least in the opening moves, was a crucial part of Operation MO. When the flying boats and seaplanes were conducting their missions, at about 0930 hours, Rear Adm. Kiyohide Shima's Tulagi Invasion Force had departed from Rabaul. The group consisted of the destroyers *Kikuzuki* and *Yūzuki*, the minelayer *Okinoshima*, the transport ships *Kōei Maru* and *Azumasan Maru*, auxiliary minesweepers *Wa-1*, *Wa-2*, *Tama Maru*, *Hagoromo Maru*, and *Noshiro Maru No 2*, and subchaser *Tama Maru No 8*. Shima's task was to seize Tulagi, Gavutu, and Tanambogo at dawn on 3 May to set up a seaplane base for the next stage of Operation MO.[12]

Once the Tulagi Invasion Force had set off, the heavy cruisers *Aoba*, *Kako*, *Kinugasa*, and *Furutaka* left Truk at 1015 hours. The 6th Sentai was part of Rear Adm. Aritomo Gotō's MO Main Force, which also included the light carrier *Shōhō* and the destroyer *Sazanami*; they departed from Truk slightly later, at 1500 hours.[13] Gotō was to pass between Bougainville and Choiseul, join his forces together, and head southeast, from where he was supposed to cover the landings on Tulagi, Gavutu, and Tanambogo. On completing this objective, the ships under his and Marumo's command were to be withdrawn west to support the invasion of Port Moresby.[14]

The last element of the Japanese preparations on 30 April included dispatching submarines *I-22*, *I-24*, *I-28*, and *I-29* from Truk. They all went on patrol southwest of Guadalcanal and were to hold that advanced line until 5 May. *I-28* also had one Glen at her disposal, which could be used to detect the Allied transport ships bound for the eastern coast of Australia.

At 0600 hours on 1 May the Fourth Fleet moved its most powerful figure from Truk: Vice Adm. Takeo Takagi's MO Kidō Butai. This force was built around Rear Adm. Chūichi Hara's 5th Kōkū Sentai, which featured the *Shōkaku*

PHOTO 4 ■ Rear Adm. Kiyohide Shima, commander of the Tulagi Invasion Force *NDL*

and the *Zuikaku*. The carriers were screened by the heavy cruisers *Myōkō* and *Haguro* and the destroyers *Ushio*, *Akebono*, *Ariake*, *Yūgure*, *Shiratsuyu*, and *Shigure*. The fuel for all of the ships was provided by one oiler, the *Tōhō Maru*. Takagi had orders to steam southward, go around the Solomon Islands from the east by 4 May, replenish the fuel supplies, and enter the Coral Sea. Passing south of Guadalcanal and Rennell Island on 6 and 7 May, the MO Kidō Butai was to operate within three hundred miles southwest of Tulagi to provide air cover for the landing operations and, most importantly, to search for any Allied naval forces and destroy them if they attempted to intervene in Operation MO. Unfortunately, it wasn't as easy as it might have looked. Takagi and Hara were also burdened with a very troublesome task. The Nippon Kaigun wanted to take advantage of the 5th Kōkū Sentai's run southward to reinforce the Tainan Kū with nine Zeros to rebuild the land-based group before the decisive fight over Port Moresby. Four extra spare fighters were boarded on the *Zuikaku* and five on the *Shōkaku*. During the route southward, the ferried planes were to be flown by the crews of the *Shōkaku* and the *Zuikaku* to Rabaul, who would return to the carriers later in seven Kates.[15]

Just a few hours after the departure from Truk, the MO Kidō Butai received a warning from the Fourth Fleet's transport plane, which had sighted one ship, possibly a submarine, about 120 miles ahead of the carriers. Since the enemy vessel was heading north, Takagi needed to remain vigilant on his route. The *Zuikaku* scrambled one *kambaku* and two *kankō* for the reconnaissance and antisubmarine patrol. However, at about 1830 hours the weather in the area suddenly worsened. Heavy rain and a strong wind prevented the aircraft from returning to the carrier, forcing the crews to head for Truk. At about 1930 hours, one Val and one Kate crash-landed on the lagoon near Lossop Island. Most of the crew members were rescued later, but the planes required maintenance. The last *kankō* landed safely in Truk but could not rejoin the *Zuikaku* because it was dark, and the following morning there was a considerable distance between the base and the MO Kidō Butai.[16]

The MO Kidō Butai's journey toward the Solomon Islands was also backed up by the Yokohama Kū, which sent three Mavises from Shortland, led by Sub-lieutenant Narita. They took off at 0705 hours and went for reconnaissance missions in three southwestern sectors. The aircraft found no enemy and returned to base at 1610 hours.[17]

Once all the wheels were in motion, at about 1700 hours the *Kashima* left Truk with Vice Admiral Inoue and his staff officers on board. The cruiser took a course toward Rabaul, where the Fourth Fleet intended to supervise the progress of Operation MO more effectively.[18]

For the Japanese, 2 May was of vital importance for two reasons. First, the MO Kidō Butai was expected to deliver nine fighters for the Tainan Kū. According to the report from the previous day, the unit had only eighteen operational Zeros and thirty pilots. Although six Zeros were being repaired and the crews could also fly on four available Claudes, additional Zeros would make a massive difference in the upcoming days.[19] Second, the Tulagi Invasion

Force was to arrive at Tulagi anchorage in the late evening, seizing the island in the following hours.

At 1215 hours, nine fighters and seven bombers took off from the *Shōkaku* and the *Zuikaku* and headed to Rabaul. However, after one hour, at about the halfway point, they were forced to return to the MO Kidō Butai due to very bad weather. All of the aircraft had landed on the carriers safely by 1400 hours. The meteorological forecast was quite bad, so the mission was abandoned for the rest of the day. But Takagi understood the significance of delivering nine fighters for the Tainan Kū. At 1700 hours he reassured the Fourth Fleet and the Eleventh Air Fleet that he was not giving up so quickly. He informed them about the bad weather and the decision to postpone the aircraft transfer to 3 May. This naturally influenced the first refueling of the MO Kidō Butai, which would be executed at Point A (4° S, 158 °E) at 0700 hours on 4 May, about 230 miles north of Santa Isabel. After the refueling, Takagi planned to bypass the Solomon Islands from the east and operate about two hundred miles south of Tulagi. The second refueling was scheduled for 8 May.[20]

During the day, Gotō queried Inoue, Takagi, and Hara about assigning three Zeros and pilots from the 5th Kōkū Sentai to the *Shōhō* to compensate for her feeble fighter group. Gotō was particularly worried about the safety of the transport ships. Inoue understood his concern, although he didn't like the idea of weakening the MO Kidō Butai. He ordered Hara to cover the convoy's approach to Port Moresby and to collaborate with the *Shōhō* as a sensible compromise to solve this issue.[21]

The initial moves in the Tulagi invasion operation were made by the Yokohama Kū, which sent two flying boats from Shortland. At 0355, long before dawn, Lieutenant Commander Tashiro's Mavises, each armed with six 60-kg bombs, went over the island to harass the enemy forces. They dropped the bombs on a motor torpedo boat sighted in the local anchorage, reporting setting the vessel on fire. In the following hours the Yokohama Kū also dispatched three flying boats to conduct reconnaissance, but they didn't spot any enemy vessels or planes.[22]

At about 0800 hours the *Shōhō* and the *Sazanami* joined the 6th Sentai in the channel north of Bougainville. Unexpectedly, the MO Main Force was sighted by an enemy flying boat. Gotō hastily ordered fighters to be scrambled from the light carrier to intercept the snooper. The description of this pursuit remains vague in the Japanese reports, although we know that PO2c Tamura's Claude was damaged and crash-landed at sea. Unfortunately, the pilot was not rescued.[23]

Having arrived at Blanche Channel at 0006 hours, the *Kamikawa Maru* provided the air reconnaissance with her six seaplanes until 1830 hours. Daves and Petes carefully studied the Allied positions on Tulagi, Gavutu, and Tanambogo, reporting the presence of only two PBYs and one motor torpedo boat. The pilots machine-gunned all targets at least three times and claimed to sink the vessel.[24]

To execute the revised plan to transfer nine Zeros for the Tainan Kū, Takagi ordered the MO Kidō Butai to steam along a square counterclockwise and return to the southern course after midnight. At 1200 hours on 3 May, nine Zeros and seven Kates took off from the *Zuikaku* and the *Shōkaku*. Again, the planes encountered terrible weather off the northeastern coast of New Ireland and decided to return to the carriers at 1310 hours.[25] Despite the heavy rain, all but one managed to land safely on the decks. Only one of *Shōkaku*'s fighters ditched near the carrier. The aircraft sank, yet the pilot was rescued. This time, however, the Japanese ships didn't reverse the course like they had on 2 May and continued to steam southward. At 2000 hours Takagi sent a dispatch to Inoue informing him about the circumstances of another failed transfer. Because the MO Kidō Butai was scheduled to refuel the following morning and the weather forecast was still bad, Takagi suggested abandoning the transfer until 5 May. The fighters and bombers were flying from much farther away, the Coral Sea, so they were to use bases on Buka Island and New Ireland to reach Rabaul. If the situation didn't allow this, other attempts would be carried out on 7 and 8 May and the MO Kidō Butai would operate south of Tulagi. The Fourth Fleet staff also analyzed this problem and agreed with Takagi's plan. Hara was instructed to detach the *Shōkaku* and two destroyers to reduce the distance to Rabaul and to proceed with the transfer when possible. The additional cables sent by Inoue instructed the MO Kidō Butai to enter the Coral Sea, sneak to Port Moresby from the northeast, and, by cooperating with the *Shōhō*, destroy the enemy base and its remaining air force up to two days before the landing. Inoue's vision probably looked

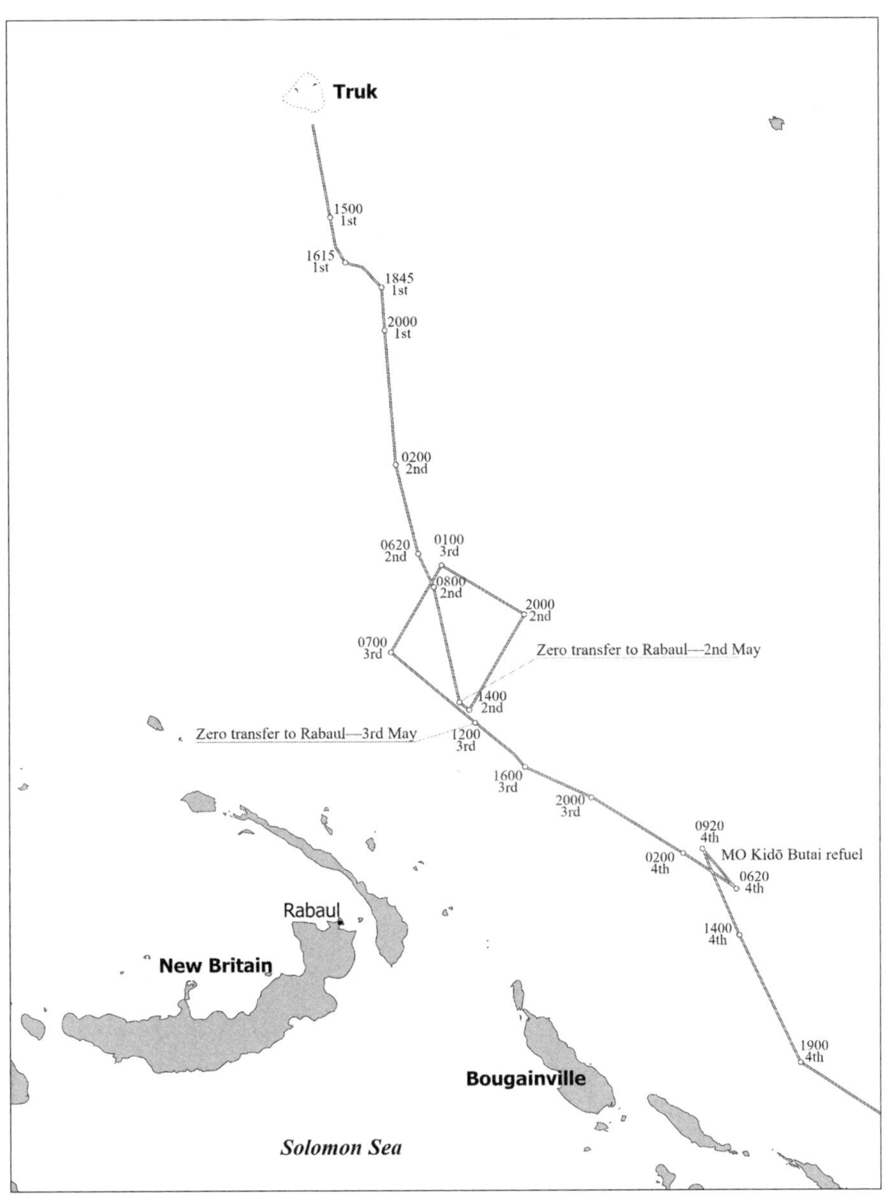

MAP 4 ■ MO Kidō Butai route from Truk, 1–4 May

compelling to his staff, but the Japanese couldn't predict that just one move by Fletcher would thwart this plan.[26]

Settling aside the MO Kidō Butai's problems, the main Japanese objective for the upcoming days was seizing Tulagi. The Allied garrison was made up of only twenty-one Australian commandos from the 2/1st Independent Company and twenty-five men from the 11th Squadron from the RAAF. There were also four Catalinas at the Gavutu-Tanambogo seaplane base. The defenders, with only four machine guns, were unprepared to defend the islands from repeated enemy air attacks or invasions. The successful raid on 30 April, which ended with one seriously damaged Catalina, proved their limited capacities. The soldiers stationed on the islands had only one task: to demolish the military installations and evacuate if the enemy appeared.[27]

On 1 and 2 May the Japanese flying boats and seaplanes appeared several times over Tulagi, dropping bombs and machine-gunning the defenders' positions, but without visible success. Three RAAF Catalinas arrived in Tulagi in the early afternoon of 1 May to help with the evacuation. Before that, the Japanese ships were sighted by a Catalina near New Georgia, steaming toward the southern part of the Solomon Islands. The base was warned about the enemy and hastened to finish the demolition and escape from the islands. As a last shot, another Catalina, armed with bombs, scrambled at dusk and went to attack the Japanese task force. Before dawn, the flying boat found the enemy ships and dropped bombs on two merchant vessels but did not secure any hits and retreated to Port Moresby.[28]

On 2 May, at 0450 and 0600 hours, the last two Catalinas took off from Tulagi to conduct reconnaissance flights on the withdrawal route to Port Moresby. When both flying boats were airborne, they saw the Japanese seaplanes raiding the base but could do nothing to help the defenders. At about 1100 hours the base received an order from Port Moresby to retain part of the fuel reserves necessary for further operations. However, a moment later, the garrison was told to destroy all installations and withdraw to Florida Island. Sirens sounded on all three islands and the Australians began planting explosives and preparing to evacuate. The soldiers had two escape plans and assumed they had to get to Florida Island, where an 80-ton, 60-foot-long vessel, the *Balus*, owned by the island trader and camouflaged and hidden amid the mangroves, was waiting for them to reach Guadalcanal. If the *Balus* was destroyed or the Japanese warships blocked the anchorage, they intended to march through the middle of Florida, along the government trail, to await help at the island's eastern tip.

As night fell, a great storm broke out over the area. The last soldiers detonated the bombs and then left Gavutu on two barges. This is how Cliff Searle recalled the escape from the island:[29]

> We decided to leave the base, as the Japanese were only sixty miles away. Took "Betty-Jane" (Petrol Barge), Bomb Scow and all the chaps to Halavo. Just reached the shore at 0630 when over came the Jap bombers. We ran for the jungle. They dropped bombs, repeat attack, then float-fighter planes sank our crash boat with cannon fire. Leading Aircraft sman [*sic*] (LAC) Keith Robinson and Peter swam ashore. I went back to the base on the scow to get the C.O. [Flying Officer Peagum, who had arrived on 20 April] and the four remaining wireless operators. More fighters came over bombing our island. We got to Halavo in the scow with secret gear, also the Wireless. Another fighter overhead at 1745. We prepared for Scorched Earth System. 2030 fires going everywhere. I stayed behind with an army chap and blew up a bomb dump. 2230 We remaining chaps travel[ed] three miles in the scow and Petrol barge to track, which would lead us to the "Balus." Blew-up petrol barge and 1700 gallons petrol, scuttled Bomb Scow and left at 0200 hours for Aola.

Having fled from Florida, the Australians picked up nineteen commandos from the southeastern tip of Guadalcanal. They retreated from Tulagi and Gavutu at the last minute before the Japanese appeared on the beaches. Despite some problems with the engine, the *Balus* headed toward San Cristóbal. This part of the trip was very tense, because they were spotted by a Japanese flying boat. The Mavis circled over the vessel for twenty minutes but took her for a local boat and didn't attack to avoid antagonizing the indigenous people. The *Balus* reached San Cristóbal safely, and a few days later she set course for Espiritu Santo. On 14 May the vessel eventually arrived at Port Vila on Efate.[30]

Regarding the Japanese part of the story, the Tulagi Invasion Force steamed for thirty-five hours toward the southern part of the Solomon Islands and sighted the Guadalcanal coast in the distance. The warships turned on the searchlights to check the surrounding waters to ensure that no enemy torpedo boats were lurking behind them. At about 2130 hours the vanguard passed north of Savo Island, and two and a half hours later the ships reached Tulagi. The minesweepers approached the harbor first, followed by the rest of the group. At midnight, under the moonlight and the fierce fire of ground installations, the 3rd Kure Special Naval Landing Force boarded the Kokosuka landing crafts.[31]

The Japanese planned to land on the beach in the northern part of Tulagi, but due to problems reaching the shore with the landing barges, the soldiers of the 3rd Company were forced to wade through water during the last section of the route. The invaders expected resistance but discovered that Tulagi, Gavutu, and Tanambogo had been abandoned by the Australians and the indigenous population.[32] Seaman Engineer Yomodama Mori of the 3rd Kure SNLF made the following notes in his diary:[33]

> We loaded our AT [antitank] guns on a large landing barge so they would be available when we faced the enemy. We packed blankets, belongings, etc., and put our name on each one and [were] ready to unload at Gavutu and Tulagi. At 1500 [on 2 May], a [minelayer, *Okinoshima*] sailed in front of our vessel, [and] reported it sighted an enemy seaplane. We recognized a four-mast warship ahead, but it was a friendly ship. At 2400 hours, we sighted island [Gavutu]. Our SNLF gathered on the stern [of the *Azumasan Maru*] and we saw something burning on the island. . . . [O] ur guard destroyers [*Kikuzuki* and *Yuzuki*] had stopped. *Okinoshima* and *Azumasan Maru* advanced. Our 120–30 men started to head for the coast in large landing craft. We placed bullets in our "I" type rifles. Approaching the coast, 500 meters, 400 meters, 300 meters, 200 meters, and 100 meters and then 50 meters and carefully landed on pier. No resistance. It seems the enemy has escaped and burned their barracks.

Tulagi, Gavutu, and Tanambogo were secured by 0700 hours. As the sun rose, the *Shōhō*'s three Zeros and three Kates appeared over the islands to provide air cover.[34] The *Kamikawa Maru*'s four Daves soon supported them. The seaplanes were organized in two flights led by Lieutenant Minematsu and Ensign Shimura, who kept their eyes out for enemy submarines close to the landing spots.[35] Before sunset, the Kiyokawa Maru's one Pete also quickly checked for any potential intruders.[36] In the meantime, the minesweepers found no mines in the local waters and the transport ships had entered the harbor by 0900 hours to unload men and supplies. Some of the Japanese soldiers found some food rations in the barracks that the Australians had failed to destroy. The commanders of individual platoons inspected their units and recorded no losses. The construction unit hastily set up the seaplane base for six flying boats and six seaplanes, and this was completed by 1945 hours.[37]

Searching for the American carrier task force south of the Solomon Islands, the Yokosuka Kū's three flying boats, led by Lieutenant Urada, took off from Shortland at 0715 hours. They found no enemy vessels or planes and had returned to base by 1655 hours. At 1140 hours the Yokohama Kū's Mavis took off from Rabaul to deliver equipment and specialists to Tulagi. The flying boat arrived at 1615 hours. By the end of the day the Japanese had already transferred three Mavises to Tulagi.[38] All the units were notified about the successful landing and the taking control of the islands, so the Japanese started the next phase of Operation MO.[39] Marumo and Gotō withdrew west to support the invasion of Port Moresby. It was also the time for the oiler *Irō* to set off from Rabaul and head to Shortland, where she was expected to refuel the screening vessels in the following days.

At 1700 hours the *Kamikawa Maru* departed Blanche Channel and headed to Shortland.[40] The *Shōkaku* and two destroyers were prepared to be detached from the MO Kidō Butai after the scheduled refueling and approached Rabaul to make a third attempt at transferring Zeros for the Tainan Kū.[41] Once the setting up of the seaplane base and refueling were completed, the *Hagoromo Maru* and the *Noshiro Maru No 2*, now formally part of the Port Moresby Invasion Force, departed from Tulagi and took a course toward Deboyne. The same evening, the *Toshi Maru No 3* and the *Keijō Maru* steamed together toward the Port Moresby Invasion Force.[42]

Chapter 4

THE *YORKTOWN* STRIKES ON TULAGI AND GAVUTU

While the Japanese soldiers and construction workers were on the beaches of Tulagi, Gavutu, and Tanambogo, Rear Admiral Fletcher was anxiously awaiting reports from reconnaissance planes sent from Allied bases to fly over the Solomon Islands and the Bismarck Islands. At about 1830 hours, TF 17 received a warning that an enemy force made up of five or six vessels had been sighted off the southern end of Santa Isabel the previous evening and was steaming toward Tulagi. Half an hour later Fletcher had another cable from the SoWePac command informing him about the progressing occupation of Tulagi. Refraining from joining Rear Admirals Fitch and Crace for the time being, he detached the *Neosho* and the *Russell* at 2030 hours. They set a southern course while he left a message for Fitch about the circumstances surrounding his changing the plans. TF 17 headed north at twenty-seven knots to attack the Japanese on Tulagi early in the morning.[1]

At dawn on 4 May, TF 17 was approximately one hundred miles south of Guadalcanal. The weather deteriorated significantly. Thick clouds obscured the sky over the Coral Sea, and the rain squalls significantly reduced visibility. The southeast wind blowing at twenty-five knots made it even harder to conduct air operations. In contrast, no heavy clouds or rainfall were observed near

Tulagi. According to the air officers in the *Yorktown*, this was the perfect occasion for a surprise raid on the island occupied by the Japanese.[2]

With her offensive potential of sixty fighters and bombers, the *Yorktown* could cause a lot of trouble for the enemy. At 0631 hours the carrier scrambled six F4Fs led by Lt. Vincent McCormack. The fighters were ordered to patrol designated areas during the day. Soon after, the first striking group, consisting of twenty-eight SBDs and twelve TBDs, was airborne. Each Dauntless was armed with one 1000-pound bomb, and each Devastator with one Mk XIII torpedo. Torpedo bombers were the first to take off from the *Yorktown*, followed by dive bombers in two batches. The group departed without escorts, because no significant threats from the enemy fighters were expected.[3]

On their route north, the striking group encountered no enemy aircraft. Flying over Guadalcanal, they soon arrived over Tulagi harbor, which was partially covered with dense clouds. Just after 0800 hours Lt. Cdr. William Burch sighted several Japanese ships. The *Okinoshima* was anchored at the pier, and one destroyer was resupplying fuel on her port side. He also located two large transports accompanied by smaller vessels and two submarine chasers in the distance. Three auxiliary minesweepers were heading northwest, probably to Shortland. All enemy units anchored off Tulagi were busy unloading supplies ashore and helping to set up the seaplane base. The Japanese were completely surprised by the *Yorktown* striking group. Most units were in the middle of their routine duties. At about 0700 hours the Yokohama Kū sent three flying boats, led by WO Takahashi, for the reconnaissance patrols in the western arc of the Coral Sea.[4] According to the plans, the *Kamikawa Maru* arrived in Shortland at 0700 hours and scrambled two Daves to investigate the local anchorage for the submarines.[5] The *Shōhō* had withdrawn west and

TABLE 4 **Composition of the *Yorktown*'s First Striking Group against Tulagi, Morning of 4 May 1942**

Unit	Commander	Planes
VS-5	Lt. Cdr. William Burch	13 SBDs
VB-5	Lt. Wallace Short	15 SBDs
VT-5	Lt. Cdr. Joe Taylor	12 TBDs

hadn't scheduled any morning patrols over the newly established base in the Solomons. This meant that the only active aircraft over Tulagi were those from the *Kiyokawa Maru* air group. At 0810 hours, right before the Americans arrived, she sent Lt. Mishiro's Pete to provide air cover.[6]

Burch's SBDs attacked first, at 0815 hours. They started the approach from approximately ten thousand feet, aiming for the *Okinoshima* and the destroyers *Kikuzuki* and *Yūzuki*. VS-5 divided tactically into two divisions. They both encountered heavy but inaccurate antiaircraft fire. The crews were believed to score four confirmed hits and one probable one on the *Okinoshima*, which they identified as the *Jintsū*-class light cruiser. In reality, all bombs missed the target due to fogged bombsights.[7]

Next were three TBDs, which targeted the *Azumasan Maru*, anchored off the northern shore of Tulagi. The other two Devastators headed for the *Kōei Maru*, moored off Gavutu and Tanambogo. The remaining seven torpedo bombers aimed for the destroyers. VT-5 attacked the enemy ships simultaneously but without apparent coordination, machine-gunning smaller vessels along the way. The TBDs dropped torpedoes from about fifty feet at about four hundred to one thousand yards from the targets. Although the crews claimed to score at least five hits on the three ships, the only success confirmed by the Japanese sources was a direct hit on the *Kikuzuki*. The fish struck straight into the starboard side, exactly at the engine room, and immobilized the ship. Twelve men were killed and fourteen slightly wounded. The destroyer was flooding rapidly so the *Toshi Maru No 3* took her in tow and beached her near the Gavutu shore.[8]

Tactically divided into three divisions, Short's dive bombers ended the onslaught. They went for the transport ships and the auxiliary vessels but didn't secure any hits. Like the attack of VS-5, VB-5's attack ended with a poor outcome due to the fogged bombsights, significantly hindering the accuracy during the dive.[9]

Once they had expended their bombs and torpedoes, all the *Yorktown*'s planes set a return course. According to the Japanese sources, the first attack lasted about twenty minutes.[10] During the strike, a TBD piloted by Ens. George E. Bottjer was damaged by the antiaircraft fire and had trouble catching up with the rest of the group. As the bombers disappeared over the southern horizon, the pilots cabled the first news about the Japanese forces in the

TABLE 5 **Japanese Seaplane Activity during the First Strike on Tulagi, 4 May**

Unit	No.	Crew members		Notes
Pete/*Kiyokawa Maru* air support	1	Sea1c Fukawa *	PO2c Mishiro *	Takeoff: 0810
Petes/*Kiyokawa Maru* air support	1	Lt. Yamada (S)	PO1c Aoyagi	Takeoff: 0830 Landing: 0930
	2	PO1c Kumazawa	PO2c Matsuzawa	
Daves/*Kiyokawa Maru* air support	1	PO2c Shibata (S)	PO2c Miyamoto	Takeoff: 0900 Landing: 1110
	2	Sea1c Uemura	PO2c Aoshima	

Source: JACAR: Kiyokawa Maru (4), 15.
* *Indicates destroyed aircraft*

Tulagi area. According to the report, the enemy had two large cargo ships or transport ships (8,000–10,000 tons), one cargo ship (5,000 tons), four gunboats (1,000–1,500 tons), a light cruiser (*Jintsū* class), two destroyers, and one large seaplane tender. There were also five seaplanes based off Makambo Island and many patrol boats and smaller auxiliary vessels.[11]

The seaplanes mentioned by the American crews belonged to the *Kiyokawa Maru* air group. Between 0830 hours and 0900 hours, two Petes, led by Lieutenant Yamada, and two Daves, led by PO2c Shibata, scrambled to defend the warships in the Tulagi area. Yamada rushed after the withdrawing bombers but soon resigned from the pursuit and had landed by 0930 hours. By that time the Japanese had lost one Pete, set on fire when it took off, but with the crew evacuated from the sinking aircraft.[12]

While the first striking group was on its way back, at 0844 hours, McCormack's F4Fs landed on the *Yorktown* and were soon replaced by six Wildcats led by Lt. Cdr. Charles Fenton. Also, to make more room for the returning bombers, another six fueled F4Fs, led by Lt. Cdr. James Flatley, were airborne. This raised the number of fighters in CAP to twelve planes.

Starting at 0931 hours the first striking group landed on the *Yorktown*. Following Fletcher's decision to launch a second attack on Tulagi, the planes were hastily refueled and rearmed. Between 1036 hours and 1120 hours, twenty-seven SBDs and eleven TBDs rose into the air. Each Dauntless was armed with one 1000-pound bomb and each Devastator with a Mk XIII torpedo. All three squadrons headed north separately; however, VS-5 and VB-5 were

TABLE 6 **Composition of the *Yorktown's* Second Striking Group against Tulagi, Morning of 4 May 1942**

Unit	Commander	Planes
VS-5	Lt. Cdr. William Burch	13 SBDs
VB-5	Lt. Wallace Short	14 SBDs
VT-5	Lt. Cdr. Joe Taylor	11 TBDs

also to scout the western and northwestern parts of Florida Island and then fly over Tulagi. The position of the enemy ships was to be reported to VT-5, which would make a decision about attacking the priority targets.[13]

Immediately after sending the second striking group, the *Yorktown* took six of Fenton's Wildcats on board and by noon had sent McCormack's section again, maintaining twelve fighters in CAP.

The American raid on Tulagi was a severe shock for the Fourth Fleet and the MO Kidō Butai, although it did not surprise Shima. Inoue had been awake since 0500 hours, and the *Kashima* was slowly approaching Rabaul.[14] Suddenly, at 0824 hours, the *Okinoshima*'s desperate warning reached all units. Shima alerted them that he was being attacked by six carrier-borne planes at 0815 hours and later by the torpedo bombers.[15] He abandoned the refueling of the destroyers and issued orders to rapidly escape southward.[16] Shima believed the American task force was within a 160-mile range from Tulagi. In the follow-up messages, he adjusted this distance to 300 miles based on the time that the enemy planes spent over the island and the lack of fighter escort.[17]

The MO Kidō Butai was in the middle of refueling, which was scheduled to end in the following two hours, when the disturbing news reached Takagi. At 0920 hours he ordered the refueling to stop and that they should head south to get close to the enemy carrier task force.[18] He planned to be about two hundred miles north of Guadalcanal by 2000 hours. At 0940 hours Inoue confirmed that the American carriers had been operating within a two-hundred-mile range from Tulagi. The MO Kidō Butai was to shorten the refueling time to proceed with Takagi's plan.[19]

This time, the Japanese intended to strengthen the air support over Tulagi if the enemy appeared again. At 1120 hours the *Kiyokawa Maru* air group

TABLE 7 **Japanese Seaplane Activity during the Second Strike on Tulagi, 4 May**

Unit	No.	Crew members		Notes
Pete/*Kiyokawa Maru* air support	1	Lt. Yamada (S)*	PO1c Aoyagi*	Takeoff: 1130 Landing: 1330
Dave/*Kiyokawa Maru* air support	1	PO1c Kumazawa	PO2c Matsuzawa	
Petes/*Kamikawa Maru* air support	1	Ens. Shimura	PO2c Kashiyama	Takeoff: 1135 Landing: 1330
	2	WO Kageyama†	Sea1c Taka†	
	3	WO Uemura†	Sea1c Takenouchi†	

Sources: JACAR: Kiyokawa Maru (4), 16; JACAR: Kamikawa Maru (2), 4.
* *Indicates destroyed aircraft*
† *Lost in action*

scrambled one Dave and one Pete. Five minutes later, the *Kamikawa Maru* sent three Petes from Shortland.

VB-5 passed over Florida Island to spot the ships escaping from Tulagi. Five miles northeast of Savo Island, they sighted three minesweepers, mistakenly identified as gunboats. The squadron split into three divisions and attacked the vessels from the stern and bow sides. The SBDs had sunk *Wa 1* and *Wa 2* within seconds. The last minesweeper, the *Tama Maru*, avoided receiving direct hits but was severely damaged by near misses and was strafed by machine guns.[20]

Most Japanese ships followed Shima's order and sought to escape from the area, but some were too slow to raise the anchor and leave on time. The second striking group caught many vessels dashing out of the Strait. At about noon, VS-5 arrived over Tulagi harbor. Less than ten minutes later, SBDs rushed against the *Okinoshima*, which was taken for the seaplane tender. The dive bombers approached the target from about twenty-five hundred feet and claimed to have scored two direct hits.[21] However, none of the bombs were accurate, and the minelayer got away by zigzagging at twenty knots.

During VS-5's attack, one of the SBD pilots noticed the Japanese seaplane trying to get close to the bombers. The enemy, the *Kiyokawa Maru*'s Pete, was machine-gunned and started to lose altitude. The Americans claimed an undisputed victory, but the air unit's report says that the aircraft was seriously damaged in the dogfight and sank after crash-landing on the sea.[22]

Flying over Gavutu, the raiders found the enemy seaplane base and the Yokohama Kū's flying boats on the water. At least two were machine-gunned and it was claimed they were damaged, although the unit records do not mention any significant losses on that day. The antiaircraft Mitsuwa Unit, stationed at Toridai Hill on Tulagi, tried to down the dive bombers with their 80-mm guns, but without success. The American planes strafed the ground installations and soldiers' positions. The 3rd Kure SNLF counted five killed men and twenty-nine wounded.[23]

The TBDs were the last ones to arrive on the stage, at 1245 hours. They split into two divisions consisting of six and five aircraft. Both groups aimed for the *Okinoshima*, but the anvil attack was not very well coordinated and they failed to score any hits due to heavy antiaircraft fire. While closing in on the target, the *Kiyokawa Maru*'s Dave engaged one of the Devastators about five miles southwest of Tulagi. The crew of the American bomber chased off the seaplane, which was badly damaged and was soon forced to ditch near Makambo.[24]

Among the planes of the second striking group, all but one TBD returned to the carrier. One Devastator, piloted by Lt. Leonard E. Ewoldt, could not find its way back to TF 17, and it was impossible to determine its position by radio.

In the meantime, the *Yorktown* recovered Flatley's section to refuel. McCormack's F4Fs continued to circle above in poor weather conditions. Fenton's section was ready to launch and was waiting for precise instructions.[25] When TF 17 got the news about the enemy seaplanes, Fletcher sent four Wildcats led by Lt. William Leonard. The fighters were airborne at 1310 hours and were told to escort torpedo and dive bombers and engage any enemy planes they encountered. Immediately after the VF-42 planes departed, twenty-one SBDs landed on the *Yorktown* and were quickly refueled and rearmed for the third strike.[26]

The Japanese garrison alarmed the other units about the second strike. The antiaircraft artillery detachment did everything to protect the base against the enemy bombers but was overwhelmed by the sheer number of intruders. The gunners wondered where the friendly carriers had been and whether they could rely on any air support.[27] Contrary to expectations, the MO Kidō Butai was too far from the Solomon Islands to send relief. Still, Takagi interrupted the

TABLE 8 **Reconnaissance Missions from the *Zuikaku*, Morning of 4 May 1942**

Unit	No.	Pilot	Observer	Radio operator	Notes
Kates/*Zuikaku* 130 degrees	1	PO1c Hori	Ens. Matsunaga (S)	PO2c Ōta	Takeoff: 1000 Landing: 1350
	2	Sea1c Morimitsu	PO2c Hiwatashi	Sea1c Tani	
Kates/*Zuikaku* 140 degrees	1	PO1c Satō (S)	PO1c Kawabata	PO2c Yoshida	
	2	Sea1c Nishitani	PO2c Matsuo	Sea1c Ōizumi	
Kates/*Zuikaku* 150 degrees	1	PO1c Ishihara	WO Kanazawa (S)	PO2c Nishizawa	
	2	Sea1c Tsubokawa	PO2c Idehara	PO2c Ikushima	

Source: JACAR: Zuikaku (1), 30.

refueling and rushed south. Hara organized a quick meeting of the 5th Kōkū Sentai staff to discuss the possible options. Mieno and Yamaoka agreed that the best they could do was to investigate the approach southward.[28] Thus, at 1000 hours, the *Zuikaku* scrambled six Kates, flying in pairs, to scout the 130-, 140-, and 150-degree sectors. The *kankō* were ordered to search at 250 miles and then 20 miles in the right outward leg.[29]

Leonard's four F4Fs arrived over Tulagi within thirty minutes. By this time, all aircraft from the second striking group had completed their attacks and set a return course. For a moment, it seemed that VF-42 had marked its presence too late. However, at 1350 hours the *Kamikawa Maru*'s three Petes unexpectedly appeared on the battlefield. Having sighted the enemy seaplanes, Leonard waved with his wings, signaling to attack. He was soon joined by his wingman, Ens. Edgar Bassett. In a short dogfight, they downed two Petes and then returned to the rest of the section. The Japanese sources confirm the destruction of two seaplanes, those piloted by WO Kageyama and WO Uemura. Although Leonard and Bassett also claimed to shoot down the third one, Ensign Shimura avoided death by escaping south.[30]

It wasn't long before the Wildcats found one of VB-5's victims, the damaged *Tama Maru*, northwest of Florida Island. Taking advantage of the vessel's critical condition, two F4Fs mercilessly strafed her, killing four men and wounding seven. The demolished minesweeper ran aground. As the fighters withdrew, they knew she was doomed. Eventually, the *Tama Maru* met her destiny near Buena Vista Island, west of Florida, two days later.[31]

Subsequently, Leonard's section came across the *Yūzuki*, which was fleeing in terror from the Tulagi anchorage. Her stern and bow were machine-gunned during a few passes, although the pilots mainly aimed at the engine room, the torpedo tubes, and the bridge. The destroyer soon began leaking oil, and a black trace was visible from above. As mentioned in the 19th Sentai war diary, ten men were killed, including the skipper, Lt. Cdr. Hirota Tachibana, and twenty-four were severely wounded. Losses on the ship included minor damage to the hull, gun No. 4 and machine guns on the port side being rendered nonoperational, a ruptured telephone line, and damaged navigation equipment. On the same day, the *Yūzuki* was ordered to return to Rabaul. It was planned that she would be hastily repaired and be ready to participate in the second phase of Operation MO.[32]

Having flown to the end of the reconnaissance sector, Ensign Matsunaga, the most senior airman sent from the *Zuikaku* that day, looked at the surface of the sea and said to his pilot, "There is no enemy. Are we coming back?"[33] The Japanese were disappointed, but at least they had all returned safely to the carrier by 1350 hours.[34] Their missions were also essential to check that the enemy hadn't set up any traps on the route southward. Ten minutes later, the Fourth Fleet ordered the MO Kidō Butai to provide air support for the Tulagi garrison as soon as possible, if it was possible at all.[35]

Returning Wildcats accidentally encountered the lost Devastator from the second striking group. They wanted to guide the friendly aircraft but could not determine the correct course because of the bad weather. Ewoldt had been circling for several hours and was slowly running out of fuel, so he turned back toward Guadalcanal, informing the rest of his decision. Due to a misunderstanding, Lt. Elbert McCuskey and Ens. John Adams followed the torpedo bomber while Leonard and Bassett eventually contacted the *Yorktown* and continued south. The latter pair were on board the carrier at 1542 hours, surprised that McCuskey and Adams did not return in the next few minutes.

At 1536 hours Ewoldt cabled TF 17, describing his difficult situation. However, his radio receiver was broken, so when he did not receive a response from the carrier, he ditched a few miles off the southern shore of Guadalcanal. He spent

TABLE 9 **Composition of the *Yorktown*'s Third Striking Group against Tulagi, Afternoon of 4 May 1942**

Unit	Commander	Planes
VS-5	Lt. Cdr. William Burch	12 SBDs
VB-5	Lt. Wallace Short	9 SBDs

the next three days in a rubber lifeboat with RM3c Raymond Machalinski, his radio operator. They finally reached the island, and a friendly indigenous population soon helped them leave.[36] As for McCuskey, he knew he wouldn't be able to go back to the carrier. Thus, he informed the team he would land on a beach in the southern part of Guadalcanal. In response, the *Yorktown* attempted to reach him on the radio, but the communications failed again. Although Adams found the correct bearing, he couldn't contact McCuskey. The winger didn't leave his companion, however, and they both headed toward the island. Two F4Fs made an emergency landing on a beach on the southern coast of Guadalcanal, near Cape Henslow.[37]

Rear Adm. William Smith proposed detaching the heavy cruisers *Chester* and *Astoria* and two destroyers to send them to Tulagi to sweep the remaining enemy ships by the end of the day. After considering this interesting option, Fletcher decided to launch the third strike. By 1400 hours, twenty-one SBDs had taken off from the *Yorktown* to sink as many Japanese units as possible that remained at Tulagi. Typically, each dive bomber was armed with one 1000-pound bomb. Soon after, Fenton's six F4Fs were sent to CAP, and the planes from the second striking group and McCormack's section landed on the carrier.[38]

At about 1500 hours, VS-5 arrived over Tulagi harbor, targeting the undamaged *Azumasan Maru*. Diving from about nine thousand feet, the bombers didn't encounter the heavy enemy antiaircraft fire. Although the crews were convinced they had pounded the transport ship hard, she was only slightly damaged by one direct hit. As a result of this explosion and several near misses, only five men were slightly wounded.[39]

Once VS-5 had expended all its bombs, it moved toward the submarine chaser, mistakenly identified as a gunboat. VS-5 machine-gunned her and changed the target to another gunboat. After several passes, SBDs sank and damaged a couple of landing craft.

In the meantime, VB-5 had located the *Kōei Maru* five miles northeast of Savo Island. She was taking on board the survivors from other ships. When the Japanese noticed enemy dive bombers, they immediately started to escape. The SBDs left her alone and followed the trail of oil. This led them to the *Yūzuki* and the *Okinoshima*, which were fleeing toward the Russell Islands. At about 1515 hours, VB-5 attacked the minelayer from the bow and starboard sides but didn't score any hits. Only two bombs exploded near the hull, slowing down the vessel by a few knots. Fourteen men were killed and sixteen wounded.[40] After recovering from the dive, Burch ordered his squadron to abandon the strafing and return. The third and final strike against the Japanese forces at Tulagi was over.[41]

The loss of one TBD and two F4Fs, particularly their crews, was regrettable news for Fletcher. He expected to engage the MO Kidō Butai in the following days, so he needed to keep his air groups intact, especially the fighter squadron, considered an essential element for defending the carrier task force. Since no enemy aircraft had been spotted nearby and TF 17 was only forty-two miles south of Guadalcanal, Fletcher sent the *Perkins* to rescue Ewoldt and Machalinski. Less than ten minutes later, the *Hammann* was also detached to find McCuskey and Adams, who were expected to be near Cape Henslow.

Once the destroyers headed toward Guadalcanal, Flatley's six F4Fs took off on CAP. The *Yorktown* accommodated twenty-one SBDs from the third striking group. Finally, at 1747 hours, the last Wildcats returned on the carrier. The upcoming dusk convinced Fletcher to abandon the idea of sending two cruisers and two destroyers to Tulagi to sweep the enemy vessels that had survived the raid. Thus, TF 17 eventually took a southerly course toward TF 11 and TF 44 to refuel at the previously designated Corn Point.[42]

Proceeding at thirty knots for almost one and a half hours, the *Hammann* sighted the outline of Guadalcanal at 1810 hours. The shallow waters around Cape Henslow and the storm prevented the destroyer from approaching closer to the coast than three miles. Still, the observers soon noticed two missing Wildcats and parachutes serving as markers. A motor whaleboat was launched for a rescue but didn't reach the shore due to the heavy surf. Finally, after many attempts, both pilots paddled out on their rubber rafts to the whaleboat and had been transported to the *Hammann* by 2048 hours. In the meantime, the *Perkins* hadn't found the Devastator and the crew despite several hours of searching. Eventually, both destroyers set a southerly course to rejoin TF 17.[43]

In the report about the air raid on Tulagi, the Americans presented a list of Japanese vessels that had been sunk or damaged by the *Yorktown*. The results could have been better at first glance, but the reality seemed even worse when compared with the Japanese records. Although the carrier had engaged her entire air group throughout the day, she only achieved a marginally significant operation. The Japanese resistance was nonexistent but the *Yorktown* still lost three planes, including one crew from the torpedo bomber. The attackers sank four ships and damaged two. The assessment of the strike on Tulagi must include another essential factor, though: as many as 22 torpedoes, 76 bombs, and more than 82,000 machine gun rounds were used.[44]

Despite the disappointing outcome, the accounts of the *Yorktown* crew show that the raid on Tulagi gave everybody the necessary training and practice to gain the self-confidence that had been lacking since the action against Lae and Salamaua in March. On learning of the first losses inflicted on the Japanese, Nimitz also decided to uplift the fighting spirit in TF 17 and congratulated Fletcher, counting on a favorable result in the upcoming carrier battle with the MO Kidō Butai.[45]

When VS-5 and VB-5 from the third striking group hunted for the Japanese vessels, the *Kiyokawa Maru* air group scrambled PO2c Shibata's Dave at 1500

TABLE 10 **Summary of the *Yorktown* Raid on Tulagi, 4 May**

Japanese losses according to the *Yorktown's* report	Actual Japanese losses
Sunk vessels: one *Jintsū*-class light cruiser, two destroyers, one transport ship	Sunk vessels: the *Kikuzuki*, *Tama Maru*, *Wa 1*, and *Wa 2*
Severely damaged: one *Asashio*-class destroyer, one seaplane tender	
Damaged: one cargo ship	Damaged: the *Okinoshima*, the *Yūzuki* Slightly damaged: the *Tama Maru No 2*, the *Kōei Maru*
Destroyed planes: five Petes Damaged planes: two Mavises	Destroyed planes: four Petes Damaged planes: one Dave

Sources: JACAR: 19 Sentai (3), 41–43; JACAR: Kamikawa Maru (2), 4; JACAR: Kiyokawa Maru (4), 15–16.

hours. The pilot felt confident he could sneak behind the enemy's back and follow the attacking bombers, which would unwittingly guide him to TF 17. However, the half-fueled aircraft could not catch up with withdrawing SBDs, so Shibata returned after thirty minutes.[46] It had been a murderous day for the Japanese seaplanes. Having lost four Petes over Tulagi, at 1700 hours the *Kamikawa Maru* sent Shimura to search for his two wingmen shot down during the early afternoon clash. The area over the island was finally clear, but there was no sign of the crews. Shimura returned with bad news at 1830 hours.[47]

The information about the end of the American raid on Tulagi reached the Fourth Fleet and the MO Kidō Butai. The enemy was unlikely to attack again and risk landing the aircraft on the carrier after dark. At 1700 hours Takagi informed all units that he would start passing the Solomon Islands from the northeast and rush south at about 0800 hours on 5 May. Once he was about 200 miles from Point "KE," Hara was supposed to send reconnaissance patrols to scout the sectors south and east of Tulagi in the early morning and provide fighter support for the garrison on the island. The Japanese search plan was also assumed to involve the 6th Sentai's seaplanes to cover the 120–205 degree arc from Tulagi at 150 miles. Inoue authorized this plan at 1820 hours. After checking the area south of Tulagi, he instructed the MO Kidō Butai to proceed with the refueling schedule. Then Takagi was ordered to deliver the fighters for the Tainan Kū again. In practice, this would happen no sooner than 6 May.[48]

The decisions made by Inoue and Takagi were only the background of a more critical Japanese move on 4 May. From 1700 to 1800 hours Rear Adm. Sadamichi Kajioka's Port Moresby Invasion Force set off from Rabaul to begin the last phase of Operation MO. The convoy consisted of twelve transport ships, six from the army and six from the navy, screened by the 6th Suirai Sentai, the minelayer *Tsugaru*, and the minesweeper *No. 20*. As well as relying on help from the MO Main Force and the MO Kidō Butai in the following days, Kajioka could count on support from ground-based air units in Rabaul and the auxiliary vessels of the 8th Base Force when he left Simpson Harbor.[49] By landing the South Seas Detachment and part of the 3rd Kure SNLF near Port Moresby on 10 May, the Fourth Fleet foresaw an end to the struggle for New Guinea, which had been stealing too much precious time from the Japanese war machine.

Chapter 5

MAY 5 AND 6 SEARCHES BY EACH SIDE FOR OPPOSING CARRIER FORCES

The raid on Tulagi triggered the Japanese to actively search for the enemy carrier task force first thing in the morning on 5 May. Even before dawn, at 0330 hours, the Yokohama Kū had scrambled three flying boats from Shortland. The group, led by Lieutenant Urada, was supposed to check the sectors south of Guadalcanal. The unit also sent Lieutenant Sakamoto's six flying boats from Tulagi at 0630 hours.

While steaming over Malaita Island and preparing to pass the Solomon Islands from the east, the MO Kidō Butai sent reconnaissance flights according to the previous plans. At 0600 hours the *Shōkaku* and the *Zuikaku* scrambled six Kates each to check the 130–80-degree sectors at 300 miles. The 5th Sentai also participated in the search missions, sending four seaplanes. The *Myōkō*'s Daves were to fly in the 105- and 130-degree sectors at 160 and 250 miles, whereas the *Haguro*'s Daves were ordered to cover the 180- and 200-degree sectors at 250 and 160 miles.[1] Due to bad weather, the 6th Sentai didn't send any aircraft for reconnaissance missions despite the initial plan to do so.[2]

Since the MO Kidō Butai had encountered unexpected complications in the first days of Operation MO, Takagi had to figure out how to return to the original plan and still be able to transfer the fighters for the Tainan Kū. In the morning he suggested that the second refueling would take place at Point

TABLE 11 ■ **Yokohama Kū's Reconnaissance Missions, Morning of 5 May 1942**

Unit	No.	Commander	Notes
Mavises / Yokohama Kū (Shortland)	1	Lt. Urada*	Takeoff: 0330 Landing: 1700
	2	Sub. Lt. Narita	
	3	Ens. Yoshida	
Mavises / Yokohama Kū (Tulagi)	1	Lt. Sakamoto	Takeoff: 0630 Landing: 1650
	2	?	
	3	WO Kubo	
	4	WO Takahashi	
	5	Ens. Ōmori	
	6	WO Ueno	

Source: JACAR: Yokohama Kū (2), 18–19.

* *Presumed killed in action* (The Yokohama Kū's report has an apparent mistake—it mentions two identical crews starting from Shortland and Tulagi.)

TABLE 12 ■ **Reconnaissance Missions from the *Zuikaku*, Morning of 5 May 1942**

Unit	No.	Pilot	Observer	Radio operator	Notes
Kates/*Zuikaku* 130 degrees	1	Lt. Satō (S)	PO1c Ōtani	PO2c Yoshida	Takeoff: 0600 Landing: 1050
	2	PO2c Fukutani	PO2c Kojima	Sea1c Hara	
Kates/*Zuikaku* 140 degrees	1	Lt. Murakami (S)	WO Baba	PO1c Miyada	
	2	PO3c Yokomakura	PO2c Kishi	PO2c Satō	
Kates/*Zuikaku* 150 degrees	1	PO3c Hatanaka	PO1c Ushijima (S)	Sea1c Morishita	
	2	PO1c Tahara	PO2c Ōnishi	PO3c Kanetō	

Source: JACAR: Zuikaku (1), 31.

Note: The *Shōkaku's* report lacks detailed information about the scouting missions on that day.

B (9° 40' S, 157° 20' E) at 0800 hours on 6 May. At 0800 hours the 6th Sentai arrived in Shortland and began replenishing fuel from the *Irō* during the next few hours.[3] Once the four heavy cruisers were ready, they were expected to rejoin the *Shōhō* and the *Sazanami*, which were already engaged in screening the Port Moresby Invasion Force. The light carrier dispatched some fighters to watch over the transport ships during the day. Although one enemy bomber tried to attack the convoy, Zeros successfully chased it off.[4] In return, the

Shōhō was unexpectedly sighted by the enemy aircraft at about 1035 hours.[5] The *Kamikawa Maru*, which had sent one Pete to circle over Shortland, could theoretically provide air support, but the pilot, PO1c Amino, didn't find the intruder. The *Kiyokawa Maru* air group, which sent one Pete and three Daves from Tulagi over Shortland to carry out an antisubmarine patrol, didn't report any intruders and had returned to base by 1045 hours.[6]

The atmosphere in the Port Moresby Invasion Force was tense. The Allied bombers and flying boats were passing over their heads, and they could only rely on one light carrier with a downsized air group. "I can feel the anxious mood of the men from the South Seas Detachment," Lieutenant Commander Sugiyama commented out loud when he recalled the moment they joined the convoy's screening.[7]

PHOTO 5 ■ Rear Adm. Sadamichi Kajioka, commander of the Port Moresby Invasion Force *NDL*

Still, the Japanese could feel the situation returning under control after the setback with the raid on Tulagi. The *Kiyokawa Maru*'s two Jakes from Rabaul roamed over the MO Invasion Force during most of the daylight hours. The *kankō* found no trace of the enemy carriers, and they were all recovered by 1100 hours. Equally, the *Myōkō* and the *Haguro*'s seaplanes reported making no contact. Still, the MO Kidō Butai kept six fighters in combat readiness to support the Tulagi garrison in case the enemy tried to raid it again.[8]

Contrary to the fears of the Japanese, Fletcher didn't intend to get close to the Solomon Islands and headed southward to join TF 11 and TF 44. On the morning of 5 May he conducted reconnaissance patrols in the northern sectors to ensure the MO Kidō Butai didn't pursue him. At about 0740 hours, one of the SBDs radioed regarding a Japanese submarine at 150 miles with a bearing of 285 degrees that was heading toward TF 17. Three TBDs hurriedly scrambled from the *Yorktown* but didn't find the enemy.[9]

Ten minutes after receiving the SBD's cable, the *Yorktown*'s CXAM radar picked up contact at 30 miles with a bearing of 252 degrees. Soon four F4Fs were airborne, and at about two thousand feet they sighted the flying boat. Lt. Urada flew the aircraft, which took off from Shortland before dawn. Wildcats ambushed the Mavis and charged together from above. The brief fight was summarized later by Lt. Walter Haas: "Art Brassfield made the first run and the rest of us straddled the thing. Just as I completed my run, it blew up in my face."[10]

Urada failed to transmit a warning to all units, but his disappearance was correctly assessed by the base at 1230 hours as probably caused by being shot down by the enemy's carrier-borne planes about 400 miles from Shortland with a bearing of 155 degrees.[11] When news about the Mavis's elimination reached the *Yorktown*, TF 17 and TF 11 sighted each other. Fletcher ordered the *Yorktown*, the cruisers, and the destroyers to refuel from the *Neosho*. The *Hammann* and the *Perkins* soon rejoined the task force with two rescued pilots. Since the carrier had lost two fighters and had only one spare, McCuskey, considered responsible for the mistake made during the raid on Tulagi, was excluded from air operations for two days.

At 1130 hours the MO Kidō Butai, located near San Cristóbal Island, finally set a southerly course. At the same time, Fletcher received a CINCPAC intelligence report that located the Japanese carriers north of Bougainville or in the Coral Sea south of the Solomon Islands. According to the cable, the enemy planned to land near Port Moresby on 10 May. Before that, on 7 and 8 May, his planes would carry out raids on the city and its military facilities. Additionally, Fletcher and Fitch quite accurately predicted the potential route of the Port Moresby Invasion Force. They believed the transport ships with screening vessels would set off from Rabaul and slowly steam south through the Louisiades, awaiting orders to begin the amphibious operation. Thus, the Japanese moves gave TF 11 and TF 17 time to refuel the following morning and head eastward to engage the enemy in a decisive carrier battle on 7 May.

At 1341 hours, TF 17 received a message from the SoWePac area about an enemy seaplane tender south of New Georgia, sighted by a reconnaissance aircraft at 1313 hours. The American and Australian planes operating from airfields in New Guinea failed to spot the MO Main Force despite conducting several scouting missions toward the Solomon Islands. On the basis of unconfirmed information, CINCPAC warned Fletcher that the *Hiryū* would likely have left Japan and that the *Sōryū* was already en route to Truk. However, before both carriers could reach the South Pacific, it was expected that the Japanese would be able to proceed with the invasion of Port Moresby.[12]

Despite this disturbing intelligence news, the rest of the day passed peacefully for the Americans. The Japanese, struggling until the evening with bad weather conditions in the area west of the Solomon Islands, had trouble recovering the seaplanes from the 5th Sentai. One Jake from the *Myōkō* was seriously damaged and became nonoperational, while one Jake from the *Haguro* overturned.[13] The problems with the weather were unfortunate, but changes in the Japanese schedule were unlikely. At 1720 hours Takagi made his decision about the refueling plan. He was told, "Sir, there is a message from the *Myōkō*." Lt. Takashi Yasumi, the *Zuikaku*'s communication officer, was called by another officer. He stood on the bridge and started reading the dispatch transmitted by the cruiser's blinker: "Da-i-ni-ji-ho-ki-yu-u-ni-ka-n-shi" ("Concerning the second refueling"). Now it was certain that the second refueling would be carried out on the morning of 6 May.[14] Hara met with Mieno and Yamaoka to discuss the air support for the entire team on 6 May. At 1845 hours he issued orders regarding the anti-torpedo plane and antisubmarine patrols but canceled the reconnaissance missions.[15] Although the MO Kidō Butai finally entered the Coral Sea and headed westward, the Japanese needed to focus on refueling to make their crucial moves in the upcoming days.

■ ■ ■

Dawn found the MO Kidō Butai approximately 150 miles south of Guadalcanal. The Japanese, steaming toward New Guinea, made the rendezvous with the *Tōhō Maru* at about 0700 hours and began refueling. The destroyers assumed defensive positions to screen the group against snoopers.[16] The entire process was carried out without unexpected obstacles, and Takagi instructed the vessels to be ready to dash westward at up to thirty-one knots.[17]

Because Hara had canceled sending the scouting planes from the *Shōkaku* and the *Zuikaku* in the middle of the refueling, the morning reconnaissance missions were entrusted to the Tulagi base. At 0630 hours five flying boats of the Yokohama Kū took off, led by Lieutenant Adachi. They went to cover the southeastern and southwestern sectors at long distances to investigate the most probable location of the enemy carrier task force.

Things started to get complicated at about 0800 hours. Two enemy aircraft—one was probably the Australian Catalina commanded by Squadron Leader G. Hemsworth—sighted the Port Moresby Invasion Force. According to the *Shōhō*'s war diary, it is possible to say that the fighters deterred the intruders.[18] Despite having direct air support from the light carrier, the convoy was in a very unfortunate position. The MO Kidō Butai was still too far away, and the *Kamikawa Maru* and the *Kiyokawa Maru* were preparing to transfer their seaplanes from Rabaul and Shortland to Deboyne, where a

TABLE 13 ■ **Yokohama Kū's Reconnaissance Missions, Morning of 6 May 1942**

Mavises / Yokohama Kū	1	Lt. Adachi	Takeoff: 0630 Landing: 1530
	2	Ens. Kiyomizu	
	3	WO Fujiwara	
	4	Lt. Sakamoto	
	5	WO Yamaguchi	Landing: 1740

Source: JACAR: Yokohama Kū (2), 20.

new seaplane base was scheduled to be set up the following morning. The only antisubmarine patrol around the Port Moresby Invasion Force was WO Aoki's Jake, sent by the former tender at 0820 hours.[19]

At 0920 hours the observers on the *Tsugaru* noticed a rubber lifeboat heading toward them. The *Oite* was detached to check on this unusual finding. It turned out that the Japanese had stumbled on the crew of the Australian flying boat—six officers and three enlisted men. They became prisoners of war.[20] All of the facts suggest that the Japanese found Hemsworth's crew, that is, the crew of the Catalina A24–20 of RAAF 20 Squadron, which was reported as missing during the action. Since the POWs didn't survive their captivity, the details of what happened to them were still a mystery at the time of writing.[21]

The Yokohama Kū's predictions about the position of the enemy proved correct. At about 1000 hours, one Mavis patrolling section "F3" found TF 17 and informed the Tulagi base about its location on the radio: "I spotted the enemy. Big task force bearing 192 degrees from the base, distance 420 miles." The flying boat commanded by WO Yamaguchi broke the deadlock and gave the Japanese this highly desirable report. It didn't take more than ten minutes for the Eleventh Air Fleet to distribute the message to all units. But that wasn't the end of the matter. Yamaguchi shadowed the Americans and transmitted more details in the following minutes: "One carrier, one battleship, two cruisers and five destroyers, bearing 192 and 420 miles from Tulagi, course 190, speed 20 knots." There was no doubt that the flying boat was in the right spot. "Clear weather in the area, visibility 50 kilometers, clouds 4–5 at 1000 meters"—the crew did their best to deliver the most precise information. The MO Kidō Butai had received all three cables by 1050 hours.[22] Yamaguchi could now potentially retreat to Tulagi, but to obtain all the necessary information, he stayed near the enemy carriers to take his chances at the right time.

At dawn on 6 May, TF 17 began steaming on a northwesterly course toward the Louisiades. They were about three hundred miles south of Takagi. The *Lexington* launched twelve SBDs early in the morning to scout the northern arc at 275 miles. At 0700 Fletcher issued Operational Order 2–42 to reorganize his fores. Five days after receiving the instructions from Nimitz, he was finally able to merge all ships in TF 17, consisting of the following:

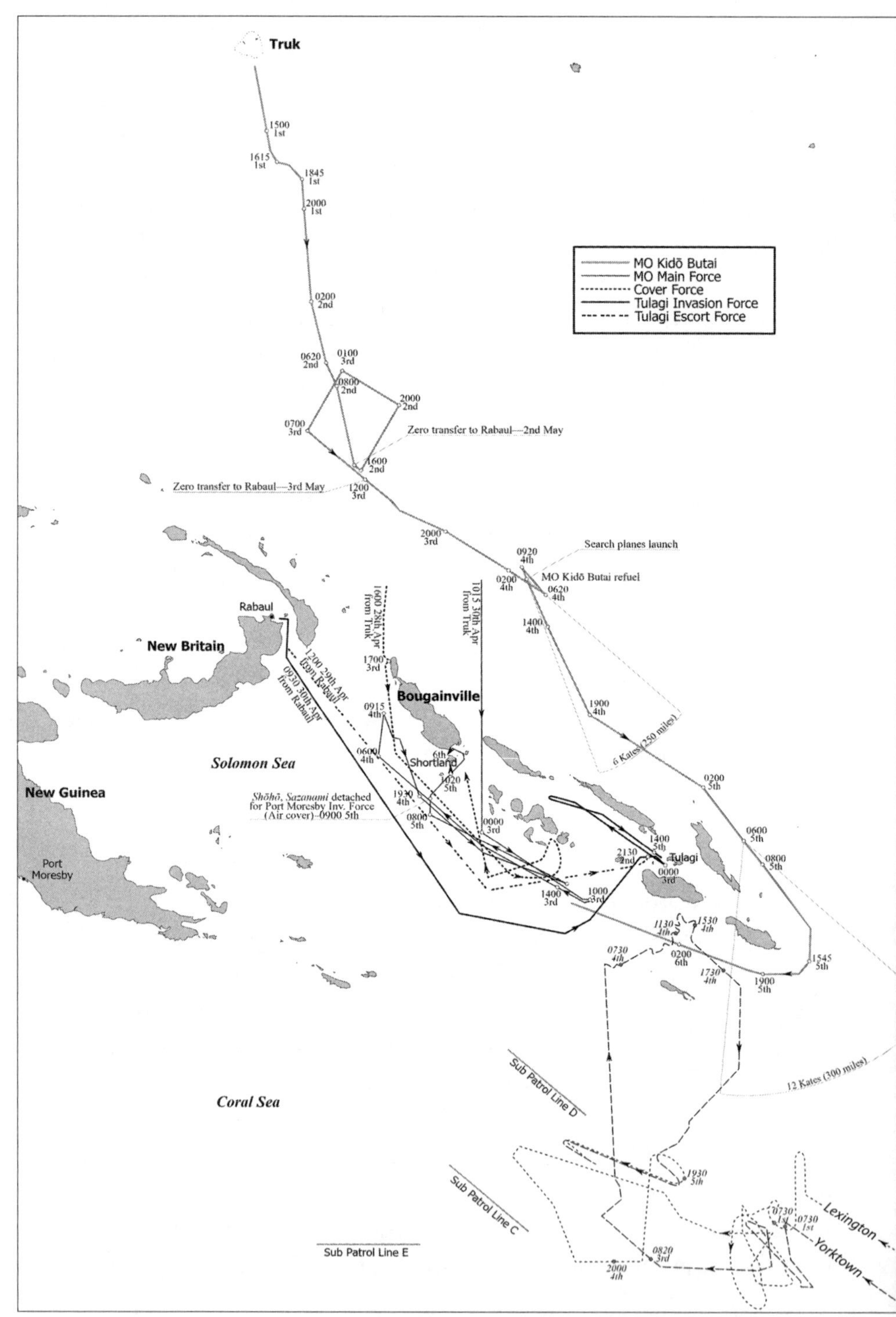

MAP 5 ■ The Battle of the Coral Sea: movements until the late hours of 5 May

1. Attack Group (TG 17.2), commanded by Rear Adm. Thomas C. Kinkaid and consisting of the heavy cruisers *Minneapolis*, *New Orleans*, *Astoria*, *Chester*, and *Portland* and the destroyers *Phelps*, *Dewey*, *Farragut*, *Aylwin*, and *Monaghan*;
2. Support Group (TG 17.3), commanded by Rear Adm. John G. Crace and consisting of the heavy cruisers *Australia* and *Chicago*, the light cruiser *Hobart*, and the destroyers *Perkins* and *Walke*;
3. Carrier Air Group (TG 17.5), commanded by Rear Adm. Aubrey W. Fitch and consisting of the carriers *Yorktown* and *Lexington* and the destroyers *Morris*, *Anderson*, *Hammann*, and *Russell*;
4. Fueling Group (TG 17.6), commanded by Captain John S. Phillips and consisting of the oilers *Neosho* and *Tippecanoe* and the destroyers *Sims* and *Worden*.[23]

Nominally, TF 17 also included Search Group (TG 17.9), commanded by Cdr. George H. DeBaun and consisting of the seaplane tender *Tangier* (12 PBYs from VP-71 and VP-72) and based at Noumea, New Caledonia.

At 0730 hours, TF 17 headed south to complete refueling. Fletcher believed that he still had several hours to prepare for the carrier battle. Weather conditions that morning, unlike during the previous few days, were fairly favorable for air operations.

Unexpectedly, at 1015 hours, the *Yorktown*'s CXAM radar picked up an enemy aircraft north of TF 17. The *Lexington* fighter director officer, Lt. Frank Gill, sent four F4Fs, two from VF-2 and two from VF-42, to intercept the bogey. Hunting it down was challenging, because, unexpectedly, thick clouds obscured the sky. Discouraged pilots gave up on their dogged search. Although a Mavis was spotted by the *New Orleans* for a couple of seconds when it emerged from the clouds, it soon disappeared again and didn't get too close to the American ships.

Fletcher knew from the beginning that the enemy had spotted him. When the snooper got away, he ordered the refueling to stop to prepare for an onslaught. Time passed, though, and the Japanese did not come, so he continued to refuel. Although TF 17 was detected, an attack by the MO Kidō Butai seemed unlikely to Fletcher. According to him and the CINCPAC intelligence bulletin, all three enemy carriers (the *Zuikaku*, *Shōkaku*, and *Shōhō*, the last mistakenly designated as the *Ryūkaku*) were located far to the northwest, near Bougainville. Those judgments were very inaccurate, because Takagi was only three hundred miles north of TF 17 at noon on 6 May.[24]

The Yokohama Kū understood the crucial role of Tulagi in the upcoming battle and decided to bring more flying boats from Shortland. At 1235 hours, two of them, led by Lieutenant Commander Tashiro, were airborne and headed toward the newly established base. On the last stretch of their route they met the returning aircraft from the reconnaissance mission and landed safely by 1545 hours.[25]

Meanwhile, having smartly outplayed the American fighters, Yamaguchi maintained visual contact with TF 17. At 1400 hours he sent an update to Tulagi disclosing the enemy formation and distances between screening ships and informing the base about thirty planes on the carrier's deck. Twenty minutes later Yamaguchi informed the base that he had set a return course and reported for the last time about the weather conditions.[26] His replacement was already on the way. At 1400 hours the Yokohama Kū scrambled a Mavis flown by Ensign Ōmori to maintain contact with the American carrier task force. Yamaguchi returned safely to Tulagi before dusk.[27]

On learning of the enemy's position, the Yokohama Kū considered sending its flying boats armed with torpedoes to attack TF 17 at the least expected moment, namely before sunset at 1815 hours. This plan, however, strongly depended on reestablishing contact with the opponent and on the weather conditions in the area. Yamaguchi's discovery greatly aroused the Japanese command, which hadn't expected that they could attack the enemy on 6 May. It is essential to add that Mori notes that Yamaguchi's report was a severe reconnaissance mistake. The Mavis warned all the units about one carrier and one battleship, but the crew should have identified two carriers. The events to come showed how every mistake accumulates and has consequences, leading to terrible decisions in a worst-case scenario.[28]

But what was happening with the MO Kidō Butai and the 6th Sentai? As for the latter, four heavy cruisers completed the refueling at about 0800 hours, and half an hour later the unit departed Shortland to join the Port Moresby Invasion Force; the *Shōhō* and the *Sazanami* were to assist the convoy by the time it was passing the Jomard Passage. However, before Gotō could reach the transport ships, they were detected by three B-17s of the 40th Reconnaissance Squadron, which had taken off from Cloncurry in the early morning and left Port Moresby on a reconnaissance patrol on a northeasterly course. American bombers sighted the enemy group steaming toward the Jomard Passage and attacked it at 1030 hours. None of the dropped bombs hit the target.[29] The Flying Fortresses reported finding one carrier about 490 miles northwest of TF 17. This message was relayed to Fletcher, who was convinced that Japanese carriers were operating near the convoy. His misconception of the whereabouts of the *Shōkaku* and the *Zuikaku* became even stronger when none of the *Lexington*'s twelve SBDs found any track of the enemy forces within three hundred miles north.

The news about spotting one carrier and one battleship heated the atmosphere in the MO Kidō Butai. Just like on 4 May, they were caught in the middle of refueling, yet there was hope that the second part of the day could be used in their favor this time. At 1100 hours Hara ordered both carriers to prepare the striking group. Less than forty minutes later Takagi told the 5th Kōkū Sentai to rush south to proceed with the attack once the *Ariake* and the *Yūgure* were refueled. He soon changed his mind and instructed the *Yūgure* to stop refueling and head south with the 5th Kōkū Sentai. The *Shōkaku* and the *Zuikaku* were already heading on a 160-degree course at twenty-six knots. The preparations to hit the enemy were at the advanced stage. At noon Hara decided that each carrier would send twelve *kankō*, eighteen *kambaku*, and nine *kansen* and that the striking group would be prepared to take off at about 1400 hours. To reduce the distance to the enemy, the 5th Kōkū Sentai, the *Ariake*, and the *Yūgure* were also ordered to be ready to speed up to thirty knots if needed.[30]

Takagi committed himself to attacking the enemy in the afternoon to such an extent that the *Tōhō Maru* was also instructed to follow the MO Kidō Butai on the route southward after finishing refueling the destroyers. The Japanese began to see an opportunity to deal a massive blow. Rear Adm. Yamada of the 25th Kōkū Sentai was equally eager to strike and notified all units that he was preparing his thirty land-based bombers in Rabaul, armed with torpedoes, to make a bold move at any time.[31]

At 1240 hours Takagi informed Inoue and Yamada that according to the reconnaissance report that had been received, the MO Kidō Butai was dashing south at twenty-three to thirty knots to "obliterate the big task force." Since the refueling of the 5th Sentai had been postponed, he intended to take the *Tōhō Maru* with him after she finished supplying the destroyers.[32]

The Fourth Fleet understood Takagi's fervor regarding attacking the "big task force" but remained vigilant against any threat to the timely execution of Operation MO. Gotō alarmed Rabaul that the Allied bombers had seen his warships and convoy several times since dawn. Undoubtedly, the Japanese knew that the Americans were aware of their plan to set up the seaplane base in Deboyne. And the MO Main Force had intercepted the enemy cable, which disclosed the location of their two cruisers, two destroyers, and one carrier.[33] Relying on this information, at 1230 hours the Fourth Fleet staff warned that the enemy carrier task force would likely powerfully strike the Port Moresby Invasion Force when it crossed the Louisiades on the morning of 7 May.[34]

By 1400 hours, owing to the last of Yamaguchi's reconnaissance reports, the Japanese knew, although not without significant errors, about the composition of the enemy's "big task force." The 5th Kōkū Sentai and the 25 Kōkū Sentai were theoretically ready to scramble, yet the flying boat also complained about imperfect weather conditions in the area, mainly thick clouds at three thousand meters and visibility only up to ten kilometers. Because the risk of sending the striking group and missing the target was too high, Hara and Yamada put their crews on hold. Notably, the 5th Kōkū Sentai needed to know more about the actual position of the enemy, but once Yamaguchi left the area, there were no updates. At about 1500 hours the probability of making the first move dropped sharply. During that time, Gotō warned all units about planes snooping on his force. Eventually, at 1630 hours, Takagi advised that there were no prospects of sending the striking group on 6 May because of insufficient information on the enemy. Instead, he planned to withdraw the 5th Sentai northward to refuel the cruisers.[35]

The sun went down at 1815 hours, and fifteen minutes later the *Myōkō* and the *Haguro* had a rendezvous with the *Tōhō Maru* and started refueling. The MO Kidō Butai was ready to reduce the distance to the enemy at thirty-one knots, but there was no need to rush anymore. The 5th Kōkū Sentai was already planning to engage in battle on 7 May. Despite the alarming news from Gotō, the Americans didn't dare to attack the convoy with the bombers. The positions in Deboyne were equally protected. At about 1510 hours, when the enemy flying boat arrived over the area to drop bombs, the *Kamikawa Maru* scrambled three Petes and one Jake. Lt. Shimura later claimed to have set the intruder afire. Besides that, from the early afternoon until 1800 hours, the *Kiyokawa Maru* air group's three Daves and one Pete, led by Lieutenant Yamada, patrolled Deboyne against submarines but didn't find anything suspicious.[36]

Yamaguchi's effort to furnish all units with in-depth information was wasted. At about 1900 hours Ensign Ōmori reached the supposed location of the "big task force" but didn't spot any vessels. He reported no enemy presence and set a return course, landing in Tulagi by 0100 hours on 7 May.[37]

The Japanese lost their last opportunity to maintain contact with TF 17 before the first day of the battle. Ōmori's failure to track down Fletcher was a significant setback. Consequently, Hara had to figure out a more complex search plan in the morning. Also, there is a high probability that if Ōmori had sighted the "big task force," he would have identified two carriers instead of only one and would have found out that Fletcher was not on a southern course but a northeastern one. This would eventually affect the entire decision-making process in the 5th Kōkū Sentai's command.

At 1930 hours Hara informed Takagi that he couldn't launch the strike on 6 May because the last report about the enemy had come in at 1100 hours. As the MO Kidō Butai's war diary evidenced, this was a very debatable explanation. Still, one could say that Hara didn't receive the necessary details of "the big task force" location after the initial cable in the morning. Nonetheless, he told Takagi that he would reach Point A at 0600 hours on 7 May to send scouting planes in sectors from 170 to 270 degrees at 250 miles. Most importantly, he reassured Takagi that if the MO Invasion Force was attacked, he would come to the rescue of Gotō and destroy the enemy carrier task force. Half an hour later the 5th Kōkū Sentai set its course to 0 degrees at 16 knots, which would be changed to 180 degrees after five hours to reach the desired coordinates on the morning of 7 May.[38]

In the *Zuikaku*'s bridge, Hara, Mieno, and Yamaoka discussed the details of the reconnaissance missions and transmitted their decision to the rest of the team at 2100 hours. The *Shōkaku*'s six *kankō* were to cover the sector in three pairs from 180 to 220 degrees at 250 miles with an additional 40 miles on the right outward leg, while the same number of the *Zuikaku*'s *kankō* would focus on 165, 235, and 250 degrees at 250 miles with an additional 30 miles on the right outward leg. In view of these plans, it is possible to state that the 5th Kōkū Sentai expected the *Shōkaku*'s aircraft to be the most likely to find TF 17. As mentioned to Takagi, the Kates were to scramble at 0600 hours. Once Fletcher's position was established, the striking group of all the remaining bombers and nine fighters from each carrier would deal the decisive blow. Hara put equal emphasis on defending the 5th Kōkū Sentai in the meantime.[39]

At 2200 hours Takagi sent the last message of the day to his team and Inoue and confirmed the plans for 7 May. He reassured them that the MO Kidō Butai would head west to support the MO Invasion Force if the enemy carrier task force wasn't found during the morning reconnaissance missions. He also informed them that the *Tōhō Maru* would await the rest of the group between New Georgia and Santa Isabel. Before the new day started Takagi wanted to gather all of his force. Thus, shortly after midnight, the 5th Sentai aborted refueling and rushed toward the 5th Kōkū Sentai. It wasn't long before the MO Kidō Butai had two carriers, two cruisers, and four destroyers again.[40]

When Fletcher finished refueling at 1800 hours, he sent the *Neosho*, screened by the *Sims*, south to the scheduled rendezvous Point Rye (16° S, 158° E) in the evening on 7 May. Then he took a northwesterly course toward the Russell Islands to halt the enemy before it crossed the Louisiades.

Undoubtedly, 6 May was a day of missed opportunities for both sides. At the time, Fletcher and Hara didn't know that their forces were separated by only seventy miles at 2000 hours, less than half an hour of flight for a carrier-borne aircraft. Fletcher at least tried to find the MO Kidō Butai during the morning, but many historians have blamed Hara for not sending reconnaissance missions during the afternoon of 5 May and all of 6 May. It is worth examining the explanation presented by S. Mori here. According to him, Hara pleaded after the war that "he avoided the detection by entrusting the scouting to the land-based air groups." One cannot disagree with Mori that it was unreasonable to believe that a limited number of flying boats at the Tulagi base could provide adequate scouting across the Coral Sea. On 6 May the Yokohama Kū strained its resources and men by sending five aircraft on long missions. When Yamaguchi sighted "the big task force," the unit brought two more flying boats from Shortland and risked the lives of nine people, namely Ōmori's crew, by sending another Mavis to maintain contact with the enemy despite the high chances of it being intercepted by American fighters. Hara complained to Takagi about there being no critical updates about "the big task force" since 1100 hours, but he could have used his torpedo bombers to scout for the 5th Kōkū Sentai and proceeded with the envisaged afternoon attack, especially since the striking groups were ready to take off. Instead, he chose to be passive and wait for news from the Yokohama Kū, postponing the battle until the next day. Poor visibility and thick clouds in the area that TF 17 was in was only a valid excuse after 1400 hours, when Yamaguchi reported that he was returning to Tulagi. Of course, Hara could be credited for "not being discovered" to some extent, but he could have contributed more to the Japanese effort to find out more details about the enemy. His reluctance to arrange additional reconnaissance missions resulted from his private vision of carrier warfare tactics. During the war, he repeatedly mentioned that he avoided as much as possible diminishing his air groups' striking potential on the eve of the decisive attack. Therefore, he genuinely believed in the importance of land-based aircraft for furnishing the carrier air groups with reconnaissance data. Future events would prove that he acted according to his convictions.

Mitigating circumstances for Hara could be found in the recurring issue of refueling the warships. The MO Kidō Butai needed to replenish its fuel supplies on 6 May and wasn't prepared for the battle for most of the day. The decision to strike the enemy could entail an American counterattack at an unfortunate moment during Operation MO. After all, it was safer to refuel the destroyers and the cruisers and try their chances the following morning than rush forward with the afternoon or dusk attack. Again, the events in the next twenty-four hours would prove that it had been sensible not to take rash actions.

Hara's plan for 7 May relied on two main factors. First, the MO Kidō Butai hadn't been discovered even once by the enemy, and Hara had some clue about the TF 17 position, so theoretically he had the upper hand in delivering the first strike. Second, the Japanese were almost sure Fletcher would shift his attention to the convoy heading toward the Jomard Passage. Nobody was willing to risk the transport ships and put Operation MO at stake, but the reality was that Hara counted on finding and destroying TF 17 before it could threaten Gotō.

As for the MO Invasion Force, establishing the seaplane base in Deboyne had been in progress since the early afternoon of 6 May. The Japanese vessels and aircraft were slowly approaching that location to provide materials and support to incorporate the base into the plan. But Gotō's men, particularly the officers in the *Shōhō*, were worried about the upcoming day. The enemy bombers and carrier-borne planes hadn't seriously attempted to attack the convoy or the screening vessels, but they knew that would change. Having read the dispatches of the MO Kidō Butai and the Fourth Fleet, the officers in the MO Invasion Force tried to comfort each other. Lt. Tadamitsu Taniguchi, the *Shōhō*'s communication officer, passed a message from Gotō to the carrier's skipper that said, "I believe that our carrier task force and land-based unit will be able to smash the enemy." Many of Izawa's men felt unconvinced by those words, but all they could do was wait for developments. The response was intended to boost the esprit de corps: "Using our full-strength utmost, we will provide air cover earnestly to progress with the operation."[41]

Contrary to popular belief, Lieutenant General Wainwright's capitulation on Corregidor on 6 May had only symbolic meaning. The fall of the last American stronghold in the Philippines freed the Nippon Rikugun from the last Southern Operation campaign but didn't influence the men fighting in the Coral Sea, particularly the Japanese crews. As shown in this chapter, morale strongly depended on the position at the time and the envisaged role of 7 May. For Gotō's men it would be a great survival test, while for Hara's men it presented a great opportunity to prove their value and become the elite of the Nippon Kaigun, admired no less than the 1st and the 2nd Kōkū Sentai, whose aircrews maliciously called the 5th Kōkū Sentai *mekake no ko* (a concubine's child).

PART 2

7 MAY 1942

Chapter 6

MORNING SEARCH MISSIONS FOR AMERICAN CARRIERS AND MOVEMENTS OF MO KIDŌ BUTAI IN RESPONSE

At 0600 hours on 7 May the MO Kidō Butai reached Point A (13° 20' S, 158° E), about four hundred miles southeast of the Louisiades.[1] According to the initial plan of Operation MO, Hara was to provide air cover to the Port Moresby Invasion Force, which slowly proceeded southward to the Jomard Passage to cross it in the evening and enter the Coral Sea.[2] The third Japanese aircraft carrier, the *Shōhō*, kept a reasonable distance from the most hazardous part of the route and took a position northeast of Misima Island to support the operation with her modest air group.

However, apart from protecting the vulnerable convoy, the MO Kidō Butai's primary objective was to find and destroy the American carriers before they could launch their attack on any friendly force. As mentioned in the previous chapter, Hara and Takagi knew about the group made up of at least one carrier and one battleship and screening vessels, which was operating approximately three hundred miles south of their positions around noon on 6 May. Of course, the distance and bearing might have changed during the long hours without updates on the enemy moves. But the Japanese were desperate to resolve the battle on 7 May and thus arranged a series of reconnaissance missions to cover the crucial sectors of the Coral Sea. The summary of the air search recorded the following actions (four additional points appear later in this section):

1. At 0600 hours, half an hour before sunrise, the *Shōkaku* and the *Zuikaku* each scrambled six Kates to search the sectors from 160 to 270 degrees at 250 miles (see tables 14 and 15).[3]

As part of the analysis concerning the 5th Kōkū Sentai's scouting missions, it is worth recalling a less-known story. When the *Shōkaku* and the *Zuikaku* arrived at the Makō naval base in Taiwan after the Indian Ocean operation on the afternoon of 18 April, air personnel had a unique chance to go ashore.[4] The Japanese airmen had only a few hours to wander around the narrow streets of the port city before the scheduled departure for the South Pacific. They could finally eat locally prepared meals, grab some fresh greens, and order a few cups of sake. The supply teams of both carriers also used the short break to load considerable portions of canned pineapple. Sweet and juicy fruits could be

TABLE 14 ■ Reconnaissance Missions from the *Shōkaku*, Morning of 7 May 1942

Unit	No.	Pilot	Observer	Radio operator	Notes
Kates/*Shōkaku* 220 degrees	1	WO Shindō	Lt. Yano (S)	PO2c Ibayashi	Takeoff: 0600 Landing: 1230
	2	Sea1c Ōtani	PO1c Yamauchi	Sea1c Gomi	
Kates/*Shōkaku* 200 degrees	1	PO1c Okimura	WO Ukita (S)	PO2c Tozawa	
	2	Sea1c Okafuji	PO1c Mimori	Sea1c Kobayashi	
Kates/*Shōkaku* 180 degrees	1	PO1c Saitō*	WO Shibata (S)*	PO3c Dōmae*	Takeoff: 0600 (emergency landing)
	2	PO1c Akao*	PO1c Ōtake*	Sea1c Sakashita*	

Source: JACAR: Shōkaku (1), 30.

* *Forced to ditch at sea but later recovered*

TABLE 15 ■ Reconnaissance Missions from the *Zuikaku*, Morning of 7 May 1942

Unit	No.	Pilot	Observer	Radio operator	Notes
Kates/*Zuikaku* ? degrees	1	Lt. Satō (S)	PO1c Ōtani	PO2c Yoshida	Takeoff: 0600 Landing: 1230
	2	PO2c Fukutani	PO2c Kojima	Sea1c Hara	
Kates/*Zuikaku* ? degrees	1	PO1c Hori	Ens. Matsunaga (S)	PO2c Ōta	
	2	Sea1c Morimitsu	PO2c Hiwatashi	Sea1c Tani	
Kates/*Zuikaku* ? degrees	1	PO1c Satō	PO1c Kawabata (S)	Sea1c Yoshimura	
	2	PO1c Tahara	PO2c Ōnishi	PO3c Kanetō	

Source: JACAR: Zuikaku (1), 42–43.

considered a delicacy for ordinary Japanese people, not to mention the crews on their long journeys with no clear vision of the next destination. Some even joked that the pineapple compensated for all the annoyances and hardships they faced on the open seas. However, this simple treat caused unexpected trouble in the following days. On 5 and 6 May one of the seasoned officers of the *Shōkaku*'s torpedo bomber squadron, whose name was not mentioned, took advantage of relatively inactive days and overate canned pineapple and drank too much Taiwanese beer. This caused him serious stomach issues on the morning of 7 May and he was unable to participate in the reconnaissance mission. The torpedo bomber's *buntaichō*, Lt. Tatsuo Ichihara, replaced him and his two companions with another much younger crew with relatively little scouting experience. After all, he did not have many alternatives. It was not uncommon for *Shōkaku*'s airmen to serve less than one year on the carrier, and they were all considered rookies compared to veterans from the *Akagi*, who could boast, in many cases, more than a decade of practice. Ichihara had a clear memory of the November training in Kyūshū before the attack on Pearl Harbor, when some of his pilots landed on a carrier's deck for the first time. Although they had improved their skills since then, they had not earned the reputation they desired yet. Ichihara certainly did not want to criticize them, so he trusted his instincts and delegated the youngest commissioned officer. However, when the Kates took off to spot the American task force, he began questioning his decision. Did sending an inexperienced crew on the crucial reconnaissance mission address the problem of having a sick experienced airman? What if the young personnel failed to locate or misidentified the enemy vessels? Still, he had a reasonable excuse if things went wrong. The *buntaichō* knew perfectly well that keeping as many senior airmen as possible for the decisive strike could significantly influence the battle. From his perspective, he was not simply facing a routine dilemma regarding whether to replace one crew with another. It was a decision that could change the MO Kidō Butai's chance to deliver a devastating blow to the enemy.[5]

Not all Japanese officers felt sure about the 5th Kōkū Sentai's scouting missions in the wide arc from 160 to 270 degrees, either. On the evening of 6 May Hara discussed the search plan, mainly with Mieno. His air officer was afraid that American carriers might try to slip away in the western direction after the detection by the Mavis and insisted on focusing on that area. "But once we commit half of our attention to the west, what if the enemy lands a hit on us from the south," Hara replied, with visible consternation. Mieno, who was more confident, tried to persuade the 5th Kōkū Sentai commander to take a different approach, saying, "[An] American carrier task force is unlikely to challenge us in the pitched battle. They will withdraw to the south to keep the distance from us for sure." Hara did not comment on this overly optimistic statement but was still doubtful about the need to concentrate on the western direction. The Japanese had at least three bases in the area—Rabaul, Tulagi, and Deboyne. Hara thought they should investigate the western sectors, while the *Shōkaku* and the *Zuikaku* would cover the southern part. Eventually, after rethinking various options, Hara picked his plan rather than Mieno's. He adopted the search in the vast sector mentioned earlier in this paragraph, focusing on locating the American task force where he thought they were most likely to operate.

Although Hara was wrong about Fletcher's position on the morning of 7 May, his decision to search in the wide arc from 160 to 270 degrees seemed the most flexible one he could make to reconcile his and Mieno's predictions. His order also had a practical basis. If the 5th Kōkū Sentai's aircraft missed American carriers, they would be found by friendly seaplanes leaving from Deboyne and from Rossel Island. Only S. Mori remains skeptical about Hara's excessive reliance on scouting planes rather than his own. The Japanese historian argues that the *Kamikawa Maru*, cruisers, and land-based units had limited air potential and could not fully relieve the 5th Kōkū Sentai from checking the most crucial parts of the Coral Sea. Nevertheless, Hara dispatched as many as twelve Kates from his carriers and still needed to keep in mind preserving the combat potential of the MO Kidō Butai on the eve of the decisive clash with the Americans.[6]

The last argument, which can be used to endorse Hara's decision, is related to pure coincidence. The Kates scrambled from the decks at 0600 hours, so the two *kankō* from the *Zuikaku* flying the 270-degree sector missed Fletcher only by a whisker. They would have noticed at least part of the enemy carrier task force if they had departed fifteen minutes earlier. Their bad luck can be seen in the charts of the Japanese reconnaissance missions that were completed on the morning of 7 May.

Returning to the other scouting runs, they can be described as follows:

2. At about 0600 hours the *Furutaka* and the *Kinugasa* (belonging to the 6th Sentai, 2nd Division, detached from the *Shōhō* escort forces for the time being and operating north of the Russell Islands) each catapulted two Alfs to investigate the sectors from 90 to 210 degrees within 150 miles of the Russell Islands. All aircraft received the order to land at Deboyne after completing the mission.[7]
3. The *Kamikawa Maru* had successfully opened the seaplane base near Deboyne early in the morning on 7 May, and the Fourth Fleet wanted to use the newly established position as an additional asset during the morning search.[8] At 0630 hours, three Jakes from the *Kamikawa Maru* took off to investigate the sector from 160 to 230 degrees for 250 miles.[9] The *Kiyokawa Maru* also sent one Jake to search the area south of Deboyne at 0745 hours. To protect the team against the enemy aircraft, the *Kamikawa Maru* had dispatched one Jake and one Pete by 0730 hours to conduct an antisubmarine patrol. The presumption that Americans would actively monitor the area proved correct, because the Jake clashed with one Dauntless west of Misima Island and was shot down. Furthermore, at 0755 hours, when the 18th Sentai left Deboyne after establishing the seaplane base and took a northward course, a lone B-17 unexpectedly appeared overhead and attacked the *Kamikawa Maru*. According to the unit's report, the enemy dropped four 60-kg bombs, which caused minor damage to the after section of the ship and wounded two men. One of the Jakes also noticed the bomber. The Japanese seaplane crew tried to chase it off, but during the short clash the Jake was hit by four bullets and withdrew from the engagement. Despite the visible damage to the aircraft, it was repaired the next day.[10]

The increased enemy activity in the area and losing one aircraft forced the *Kamikawa Maru* to scramble two more Petes at 1230 hours. They did not, however, encounter any American bombers or other planes and returned safely by 1530 hours.[11]

4. Besides the ship-borne planes, the Nippon Kaigun's base units also contributed to scouting missions. At 0630 hours the 4th Kū sent three Bettys from Vunakanau to search the sectors from 160 to 180 degrees for seven hundred miles. On reaching the end of their patrol lines, the bombers were to fly an additional sixty miles on the outward legs and then return to base.[12]

At 0700 hours the Yokohama Kū sent four flying boats from Tulagi to search the sectors from 175 to 225 degrees at 650 miles.

While several aircraft conducted reconnaissance missions in the Coral Sea, the MO Kidō Butai continued a southwestern course to prepare for an immediate attack on the enemy carriers that had been spotted. Although Hara knew that the Americans would also order intensive searches that morning and his task force might be discovered, he was determined to resolve the battle in his favor.

Hara's shy predictions about the location of the American carriers proved correct when a long-awaited reconnaissance report from torpedo bombers reached the MO Kidō Butai at 0735 hours. One of two Kates from the *Shōkaku*, commanded by WO Masanobu Shibata and PO1c Tomi Ōtake, who investigated the 180-degree sector, confirmed that it had spotted the enemy carrier task force at 0722 hours proceeding on a course of 25 degrees at 20 knots.[13] The torpedo bomber's crew coded the location of the Americans ("U, 4, TSU, TSU"). A quick decryption at the *Shōkaku*'s bridge made it possible to indicate a bearing of 182 degrees and 163 miles from the position of the 5th Kōkū Sentai at 0600 hours.[14] The excitement among the officers drowned out the routine communications between other staff members. When Hara heard about the report for the first time, his only comment was "As I thought." The Japanese officers got a glimpse of his satisfied, smiling face that reflected his pleasure at exercising good naval aviation tactics.[15] At 0740 hours he changed the course to 90 degrees at twenty knots to prepare to launch the striking group and avoid a counterattack.[16] But the situation became more dynamic. Five minutes later the *Shōkaku* got additional information about the enemy force from her *kankō*: "Enemy carrier task force composed of one carrier and one heavy cruiser as a core, accompanied by three destroyers, course 0 degrees, speed sixteen knots."[17]

Table 16 ■ Activity of the *Kamikawa Maru* and *Kiyokawa Maru* Air Groups, Morning of 7 May 1942

Unit	No.	Crew members			Notes
Jakes / *Kamikawa Maru* air reconnaissance	1	Ens. Yoshida	PO1c Kōno	Sea1c Takase	Takeoff: 0630 Landing: 1145
	2	Sea1c Todokoro	WO Aoki	Sea1c Sudō	
	3	PO1c Asanaga	PO2c Hirao	Sea1c Ishida	
Jakes / *Kiyokawa Maru* air reconnaissance	1	Ens. Kozaki	PO2c Aota	Sea1c Ishii	Takeoff: 0745 Landing: 1325
Jakes / *Kamikawa Maru* antisubmarine	1	Sub. Lt. Ogata†	WO Harigae†	Sea1 Nishioka†	Takeoff: 0630 (lost)
Petes / *Kamikawa Maru* air cover	1	Ens. Shimura		PO2c Kashiyama	Takeoff: 0730 Landing: 1030
	2	Lt. Minematsu		PO1c Hasano	Takeoff: 1230 Landing: 1530
	3	PO1c Ueki		Sea1c Sasaki	

Source: JACAR: Kamikawa Maru (2), 6; JACAR: Kiyokawa Maru (4), 20.

† *Lost in action*

TABLE 17 ■ 4th Kū's Reconnaissance Missions, Morning of 7 May 1942

Unit	No.	Commander	Notes
Bettys / 4th Kū	1	PO1c Hattori	Takeoff: 0635 Landing: 1350
	2	WO Koseki	Takeoff: 0630 Landing: 1605
	3	WO Yano (S)	Takeoff: 0635 Landing: 1705

Source: JACAR: 4 Kū (1), 13.

TABLE 18 ■ Yokohama Kū's Reconnaissance Missions, Morning of 7 May 1942

Unit	No.	Commander	Notes
Mavises / Yokohama Kū	1	Lt. Sakamoto †	Takeoff: 0700 Landing: 1330
	2	WO Ueno	
	3	WO Takahashi	
	4	WO Miwa	

Source: JACAR: Yokohama Kū (2), 24.

† *Lost in action*

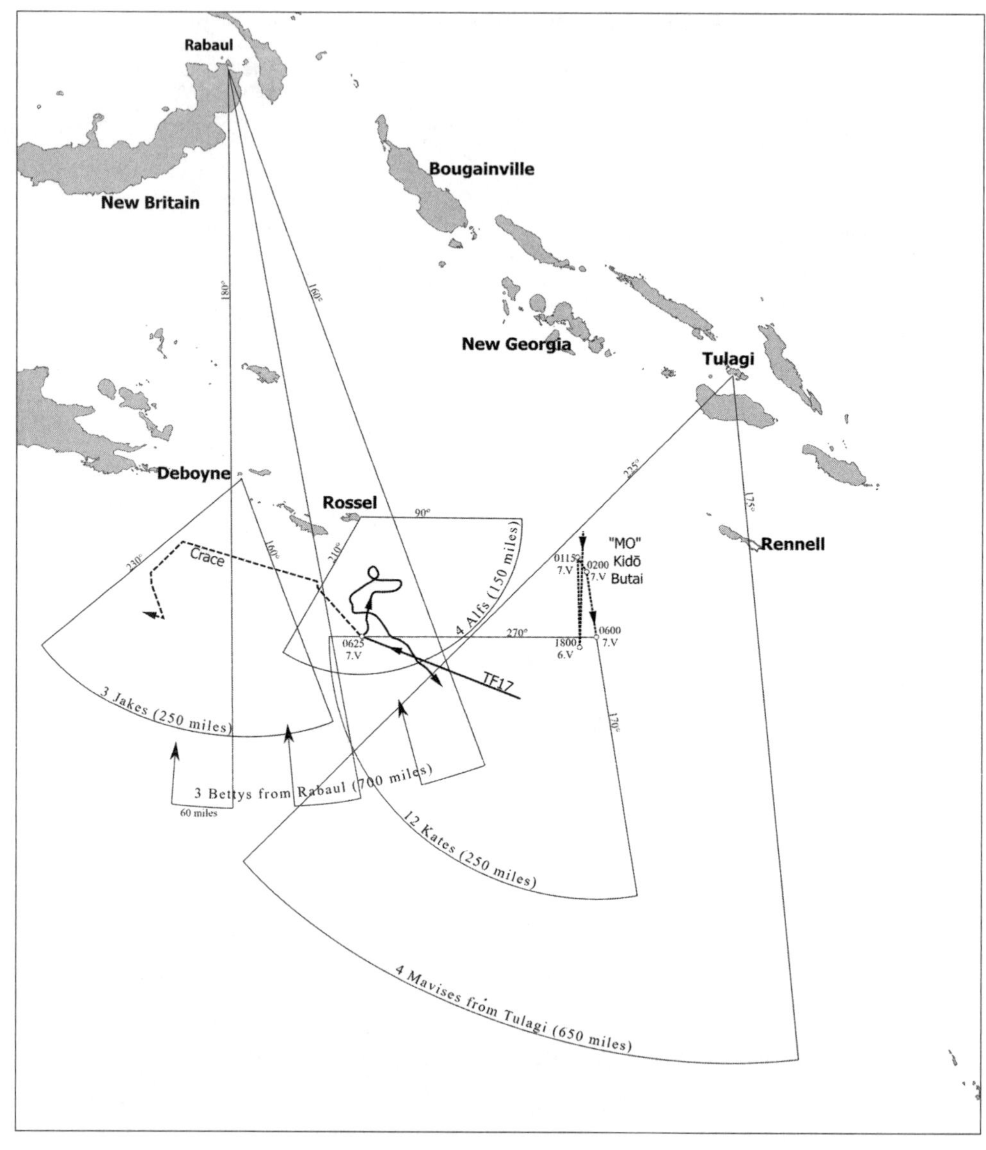

MAP 6 ■ Japanese reconnaissance missions, morning of 7 May

On hearing the second sighting report, Cdr. Hisao Shimoda, the *Zuikaku*'s flight officer, ran out of the bridge and dashed toward the ready room. The rays of the slowly rising sun covered the carrier and revealed the silhouettes of the planes lined up on the deck. Maintenance Officer Cdr. Eiji Harada climbed up to the bridge and confirmed that all necessary preparations for the takeoff had been completed. As an officer transferred to the carrier less than a month before, during the short break at Makō, he had a concise service record on the *Zuikaku*. Still, Harada did everything he could, including making his men work during a few busy nights, to meet the Nippon Kaigun's high expectations and deliver flawless aircraft for the strike. All the efforts paid off—engine and oil pressure checks, loading bombs and torpedoes in advance, and, finally, test runs—and the flagship of the 5th Kōkū Sentai was more than ready to enter the battle.[18]

Soon after, at 0758 hours, the Japanese also had the current data on the weather near the enemy task force. The torpedo bombers' crews confirmed they encountered a clear sky, a southeastern wind of ten meters per second, moderate clouds at eight hundred meters, and visibility of up to twenty miles in the area.[19] Air operations were likely to begin at any moment. The officers felt that all stars were aligned. The 5th Kōkū Sentai could now outshine the 1st and the 2nd Kōkū Sentai's achievements in one battle and go down in history despite its unfavorable reputation in the Nippon Kaigun.

The two cables from the *Shōkaku*'s scouting planes could have made the Japanese feel that Mieno was wrong to argue with Hara, because the enemy was not in thé west and the battle could not be avoided. It was quite the opposite—Fletcher reduced the distance to seek an open confrontation. Thus, the MO Kidō Butai command could generally believe that fate put American carriers on the table for them. Hara, now convinced he could destroy the enemy task force in a single blow, ordered the skippers of the *Shōkaku* and the *Zuikaku*, Capt. Takatsugu Jōjima and Capt. Ichihei Yokokawa respectively, to pass the word to their aircrews about the immediate takeoff. Beginning at 0808 hours, seventy-eight aircraft scrambled from both Japanese carriers within fifteen minutes. All Kates were armed with one 800-kg Type 91 aerial torpedo (*kyū ichi shiki gyorai*), while all Vals departed with one 250-kg ordinary bomb (25-*ban tsūjō bakudan*) with a 0.2-sec delay fuse.[20]

Since the striking group had two senior commissioned officers ranked as *hikōtaichō*, forty-one planes from the *Shōkaku* were led by Lt. Cdr. Kakuichi Takahashi and thirty-seven planes from the *Zuikaku* by Lt. Cdr. Shigekazu Shimazaki. Still, Takahashi was more senior than Shimazaki, so according to the Nippon Kaigun procedures, he retained *sōshiki* (overall tactical command). By a strange twist of fate, both *hikōtaichō* were close family, because the younger sister of Takahashi's wife married Shimazaki in October 1940. Despite having equally good reputations and both being assigned to serve on the newly commissioned carriers just before the outbreak of the war, they were completely different people. Rather tall and slim, Shimazaki was described by his men as a relatively tender and open-hearted leader. In contrast, short and stocky Takahashi had the opinions of a rigid and down-to-earth officer.

PHOTO 6 ■ Lieutenant Commanders Shimazaki and Takahashi (*far left and standing, respectively*) in China when they were both still lieutenants. Mori, *Akatsuki*

Although the South Pacific campaign was not their first combat experience, their traits played a particular role in the Battle of the Coral Sea.

However, no more than a few minutes after the departure of the striking group, the Japanese vision of a clean opening blow became more obscure. The *Shōkaku*'s two Kates, which had previously spotted the carrier, now located an enemy tanker and one destroyer bearing 150 degrees and 25 miles from the initial contact.[21] The message caused great concern in the 5th Kōkū Sentai command, because the torpedo bomber had probably found the ship or a group of ships supporting the main U.S. Navy task force operating nearby. But the real complications for Hara and Takagi appeared out of the blue. At 0838 hours the *Furutaka*'s No. 1 seaplane also reported spotting the enemy's force at 0820 hours, which looked like a carrier task force. Its position was

TABLE 19 ■ MO Kidō Butai Striking Group, Morning of 7 May 1942

Unit	No.	Pilot	Notes
1st shōtai Zeros/*Zuikaku*	1	Lt. Kiyokuma Okajima (B)	Takeoff: 0808 Return: 1230
	2	PO1c Komiyama	
	3	PO2c Sakaida	
2nd shōtai Zeros/*Zuikaku*	1	WO Sumita (S)	
	2	PO1c Tsukuda	
	3	Sea1c Fujii	
3rd shōtai Zeros/*Zuikaku*	1	PO1c Iwamoto (S)	
	2	PO1c Itō	
	3	Sea1c Mae	
11th shōtai Zeros/*Shōkaku*	1	Lt. Takumi Hoashi (B)	Takeoff: 0815 Return: 1310
	2	PO1c Miyazawa	
	3	PO3c Komachi	
12th shōtai Zeros/*Shōkaku*	1	Ens. Abe (S)	
	2	PO1c Kawanishi	
	3	PO3c Tanaka	
13th shōtai Zeros/*Shōkaku*	1	PO1c Minami (S)	
	2	PO2c Okabe	
	3	PO2c Ichinose	

TABLE 19 **MO Kidō Butai Striking Group, Morning of 7 May 1942** (*continued*)

Unit	No.	Pilot	Observer	Radio operator	Notes
41st shōtai Kates/*Zuikaku*	1	Lt. Cdr. Shigekazu Shimazaki (H)	Lt. Iwami (C)	PO1c Yoshinaga	Takeoff: 0808 Return: 1230
	2	WO Yaegashi	PO1c Himeishi	Sea1c Ōuchi	
	3	PO3c Nozawa	PO1c Kawahara	Sea1c Honda	
42nd shōtai Kates/*Zuikaku*	1	Lt. Murakami (S)	WO Baba	PO1c Miyada	
	2	PO3c Yokomakura	PO2c Kishi	PO2c Satō	
	3	Sea1c Nishitani	PO2c Matsuo	Sea1c Ōizumi	
45th shōtai Kates/*Zuikaku*	1	Lt. Tsubota (B)	PO1c Kosakada (S)	PO1c Endō	
	2	PO1c Sugimoto	WO Ni'ino	Sea1c Hasegawa	
	3	Sea1c Tsubokawa	PO2c Idehara	PO2c Ikushima	
46th shōtai Kates/*Zuikaku*	1	PO1c Ishihara	WO Kanazawa (S)	PO2c Nishizawa	
	2	PO3c Hatanaka	PO1c Ushijima	Sea1c Morishita	
Unit	**No.**	**Pilot**	**Observer**	**Radio operator**	**Notes**
41st shōtai / 1st chūtai Kates/*Shōkaku*	1	Lt. Tatsuo Ichihara (B)	WO Saitō	PO1c Munakata	Takeoff: 0815 Return: 1310
	2	PO2c Itakura	PO1c Matsuyama	Sea1 Morishita	
	3	PO2c Orikasa	PO2c Shigeta	Sea1c Itō	
42nd shōtai / 1st chūtai Kates/*Shōkaku*	1	PO1c Satō	WO Isono (S)	PO2c Ishihara	
	2	PO2c Toda	PO1c Kodama	PO2c Abe	
43rd shōtai / 1st chūtai Kates/*Shōkaku*	1	PO1c Gotō	WO Kanno (S)	PO2c Kishida	
	2	Sea1c Itō	PO3c Satō	PO3c Takada	
44th shōtai / 2nd chūtai Kates/*Shōkaku*	1	PO1c Ishikawa	Lt. Hagiwara (C)	PO2c Sagara	
	2	Sea1c Murakami	PO1c Takahashi	Sea1c Kodama	
45th shōtai / 2nd chūtai Kates / *Shōkaku*	1	Lt. Iwamura (S)	PO1c Shirai	PO2c Misumi	
	2	PO3c Irimi	PO2c Akaishi	PO2c Shimomichi	
46th shōtai / 2nd chūtai Kates/*Shōkaku*	1	WO Yonekura (S)	PO1c Nakamura	PO2c Fukushima	
	2	PO2c Yoshitomo	PO2c Tanaka	PO2c Ōta	

TABLE 19 ■ **MO Kidō Butai Striking Group, Morning of 7 May 1942** (*continued*)

Unit	No.	Pilot	Observer/navigator	Notes
21st shōtai /1st chūtai Vals/*Zuikaku*	1	Lt. Tamotsu Ema (B)	WO Higashi	Takeoff: 0808 Return: 1515
	2	PO1c Hatakeyama	PO2c Fujioka	
	3	Sea1c Egusa	PO3c Matsushita	
22nd shōtai / 1st chūtai Vals/*Zuikaku*	1	Lt. Kuzuhara (S)	PO1c Kawase	
	2	PO1c Hori	PO2c Uetani	
	3	Sea1c Kakuta	Sea1c Miyake	
23rd shōtai / 1st chūtai Vals/*Zuikaku*	1	PO1c Nakanishi	WO Izuka (S)	
	2	PO1c Katō	PO2c Fukugaki	
	3	Sea1c Matsumoto	Sea1c Tsuji	
24th shōtai / 2nd chūtai Vals/*Zuikaku*	1	PO1c Andō	Lt. Ōtsuka (C)	
	2	PO1c Igata	PO1c Shirakura	
25th shōtai / 2nd chūtai Vals/*Zuikaku*	1	WO Fukunaga (S)	PO1c Ishikawa	
	2	PO2c Ishizuka[†]	PO3c Kawazoe[†]	
	3	PO1c Kamioka	Sea1c Izumi	
26th shōtai / 2nd chūtai Vals/*Zuikaku*	1	PO1c Fukugaki	WO Koyama (S)	
	2	PO2c Sakamaki	PO2c Negishi	
	3	PO1c Yamanaka	Sea1c Nakane	

TABLE 19 ■ **MO Kidō Butai Striking Group, Morning of 7 May 1942** (*continued*)

Unit	No.	Pilot	Observer/navigator	Notes
20th shōtai / 1st chūtai Vals/*Shōkaku*	1	Lt. Cdr. Kakuichi Takahashi (H)	Ens. Nozu	Takeoff: 0815 Return: 1310
	2	PO1c Shinohara	PO1c Someno	
	3	PO1c Fukuhara	PO2c Suzuki	
21st shōtai / 1st chūtai Vals/*Shōkaku*	1	Lt. Yamaguchi (S)	Ens. Naka	
	2	PO1c Ueshima	PO1c Kōda	
	3	Sea1 Odagiri	PO2c Hajime	
22nd shōtai / 1st chūtai Vals/*Shōkaku*	1	PO1c Itō	Lt. Koizumi (S)	
	2	PO1c Shirai	PO1c Koitabashi	
	3	PO3c Harashima	PO3c Tanaka	
23rd shōtai / 1st chūtai Vals/*Shōkaku*	1	PO1c Suzuki	WO Kokubu (S)	
	2	PO2c Katō	PO2c Kushima	
	3	Sea1c Ōgawa	PO3c Ōura	
24th shōtai / 2nd chūtai Vals/*Shōkaku*	1	Lt. Mifuku (C)	PO1c Imada	
	2	PO2c Ikeda	PO1c Nagasawa	
	3	PO2c Sugimura	PO3c Yoshinaga	
	4	Sea1c Okada	Sea1c Matsuda	
25th shōtai / 2nd chūtai Vals/*Shōkaku*	1	WO Matsuda (S)	PO1c Nobe	
	2	PO1c Nakasho	PO2c Togashi	
	3	PO3c Hanawa	PO3c Yamauchi	

Sources: JACAR: Shōkaku (1), 31–36; JACAR: Zuikaku (1), 32–37; JACAR: Gunkan Zuikaku (2), 36–38.

From largest to smallest unit size: (H) *hikōtaichō*; (B) *buntaichō*; (C) *chūtaichō*; (S) *shōtaichō*.

† *Lost in action*

far from the one noted in the previous cables—bearing 152 degrees and 150 miles from Deboyne. This report was neither a coincidence nor a mistake. At 0840 hours the *Kinugasa*'s No. 1 seaplane sent a message about spotting the enemy task force at 0800 hours that was composed of one battleship, two heavy cruisers, seven destroyers, and, more importantly, "one vessel appearing to be a carrier," all proceeding on a 30-degree course at 20 knots. Five minutes later the crew confirmed the bearing and distance—170 degrees and 82 miles from Rossel Island.[22] After sending their dispatches, two Alfs remained at a safe distance to provide further data on any changes in the course or composition of the enemy force. At 0844 hours the *Shōkaku*'s plane informed the team that the shadowed enemy carrier had changed its course to 150 degrees at 0820 hours.[23]

At first sight, the two contacts reported by the 6th Sentai's seaplanes were separated by forty miles, but the MO Kidō Butai command assumed they were the same task force.[24]

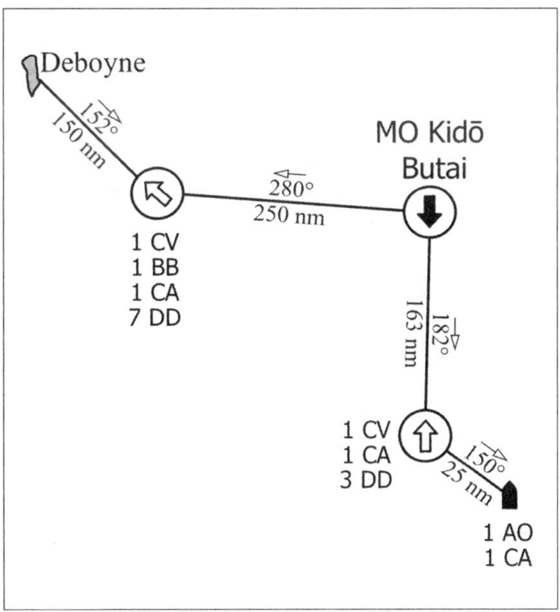

MAP 7 ■ Potential targets for the MO Kidō Butai according to the recon reports, morning of 7 May

The Japanese, having data on the two optional targets of the MO Kidō Butai, the first 163 miles south (spotted by torpedo bombers) and the second 250 miles west (spotted by seaplanes), deduced that the Americans had divided two carriers into two independently operating task groups.[25] They also quickly realized that attacking the second target could bring more promising results. This crucial information shaping their assessment came, again, from the 6th Sentai's seaplanes. Between 0830 and 0840 hours they reported sighting five aircraft bearing 45 degrees and forty-five miles from Deboyne at 0800 hours and thirty-five fighters passing close by at 0825 hours.[26] Almost three dozen aircraft could mean only one thing: the most active American carrier was operating in the west. Although the contact information seemed accurate, Hara had already sent the first striking group against the group located in the south. Most Japanese air officers would not have realized the importance of this target. Yet it was much closer to the MO Kidō Butai, and what was equally important in the calculation was that it also included one carrier. Thus, the southern group had to be destroyed before the clash with the task force located in the western direction took place. In view of the MO Kidō Butai's report, Takagi's decision can be grasped by quoting his order: "It is apparent that the enemy located in the west launched an attack against our friendly forces, but we are now committed to striking the enemy carrier task force in the south with our full strength. Once we destroy the enemy in the south, we will go for the group located in the west."[27] During that memorable moment, Hara also made confident statements to his men, who were gathered at the bridge, saying that the first American carrier would be slaughtered and the second in the west would be struck. No one doubted the victory of the Nippon Kaigun in the upcoming battle.[28]

At 0900 hours Takagi also sent a cable to the Fourth Fleet, informing Inoue of the "progressing strike against the American task force composed of one carrier, one cruiser and three destroyers with all available aircraft [*zenryoku o motte*]."[29] Almost simultaneously, the commander of the 5th Kōkū Sentai forwarded the message to all units involved in Operation MO.[30] The only thing that Takagi and Hara could do at that time was to keep their fingers crossed and await the first report with the attack results on the southern group. One can only guess what was happening in their heads, but their thoughts about

PHOTO 7 ■ The 5th Kōkū Sentai staff. *Seated, left to right*: Commander Yamaoka, Rear Admiral Hara, and Lieutenant Commander Mieno. *Standing, left to right*: Commander Yoshida and Lieutenant Commander Ōtani. *Senshi Sōsho*, vol. 49

the next move, namely the next strike on the second group in the west, had probably already ripened. The most desirable sequence of events included the sinking of the first American carrier, the safe return of the striking group to the decks, the quick refueling and rearming of aircraft, and, finally, taking off for the next target. The Japanese had proved in the Indian Ocean that they could send a carrier to the bottom of the sea in less than a quarter of an hour. Surely they could repeat this feat in the Coral Sea? The 5th Kōkū Sentai had still not been spotted by the enemy scouting planes—at least there was no indication that it had been. Therefore, once the second American flattop had also been destroyed and the striking group had returned to the MO Kidō Butai before sunset, Takagi and Hara could call themselves admirals who had surpassed the victory near Kuantan, where Japanese bombers surprised and sank two British capital ships, *Prince of Wales* and *Repulse*. It was less than a quarter of an hour before they witnessed an ideal scenario collapse like a house of cards.

Chapter 7

MORNING RECONNAISSANCE MISSIONS AND MOVEMENTS OF TASK FORCE 17

After maintaining a northwestern course all night, at dawn on 7 May, TF 17 arrived at latitude 13° 25.5' S, longitude 154° 48' E, near the Louisiades, then proceeded on a course of 270 degrees at 22 knots. At 0625 hours the course was changed to 25 degrees at 15 knots.[1] That morning, Rear Admirals Fletcher and Fitch expected to find the Japanese invasion force supported by three carriers. Two of them, recognized as the 5th Kōkū Sentai, were reported in the vicinity of Bougainville on 6 May.[2] But the position of the MO Kidō Butai remained a guess and could only be confirmed by scouting planes. Despite several successful air strikes against enemy bases in previous months, neither Fletcher nor Fitch had experienced fighting with aircraft carriers. The upcoming battle was a great baptism of fire for them and the U.S. Navy. Yet Fletcher was aware that adopting simple tactics might bring a conclusive victory—finding the Japanese before they located his carriers and destroying them with a single massive blow, sending as many planes as he could at the time. If Port Moresby had to be saved from the landing of the enemy force in the following days, TF 17 was left with no other option than to neutralize the MO Kidō Butai at all costs.

Anticipating that the carriers of both sides would be engaged in combat, the Americans wanted to ensure that the Japanese invasion force did not enter the Coral Sea and approach Port Moresby unnoticed. TG 17.3 with *Farragut* was detached from TF 17 to avoid this scenario. At 0625 hours it took a western course toward the Louisiades. Crace was supposed to destroy enemy transports and light cruisers reportedly headed toward Jomard Passage the preceding night.[3]

S. Morison and R. Bates argue that delegating TG 17.3 to halt the Japanese invasion force at the southern end of the Jomard Passage was one of Fletcher's biggest mistakes during the Battle of the Coral Sea. The group did not receive any air support, and although each of the three cruisers disposed of one or more seaplanes, putting them into action required more time due to the complicated recovery process. Crace had to rush westward for most of 7 May to be on time at the designated point (because he was 150 miles away when detached) in view of TF 17's instruction about conserving fuel. Since he decided not to catapult seaplanes and relied on his cruisers' radars to spot the enemy, the Japanese could hit him anytime and without risking a confrontation with the carriers. Although TF 17 was to remain south of the Russell Islands to focus on air operations against the MO Kidō Butai that day, Fletcher should not have put three cruisers and three destroyers in such an isolated position. Sending Crace off to block the Jomard Passage also cut the number of destroyers in the American carriers' escort from ten to seven and cruisers from eight to five, significantly influencing the entire team's antiaircraft potential.[4] S. Mori agrees with Morison and Bates that a lonely group of warships with no TF 17 air support would become an obvious target for the Japanese land-based bombers, especially if American carriers lost the Battle of the Coral Sea.[5] However, other American historians also underline that detaching Crace's force was a calculated risk that it was thought could pay off if the Japanese transport ships were intercepted south of Jomard Passage, especially because the American and Japanese carrier task forces excluded each other from the battle.

Regardless of historians' opinions concerning the rationale behind and execution of Crace's mission, at 0619 hours the *Yorktown* scrambled 10 SBDs from VB-5 to search the 325 to 85 degree sectors (on a median of 25 degrees) for a distance of 250 miles.[6] Starting at 0703 hours the *Lexington* also sent up four F4Fs, led by Lt. Noel Gayler, for the first CAP of the day and, most likely, two SBDs from VB-2 and six from VS-2 for anti-torpedo plane patrol.[7]

Immediately after that, Fletcher changed course to 355 degrees to head toward the Russell Islands at 20 knots. He had a total of 128 operational planes at his disposal. Some of them were already being prepared for a fast takeoff in response to the reconnaissance patrol reports indicating the enemy's position. American pilots were also ready to fight; the only thing they were waiting for was the final call for action. At 0700 hours Fletcher placed Operation Order 2–42 into effect and detached the *Neosho* and the *Sims*. Both ships were to proceed to the prearranged rendezvous fueling point, because the tankers' presence was unnecessary during a hunt for the enemy carriers.[8]

American scouting planes also located the enemy ships in their morning search. At 0735 hours, a VB-5 SBD, piloted by Lt. Keith Taylor, reported two heavy cruisers (the *Kinugasa* and the *Furutaka*) at coordinates 10° 40' S and 153° 15' E (northeast of Misima Island) proceeding on a course of 310 degrees at 12 knots. The Japanese ships also sighted the SBD, and they challenged it with two long flashes on the searchlight. In the meantime, another two scouts reported that they had shot down one twin floatplane each (described as a Kawanishi Type 94 torpedo plane) over Misima Island, about 250 miles east of the Louisiades.[9] In fact, they destroyed only one of the *Kamikawa Maru*'s Jakes, confirmed as lost by the seaplane tender and soon replaced by two Petes.[10]

Fletcher expected the two vessels to be part of a larger force that operated near Misima Island. He told Fitch and Kinkaid that TF 17 should continue its course to the northwest until 1030 hours. If the Japanese carriers were not found by then, he intended to change the course to the northeast at twenty knots. At 0815 hours, however, the *Yorktown* got the message Fletcher had been

TABLE 20 ■ **Composition of the American Carrier Air Groups, Morning of May 7**

Lexington Air Group (LAG)	*Yorktown* Air Group (YAG)
Commander: Cdr. William B. Ault (CLAG)–1 SBD-3 (1)	Commander: Lt. Cdr. Oscar Pederson (CYAG)
VF-2: Lt. Cdr. Paul H. Ramsey–21 F4F-3/3As (19)	VF-42: Lt. Cdr. Charles R. Fenton–17 F4F-3s (17)
VB-2: Lt. Cdr. Weldon L. Hamilton–18 SBD-2/3s (17)	VB-5: Lt. Wallace C. Short–18 SBD-2, 3s (18)
VS-2: Lt. Cdr. Robert E. Dixon–17 SBD-3s (17)	VS-5: Lt. Cdr. William O. Burch Jr.–17 SBD-2/3s (17)
VT-2: Lt. Cdr. James H. Brett Jr.–12 TBD-1s (12)	VT-5: Lt. Cdr. Joe Taylor–13 TBD-1 (10)
Total: 69 planes (66 operational)	**In total**: 65 planes (62 operational)

Sources: NARA: USS *Yorktown*, May 8, 29; Lundstrom, *First Team*, 190.

expecting for a long time. Lt. John Nielsen had found two fleet carriers and four heavy cruisers at coordinates 10° 03' S, 152° 27' E, barely 200 miles northeast of TF 17, proceeding on a course of 140 degrees at 20 knots.[11] The *Lexington* was informed about the sighting at 0835 hours. Other scouting planes did not report anything, except one pilot complaining about low visibility in the easternmost arc. After flying for 150 miles he was forced to return, and the rest of his sector was not searched.[12]

The contact provided by Nielsen was in line with the prediction of Fletcher and Fitch of the Japanese positions, described in the TG 17.5 report as "running southward from the vicinity of Bougainville."[13] The message indicated two fleet carriers, which also perfectly matched the 5th Kōkū Sentai and its task of providing air cover for the invasion force heading to Port Moresby, the main objective of Operation MO. The Americans felt confident they could launch their first strike, a combined attack from the *Lexington* and the *Yorktown*. Preparations for the takeoff were already advanced. However, at 0833 hours a minor incident made the Americans uneasy. An unidentified radar contact appeared on the screen, bearing 295 degrees and 30 miles away. Despite the clearly outlined offensive plan, the contact could not be ignored. Lt. (jg) Howard Clark from the morning CAP was vectored out to intercept it. Soon after, Captain Frederick C. Sherman, the *Lexington*'s skipper, told him to return, believing it was a friendly aircraft. The mysterious plane, however, kept its distance and did not approach TF 17, which was quite suspicious. Clark's section finally received permission to recheck the situation, but it encountered bad weather during the pursuit and was forced to return. The disappointed F4Fs' pilots were sure the opponent was a Japanese plane.[14] The intruder disappeared off the radar screen at 0859.[15] In view of what is described in the preceding part of this chapter, it can be concluded that the radar picked up one of the Alfs that had found TF 17 and informed Hara and Takagi about the enemy carrier task force operating in the west.

A single bogey could not obstruct the most crucial part of TF 17's plan for the following hours. At 0915 Fitch issued Air Group Operation Order Number One, pointing to the Japanese carriers as the primary objective but mentioning other enemy naval units as targets that were just as valuable. However, since TF 17 was 210 miles from the Japanese carriers, the *Yorktown*'s aircrews started questioning sending short-legged fighters and torpedo planes. Eventually, the discussion was cut off at 0920 hours when Fitch replied that he would send all the planes he had at hand. J. Lundstrom underlines that Americans were sending the carrier air groups against opposing carriers for the first time, which were believed to be well-defended targets. The U.S. Navy had still not developed a sophisticated fighter escort theory, and each fighting squadron and air group generally used its own procedures. This made the first battle of the carriers a testing ground for future developments, which would change air-naval tactics beyond recognition in the following months.[16]

Beginning at 0925 hours, the *Lexington* striking group scrambled from the deck. Each of VB-2's SBDs was armed with one 1000-pound bomb, and each of VS-2's SBDs with one 500-pound bomb and two 100-pound wing bombs, commonly known as "firecrackers." In total, "Lady Lex" contributed twenty-eight dive bombers. Only eight were retained at the ship for the anti-torpedo plane patrol.[17] Each of Lt. Cdr. James Brett's twelve TBDs went for the Japanese armed with one Mark 13 torpedo. Finally, Lt. Cdr. Ramsey's ten F4Fs were to furnish fighter protection for dive and torpedo bombers during their approach and attack. The entire striking group was in the air by 0945 hours. It departed two minutes later as crews did not want to wait for colleagues from the slower *Yorktown*. Twenty-five SBDs, escorted by four F4Fs from Lt. Fred Borries' 3rd Division, climbed to 16,000 feet. Lt. Cdr. William Ault and the last two dive bombers, accompanied by Ens. Bill Eder's section of two Wildcats, proceeded at about 10,000 feet. Below them, all TBDs were covered by Ramsey's four F4Fs. Since the first CAP and anti-torpedo-plane patrol had already been in the air for a long time, Gayler's four Wildcats and one Dauntless returned to the carrier once the *Lexington*'s deck was cleared.[18]

Due to the smaller deck of the *Yorktown*, its takeoff was prolonged to 0944 hours. For the strike, she prepared VS-2's and VB-2's twenty-five SBDs, VT-5's ten TBDs and VF-42's eight F4Fs. Each dive bomber was armed with one 1000-pound bomb, and each torpedo bomber with one Mark 13 torpedo. Like the *Lexington*'s counterparts, Wildcats were to furnish the bombers with fighter protection. However, in contrast to the practice of the commander of Lexington's air group, CYAG's Lt. Cdr. Oscar Pederson remained in the carrier to serve as fighter director officer.[19]

Since the SBDs of Lt. Walter C. Short and Lt. Cdr. William O. Burch took off first, they slowly climbed to 18,000 feet and were told to circle above the ships and wait for the other planes. Lt. Cdr. Joseph Taylor's TBDs came after the SBDs and immediately left for the target in a single formation at five hundred feet. Eventually, Lt. Cdr. James H. Flatley's F4Fs also took off and divided into two groups in order to escort the SBDs and TBDs. Lt. Vincent McCormack's four Wildcats were to join the dive bombers, but due to confusion surrounding the takeoff Ens. Walter Haas joined the fighters from the torpedo bomber escort. Thus, Flatley headed to the target with five F4Fs, while McCormack was left with only three.[20] All aircraft remaining near the *Yorktown* set off for the Japanese after the last Wildcat left the carrier's deck at 1013 hours.[21] Much slower Devastators, which like the *Lexington*'s had already departed, were caught up by the dive bombers and fighters after twenty minutes. Once Flatley spotted the TBDs flying just above sea level, he positioned his group at 6,000 feet, sunup from the obsolescent torpedo planes. The dive bombers and McCormack's Wildcats remained at 18,000 feet.[22]

Besides the previously mentioned eight SBDs, Fletcher left eighteen F4Fs with TF 17, half of his fighter potential, as a defensive measure against any possible Japanese threat. At 1019 hours the *Yorktown* took advantage of an empty deck

TABLE 21 ■ ***Lexington* and *Yorktown* Striking Groups, Morning of 7 May 1942**

Unit	Commander	Aircraft
CLAG Section	Lt. Cdr. William B. Ault	3 SBD-3s
VF-2	Lt. Cdr. Paul H. Ramsey	10 F4F-3s
VB-2	Lt. Cdr. Weldon L. Hamilton	15 SBD-2/3s
VS-2	Lt. Cdr. Robert E. Dixon	10 SBD-3s
VT-2	Lt. Cdr. James H. Brett Jr.	12 TBD-1s
Unit	**Commander**	**Aircraft**
VF-42	Lt. Cdr. James H. Flatley Jr.	8 F4F-3s
VB-5	Lt. Walter C. Short	8 SBD-3s
VS-5	Lt. Cdr. William O. Burch Jr.	17 SBD-3s
VT-5	Lt. Cdr. Joseph Taylor	10 TBD-1s

Sources: NARA: USS *Lexington*, May 7 and 8, 1; NARA: USS *Yorktown*, May 7, 3; Lundstrom, *First Team*, 195.

and relieved the *Lexington* of CAP duties by sending up Lt. Cdr. Charles R. Fenton's section of four Wildcats. Then she swiftly recovered the SBDs returning from the scouting patrols and changed course to 290 degrees at 23 knots.[23]

After TF 17 had launched the first striking group and was well on the way to finishing accommodating planes from the morning scouting missions, the American vision of an excellent day started getting complicated. At 1021 hours Fletcher received an urgent message from the *Neosho*, repeatedly stating that three two-engine bombers were harassing the Refueling Group at coordinates 16° 38' S and 158° 28' E.[24] Attacking planes had separated from a bigger group of ten aircraft and were approaching from 150 degrees, commencing a horizontal bombing attack. The direction of the bombs was observed closely, and since the ship was swung hard right, they all fell to the starboard as near misses. It was not the tanker's first contact with an enemy. At 0925 hours she had noticed a formation of fifteen planes approaching from 25 degrees, but they made no attempt to attack and flew parallel to the ship's course at a high altitude. Although the *Neosho* did not inform the task force about their specific type or model, Fletcher and Fitch noticed that she was bombed in a location beyond the range of land-based bombers from Rabaul. Therefore, the planes were probably carrier-borne.[25]

Fletcher did not have much time to focus on the *Neosho* because at 1022 hours he was notified about a cable from ComSoWePac. General MacArthur's command sent a reconnaissance report advising that at 0748 hours three Army B-17Es, which had departed from Fremantle, had located one carrier, sixteen miscellaneous warships, and ten transport ships at coordinates 10° 54' S and 152° 36' E, proceeding on a course of 285 degrees.[26] The actual sighting and the reception of the dispatch were delayed by more than two and a half hours. However, the TF 17 command assumed that the Flying Fortresses probably met the same force or part of the same force that the *Yorktown*'s SBD had reported, although the two contacts were separated by about thirty-five miles.[27] MacArthur also furnished Fletcher with an additional B-17 report from 0800 hours, which said that about four destroyers and three large transport ships were proceeding on a course of 285 degrees, ten miles southwest of Misima Island.[28] TF 17 did not find this cable more compelling than the VB-5's sighting from 0815 hours.

Despite the alarming dispatches from the Fueling Group and new data on the enemy, Fletcher did not face any real trouble until scouting planes landed on the *Yorktown* and pilots started to submit their reports. One of them was Nielsen, who located the Japanese task force and thus initiated the events leading to the launching of the first striking group. To his great surprise, he knew nothing about the spotting of two carriers two hours previously. "What carriers?" Nielsen asked when he dropped a message on the carrier's deck about his finding, because he had only seen four light cruisers and two destroyers. It quickly became clear that he had made an unfortunate mistake, caused by the fact that the contact pad did not line up with the holder, so when the pilot checked what he thought was a destroyer, he was checking a carrier. The promising report of contact was erroneous. It should have indicated two DDs instead of two CVs.[29] As J. Lundstrom describes, it was "a traumatic moment for Fletcher and his advisors." Nielsen ran to the flag plot to explain the situation again, but the commander of TF 17 was already upset. Flailing his hands around, he yelled at the SBD's pilot: "Young man, do you know what you have done? You have just cost the United States two carriers!"[30]

To spare Nielsen from unfair blame, it is worth taking a closer look at his point of view, which is covered in S. Ludlum's book. At about 0800 hours the pilot spotted a Japanese cruiser south of Tagula Island, or at least what he believed was a cruiser. After closely examining the speed and the course based on what he thought was the ship's wake, he handed the scouting report to his rear seat man, Straub, who was responsible for transmitting it to the *Yorktown*. However, before sending the report to the carrier, Nielsen noticed something odd about the vessel's bearing. He went down and flew across her course to investigate. To his surprise, she was not a cruiser but a small island, one of the thousands of objects that looked like a ship from higher altitudes. A bit disappointed, Nielsen decided to approach Misima Island from twenty-five hundred feet. This is where his long story began. It is possible to understand the circumstances of the unfortunate scouting mission by quoting the SBD pilot's words:[31]

> Suddenly, thousand yards off to port, ahead a bit, and about 500 feet above us, I spotted a twin-float, three-place Jap plane. He was diving at us and coming like a bat out of hell. I pulled up hard, changed the prop

> to low pitch for more power, turned on my gun switch, set my mixture control, shifted gas suction to a full tank, poured on the coal, and the SBD went up on its tail.
>
> The Jap plane was coming down so fast he would have had to pull too many G's to zoom and try to follow us up. He shot below, scissored under us and came out going away in the same direction he came from. We were hanging on our prop, having gained about 800 feet in our climb, and I had to nose down before we stalled. We had about 500 feet of altitude on the Jap, but he had picked up a lot of speed in that dive, and I couldn't catch him flying level. I nosed over and went after him, telling myself "Got to get him. Got to get him . . . before he reports!"
>
> If the Japs spotted a carrier-based plane, they'd know we had a carrier within 300 miles, and that was something we didn't want them to know. I had to get that guy; that's all there was to it.

Nielsen recalled that chasing and machine-gunning the floatplane from a point-blank range took him three long minutes, during which he almost collided with his prey, which was biting back. Finally, he saw the clear splash on the water's surface, so confirmation of the victory was unnecessary. He decided to fly away, because many other Japanese planes were lurking in the area. Then the memorable sighting occurred:[32]

> The mountain that runs the length of Misima Island is just like the roof of a barn, just as steep and just as sharp at the ridge. I poured on the coal and we climbed that roof. When we got to the top, I'd ease up to the ridgepole and sneak a look over, then slide back, keeping out of sight. We didn't see anything except a hut or two; no ships or planes or installations. So over we went.
>
> We got back on our search course, with the sun off our starboard bow, which cut down visibility in that direction to about two miles. In 15 minutes or so Straub reported over the intercom, "They're shooting at us."
>
> Up to that point I hadn't seen any ships, but as Straub spoke I saw the flashes down on the water and directly up sun. They couldn't have been shooting fused ammunition, for I didn't see any shrapnel bursts at all, and I couldn't tell how close they were coming to us.

> We flew around to get up sun from the Jap ships and made out two destroyers and four cruisers. As soon as they spotted us, they turned east. Once we were certain of the force, we broke radio silence, only to discover that our trailing antenna had been shot away in the brush with the Jap plane. We put the report on CW [continuous wave] and sent it out over the short-range fixed antenna. It was 8:30. We were 200 miles from the *Yorktown* and we headed back full gun, but leaned out. I didn't know how close we'd have to get to our ships before they could pick up our report off the fixed antenna; so we sent it out every few minutes. It wasn't until we were 125 miles from the carrier that we got a "Roger." We were just crossing Tagula Island when they acknowledged.

Nielsen's version did not change the fact that Fletcher and Fitch faced a huge dilemma which had to be solved quickly. Even worse, at 1044 hours the *Lexington*'s radar picked up an unidentified plane bearing 45 degrees at forty-one miles.[33] Fighter Direction Command delegated two pilots from VF-42, Lt. (jg) Richard G. Crommelin and Ens. Richard Wright, to intercept the snooper. The weather in the indicated area was terrible, but they had a lot of luck. After flying for about eight miles, they broke into a clear sky and, on the opposite side, came across a flying boat seven miles off, cruising at 1,500 feet. Using their speed and position advantage, the two F4Fs surprised the lonely Japanese aircraft, attacking from behind and port. The Mavis' fuel tanks started spraying gasoline, and the flames forced the crew to go down. The burning plane crashed into the sea ten miles northeast at 1100 hours.[34] There is no doubt about the victim's identity. She was one of the four flying boats that took off from Tulagi to find the American carriers. As is known from the Yokohama Kaigun Kōkūtai's report, Lieutenant Sakamoto was her commander. At 0840 hours he received the order to maintain visual contact with the enemy task force west of the MO Kidō Butai, located by the 6th Sentai's seaplanes. Because the Tulagi base did not hear back from him for some time, at 1130 hours the nine-man crew was presumed lost during the reconnaissance mission.[35]

The Americans were now sure that the Japanese knew about TF 17's location, and thus, at 1100 hours the *Yorktown* launched VB-5's ten SBDs, rapidly refueled after their morning scouting runs. These freshly scrambled dive bombers and four F4Fs led by Lt. (jg) William N. Leonard of VF-42, who left the deck soon after, would reinforce the anti-torpedo plane patrol and CAP if the enemy was about to attack.[36]

One cannot deny that the CAP activity was overshadowed by Fletcher's consideration of what to do with the striking group, which was well on its way to hitting the secondary target. The TF 17 commander was left with three alternatives: carry out the attack against four cruisers and two destroyers, change the target, or recall the entire group. Despite some suggestions from his officers, the last option was ruled out as the least rational one. Since the Americans anticipated the incoming Japanese hit, keeping carriers' decks and hangars empty was a wiser decision. Additionally, if the planes returned moments before the enemy's blow, this would undeniably lead to a disaster. However, sticking to the original target could not produce outstanding results. The thirty-minute-old ComSoWesPac cable, initially underestimated as an additional scouting report from the other source, suddenly became a crucial hint. It indicated that there was one carrier accompanied by many vessels, so at least it allowed Fletcher to cause a painful loss to the Japanese, assuming his airmen would find the carrier. Therefore, at 1053 hours a message was sent to the *Lexington* and the striking group to redirect the attack to the contact as given by the Army bomber.[37] Despite diverting all planes from one target to another according to the TF 17 calculations, the group was due to arrive at the relevant location shortly. Just like Hara and Takagi, Fletcher and Fitch had to wait the longest and most nervous minutes of 7 May to receive confirmation that the enemy carrier had been attacked.

Chapter 8

SINKING OF THE *NEOSHO* AND THE *SIMS*

The 5th Kōkū Sentai's dream of becoming an equal counterpart to the renowned 1st Kōkū Sentai and the 2nd Kōkū Sentai was never closer to coming true than on the morning of 7 May. The striking groups of the *Shōkaku* and the *Zuikaku* were already on their way to attack the American task force. In the meantime, Hara maintained radio contact with the pair of Kates circling close to the target to acquire the most accurate data. At 0900 hours the *Shōkaku* asked them whether they could see any battleships. Since communication between the vessel and the aircraft usually took some time, it wasn't until 0915 hours that the carrier received two messages sent at 0905 hours. The first informed Hara about one transport ship accompanied by one heavy cruiser and the second about one carrier changing its course to 90 degrees.[1] The weather conditions in the area were described as good, with a generally clear sky, moderate southwestern wind, clouds at eight hundred meters, and visibility up to 20 miles. The 6th Sentai's commander almost simultaneously repeated that his seaplanes were sure about the American carrier force bearing 145 degrees and 165 miles from Deboyne.[2]

Finally, after more than an hour of stressful anticipation, the 5th Kōkū Sentai received a cable from the striking group at 0930 hours. Two short messages arrived individually and cheered up the Japanese officers: "We see the enemy" and "We see the enemy carrier task force."[3] Hara let out a sigh of relief. On seeing the enemy, the Japanese airmen suddenly heard "totsure, totsure" on the radio—an order from Takahashi to prepare an attack formation. Those flying close enough to each other waved their wings to pass on the instructions just in case. Torpedo and dive bombers gradually took their positions to approach the target. While executing these well-rehearsed maneuvers, the two Kates on the scouting mission confirmed they saw no battleships.[4] Thus, the Japanese planes had good news: they did not have to worry about the intimidating amount of antiaircraft fire a battleship could produce.

However, Hara did not know then that his airmen had been too hasty with their reports when they established visual contact with the American ships from a long distance away. It did not take more than a few minutes for them to realize that something was wrong with the enemy carrier. Takahashi shared his doubts with two companions sitting in the cockpit: "For a carrier, it has a different silhouette. Let me think. . . . Neither can I see any screening warships." He did not need much time to make a final assessment. "It doesn't look like a carrier" was the discouraging message he passed to all the *chūtaichō*, and then it quickly spread among other planes. Some officers commented that the group would likely be recalled soon.[5]

Since the attack was supposed to be directed at a carrier, the Japanese aircraft ignored the American ships and split into smaller groups. They did not give up and nervously searched the area, hoping to find the enemy task force.[6] The *Zuikaku*'s report perfectly reflects the endeavor to locate the core of the TF 17; the various *chūtai* declared negative results one by one. The striking group eventually decided to ask the 5th Kōkū Sentai if it knew the precise position of the enemy carrier spotted by the torpedo bomber. "The enemy carrier is bearing 330 degrees and twenty-five miles distant from the tanker," the *Zuikaku* replied at 1015 hours.[7]

Contrary to the expectations from one hour previously, the mood in the *Shōkaku*'s bridge had become tense. The communications personnel were ordered to contact the two scouting bombers one more time to work on the position of the enemy carrier. So far they had not added anything new and persistently claimed that the carrier should be near the tanker. However, after more than three hours of lurking near the American ships, they finally admitted their fatal mistake and sent a sobering cable to the MO Kidō Butai: "Our established contact is a mistakenly recognized tanker. From now on, we are preparing to return." This message, received at 1045 hours by the 5th Kōkū Sentai, eventually buried the hope of finding the enemy carrier southward.[8] "Besides the tanker, no enemy ships [carriers] are present in the northwest," the *hikōtaichō* announced at 1050 hours. On hearing this message, Hara had to reconsider the next move immediately. Since one of the *Shōkaku*'s planes had already recommended sinking the oiler regardless of the circumstances at 1038 hours, he acceded to this plan. At 1100 hours he transmitted his instructions and calculated that the striking group would return by 1330 hours.[9]

The dilemma caused by the canned pineapple and the stomach issues of the senior airman in the morning returned to Ichihara like a boomerang. He was in the air with the striking group and knew that the torpedo bombers from his *buntai* (squadron) had thwarted the whole mission. If he could turn back time, he would have sent more experienced crews on a scouting mission. Still, the grim reality was evident to him—the MO Kidō Butai had irretrievably lost one of the best opportunities to destroy the enemy carriers without taking a hit in return.

Because Nielsen's mistake was explained by the incorrect lining up of the contact pad, mentioned earlier, which was discovered soon after he landed on the *Yorktown*, Japanese historians have tried to find other reasons for the clear failure of their crews. How had the *Shōkaku*'s two Kates, with six men on board, circled two ships for more than three hours and not realized their crucial mistake until queried by their ship? Insufficient training in recognizing vessels was a primary factor, making them believe that a tanker's flat silhouette resembled a carrier from a long distance away. But there was another explanation. Japanese pilots were taught that during scouting missions they must hide in the clouds after spotting enemy ships to follow the target unnoticed and avoid interception by the CAP planes. On 7 May the dense and scattered clouds obstructed the view of the two Kates for too long from the initial contact, mistakenly reported as a group with a carrier. Then, when they ran into the enemy ships for the second time, they identified the American group accurately by pointing out a tanker and a destroyer. What Shibata and Ōtake were not aware of, however, was the fact that they met the same American group two times. They could have deduced this later, but their excitement at the initial contact, soon lost and not reencountered, overshadowed their rational assessment. Once the *Shōkaku* pressed both torpedo bombers to confirm the location of the American carrier to redirect the striking group, they finally got to the truth of the situation.[10]

The two crews that misled the entire Fourth Fleet were probably so stressed about their failure that they made another rookie mistake. After they set a return course, they could not find the proper bearing for the 5th Kōkū Sentai and were forced to ditch at the Indispensable Reefs, about one hundred miles north of the *Shōkaku*'s actual position. Despite their obvious responsibility for this outcome, all air personnel, especially from the carriers, were worth their weight in gold to the Nippon Kaigun, so Hara detached the destroyer *Ariake*, which rescued all six airmen by the morning of 8 May.[11]

At 1100 hours Takagi sent the official dispatch to the Fourth Fleet to avoid further confusion with the circulating reports indicating that there was one American carrier south of the MO Kidō Butai. After a long ruckus, he informed Inoue that the 5th Kōkū Sentai had not found the American task force and that the tanker had mistakenly been reported as a carrier. In the next move, Takagi planned to proceed rapidly toward the second carrier task force, spotted southwest of Rossel Island.[12]

Takagi and Hara quickly realized they should have attacked the American carrier task force spotted in the west. However, the striking group had already been in the air for more than two hours, so they could use this advantage to achieve gains during the luckless morning. A tanker and a destroyer seemed secondary targets, yet they were better than nothing. Takahashi also wanted to compensate the sortie because he was concerned about the morale of the 5th Kōkū Sentai. Still, committing all aircraft could be considered an excessive involvement of the MO Kidō Butai on the eve of the clash with the second American group southwest of Rossel Island. Therefore, at 1120 hours Takahashi ordered all Kates and Zeros to set a return course while he led more flexible Vals against the two lonely American ships.[13]

At 1126 hours, thirty-six *kambaku* approached their prey from about 15,000 feet.[14] Two targets were described in the report of the *Zuikaku* air group as a destroyer and a 20,000-ton tanker.[15] Takahashi decided to focus on the *Neosho*, and the Vals instantly turned on her in three separate waves from different bearings. During that time the *Sims* sped up to flank speed and turned left to take a position on the port quarter of the tanker. Her 5-inch gun batteries opened fire when the planes came within range and the ship reported a direct hit on one bomber with a 5-inch shell, which ripped the plane up in the air. The destroyer kept her 20-mm guns in action, but the projectiles failed to burst and did not destroy the aircraft flying overhead. One of the forward 20-mm guns jammed early in the action and was not cleared during the remainder of the engagement. The *Neosho* soon joined the desperate defense with her Oerlikons. Despite American crews seeing several direct hits on the planes, all three formations of dive bombers remained intact and got close enough to both ships to start a dive.[16]

As the *Sims*' report depicted, four planes broke off from one wave of the *Neosho* attackers and directed their attack at the destroyer, diving on her from astern. It is clear from the Japanese documents that they were Vals from the *Shōkaku,* and some other sources also claim that Takahashi himself led this small formation.[17] The first bomber released a bomb, which proved to be a near miss as it landed in the water about adjacent to the port side midships section. Several seconds later the second plane scored a direct hit on number two torpedo mount. The bomb exploded in the forward engine room, violently shaking the ship's forward section and causing a complete loss of power. The *Sims* became a sitting duck with its lights turned off. The crew started the auxiliary diesel generator, which brought to life the electrical load on units with undamaged power supply cables. The other effect of the first direct hit was damaging the radar antenna. It fell from the mast and landed in the port motor whaleboat. The survivors also recalled flames shooting about 150 feet in the air and the explosion knocking people over. When the repair party was doing its best to secure the boilers, the second bomb hit the after upper deck house. It penetrated several compartments and exploded in the after engine room. Finally, the fourth bomber hit number four gun, yet this score remains debatable because it is based on the testimony that everyone in the gun crew had been killed and the gun was wrecked. Because all three direct hits on the *Sims* came in fairly close succession, the survivors could not accurately recall the events. The skipper ordered everyone off the bridge except himself and the chief quartermaster when the attack was over. All surviving crew members assisted the repair party to jettison the topside weights. The ship fought to the bitter end but broke in half and sank twenty minutes after the first hit. As the water level reached the top of the stack and began running into it, a tremendous explosion raised what was left of the ship almost fifteen feet up. The chief was only able to pick up fourteen survivors in a damaged whaleboat. Then he began looking for life rafts to tow. He recalled that the commanding officer was standing on the bridge when the explosion blew up the ship.[18]

The speed with which four Vals dealt with the *Sims* is perfectly reflected in the Japanese word *gōchin* (an instant sinking of the ship). Regardless of this clear success, it was only part of the strike. Most of the dive bombers threw themselves at the *Neosho*. Her action report mentions about twenty-four enemy planes at high altitudes that made continual dive-bombing attacks from all directions. Despite putting the 20-mm guns into action, the crew knew the enemy had an overwhelming numerical superiority and that the ship could not be saved. Still, the antiaircraft fire forced some planes diving toward the *Neosho* to deliver their attacks at a high altitude, and only three or four got to within a few hundred feet of her masts. Also, the constant maneuvering and crosswind sometimes caused the Japanese bombers to miss the target. The *Neosho* could not escape her fate anyway, and the enemy finally started to score hits one after another. The lethal dose comprised seven or eight direct hits and eight near misses.[19] Most attacks were delivered to the bridge and at the after section with the engineering installation. Three bombs hit directly and several near-missed the bridge. Two bombs slammed into the after part of the ship and blew up at least two boilers. The unexpected coup de grâce came from one aircraft damaged by the antiaircraft fire, which allegedly crashed into Gun Number 4's enclosure. The *Zuikaku* dive bombers' *buntaichō*, Lt. Tamotsu Ema, remembered this remarkable moment, touching and shocking at once, for the rest of his life:[20]

> Faced with the domination of our dive and torpedo bombers, the enemy tanker was desperately trying to escape the inevitable death by maneuvering, but the dive bombers, one by one, came in from above and dropped their bombs. Despite many direct hits, they did not set fire to the ship. The torpedo bombers did not participate in this attack.

> The enemy anti-aircraft guns fired at us furiously. The attack of my group was over, and I saw the bursts of the enemy anti-aircraft fire while moving away. Then I noticed that one of the dive bombers was suddenly hit during the pull-up and started to burn.
>
> "Oh, they got him!" I thought to myself, and at the same time, the plane in flames reversed the course and crashed into the deck of an enemy tanker. At that moment, the wave of fire went out of the ship. So far, none of the scored bombs could set her on fire, but the collision with one burning suicidal plane instantly turned the deck into an inferno.
>
> This was the first suicidal crash I had ever seen, and it impressed me greatly.

The Val crashing into the *Neosho* was piloted by Petty Officer Third Class Ishizuka, and his observer was Petty Officer Third Class Kawazoe. Once the Japanese ended the attack, the commanding officer, CPO Oscar V. Peterson, ordered his people to prepare to abandon the ship and wait for further instructions. The communications officer was instructed to destroy all the classified material to prevent it from falling into Japanese hands. Due to the mess and miscommunication between Peterson and the executive officer regarding the order to evacuate the *Neosho*, at about 1200 hours Peterson instructed that two motor whaleboats should be lowered down to pick up personnel who had abandoned the ship in panic and that all seven life rafts should be towed back to the ship. It remains unknown how many severely burned or injured people jumped over the side because of the fear of being trapped in the after part of the ship when the fire broke out and the smoke made it hard to find a way out. The two motor whaleboats placed men on the rafts and saved as many men as possible. The arduous rescue action took the entire afternoon. The late inspection revealed that sixteen officers and ninety-four men had survived the attack. One officer and 19 men were known to be dead, and 4 officers and 154 men were missing. In the meantime, the *Neosho* also took on board fifteen enlisted survivors of the *Sims* on 9 May.[21]

The Japanese left the tanker in bad shape and without power. Yet she was still afloat. The skipper did not believe his ship could survive the night on the rough sea, but the *Neosho* was sturdier than anyone could have predicted.

PHOTO 8 ■ The *Neosho* after the crash of one Japanese dive bomber Mori, *Akatsuki*

The damage control teams tried to stop the heavy listing, which was finally controlled at 30 degrees. The tanker remained afloat but in a sinking condition for the following days. Her drama and that of those who survived were to continue even after the Battle of the Coral Sea.[22]

Despite the *Neosho*'s and the *Sims*' claims that at least four Japanese bombers had been shot and several damaged beyond repair, the striking group lost only a single *kambaku*, the one that had intentionally crashed into the tanker. The heavy antiaircraft fire of the American ships damaged six Vals—four from the *Zuikaku* and two from the *Shōkaku*—but neither carrier described them as mauled. The Japanese did not report additional losses among the air personnel either except for two men making a suicidal run against the enemy. At 1205 hours Takahashi sent a cable to the MO Kidō Butai saying that he had destroyed the enemy group and that the striking group had set a return course.

The striking group scored ten or eleven hits out of thirty-six dropped bombs, which gave a hit ratio of between 28 and 31 percent. Given the intense antiaircraft fire of the *Neosho* and the *Sims*, it was a decent result. Indeed, it could have encouraged Hara to think positively before the decisive clash with

TABLE 22 ■ **Summary of the Japanese Attack on the *Neosho* and the *Sims*, 7 May 1942**

Carrier	Losses	Bombs and ammunition	Claims
Shōkaku	Two bombers damaged	19 × 250-kg bombs dropped	Sinking one destroyer of a bigger class, setting fire to and sinking one big tanker (six direct hits in total)
Zuikaku	One bomber lost, one bomber ditched, four bombers damaged	17 × 250-kg bombs dropped, 1600 x 7.7-mm rounds expended in total	Moderate/serious damage and immobilization of a 20,000-ton tanker, sinking one destroyer (five direct hits in total)

Sources: JACAR: Shōkaku (1), 31–32; JACAR: Zuikaku (1), 34–35.

Fletcher's carriers. Despite the initial setback in identifying the enemy task force and "killing a baby bird with a butcher's knife," the Japanese destroyed the cumbersome group in the south while keeping the 5th Kōkū Sentai's offensive potential intact.[23] All the MO Kidō Butai had to do was to recover the planes, reconfirm the position of the second American carrier task force, and rapidly proceed westward to send the next striking group against the primary target.[24] Although this plan might have looked compelling, the Japanese did not have much room for mistakes if they were to conduct it before sunset. Their race against time had begun.

Chapter 9

SINKING OF THE *SHŌHŌ*

While the pilots of the *Shōkaku* and the *Zuikaku* were desperately searching for enemy carriers over the area indicated by the reconnaissance bomber, the *Lexington* striking group arrived over Tagula Island. As they passed its northwestern tip, the Americans emerged from the clouds, closely observing the horizon. The formation was led by VS-2's SBDs, which were to attack first, clearing the way for the remaining planes.

At about 1040 hours Lieutenant Commander Hamilton noticed wakes forty miles northward through his binoculars. He shared his finding with Dixon, who quickly passed the word to Ault and Brett. Hamilton recognized a flight deck as the *Lexington* striking group veered to the right. Undoubtedly, the Japanese had at least one aircraft carrier in the group. VB-2's leader also spotted the silhouettes of two or three heavy cruisers and one or two destroyers.[1] The American strike was intended to find the MO Kidō Butai; instead, it ran across the MO Main Force. Also, if Hamilton had proceeded northward for several minutes more, he would have spotted the Port Moresby Invasion Force, just twenty-five miles north-northeast.[2]

The *Shōhō* crew would find it hard to believe that they were the first victims of the Americans on the morning of 7 May. As Shirō Ishikawa, *Shōhō*'s fighter pilot, recalled in his memoirs, the light carrier shouldn't even have been there directly supporting the convoy. Before launching Operation MO, the Fourth Fleet and the 5th Kōkū Sentai officers strongly argued about using the *Shōhō*. The latter insisted on grouping all three carriers in one task force to maximize the striking potential of the MO Kidō Butai. Admiral Inoue disagreed but eventually acceded to the views of his cruisers' commanders and assigned her to screen the vulnerable transport ships. Ishikawa writes that although the MO Main Force gained the coveted air support, this was also the reason for the Nippon Kaigun losing the carrier, which was, importantly, the first one lost in the Pacific War.[3]

In an interview for a Japanese magazine, another of the *Shōhō*'s fighter pilots, PO2c Mitsuo Nakayama, said that the B-17s, which appeared overhead, weren't a good sign. As they passed near the group, he looked nervously into the air, anticipating the enemy's striking group. Nakayama described his feelings as "being caught in the trap and becoming a decoy."[4]

Yet the *Shōhō* was there, far away from the MO Kidō Butai, performing her less flashy duties for the Fourth Fleet. The weather was perfectly calm and the sea's surface looked like a lake.[5] At 0730 hours, four fighters and one Kate scrambled from the deck and went on routine anti-torpedo plane patrol.[6] Merely one hour later, the *Aoba* copied the cable about the location of the American carrier task force, which should have been 140 miles from Deboyne with a bearing of 160 degrees. However, just after 1000 hours the situation in the MO Main Force suddenly changed. The *Kinugasa*'s Alf warned all units about many planes scrambling from the enemy carriers. Quick calculations indicated that the Americans would hit Gotō's group at about 1120 hours. Thus, at 1015 hours the 6th Sentai commander ordered the seaplanes to maintain contact with the enemy carrier task force and monitor its moves on an ongoing basis. The *Shōhō* had about one hour to prepare her counterattack. At 1020 hours the *Kinugasa*'s seaplane made contact again and gave information about two carriers—one *Saratoga*-class and one unspecified.[7]

This exciting news arrived at the MO Main Force with the order to prepare all available Kates and Zeros to strike the enemy. Before that, at 1030 hours, the *shōtai* of three Claudes piloted by PO2 Tadao Aoki, PO2c Takeo Inoue, and PO3c Shirō Ishikawa respectively rose into the air to form a CAP.[8] Soon after, all five planes from the morning patrol landed on deck. In the meantime, the *Aoba* catapulted seaplane No. 2 and the *Kako*'s seaplane No. 1 to relieve the pilots from the *Kinugasa* and the *Furutaka*, who had already been in extended contact with the American task force. The crews even complained about the enemy fighters trying to shoot them down. Still, all four *94 no baka karasu*, maliciously nicknamed "stupid crows," used their flying skills to avoid destruction and held on to the warships below.[9]

Next, the *Shōhō* was to arm her torpedo bombers, which had to depart hastily. Captain Izawa changed course to the northwest and began preparations to launch the planes. All he could contribute to the battle was six Kates with a petite escort. Still, this force was better than nothing. Hanging the torpedoes under the belly of the bombers turned out to be time-consuming, because the day began with patrol missions and no promise that the *Shōhō* would take part in the main clash of the carriers.[10] Her smaller deck limited the speed of flight operations, and her crew was still inexperienced, especially compared to those of the other Japanese carriers.

PO2c Nakayama's awful hunch wasn't an exaggeration. At about 1050 hours observers in the carrier spotted a group of more than fifteen enemy planes approaching from the port side, a distance of 40,000 meters with a bearing of 110 degrees.[11] "Taikū sentō, taikū sentō!"—the order to the antiaircraft artillery stations was passed on to the *Kako* and the other screening vessels.[12]

Although the Japanese radio communications weren't working at their best at this point, the fighters in the air also quickly noticed the incoming wave of aircraft.[13] According to PO2c Nakayama, sitting with his colleague from the fighter group close to the antiaircraft machine guns at the starboard beam, two Claudes had already left and had gone north to protect the convoy.[14] The Americans came faster than expected. The Japanese still needed at least a quarter of an hour to prepare the Kates for departure. Now it was too late. All they could do was strengthen their CAP to defend the *Shōhō*.

Ault led the formation, and right behind his section were ten more SBDs from VS-2. The Americans planned to break through antiaircraft fire and approach the target from the bow side to attract attention. At the same time, VB-2 headed east to wait for the slower Devastators to launch a coordinated anvil attack from the stern and both sides. Four Wildcats led by Lt. Fred Borries took their positions above, escorting the dive bombers. Lt. Cdr. Ramsey's

Wildcats, covering torpedo bombers, approached the Japanese carrier at about five thousand feet. Near Misima Island, just over the water, they came across one of the two Alfs catapulted from the 6th Sentai early that morning.[15]

Ramsey delegated his second section, led by Lt. (jg) Paul Baker, to intercept the enemy seaplane. The two F4Fs surprised the Alf and forced the Japanese pilot to ditch a few miles off Misima. Baker did not have time to confirm his victory and quickly headed toward Ramsey to escort the dive bombers during a strike against the carrier. However, as it turned out, half an hour later there was no evidence that the Japanese seaplane had been shot down. The Americans suspected that the aircraft might have sunk, but the pilot managed to withdraw from the area and, after less than an hour, headed for Deboyne.[16]

Awaiting the attack of the enemy planes, the MO Main Force took a defensive posture and formed a tight *rinkejin* (circle formation). Gotō put the *Shōhō* in the center. The heavy cruisers *Aoba*, *Kinugasa*, *Kako*, and *Furutaka*, armed with the most potent antiaircraft artillery, were placed at about fifteen hundred meters in four corners. The last element of this formation was the destroyer *Sazanami*, which sailed astern of the carrier.

Once the news about the incoming strike of the American carrier-borne force on the MO Main Force reached Rabaul, Inoue didn't have any second

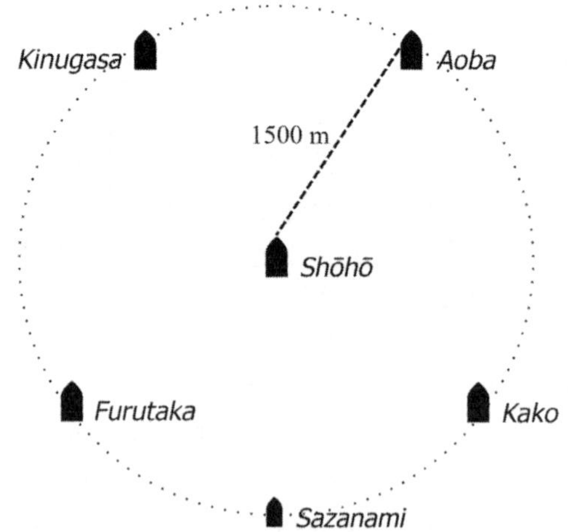

MAP 8 ■ *Rinkeijin*, or "circle formation," of the MO Main Force during the attack on the *Shōhō*

PHOTO 9 ■ Rear Adm. Aritomo Gotō, commander of the Main Force *NDL*

thoughts about the immediate reaction. Just after 1100 hours he ordered the Port Moresby Invasion Force to head northward to wait out the main enemy attack. The next move strongly depended on what happened during the following hours, namely after the exchange of blows between Fletcher and Hara. The Fourth Fleet had just learned about the erroneous identification of the American carrier by the torpedo bomber crew, and there was not much left to do but patiently wait for the first combat reports.[17]

The MO Main Force probably had more concerns at the time than the chess game being played by staff officers. At 1107 hours Captain Izawa ordered a sharp turn to the port to outmaneuver the approaching enemy aircraft. On the *Shōhō*'s deck, the crew was frantically preparing Zeros for takeoff, but the SBDs led by Ault turned out to be faster. At 1110 hours, three American dive bombers began their approach from eighty-five hundred meters. None of the Japanese fighters interrupted this run, because they were well behind the main part of VS-2. However, the carriers' evasive maneuvers played their role. Ault's section had a clear path, but all bombs missed the vessel, despite the claim about one direct hit. Parallel to his dive, ten VS-2 SBDs made a circle up north, approaching the *Shōhō* from the sun and wind direction.[18] The Americans focused on the primary target and avoided dogfights with the Claudes, which were now concentrating on defending their carrier. At least two of them were trying to chop into Dixon's formation to disturb his approach. One of the pilots joined the defense of the *Shōhō* and badly shot up Ens. Anthony J. Quigley's dive bomber, which almost lost the control wires, but the ailerons jammed. The pilot informed the *Lexington* by radio that he would fly to Rossel Island.[19] Still, the SBDs continued the run and released their 500-pound bombs at two thousand feet. Again, VS-2 reported three direct hits on the carrier, but the reality was far more fortunate for the Japanese. The *Shōhō*'s report depicts the dramatic course of action and the bombs falling one by one around the carrier without damaging her.[20]

After the first two unsuccessful passes, Dixon and his SBDs were to climb up and use the remaining 116-pound bombs against the screening warships to distract the antiaircraft guns from the approaching VB-2 and VT-2. Despite being vastly outnumbered, the Japanese pilots showed they also had fangs. One of them took advantage of his position and caught one Dauntless pulling out of his dive. Lt. Edward H. Allen with ARM2c Charles W. Rouser Jr. crashed with their SBD behind the *Shōhō*'s stern. They didn't have much chance of surviving.[21] The two fighters from CAP briskly chased after the remaining dive bombers, and thus only Ens. John A. Leppla dropped his bombs on one of the cruisers. He radioed a hit, but it had only occurred in his imagination.[22]

Just after VS-2 completed their attack, Captain Izawa used a precious moment of peace to strengthen his CAP. At 1117 hours, three Zeros led by Lt. Kenjirō Nōtomi scrambled from the *Shōhō*.[23] At least for a while, Izawa felt the situation was under his control and that the carrier could survive this massive assault. However, he did not realize that VB-2 had refrained from approaching the target until VT-2 took up a convenient position from which to charge. What was worse for him was that the *Yorktown* striking group was also gradually arriving on the battlefield. At 1100 hours the flyers from the second American carrier spotted the wakes of six vessels and the explosions

TABLE 23 ■ ***Shōhō* CAP during the American Attack**

Unit	No.	Pilot	Notes
1st shōtai Claudes/*Shōhō*	1	PO2c Aoki (S)†	Takeoff: 1030
	2	PO2c Inoue†	
	3	PO3c Ishikawa	
2nd shōtai Zeros/*Shōhō*	1	Lt. Nōtomi (S)	Takeoff: 1117
	2	PO1c Imamura†	
	3	Sea1c Ban'no	

Sources: JACAR: Shōhō (2), 30; JACAR: Gunkan Shōhō (8), 12–13; Ishikawa, 143; Kudo, 133; Mori, *Akatsuki*, 210; Hata, Izawa, Shores, 387.
† *Lost in action*

of antiaircraft projectiles about twenty miles northeast of Misima Island. Initially, they saw one fleet carrier and one light carrier but quickly figured out that the enemy had only one flattop, which to them resembled the *Ryūjō*.[24]

Just one minute after the Zeros took off from *Shōhō*, Lieutenant Commander Hamilton gave the signal to attack. Fifteen of VB-2's SBDs began their approach from 12,000 feet. At about 8,000 feet, one Claude appeared behind Hamilton, trying to prevent or at least hinder the run. The Japanese pilot's efforts were in vain, because at 2,500 feet Hamilton released his bomb, which hit the *Shōhō*'s flight deck near the after elevator at about 1120 hours. Several seconds later, another bomb hit the flight deck, closer to the forward elevator. The bombs had penetrated the *Shōhō*'s hangar deck, where they started a massive fire of refueled and armed torpedo bombers. Ironically, the Kates were just prepared for the strike against the Americans. The carrier burst into flames and a thick column of black smoke emerged from huge holes in the flight deck. Although VB-2 scored only two of the five claimed hits, both had fatal consequences for the vessel. The *Shōhō*'s report discloses that the explosion in the forward hangar deck had turned it into an inferno.[25]

Petty Officer Third Class Ishikawa described his participation in the defense of the carrier after VS-2's attack as follows:[26]

> Then I saw them [the enemy]. Many black dots were floating in the distant sky. They gradually became larger and took the distinct shape of

an aircraft. I noticed that three Zero fighters hurriedly took off from the carrier. Immediately after that, before my eyes, I saw a loose formation of planes on the opposite course, which spotted the carrier and were about to start a plunge. The attack has begun.

Like in a dream, I went down after those dive bombers, which commenced their run. However, unlike a Zero fighter, I couldn't catch up with my obsolete Type 96 fighter, and they were finally able to escape. Moreover, there was already a big hole in the carrier's deck. I veered my plane down and dove into the enemy aircraft.

There were enemies everywhere around me. I was firing a machine gun but quickly ran out of ammo.

The black smoke was already pouring from the carrier, and she was about to sink into the Coral Sea. There was no longer a ship to whom I could return.

To outmaneuver the enemy dive bombers, Captain Izawa passed the word to execute *torikaji* (a sharp turn to the port). However, immediately afterward, he noticed the wakes of torpedoes, so he ordered *omokaji* (a sudden change of course to the starboard). This was the moment when VB-2 pinned down the carrier. The immediate result of two direct hits and a massive fire was the damage to the *Shōhō*'s main power generator. The communications system went down and the carrier's rudder jammed in one position. The ship started to head helplessly southeast, making a wide circle to port. The fire spread throughout the entire vessel, slowly detonating the stored ammunition. The damage control team tried to extinguish the flames and remove the combustible objects, but this wasn't the end of the tragedy.[27]

It is difficult to use the *Shōhō*'s report, which covers the entire attack of dive and torpedo bombers on just three pages, to reconstruct the sequence of events and the effects of each American hit on the ship's technical condition unambiguously. However, before the first bomb slammed the carrier's deck, VT-2 split into two sections of six TBDs each to execute the anvil attack they had been training for over a long period. At about 1115 hours the Devastators began approaching the helpless target from the southwest, descending from approximately four thousand to just one hundred feet. The last bump in the road was the antiaircraft fire, because Lieutenant (jg) Baker claimed to surprise and shoot down two Japanese fighters defending the damaged carrier. The other Wildcats secured an area closer to the *Shōhō*, but after a while they were forced to move to a safer distance due to the heavy antiaircraft fire.[28]

Although the torpedo attack carried out by VT-2 against an enemy aircraft carrier was the first of its kind in the history of the U.S. Navy, its course and result became a textbook example of a successfully coordinated action that significantly contributed to the sinking of the enemy ship. The first group of Devastators, led by Lieutenant Commander Brett, passed around the *Shōhō*'s stern and placed themselves in front of her port side. The second group of TBDs, led by Lt. Edwin W. Hurst, headed for the starboard side.

At 1119 hours Brett opened Pandora's box by releasing a torpedo into the water, aiming at the port quarter. The other Devastators dropped their torpedoes within the next two minutes, cutting off any means of escape. Lt. (jg) Leonard Thornhill, whose fish slammed into the starboard quarter, was the first to score a hit. At this stage, the *Shōhō* could not avoid further blows. A few seconds later Lt. (jg) Lawrence F. Steffenhagen's torpedo struck the port beam, followed by Lt. Robert F. Farrington's hit on the port bow. The fourth clear hit, forward of the port beam, was probably dropped by Lt. (jg) Harold R. Mazza, although his name was not listed in the *Lexington*'s report.[29] This is how he remembered the moment of his approach:[30]

> We dove to the surface at 160 knots and fanned out–myself being furthest to port. A ten-mile approach at 130 knots was made under heavy main battery gunfire from two heavy cruisers on either beam. The carrier was enveloped with smoke from bomb hits, and anti-aircraft fire was practically nil. I approached the carrier, which was heading east, went in to about 900 yards and dropped at 100 knots, 50 feet altitude, target angle 60 degrees. I then circled left and saw my torpedo was heading true and swung around the bow in retirement. I saw my torpedo explode forward of the beam, and I retired south, meeting Yorktown torpedo planes approaching–also an enemy fighter coming head-on. But he showed a reluctance to press home an attack. I joined up with the captain and returned to base and landed aboard.

The final punch came from ACOM Harley Talkington. His torpedo exploded on the starboard beam. Brett's men claimed nine hits, but five was a sufficiently good result.[31]

The *Shōhō* had enough troubles before the torpedo bombers attacked. Now she was left with a rapidly flooding bow, though with her engines still working to some extent. The water that poured inside didn't help the damage control team contain the situation in the hangar deck, which looked even more terrible. Thick, acrid black smoke made breathing almost impossible. Dead bodies lay around, and the fight to save the ship turned into a struggle for life. But this wasn't the last word from the Americans.[32]

Descending from 18,000 feet, Lieutenant Commander Burch led 17 SBDs against a half-alive enemy carrier. He didn't know that her rudder was jammed, and he radioed VT-5 to inform them about his decision to attack. Lieutenant Commander Taylor was against this and argued that his torpedo bombers needed at least five minutes to get into position. Burch, however, didn't want to wait for the Devastators, because the *Shōhō* was going into the wind, giving the SBDs a perfect opportunity to score hits on the entire length of the deck. At 1125 hours VS-5 ignored the enemy CAP chasing other aircraft and started the approach. In hardly any time at all they had dropped their 1,000-pound bombs on the helpless carrier, except for two pilots, who experienced some problems. Soon after Burch's squadron had attacked, VB-5's eight dive bombers turned against the *Shōhō* and ruthlessly took advantage of her state. Of all the bombs dropped by the SBDs, at least six, although Japanese sources mention as many as eleven, smashed the carrier's deck. The crews claimed fourteen, but perhaps the precise number will always remain a mystery.[33]

The attack of the *Yorktown*'s SBDs made a profound impression on Flatley, who recalled that moment as follows:[34]

> I was sitting upstairs at 5,000 feet watching them come down. The heavy bombs began exploding at three and four-second intervals. Fire, flames, and seawater were being thrown hundreds of feet high, from each explosion. The 1,000-pound bombs seemed to be pattering down like rain and those big babies do four times as much damage as the 500 pounders.

> The sight of those heavy bombs smashing that carrier was so awful it gave me a sick feeling. Every second bomb was landing and exploding aboard the ship. Those powerful blasts were literally tearing the big ship apart. She burst into flames from bow to stern. I don't see how anybody aboard that ship could have survived.

One may feel that the attack of VS-5 and VB-5 wasted their striking potential on a dead target. While pulling up from a dive, two of the *Yorktown*'s SBDs were damaged by two Zeros from the CAP, which were trying to get back at the enemy. However, there was more to come from the Americans. Ten VT-5 Devastators, escorted by Flatley's Wildcats, descended from approximately ten thousand feet and began their approach. Passing one of the heavy cruisers, the torpedo bombers headed for the *Shōhō*'s starboard side. The carrier was listing to starboard and burning fiercely at this time. Thick black smoke was emerging from the ship, covering the run from the antiaircraft artillery. But VT-5 could see the bow and dropped their torpedoes. Out of ten fish, the crews reported ten hits.[35] The *Shōhō*'s report shows only two, though.[36] After the attack, the Devastators headed south to meet with VT-2 and take a return course. Ramsey and his wingman also withdrew with the torpedo bombers to protect them if they encountered any Japanese planes arriving on the battlefield.[37]

After the *Yorktown*'s attack, the *Shōhō* was doomed. It was 1131 hours, and Captain Iwaza ordered all men to abandon the ship. The evacuation from the burning wreck, still afloat, wasn't easy. Some crew members were wounded and had to jump into the water.[38] PO3c Nakayama remembered those moments in the following words:[39]

> Smoke violently emerged from every gap in the ship, and the angry cries of wounded officers and petty officers caused a lot of chaos. All planes in the afterpart were blown off, so I ran towards the forward crane on the port side. Even in the forward part, the elevators on the flight deck had been blown away and stuck out like a mountain.

Nakayama, accompanied by several men, started lowering the lifeboat from the crane. However, a blast from the bomb explosion knocked them into the sea. Nakayama used his best swimming skills to escape from the ship and avoid being dragged under the water:[40]

> Even while we were swimming, the enemy planes were firing at us mercilessly. When I looked back at the *Shōhō*, I saw that some of her machine guns were still shooting like crazy. Suddenly, the *Shōhō* rolled upside down, and the men remaining on the flight deck slid down. I was so regretful that I could not protect the *Shōhō* whose silhouette quickly disappeared from the sea's surface.

The testimony about machine gunning the survivors is consistent with the carrier's report, though the entry is laconic.[41] The *Shōhō* sank at 1135 hours, about fifty-three miles northeast of Deboyne.[42] According to Japanese sources, she got hit by thirteen bombs and seven torpedoes between 1120 and 1130 hours. Surprisingly, the crew also reported one enemy bomber deliberately smashing into her flight deck at the starboard side.[43]

Only five Wildcats from VF-42 remained on the battlefield when the bombers set a return course. They engaged in a dogfight with the Japanese CAP circling over the burning *Shōhō* and chasing the last American bombers fleeing south. The attack on the enemy fighters was led by Flatley, who targeted one of the two Claudes. Taking advantage of his altitude, he soon found himself on the tail of the Japanese plane. The enemy fighter was seriously damaged and

TABLE 24 **Comparison of Claimed and Recorded Hits during the Attack on the *Shōhō***

	Claimed	Scored
VS-2	2	0
VB-2	5	2
VS-5	9	6–11
VB-5	5	
Total	**21**	**8–13**
VT-2	9	5
VT-5	10	2
Total	**19**	**7**

Sources: NARA: USS *Lexington*, May 7 and 8, 2; NARA: USS *Yorktown*, May 7; JACAR: Gunkan Shōhō (9).

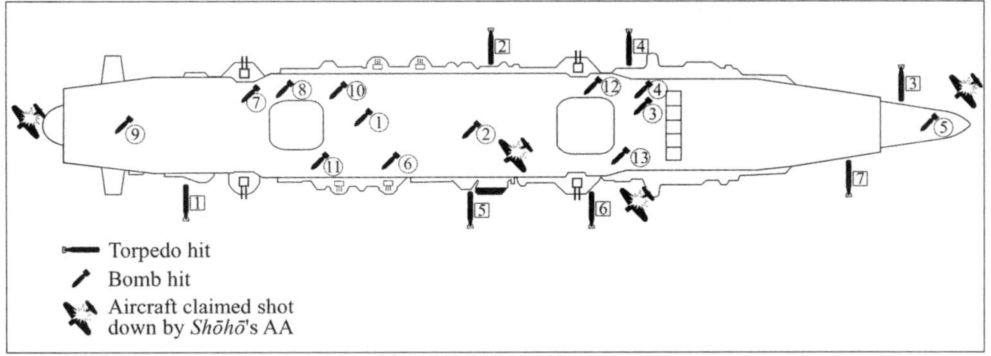

FIGURE 1 ■ Bomb and torpedo hits scored on the *Shōhō*. It is worth noting that there were as many as thirteen bomb hits in total. Additionally, the Japanese marked four American planes downed by antiaircraft fire, including one that allegedly crashed into the flight deck. *Source:* The figure can be found in *Senshi Sōshō*, 49:285, but the original source is the *Shōhō's* detailed report. See JACAR: Gunkan Shōhō (9), 12.

fell into the water after just one pass. Lt. (jg) Brainard T. Macomber witnessed Flatley's victory and later emphasized the Claudes' incredible maneuverability.

After the duel was over, the rest of the Japanese planes scattered and regrouped. Of the five F4Fs, only Flatley's climbed up to regain an altitude advantage. At the same time, his wingman, Lieutenant (jg) Baker, was busy chasing prey. The remaining three pilots split up to search for enemy fighters at about two thousand feet. However, one of them, Lt. (jg) Brainard T. Macomber, quickly attracted WO Imamura's attention. This was one of the first dogfights between Wildcats and Zeros. It would have ended badly for the American pilot if he hadn't gotten help from Ens. Edgar R. Bassett. Already cornered, Imamura was unaware that the third Wildcat was going for him. Lt. (jg) Walter A. Haas caught the Japanese veteran from China at a few hundred feet above the water and hit his fuselage. Imamura wanted to bail out, but his aircraft crashed into the sea before he could open the canopy. All three VF-42 pilots had just participated in the first U.S. Navy victory over a mythologized Zero fighter.

In another dogfight, Baker managed to get behind another defender, mistakenly identified as a Zero, and fired a series of bursts from his machine gun.

The enemy plane started to smoke and fall rapidly. Just when Baker thought the Japanese aircraft was about to crash into the water, the pilot unexpectedly regained control of his aircraft and began escaping. However, Haas observed this chase and decided to intervene. Rushing toward the enemy, he was soon on its tail and pulled the trigger. After a few seconds the Japanese fighter exploded in the air. But Haas and Baker did not have time to enjoy the victory because their victim had lured them into a heavy cruiser's antiaircraft fire. The Americans managed to get out of the trap, but their fighters were slightly damaged.

While looking for the next target, Flatley spotted another Zero at about one thousand meters. His rival noticed the Wildcat. However, seeing VF-42's advantage, the Japanese pilot decided to climb up and escape a fight that was pointless since the *Shōhō* had sunk. After a few seconds Flatley realized that his F4F was much slower than the Zero and gave up the pursuit.[44]

The half-hour dogfight over the *Shōhō* ended in American success. The attacking group shot down one Zero and two Claudes without sustaining any losses. Although the crew claimed more confirmed victories, including the nonpresent "VSB planes," Flatley could feel satisfied with this result. More importantly, he seemed to figure out the weakness of the famous "Zeke"—the lack of self-sealing fuel tanks. When a Zero got hit by a well-aimed machine gun salvo, it usually got set on fire and lost its exceptional maneuverability. The method of defeating the invincible Japanese fighter was best described by Flatley, who later shared his tactics:[45]

> The most effective attack against a more maneuverable fighter is to obtain altitude advantage, dive in, attack, pull up using speed gained in dive to maintain altitude advantage. The old dogfight of chasing tails is not satisfactory and must not be employed when opposing the Jap VF planes. On this occasion the enemy fighters resorted to steep wing-overs, rolls and loops at low altitude. They are extremely clever aerobats [*sic*] and apparently have found some way to overcome the effects of "blacking out." However, their planes can climb away from our own, and it is thought that they will soon get the news. In the engagement, the leader [Jimmy] tried to overtake a Jap VF that was running for it. He climbed rapidly away without any difficulty.

The attack on the *Shōhō* also had apparent shortcomings, as highlighted in the American documents and testimonies. All but two aircraft from the *Yorktown* headed for the carrier, which *Lexington* planes had sufficiently damaged. In such circumstances, only a few bombers were needed to hit the carrier with the coup de grâce, and the remaining part of the group should aim for the screening vessels. To avoid such a concentration on one target in the future, Flatley received permission to coordinate the attacks of the *Yorktown* striking group from his plane while observing the battlefield from above.

According to the *Shōhō*'s report, 631 crew members went down with the carrier. The number of wounded was 72 men, while 132 escaped without injuries.[46] Still, they had to wait for a rescue for several hours. Despite having intact screening vessels, Rear Admiral Gotō had to abandon the survivors and hastily withdrew north, carrying out Inoue's order to avoid the second American carrier-borne attack.[47] Before leaving the area, though, all the warships threw wooden logs, boards, barrels, and additional lifesaving equipment into the water. The message to the *Shōhō* survivors by flag semaphore was "Take care. We'll return for you later."[48] Gotō kept his promise. At about 1415 hours he was confident enough about the safety of his group and detached the destroyer *Sazanami* to dash for his companions. After heading south for more than three hours, the observers noticed overloaded lifeboats barely floating on the water. Captain Izawa and almost one hundred survivors were taken on board.[49] This wasn't easy since the men were scattered around a vast area, many floating on single wooden logs. Some of the wounded had already passed away. Still, the Japanese were genuinely committed to the rescue operation and sent reinforcements to help after dark. Rear Admiral Kajioka detached the light cruiser *Yūbari* and the destroyers *Mutsuki*, *Yayoi*, and *Mochizuki*, which arrived at the spot at 2055 hours. Due to communication issues, they almost mistakenly fired on the *Sazanami*. However, the additional effort paid off. The *Yayoi* even managed to find two fighter pilots, PO1c Okugawa and PO2c Okazaki.[50] Eventually, 205 men were saved.[51] The prolonged wait for rescue was vividly described by PO3c Nakayama:[52] "I thought it would be better to die from excessive bleeding than to be eaten by fish. After swimming for about nine hours, I was rescued with PO2c Hayashida (from the 4th pilot class) by the Sazanami before it got dark."

TABLE 25 **Summary of the *Shōhō* Air Group's Losses on 7 May 1942**

Planes	Result
6 × Kates 7 × Zeros (including disassembled) 2 × Claudes (spares)	Lost with the carrier
2 × Claudes 1 × Zero	Lost in the dogfight
2 × Zeros 1 × Claude	Ditched near Deboyne
Total: 21 planes (including spares)—100%	

The *Shōhō*'s survivors were transferred to the oiler *Irō*, which headed for Truk. After one week, they were boarded on the heavy cruisers *Myōkō* and *Haguro* and departed for Kure.[53]

All of the Japanese reports underline that six fighters did their best to defend the *Shōhō* against a cluster of intruders.[54] The pilots of the Zeros and Claudes shot down five enemy planes, including one unconfirmed victory. They received a helping hand from the antiaircraft artillery, which claimed that it downed four enemy bombers.[55] As we know, however, the American losses were significantly smaller, whereas the outcome of the attack was more than disastrous for the *Shōhō* air group. Fifteen planes, including all six Kates, either burned to ashes on the hangar deck or went down with the carrier. Out of six CAP fighters, three were missing, which meant that Wildcats had shot them down. The only surviving aircraft were two Zeros piloted by Lt. Nōtomi and Sea1c Ban'no and one Claude piloted by PO3c Ishikawa. According to Ishikawa, they received an order by radio to head to Deboyne. Since he didn't know how to find the newly established seaplane base, he followed two Zeros and ditched safely in the local lagoon.[56] Soon after, the repair ship *Shōei Maru* rescued all three pilots.[57] Detailed information about the fate of the *Shōhō* air group members can be found in appendix 4.

Chapter 10

THE 25TH KŌKŪ SENTAI ENTERS THE FRAY

The Fourth Fleet headquarters was nervously awaiting information regarding the strike on the enemy vessels, mistakenly reported as carriers, and the update on the defense of the *Shōhō*. At 1120 hours the first bad news arrived: "*Shōhō* is fiercely burning." After twenty-five minutes an even worse cable about her loss reached the *Kashima*. When the staff officer read aloud the dispatch, everyone in the room fell silent. Cmdr. Hideo Iida then passed the note to the senior staff officer, Capt. Iwao Kawai; the chief of staff, Capt. Shikazō Yano; and Admiral Inoue himself. They all read the note and didn't say anything. The Fourth Fleet commander was perfectly aware that his decision to allocate the vessel to the convoy had now taken its toll. The Nippon Kaigun had just lost its first aircraft carrier in the war.[1] Despite all this, he tried to stay calm or, at least, not show his nerves. As noted in his diary, he continued to sit in his chair and blow smoke from his cigarette as if nothing had happened. Inoue wished he could have been as serene as Adm. Heihachirō Tōgō when he lost two battleships, the *Yashima* and the *Hatsuse*, on 15 May 1904 during the war with Russia after they struck mines. "No matter how much I apologize, I think it was just bad luck, unfortunate," he wrote in his diary on the Battle of the Coral Sea.[2]

Inoue's order to the Port Moresby Invasion Force to proceed north for the time being was already in force. In addition to the sinking of the *Shōhō*, Gotō also lost seaplanes from the *Kinugasa* and the *Furutaka*, which were later forced to land at Deboyne to avoid the clash with the American fighters.[3] From 1000 hours the Fourth Fleet had a clearly defined plan: all Japanese groups, including the 25th Kōkū Sentai, were to attack the enemy carrier task force located 165 miles south of Deboyne.[4] This included the improvised vision of the night surface attack by the 6th Sentai and the 6th Suirai Sentai. Inoue believed the cruisers and the destroyers could catch the enemy carriers off guard and contribute to the battle in an alternative way. The seaplanes were instructed to maintain contact with the Americans and continually report on their position to achieve this. In the meantime, the MO Kidō Butai was to proceed southwest and recover the first striking group. Inoue issued the Fourth Fleet Secret Operational Order No. 371, a summary of his plan, at 1210 hours:[5]

1. The 6th Sentai and the 6th Suirai Sentai, following the orders of the MO Invasion Force commander, will prepare for the night surface attack against the enemy carrier task force.
2. The MO Kidō Butai will quickly establish and maintain contact with the enemy carrier task force to conduct the air strike.
3. The Port Moresby Invasion Force, following the orders of the MO Invasion Force commander, will diligently screen the convoy with troops and temporarily head north.

The second strike of the MO Kidō Butai was initially scheduled for 1430 hours, assuming that all aircraft that took part in the attack on the *Neosho* and the *Sims* would return to the carriers in the following hour. However, as S. Mori writes, the mood in the 5th Kōkū Sentai was terrible. The Japanese had lost one carrier, and Hara perhaps revealed his position to the enemy. But a light appeared at the end of the tunnel—an opportunity to reverse the back luck. At 1220 hours, observers in the *Zuikaku* noticed black dots on the horizon.[6] Thirteen Kates and nine Zeros landed on the deck within ten minutes. By 1310 hours the first striking group was back on the *Shōkaku*, but Lieutenant Ema's dive bombers were still missing.[7] The Japanese heard from other pilots that the *Zuikaku*'s Vals had navigational problems on the return route due to poor weather. Rear Admiral Hara, who wished to attack the Americans again that day, could not leave his crews and patiently waited for their return. It was a difficult decision for him, because his Kates were already in the middle of being armed with torpedoes. Hara predicted the enemy carriers would move west and soon be out of the MO Kidō Butai's range.[8]

Meanwhile, on its way back, the American striking group shared the positive news about the result of their attack. At 1210 hours Dixon broke radio silence and sent a message to the *Lexington* that would go down in history: "Scratch one flattop! Signed Bob." On hearing that cable, everybody burst out joyfully. They had done it. They had sunk the first Japanese carrier in the war. However, there was not much time for celebration. Due to deteriorating weather and strong winds, at 1234 hours the *Lexington* sent off four F4Fs, led by Lt. Albert O. Vorse, and seven SBDs, for CAP and anti-torpedo plane missions. Ault and his men now had an empty deck to land on after the successful venture.

From 1239 to 1316 hours, fourteen F4Fs (including Gayler's four from CAP), twenty-six SBDs, and twelve TBDs landed on the *Lexington*. At the same time, twelve F4Fs (including Fenton's four from CAP), twenty-four SBDs, and ten TBDs landed on the *Yorktown*. The striking group's losses accounted for three dive bombers—two from VS-2 and one from VB-5. Although the Japanese shot down only Allen's plane and Quigley ditched near Rossel Island, the Americans also lost another aircraft.[9] After the attack on the *Shōhō*, Ens. John W. Rowley from VB-5 began chasing one of the Japanese fighters. When it turned out that the enemy was moving too fast to catch up, he turned back and realized that he had lost sight of his group. He spent an hour fruitlessly searching for the return route but then came across the Crace group. They directed him toward Port Moresby. However, Rowley's SBD was running out of fuel, so he ditched off the southern coast of New Guinea. With ARM3c David Musgrove, they managed to get to shore in a rubber boat, where some friendly indigenous people found them. Both pilots were rescued later by the U.S. Navy.[10]

In addition to losing two dive bombers, the *Lexington* reported three slightly wounded VS-2 crew members. One Japanese fighter pierced the windshield of an SBD piloted by Lt. (jg) William E. Hall and then injured the arm of his gunner/radio operator, ARM3c D. C. Phillips. Ens. Arthur J. Schultz sustained superficial shrapnel wounds to his right forearm and thigh.

Ens. J. A. Leppla had several small fragments of shrapnel removed from his left thumb and forearm later.[11]

After the landing the crews were interviewed regarding the course and results of the attack on the Japanese task force. The Americans established that they had sunk one *Kōryū*-class carrier (later referred to as the modified *Ryūjō*-class, and ultimately as the *Ryūkaku*-class carrier) and one light cruiser and had damaged one heavy cruiser. In a dogfight, VF-42 and VF-2 reported shooting down five Claudes and one dive bomber. Although the actual result was limited to one light carrier and the shooting down of three fighters, the Americans could feel satisfied with the outcome of the morning action.[12]

By 1420 hours all dive and torpedo bombers had been refueled and rearmed. Sherman suggested to Fletcher that he could send another striking group to attack the surviving Japanese vessels. However, the commander of TF 17 was against this idea since he intended to find and sink the carriers of the MO Kidō Butai. Theoretically, the SBDs could have located them during their afternoon reconnaissance missions. Still, even if they had found the enemy, the second striking group would have had little time before sunset, and an attack in the dark could have resulted in losing the planes. After examining all options, Fletcher decided to give his men time to rest, taking advantage of the cover of thick clouds. At 1429 hours he informed Fitch and Kinkaid that the TF 17 "will hold off awaiting information from Army hoping to repeat in the morning this day's excellent work." Fitch backed up this plan. Despite Sherman's protests that they "should make another attack or send out a search," it was decided that further reconnaissance patrols and all air offensive operations would be resumed the following morning.[13]

Unlike the Americans, the Japanese still hoped they would be able to attack the enemy one more time that day. Relying on morning reports from the *Kinugasa*'s No. 1 seaplane indicating the presence of one probable carrier, one battleship, two cruisers, and two destroyers south of Rossel Island, Rear Adm. Yamada decided to make his move in the Battle of the Coral Sea. At 0915 hours, twelve Bettys of the 4th Kaigun Kōkūtai, led by Lt. Kuniharu Kobayashi, took off from the *yama no ue hikōjō* (airfield on the top of the mountain)—better known as Vunakanau in Allied sources. All land-based bombers were armed with 800-kg Type 91 mod. 2 aerial torpedoes. They had only one seemingly simple task—to find and sink the enemy carriers. However, the memory of the disastrous action off Bougainville was still alive among the crew members, so the pressure to redeem themselves was exceptionally high.[14]

Just ten minutes after the departure of the 4th Kaigun Kōkūtai, a Betty commanded by Lt. Tadayoshi Koseki, sent from Rabaul in the morning to

TABLE 26 **4th Kū Strike against the American Forces South of Russell Islands, 7 May 1942**

Unit	Pilots	Navigators	Radio operators	Mechanics
1st shōtai / 1st chūtai Bettys /4th Kū	WO Nakayama† PO2c Furuta†	Lt. Kobayashi (B)† PO1c Ichinose† Sea1c Furuta†	PO2c Asahi† Sea1c Tamura†	AM1c Furukawa†
	PO1c Toyama PO1c Kurimoto	PO2c Nakamura Sea2c Kajinaka	PO3c Katagiri Sea1c Tajinaka	AM2c Fukura
2nd shōtai / 1st chūtai Bettys / 4th Kū	PO1c Kambe† Sea1c Suzuki†	WO Gotō† Sea2c Tominaga†	PO2c Shiratsuchi† Sea1c Sanbongi†	AM1c Igarashi†
	PO3c Aihara† Sea1c Sakata†	PO2c Kaiwa† Sea2c Takahara†	Sea1c Matsui† Sea1c Tezuka†	AM1c Tanaka†
3rd shōtai / 1st chūtai Bettys / 4th Kū	WO Nishimura Sea1 Ishijima	PO1c Morisaku Sea2c Kakumoto	PO3c Yajima Sea1c Minamiyashiki	AM1c Ikeda
	PO1c Ozawa Sea1c Kagami	PO1c Mitori Sea2c Shimotsuura	PO3c Kamura Sea1c Okada	AM2c Yajima
1st shōtai / 2nd chūtai Bettys / 4th Kū	WO Toriumi PO2c Suita	Sub Lt. Koseki (C) Sea2c Kawai	PO2c Onishi Sea1c Ōsone	AM1c Kikuchi AM3c Kurihara
	PO1c Oyokawa† PO2c Satō†	PO3c Kase† Sea2c Doi† Sea2c Ono†	PO3c Kumobayashi† Sea1c Masuda†	AM1c Fujiwara†
2nd shōtai / 2nd chūtai Bettys / 4th Kū	PO1c Katsuta Sea1c Kitō	WO Tanaka Sea2c Kusano	PO2c Itō Sea1c Koshikawa	AM1c Andō
	PO1c Miyazaki Sea1c Hoshino	PO2c Hagino Sea2c Takahashi	PO3c Tsuboi Sea1c Komoribayashi	AM1c Wakabayashi AM1c Tomizawa
3rd shōtai / 2nd chūtai Bettys / 4th Kū	PO2c Kobayashi PO3c Watanabe	WO Okabe Sea2c Fujimori	PO2c Nishimaru Sea1c Kobayashi	AM1c Senuma AM3c Uchiyama
	PO2c Naga# PO2c Morita	PO1c Sugii Sea2c Ishihara	PO3c Takahashi† Sea1c Hirano	AM1c Kawamura AM2c Matsumoto

Sources: JACAR: 4 Kū (1), 14–15; Onishi, 195–96.

† *Lost in action*

Seriously wounded

provide the reconnaissance of the 170-degree line, cabled about spotting two battleships, two heavy cruisers, and two destroyers eighty-five miles south of Deboyne, proceeding at 20 knots toward the Jomard Passage. On hearing this news, Lt. Cdr. Matsunaga from the staff felt that the morning patrols had done a great job, and commented out loud, saying, "We are lucky."[15] Thirteen minutes later, another bomber from 4th Kū patrolling the 190-degree line reported contacting the enemy. But the crew could not remain in the area longer because they ran out of fuel and had to return to base.[16]

In February the Japanese had learned a valuable lesson when they sent slow land-based bombers against the *Lexington* without an escort. This time, things were supposed to be different. At 0945 hours, eleven Zeros from the Tainan Kaigun Kōkūtai led by Lt. Cdr. Tadashi Nakajima scrambled from Lae. The pilots took off believing that they would be forced to ditch at sea on the return route since their planes had limited range. Fortunately, the command presented them with three optional spots where friendly ships would rescue them immediately.[17] Additionally, to guide the fighters to the target without any delays, at 0940 hours the 4th Kū sent one Betty commanded by Ens. Murako from Vunakanau. He linked up with ten fighters in about ten minutes and they flew southeastward together.[18]

TABLE 27 **Tainan Kū Escort Mission, 7 May 1942**

Unit	No.	Pilot	Notes
1st shōtai / 1st chūtai Zeros / Tainan Kū	1	Lt. Cdr. Nakajima (B)	Takeoff: 0945 Ditched: 1630
	2	PO1c Ōshima	
	3	Sea1c Suizu	
2nd shōtai / 1st chūtai Zeros / Tainan Kū	1	WO Yoshino (S)	
	2	Sea1c Kokubun	
1st shōtai / 2nd chūtai Zeros / Tainan Kū	1	Lt. Kawai (C)	
	2	PO2c Yoshida	
	3	Sea1c Yamamoto	
2nd shōtai / 2nd chūtai Zeros / Tainan Kū	1	Sub. Lt. Yamaguchi (S)	
	2	PO3c Ishikawa	
	3	PO3c Arai	

Source: JACAR: Tainan Kū (3), 22–23.

By 1100 hours all Japanese forces in the area were aware that the 5th Kōkū Sentai had not encountered an enemy carrier but only an oiler. Since it was known for almost an hour that the most promising target was now located south of Deboyne, the 25th Kōkū Sentai decided to commit most of its bombers. At 1100 hours, twenty Nells of the Genzan Kaigun Kōkūtai led by Lt. Kauro Ishihara scrambled from Vunakanau. The bombers were armed with 250-kg bombs—some of them departed with only one and some with two.[19] Ishihara intended to link up with Bettys from the 4th Kū to reach the fighters' escort and carry out a well-coordinated attack. When the Alfs from the *Furutaka* and the *Kinugasa* were finally forced to break away from the enemy warships and return to Deboyne, the land-based bombers would be ready to pick up the slack.

At about noon Lt. Cdr. Nakajima's Zeros and one Betty flew over Misima Island and passed five friendly ships, most likely the MO Main Force heading north. The fighters crossed Tagula Island and caught up with the main formation of the Bettys from the 4th Kū.[20] Ensign Murako's bomber was not needed anymore, and since his aircraft hadn't been armed with a torpedo, he turned back toward Rabaul.[21]

The Japanese were trying to keep track of the enemy task force, and at 1315 hours the Jake from the *Kamikawa Maru* cabled about spotting one carrier 115 miles from Deboyne with a bearing of 250 degrees. The seaplanes had already covered the 180-mile sector, with a bearing of 180 to 230 degrees from Deboyne, but no other carriers were found. Nakajima, who had already separated from the bombers, rushed to the indicated area to see the enemy warships with his own eyes. His fighters reached the spot at 1345 hours and found only screening vessels. The Tainan Kū quickly reported spotting one battleship, two cruisers, and three destroyers. Zeros tried to close the distance, but at 800 meters they were deterred by antiaircraft fire. Their cable was more or less consistent with two other dispatches. The first one was from the *Kamikawa Maru*. At 1345 hours the seaplane crew messaged about "two battleships, two cruisers and five destroyers eighty miles from Deboyne, bearing 170 degrees."[22] The second one was from the *Aoba*'s seaplane No. 2, which came across the group of American battleships at 1400 hours. This aircraft, however, didn't send any follow-up cables to Gotō for the next two hours.[23]

TABLE 28 ■ **Genzan Kaigun Kōkūtai Attack Mission, 7 May 1942**

Unit	Pilots	Navigators	Radio operators	Mechanics
1st shōtai / 1st chūtai Nells / Genzan Kū	Ens. Oyaizu PO1c Hasuda	Lt. Ishihara (B) Lt. Nomura PO1c Itazaki	PO2c Sumie Sea1c Ikeda	AM1c Matsubara AM2c Nakahara
	PO3c Uchiyama Sea1c Oda	PO2c Utsumi	PO3c Nakakusu Sea1c Tomita	AM2c Matsumoto AM2c Usui
	PO1c Ōtake* Sea1c Ashida*	PO2c Nagatani*	PO2c Watanabe* Sea1c Chikami*	AM2c Yasui*
2nd shōtai / 1st chūtai Nells / Genzan Kū	WO Nibu Sea1c Ōbayashi	WO Hasegawa (S)	PO2c Yamamoto Sea1c Katō	AM2c Inoue AM1c Mukai
	PO2c Satomi Sea1c Fujiwara	PO1c Uetake	PO2c Nozaki PO2c Kaneda	AM2c Ozawa
3rd shōtai / 1st chūtai Nells / Genzan Kū	WO Onuma (S) Sea1c Sakai	PO1c Tomita	PO2c Tomii PO3c Aso	AM1c Ogawa AM2c Shimizu
	PO2c Takano (S) Sea2c Gotō	PO1c Ōda	PO3c Agata Sea1c Nakamura	AM1c Niiyama AM3c Inamine
1st shōtai / 2nd chūtai Nells / Genzan Kū	Lt. Nikaidō (C) PO3c Sasawara	PO1c Miyakoshi PO3c Ebira	PO1c Tsujimura PO3c Takamori	AM1c Usui AM2c Inoue
	WO Ichinose (S) Sea1c Haruna	PO1c Amamiya Sea2c Yano	PO1c Hirai PO3c Uematsu	AM1c Nonaka AM3c Takahashi
	PO1c Muramatsu Sea1c Ōhira	PO1c Hirabayashi Sea2c Ishikawa	PO3c Nakajima	AM1c Taniguchi AM2c Kurihara
2nd shōtai / 2nd chūtai Nells / Genzan Kū	Sub. Lt. Sasawara (S) Sea1c Wake	WO Miyo Sea2c Takarabe	PO1c Kawakami PO3c Kōno	AM1c Tokunaga AM3c Yamashita
	PO1c Ogawa Sea1c Murase	PO1c Murakami Sea1c Wada Sea1c Aoki	Sea1c Yasuda	AM1c Wakizaka
3rd shōtai / 2nd chūtai Nells / Genzan Kū	PO3c Matsuoka Sea1c Mishima	PO1c Maegawa (S) Sea1c Yamamoto	PO1c Ōe PO3c Sugino	AM1c Takeshima
	PO1c Sasaki PO3c Ōtsu	PO1c Muraoka Sea1c Yamamoto Sea2c Inagaki	PO2c Ōno	AM1c Iwasaki AM1c Kuroishi

TABLE 28 ■ **Genzan Kaigun Kōkūtai Attack Mission, 7 May 1942** *(continued)*

Unit	Pilots	Navigators	Radio operators	Mechanics
1st shōtai / 3rd chūtai Nells / Genzan Kū	Sub. Lt. Tanaka (C) PO1c Mukohira	WO Arano Sea2c Matsumoto	PO2c Mori Sea1c Ebihara	AM1c Okamoto AM1c Takakura
	PO3c Yamamoto Sea2c Yoshimura	WO Hiramatsu (S) Sea1c Fuse	PO2c Kunibe Sea1c Tanaka	AM1c Ishimaru
	PO2c Yamada Sea1c Nakamura	PO1c Kunizawa Sea1c Nishida	PO3c Inoue Sea1c Okada	AM2c Suzuki AM3c Matsuda
2nd shōtai / 3rd chūtai Nells / Genzan Kū	WO Terajima Sea1c Kaneko	Ens. Kaneda (S) Sea2c Kurishima	PO3c Matsui Sea1c Ōtsuka	AM1c Eda AM2c Nishiura
3rd shōtai / 3rd chūtai Nells / Genzan Kū	WO Tsuchiya Sea2c Deguchi	WO Itamura (S) Sea1c Kojima	PO3c Watanabe Sea1c Kajiuchi	AM1c Taniguchi AM2c Hane
	PO1c Tanaka PO3c Hinata	PO1c Iwata Sea2c Watanabe	Sea1c Itagaki Sea1c Katō Sea1c Ichimura	AM1c Hano

Source: JACAR: Genzan Kū (4), 8–9.
* *Forced to return due to engine damage*

Since the Tainan Kū fighters had started running out of fuel, at 1415 hours Nakajima decided they had to return. No carriers seemed to be in the area, so the bombers could proceed with the attack alone, without the escort. The Zeros still had more than two hours of flight time left before they could ditch safely near the friendly ships.[24]

On their way to the target, the Genzan Kū passed over the heads of the 6th Sentai. Less than an hour later, one Nell reported a damaged left engine and was forced to return to Rabaul.[25] However, the central part of the bombers' role was about to begin. At 1430 hours the 4th Kū finally spotted the enemy vessels. They had already formed a defensive formation and looked ready to fight. Changing the direction to the southwest to avoid the antiaircraft fire, twelve Bettys slipped beneath the clouds and divided into two groups to carry out the anvil attack.[26]

The Japanese had eventually located the target. It was Crace's group. He was not surprised to see the enemy striking his vessels. At 1300 hours the lookouts noticed the Japanese "carrier-based dive bombers," but they retired without attacking. After a while, it was assumed that the planes were fighters from

Rabaul that had become separated from the bombers and torpedo planes they had been escorting. At 1345 hours the *Chicago*'s CXAM radar made contact with a group of planes twenty-eight miles away. Twelve minutes later the screen revealed ten single-engine monoplanes. They were Zeros from the Tainan Kū, soon chased away by the antiaircraft defense. However, at 1415 hours radar indicated another group of planes seventy-five miles away with a bearing of 30 degrees. The formation was moving toward Crace, because it was thirty miles closer at 1426 hours. Finally, six minutes later, the Japanese planes were sighted at twelve miles due to the flashing of reflected sunlight.[27]

When Lieutenant Kobayashi gave the order to attack, two groups of Bettys were already steadily approaching the enemy warships. However, their timing wasn't the best. A few minutes before, Crace's group had chased away the Zeros, so the antiaircraft defense was ready to repel the next attack. PO2c Ryōkichi Onishi, a navigator from the 2nd *chūtai*, remembered that moment as follows:[28]

> The enemy warships fired with the main armament, secondary armament, anti-aircraft guns and machine guns—every weapon was shooting at us. From the bow to the stern of each vessel, like a river of fire. Please don't hit me. . . . At least protect our plane until we drop the torpedo.
>
> I hadn't believed in God, but I had some prayers when seriously troubled. This prayer must have guided our plane, which descended above the sea's surface. We rushed against the first enemy battleship in the formation.
>
> I was sent to the forward machine gun and started shooting. I aimed for the upper deck and the bridge of the screening vessel and fired frantically. Of course, the enemy ship was also repeatedly firing at us.
>
> Finally, I lost sight of the silhouette of the enemy battleship, which burst with a fire pillar. I noticed one of our planes attacking something like the heavy cruiser. It was probably one of the planes from the *shōtai* closing the formation.

This testimony alone shows the firepower of Crace's antiaircraft defense. Although Onishi's plane didn't score a hit, it survived the attack. The other bombers weren't so lucky. Despite the well-conceptualized pincer maneuver, the screening warships immediately shot down four Bettys, including

Lieutenant Kobayashi's aircraft. Even worse, all the dropped torpedoes missed their targets—the *Chicago* and the *Australia*. The former cruiser's report reflects the endeavor to dodge three torpedoes coming in from both sides. It also provides information about the downed bombers.[29] According to some Japanese sources, one of them deliberately crashed into the *Australia*. The crews reported that although one Betty only slightly hit her main mast, she was left burning heavily and listing. The second in command, Sub-lieutenant Ozeki, who was in Rabaul, added confusion to the planned action by mentioning the sinking of one battleship.[30]

The 4th Kū attack was over at 1440 hours when the last bomber dropped a torpedo. The surviving Bettys did not risk staying longer and turned back to Rabaul. Since some of them were severely shot up, it was questionable whether they could make it without additional losses. Their runs were observed from above by the Genzan Kū, which appeared at the site at 1432 hours. The Nells spotted two battleships, two cruisers, and two destroyers, but no carriers. Still, there was not much time left to do anything, and Lieutenant Ishihara decided to attack. "We count on you!" were his words of encouragement that were passed among the crews.[31] The Japanese didn't want to test the effectiveness of the enemy antiaircraft fire, so they remained at 13,000 feet to carry out horizontal bombing. In the following twelve minutes, they dropped most of their bombs and claimed two direct hits on the *Augusta*-class cruiser. The unit's report says the ship was heavily damaged, but the reality was different.[32] Crace's group had just survived a massive strike from the land-based bombers and hadn't received any torpedo or bomb hits. The antiaircraft guns ceased firing when the last Japanese aircraft took a return course.[33]

The Japanese losses, especially among the 4th Kū, were painful. Apart from four downed bombers, at 1740 hours another ditched near Panaeati Island (Deboyne lagoon) due to a damaged engine and rudder, and another one, riddled with bullets, landed at Lae. Only half a dozen Bettys returned to Vunakanau at 1705 hours, including five slightly damaged ones. Thirty crew members were lost with the planes and one gunner was killed on board. Three men were wounded, one of whom was in critical condition.[34] The Japanese later widely commented that "yon-kū wa shi-kū ka shita," which meant "the 4th Kū turned into the death squadron."[35]

The more fortunate Genzan Kū had returned without losses to Vunakanau by 1745 hours. Only four bombers were slightly damaged, but the price for security was inaccurate horizontal bombing. The crews were sure they had scored at least several hits, but these later turned out to be only in their imaginations.[36]

The 25th Kōkū Sentai's unsuccessful participation in the Battle of the Coral Sea ended up creating some challenges for the Tainan Kū's fighters. At about 1600 hours the Zeros approached Lae, where they planned to land. However, the local antiaircraft defense took the damaged fighters for enemy planes and opened fire. Soon after, three Zeros on a patrol mission around the base started attacking Nakajima's group vigorously. The numerous calls—"Stop shooting, morons!"—didn't help, and the frustrated pilots had to fly away to avoid being shot down by their companions. Eventually, all eleven fighters ditched safely near Gasmata at 1630 hours, where friendly ships rescued the men.[37]

The results of this bombing mission are probably one of the best examples of wartime exaggeration. The initial report, made on the return from the strike against the Allied warships, contained information about sinking one battleship of an unknown class and severely damaging one heavy cruiser. However, when crews from the 4th Kū and the Genzan Kū started to combine their claims during the evaluation meetings, the description confirmed that they had sunk one *California*-class battleship, heavily damaged and set on fire one *Canberra*-class heavy cruiser, and left one *Warspite*-class battleship in a sinking condition.[38] Having hastily shared this information with other units, the Secret 25th Kōkū Sentai Dispatch No. 314 created an impression of the second battle of Kuantan. The mood of joy was utterly groundless, but the Japanese believed it had strong foundations, because the success was directly corroborated by two independent groups of crew members and confirmed by photos taken during the action. S. Mori explains in his monograph in detail how this could have happened. The 4th Kū arrived at the relevant location first and recognized eight warships. However, when the Genzan Kū started to drop their bombs, they could count only six vessels. Thus, two missing ships were automatically considered sunk by Bettys in the torpedo attack. Some staff officers, including Rear Admiral Yamada, asked difficult questions to verify the result but could not openly challenge the report on the eve of its planned announcement by the Imperial Headquarters.[39]

The 25th Kōkū Sentai's strike against Crace's group resulted in two men being killed and five wounded on the *Chicago*.[40] But that wasn't the end of the troubles. Attracted by Japanese planes, three B-17s led by Capt. John Roberts arrived unexpectedly on the battlefield at 1457 hours. They made a huge mistake and took Nells for Liberators, which were attacking an enemy convoy. The Flying Fortresses also dropped their bombs on the targets below, reporting one enemy transport hit and set on fire. Fortunately for the Americans and Australians, the attack turned out to be unsuccessful, which Crace later commented on, saying, "Compared to the Japanese strike several minutes ago, this was fortunately carried out with tragic accuracy."[41]

Although Crace survived the attacks of enemy and friendly bombers, he was irritated. His view was that the Japanese had just launched an all-in attack against the American carriers, so Fletcher would counterattack in the following hours. Additionally, at 1526 hours, TG 17.3 sent a cable to TF 17 advising that the group would not perform the assigned task without air support. Fletcher, who maintained radio silence, did not respond, because he did not want to give away the position of his carriers.

Fearing further air attacks, Crace withdrew south, approximately 220 miles southeast of Port Moresby, to increase his distance from the Japanese bases and carriers. At the same time he planned to remain close enough to New Guinea to attack any enemy forces that attempted to cross the Louisiades or go through the Jomard Passage or the China Strait. However, Crace's situation was complicated. His group had been struggling since early afternoon with dwindling fuel supplies and had no knowledge of the location of the friendly carriers or Fletcher's intentions.

At 1518 hours the Americans received a short but extremely critical cable through a broadcast station that had copied the *Neosho*'s signal: "Sinking." The severely damaged tanker, unable to communicate with either the base or Fletcher for just under four hours, was begging for help. TF 17 was left with only one operational tanker in the area. The *Tippecanoe*, however, was stationed at Efate at that time and used the last fuel supplies to supply local vessels.

Due to a problem with the fuel supply for TF 17, at 1645 hours CINCPAC warned the *Tippecanoe* of Japanese submarines near New Caledonia and informed her about the probable sinking of the *Neosho*. According to the order, *Tippecanoe* was to "take all possible precautions" to remove new fuel from the tanker *E. J. Henry* and then proceed to TF 17. CINCPAC did not know, however, that the *E. J. Henry* had only arrived in Suva at noon three days later than expected. It would take several days to unload the *E. J. Henry* and transport the fuel supplies to the *Tippecanoe* at Noumea. All of this made the plan to refuel TF 17 purely theoretical.[42]

Unexpectedly, at 1718 hours Fletcher and Fitch received another cable from the *Neosho* informing them that she had been "heavily bombed." Her location seemed to be 275 miles southeast of TF 17. The message also indicated that the *Sims* had been sunk and the *Neosho* was drifting northwest in a critical condition.

On learning of the tragedy of the Fueling Group, Fitch suggested sending one destroyer south to collect essential information and rescue the survivors. Fletcher expressed readiness for this plan, but TF 17 suddenly received a ComSoWePac radiograph at 1700 hours. MacArthur's staff warned that three enemy warships and transports had been spotted twenty-five miles southwest of the Jomard Passage at 1445 hours. What Fletcher didn't know, however, was that this report came directly from B-17s, which had mistakenly bombed Crace's group. Having no idea where TG 17.3 was and believing that the Japanese had crossed the Louisiades, Fletcher sent Fitch a message at 1721 hours saying,[43] "I expect that situation has changed and most of Japs will be through the pass headed for Moresby tomorrow. Therefore propose to head west tonight and suggest you search to northward and that option be west at speed eight."

Due to the loss of the *Neosho*, TF 17 had to save fuel overnight, because the situation might require the American carriers to remain in the Coral Sea for several days longer. Fletcher hesitated for the last time about whether to surprise the Japanese in a night battle or attack in the morning. After thinking about his options, he realized that the ComSoWePac report indicated Crace's group and that the nearest enemy ships were probably north of the Louisiades. Ultimately, TF 17 would head west to resume the search for the MO Kidō Butai in the morning and prevent an invasion of Port Moresby. At the same time, Crace, who was heading south and struggling with fuel supplies on the *Hobart* and the destroyers, could only hope that Fletcher was not far to the east and would send his instructions first thing in the morning.

Chapter 11

"LET'S GO FOR IT!"—DUSK ATTACK BY THE 5TH KŌKŪ SENTAI ON TF 17 CARRIERS

When the cable about the sinking of one battleship and one heavy cruiser and the severe damage to another battleship reached the Fourth Fleet staff, the mood changed entirely again. "We got it!"—Admiral Inoue's shout of joy cheered up other officers who were probably still thinking about the fate of the *Shōhō*. He and Lieutenant Commander Yamaguchi dashed toward the operations room to follow the news about the planned afternoon strike of the 5th Kōkū Sentai.[1]

The Japanese were now seriously committed to finding the American carriers and tipping the battle in their favor by the end of 7 May. At 1300 hours the Yokohama Kū sent one flying boat from Tulagi commanded by Lieutenant Adachi to investigate the most probable position of the enemy task force. As conveyed by the 25th Kōkū Sentai, the brave actions of land-based bombers also inspired the squadron to arm three Mavises with torpedoes. Led by Lt. Cdr. Tashiro, they took off at 1500 hours to chance their luck in the chaotic air operations in the Coral Sea. Yet, as the next few hours would show, they would not play any role in the battle. On arriving at the indicated location, Tashiro's flying boats would not find the enemy because of the bad weather and would take the return course to Tulagi at 1930 hours.

Takagi and Hara, who gradually became impatient, had to act decisively to carry out the second strike by sundown. At 1400 hours the 5th Kōkū Sentai sent a query about the precise location of the American carrier task force to all units. The first answer came at 1407 hours when the *Zuikaku* received a cable from the *Aoba*'s seaplane No. 2. The crew reported that they had been following the American task force. At 1445 hours they supplemented the message with information about two big cruisers, three destroyers, and one carrier. Soon after, the enemy group changed its course to 120 degrees. Relying on the analysis of a few reconnaissance reports that mentioned at least one carrier, Takagi determined that the American carriers were 420 miles away and the battleship 380 miles away. No matter how hard the MO Kidō Butai wanted to hit the enemy, the distance excluded any air operations on the same day, especially when the dive bombers hadn't returned yet. Thus, at 1500 hours Takagi sent a message to the Fourth Fleet and the 25th Kōkū Kantai saying that he had no plans to proceed with the second strike.[2]

However, this early assessment wasn't entirely accurate, as future events showed. At 1510 hours the lookouts spotted the returning Vals. Although four of them were damaged, Hara felt relieved. The missing part of the striking group had landed on the deck by 1515 hours, except for one seriously damaged dive bomber, which ditched about three thousand meters from the *Zuikaku*. The crew was rescued by the *Shiratsuyu* in less than ten minutes.[3] Hara immediately ordered four Kates to be sent from both the *Zuikaku* and the *Shōkaku*. He initially wanted to scout the sector from 230 to 290 degrees at 200 miles and 20 miles in the outward left leg but cancelled sending the planes from the *Shōkaku*. Thus, the *Zuikaku*'s Kates covered only the 270- and 290-degree sectors.[4]

TABLE 29 ■ **Yokohama Kū's Reconnaissance Flights, Afternoon of 7 May**

Unit	No.	Commander	Notes
Mavises / Yokohama Kū	1	Lt. Adachi	Takeoff: 1300 Landing: 0130
Mavises / Yokohama Kū	1	Lt. Cdr. Tashiro	Takeoff: 1500 Landing: 0115
	2	WO Fujiwara	
	3	WO Hamano	

Source: JACAR: Yokohama Kū (2), 25–26.

TABLE 30 **Reconnaissance Missions from the *Zuikaku*, Afternoon of 7 May 1942**

Unit	No.	Pilot	Observer	Radio operator	Notes
1st shōtai Kates/*Zuikaku* 270 degrees	1	PO1c Ishihara	WO Kanazawa (S)	PO2c Nishizawa	Takeoff: 1515 Landing: 1835
	2	PO3c Hatanaka	PO1c Ushijima	Sea1c Morishita	
2nd shōtai Kates/*Zuikaku* 290 degrees	1	PO1c Hori	Ens. Matsunaga (S)	PO2c Ōta	
	2	PO1c Satō	PO1c Yamada	PO2c Moriki	

Sources: JACAR: Zuikaku (1), 42–43; JACAR: Sangokai Shiryō (1), 23–24.

TABLE 31 **The *Kamikawa Maru*'s Reconnaissance Missions, Afternoon of 7 May**

Unit	No.	Crew members			Notes
Jakes / *Kamikawa Maru* air reconnaissance	1	Ens. Yoshida	PO1c Kōno	Sea1c Takase	Takeoff: 1530 Landing: 1900
	2	WO Aoki	Sea1c Todokoro	Sea1c Sudō	

Source: JACAR: Kamikawa Maru (2), 7.

The Support Group also made a last effort to find the enemy before dark. At 1530 hours, for the last time that day, two Jakes from the *Kamikawa Maru* air group flew up into the air. The seaplanes were supposed to search the 172-degree sector within 180 miles of Deboyne and maintain contact for as long as possible with the task force that had been spotted.

The moment of sending the Kates for the reconnaissance mission coincided with the discussion in the *Zuikaku*. Since Hara was visibly upset about a closing window for another attack, Lieutenant Commander Mieno started to analyze the report of the *Aoba*'s seaplane about the enemy's carrier task force and its course and speed. He quickly calculated that Fletcher would be about 380 miles from the MO Kidō Butai at 1830 hours. This meant that he was unwittingly going into the strike range of the Japanese carriers. However, because sunset would be at 1816 hours, the attack would be delivered at dusk and the group would have to return in the dark. Unlike the crew of the 1st and 2nd Kōkū Sentai, not every crew member from the 5th Kōkū Sentai was trained to land at night. Notably, the MO Kidō Butai could only send torpedo and dive bombers. Zeros were not equipped with a homing device, so if they got engaged by the enemy fighters, there was a considerable probability that a significant part of them would lose their way and wouldn't return to the carriers. Everybody knew that the risk associated with the attack was tremendous.

Mieno's suggestion unintentionally roused Yamaoka, though, who was known for his strong personality and sharp comments. He started agitating for a decisive move: "There is no way that we stand by like this. Air Officer, what if we give it a shot?" Mieno's unconvincing reply was, "But we don't have too many crew members able to attack at night. We already decided to go for the battle without the proper training to land on the deck in the dark." Yamaoka was tenacious and convincing: "So, what about selecting crews with those skills? Air Officer, let's send the striking group!" Eventually, Hara leaned toward Yamaoka's vision, although he had reservations, saying, "I worry about the return, but it cannot be helped."

The discussion might have seemed finished once Hara had expressed his view, but Mieno was responsible for planning the air operations. "Let's ask the crews about their opinions," he suggested, so they went outside the bridge to discern the mood among the senior airmen. Commander Shimoda was also puzzled when he spoke with Mieno about sending Kates and Vals without Zeros. After a while, the *hikōtaichō* and all of the *buntaichō*—Shimazaki, Ema, Tsubota, and Okajima—stood beside Mieno. They disclosed their concern on hearing the plan: "How do we go for the second strike? Shall we attack despite no fighter cover?" Short-tempered Tsubota commented, "There's no way we won't attack if we see the enemy." Everybody felt the same fear yet was sincerely willing to go. The senior Shimazaki finally said, "Okay, Let's do this!" Ema nodded his consent, and Okajima, whose fighters were not planning to go anywhere, was the last to give the green light, or rather, to accede to the others.

Mieno felt like an enormous weight had been lifted. He didn't like the idea of the second strike, but everybody was eager to proceed with it. Almost everybody. Some torpedo bombers' crews asked Shimoda whether it would be reasonable to attack without the fighter escort. He couldn't find a single word to answer this question, because the Japanese plan had too many flaws and only a vague prospect of success. Shimoda put his faith in the *hikōtaichō*'s skills. "As for experienced Commander Shimazaki, if he will use the weather to his advantage, everything should go just fine," he reassured himself. Shimazaki

PHOTO 10 ■ Lt. Kiyokuma Okajima, *buntaichō* of the *Zuikaku* fighter group Mori, *Akatsuki*

approached him and said, "Flight Officer, I'll immediately start preparations for the departure."[5]

The dispatch of the *Kamikawa Maru*'s seaplane bolstered the Japanese vision of a successful strike. At 1610 hours WO Aoki reported that three fighters were chasing his aircraft. The Jake's position was eighty miles from Deboyne with a bearing of 170 degrees. If the enemy had CAP in the area, there was a huge probability that the carriers were also nearby.[6]

Starting from 1615 hours the *Zuikaku* scrambled six dive bombers and nine torpedo bombers. Shortly after, the *Shōkaku* added six dive bombers and six torpedo bombers. Typically, Kates were armed with Type 91 torpedoes and Vals with 250-kg ordinary bombs. As debated and agreed previously, the Japanese sent only suitably experienced crews who could land on the carrier in the dark.[7] In the *Shōkaku*, Lieutenant Commander Takahashi and Lieutenant Ichihara personally selected the personnel by discussing the possible threats with crew members on the deck.[8]

In the meantime, the MO Kidō Butai's commander cabled Inoue about the progressing takeoff and departure of the striking group scheduled at 1630 hours. He also presented the most accurate calculations—at 1600 hours the enemy carriers were supposed to be 360 miles away and battleships 330 miles away.[9] The 5th Kōkū Sentai sped up to thirty-one knots, later thirty-three, to close the distance between the opposing forces. The Fourth Fleet was aware of the risky plan to attack at dusk yet didn't comment on it.[10]

Right after the striking group had scrambled from the carriers, at 1630 hours the *Aoba*'s No. 2 seaplane sent a cable from the reconnaissance mission. "One battleship, two cruisers, three destroyers 130 miles from Deboyne, bearing 200 degrees, course 100 degrees, speed 16 knots"—the report did not indicate any carriers.[11] However, the long-awaited dispatch came from Lt. Adachi's flying boat. At 1710 hours he said his Mavis had spotted the enemy carrier task force 185 miles from Rossel Island with a bearing of 246 degrees. The group proceeded on a course of 180 degrees at an unknown speed.[12] Unfortunately for the MO Kidō Butai, the Kates had found no vessels and were on the return course. Because the first striking force had only partial

PHOTO 11 ■ Briefing on *Shōkaku*'s deck before departing for dusk attack mission Fukuchi, *Kūbo Shōkaku Kaiseki*

TABLE 32 ■ **MO Kidō Butai Striking Group, Afternoon of 7 May 1942**

Unit	No.	Pilot	Observer	Radio operator	Notes
41st shōtai Kates/*Shōkaku*	1	Lt. Ichihara (B)	WO Saitō	PO1c Munakata	Takeoff: 1630 Landing: 2020
	2	WO Shindō	Lt. Yano	PO2c Ibayashi	
	3	PO1c Okimura	WO Ukita	PO2c Tozawa	
44th shōtai Kates/*Shōkaku*	1	WO Yonekura†	Lt. Hagiwara (S)†	PO2c Sagara†	
	2	PO3c Irimi†	PO1c Shirai†	PO2c Shimomichi†	
	3	Sea1c Murakami†	PO1c Takahashi†	Sea1c Kodama†	
41st shōtai Kates/*Zuikaku*	1	Lt. Cdr. Shimazaki (H)	WO Ni'ino	PO1c Yoshinaga	Takeoff: 1615 Landing: 2000
	2	WO Yaegashi	PO1c Himeishi	Sea1c Ōuchi	
	3	PO3c Nozawa†	PO1c Kawahara†	Sea1c Honda†	
42nd shōtai Kates/*Zuikaku*	1	Lt. Murakami (S)†	WO Baba†	PO1c Miyada†	
	2	PO3c Yokomakura	PO2c Kishi	PO2c Satō	
45th shōtai Kates/*Zuikaku*	1	Lt. Tsubota (B)†	PO1c Kosakada (S)†	PO1c Endō†	
	2	PO1c Sugimoto†	PO3c Kojima†	Sea1c Hasegawa†	
46th shōtai Kates/*Zuikaku*	1	Lt. Satō (S)	PO1c Ōtani	PO2c Yoshida	
	2	PO1c Tahara	PO2c Ōnishi†	PO3c Kanetō†	

Unit	No.	Pilot	Observer/navigator	Notes
21st shōtai Vals/*Zuikaku*	1	Lt. Ema (B)	WO Higashi	Takeoff: 1625 Landing: 2100
	2	PO1c Fukugaki†	WO Koyama†	
	3	Sea1c Egusa	PO2c Fujioka	
22nd shōtai Vals/*Zuikaku*	1	PO1c Andō	Lt. Ōtsuka (S)	
	2	WO Fukunaga	PO1c Ishikawa	
	3	PO2c Sakamaki	WO Izuka	
20th shōtai Vals/*Shōkaku*	1	Lt. Cdr. Takahashi (H)	Ens. Nozu	Takeoff: 1630 Landing: 2020
	2	PO1c Shinohara	PO1c Someno	
21st shōtai Vals/*Shōkaku*	1	Lt. Yamaguchi (S)	Ens. Naka	
	2	PO1c Ueshima	PO1c Kōda	
22nd shōtai Vals/*Shōkaku*	1	WO Matsuda (S)	PO1c Nobe	
	2	PO2c Ikeda	PO1c Nagasawa	

Sources: JACAR: Shōkaku (1), 37–38; JACAR: Zuikaku (1), 38–41; JACAR: Gunkan Zuikaku (2), 39–40.

† *Lost in action*

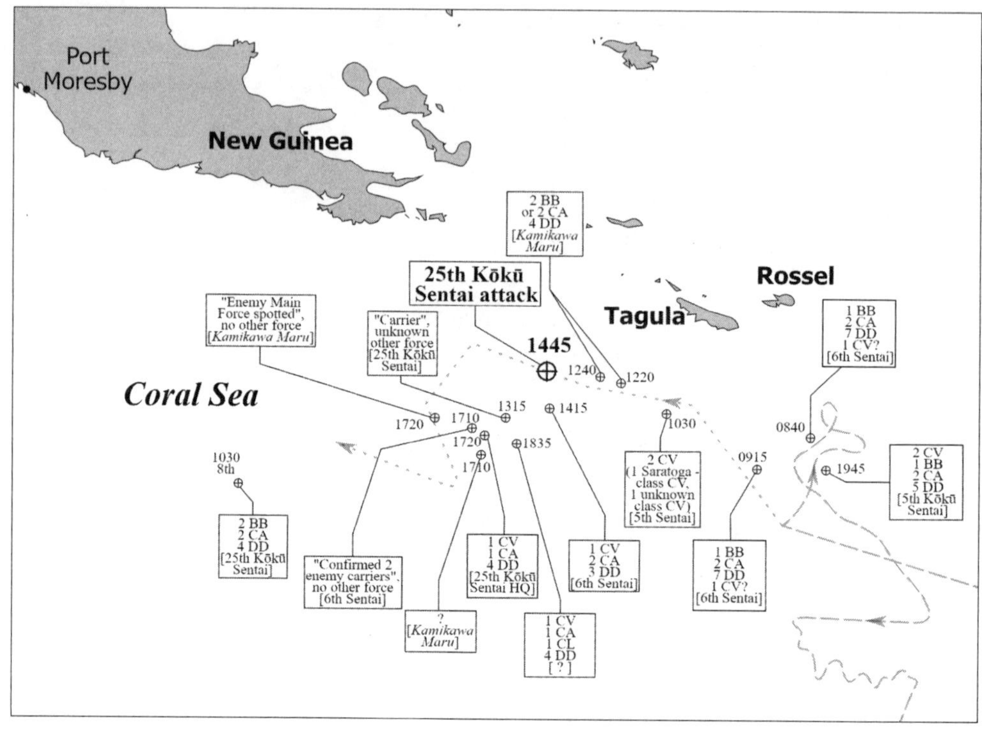

MAP 9 ■ Summary of Japanese reconnaissance contacts on 7 May

information, including some contradictory locations, everything remained in the hands of the second striking group.

Despite the favorable course of the morning mission against the *Shōhō*, the Americans were far from victory in the battle or even a successful day of air operations. At 1502 hours the *Lexington*'s CXAM-1 radar picked up a single aircraft that was maintaining a particular distance to TF 17. At the same time, the skippers of both carriers decided to replace CAP and let the dive bombers land on the decks. At 1520 hours the *Lexington* turned into the wind and sent up two fighter sections, led by Lieutenant Commander Ramsey and Lt. Richard S. Bull Jr. Four F4Fs and seven SBDs returned to the carrier in less than half an hour. At the same time, four of Lieutenant McCormack's Wildcats scrambled from the *Yorktown*, followed by four F4Fs and ten SBDs, which ended their missions.

The weather around TF 17 proved boisterous in the afternoon, when the frequent rain squalls made visibility almost zero. Fletcher, however, wasn't perfectly safe from the Japanese snoopers, and he was aware of that because of the enemy's intercepted cables that showed his approximate position, course, and speed. At 1653 hours the *Yorktown*'s CXAM radar showed contact with a single aircraft, eighteen miles southwest, coming in on a bearing of 250 degrees. Six minutes later the lookouts noticed the bogey just nine miles northwest and identified it as a seaplane. McCormack's section was dispatched to intercept the intruder, but it escaped northward into the thick clouds. The CXAM radar finally lost contact with the seaplane at 1717 hours.[13]

The Japanese, however, would appear again. At 1745 hours, close to sunset, the *Lexington*'s CXAM-1 radar picked up a large group of enemy aircraft. Two minutes later the *Yorktown*'s radar made contact with the same formation at 18 miles with a bearing of 144 degrees. The *Lexington*'s fighter director vectored out her fighters to make the first move. Soon after, he also ordered six F4Fs to scramble to defend the task force. Ramsey's section, which had enough fuel and IFF electronics, rushed toward the enemy. The remaining eight Wildcats circled over TF 17, expecting the long-awaited Japanese counterattack. Within five minutes, six of Lieutenant Gayler's fighters from the *Lexington* were already in the air. The *Yorktown* quickly added Lieutenant Commander Flatley's twelve F4Fs, including the one flown by Lieutenant (jg) McCuskey, and thus the number of fighters rapidly reached thirty in less than a quarter of an hour. At 1803 hours the *Yorktown* vectored out her seven freshly scrambled Wildcats to check on the Japanese formation. Most of the fighters were kept around the two carriers in anticipation of the enemy's evening strike.[14]

Before the *Yorktown*'s F4Fs rushed north, however, Ramsay, at about 1800 hours, was the first to spot the enemy. Despite poor visibility, he saw nine Japanese aircraft at one thousand feet, about thirty miles from TF 17. He mistakenly identified them as Zero fighters. They were in fact the *Zuikaku*'s torpedo bombers at the back of the formation. Still, there was not much time for consideration. Attacking from five thousand feet, the Wildcats surprised the enemy formation, which was unprepared for the sudden emergence of the fighters. As S. Mori writes, the crews were already tired, and some hadn't even had a proper meal before departing for the mission. A moment previously,

WO Ni'ino had commented to Shimazaki, "Taichō, we are closing to the supposed location of the American carriers." "That's right. Let's pass the word to all planes to stay cautious," Shimazaki replied. The *Zuikaku*'s dive bombers, slightly at the front of the formation, were also cutting through the thick clouds and rain squalls. "I don't see any ship's wakes," said WO Higashi to Lieutenant Ema. The *buntaichō* confirmed his observer's words, saying, "There's nothing here."[15]

J. Lundstrom claims that the Japanese planes were taken aback because they had closed their cockpit canopies to hide from the rain squalls. But the Japanese sources don't confirm this, mentioning only that they flew near the rain clouds.[16] The Wildcats were lucky to find themselves behind the enemy torpedo bombers when they were desperately looking for the carriers, and they loosened up their formation. In the first pass, Ramsey, followed by his wingman, Ens. George Hopper, targeted the rearmost Kates. Their attack was successful; Ramsey managed to torch two planes, which started to fall. Once they had machine-gunned the easy prey, Ramsey tried to regain an appropriate attitude to continue the fight. In the meantime, Lt. (jg) Paul Baker and his wingman, Ens. William Wileman, ambushed the next section of the enemy torpedo bombers. After their passes, they claimed to have shot down one aircraft and set another on fire.

The Japanese later admitted that the F4Fs approached from a blind spot, attacked from point-blank range, and aimed well at the fuel tanks. The sudden loss of four Kates, including the one piloted by the *Zuikakū*'s buntaichō, Lieutenant Tsubota, and another piloted by experienced Lieutenant Murakami, could not be taken lightly. The manuals say that the bombers, when defending themselves against fighters, should tighten their formation and "work together as a flying stronghold." This time, however, the first American pass was so effective that some Japanese crews started panicking. The *Zuikaku*'s dive bombers noticed the Wildcats at the back yet couldn't help their colleagues. The lack of escorts was backfiring on them. All they could do was escape into the thick clouds. At 1803 hours one of the planes reported to the *Zuikaku* about the attack of the enemy fighters and the destruction of the striking group.[17]

Lieutenant (jg) Baker was encouraged by his first victory, so he decided to chase the fleeing bombers. Confident of his advantage, he made a fatal mistake and got too close to one of his would-be victims. It remains unknown whether he misjudged the distance or whether his salvo detonated the Japanese plane, but Wileman soon saw a flash in the clouds. Baker was never seen again. At 1808 hours Ramsey sent a message saying that his section had shot down five fighters. It was the end of their fight, because the *Lexington*'s fighter director officer, Lt. Frank F. Gill, ordered all Wildcats to return to the carrier because they were running out of fuel. No matter how tempting it might be to destroy more Japanese aircraft, TF 17 could not afford to lose its fighters in pursuit.[18]

Flatley's seven Wildcats, flying on a bearing of 240 degrees to replace Ramsey's section at 1808 hours, spotted two Japanese planes spinning toward the water about thirty miles south of TF 17. The VF-42 pilots thought that VF-2 could be nearby. Suddenly, six aircraft emerged from the clouds below, heading in the opposite direction. Initially, Flatley believed he had passed the friendly Wildcats and soon decided to confirm this on the radio. After a while, Ramsey replied that he had encountered the enemy fighters. After looking closer at the planes, Flatley realized they had the famous "meatballs" on the wings. They were Kates from the *Shōkaku* that had avoided the clash with VF-2.

Without waiting for orders, Ens. Leslie Knox and Lt. (jg) William S. Woollen rushed to attack. Knox shot down one torpedo bomber in the first pass. After spotting the Wildcats, the rest of the group decided to split up immediately. Both VF-42 pilots chased them, though, each heading in a different direction. Woollen stubbornly machine-gunned one of the Kates, but it eventually escaped. After a few minutes he realized he was sixty miles from TF 17 and had to turn back. In the meantime, Knox secured another victory but could not find the way back to the carrier because of a malfunctioning radio. His death was the price for scattering the second formation of Japanese torpedo bombers.[19]

When Knox and Woollen were chasing Kates, the rest of the Wildcats spotted a group of dive bombers below. Taking advantage of their altitude, Flatley, Lt. (jg) Brainard T. Macomber, Ens. John Baker, and Ens. Harry B. Gibbs charged the enemy planes but did not achieve results that were comparable to those scored in relation to the torpedo bombers. Macomber destroyed one Val from the *Zuikaku*, but Flatley could not locate any new targets in the dark, so he regrouped and headed toward where Knox and Woollen had disappeared. He hoped to find more Japanese planes but gave up the pursuit after flying about twenty-five miles. He ordered Baker to tune his homing beacon and guide the F4Fs to the *Yorktown* instead. He did well, and all of the Wildcats (except for the one piloted by Lt. (jg) Paul Baker) returned safely to the carrier.[20]

The dusk ambush on the Japanese striking group lasted for less than fifteen minutes yet had enormous consequences, although they would not be visible until the following day. The formation lost seven Kates and one Val. More importantly, it was forced to scatter and escape into the clouds. Shimazaki's cable, sent at 1803 hours, reached Hara at 1818 hours: "The striking group was annihilated by the enemy fighters." Hara was speechless.[21] Lieutenant Commander Ōtani recalled that the commander of the 5th Kōkū Sentai "was shocked like someone dropped a bombshell." But this was only the beginning of the bad news.[22]

Seeing the carnage caused to the Kates, Takahashi and Shimazaki agreed to abandon the mission. It was already a few minutes after sunset and the probability of finding the American carriers was very low, so Takahashi ordered the bombs and torpedoes to be dumped. His decision was hard but reasonable. He could not expect a magical reversal of the situation, because he could see the thin smoke trail emerging from several surviving planes' fuselages. Even Shimazaki suffered in the dusk action, although he kept control over his aircraft. "What if we now find the American carriers? Are we going to attack them?" asked one Kate's crew members. "We gonna ram them!" Lt. Zen'ichi Satō answered firmly. "Sure thing," his pilot, PO1c Ōtani, agreed without hesitation.[23]

At 1825 hours Lt. Hagiwara informed the *Shōkaku* that "the enemy fighters attacked us, and I was hit. My fuel tank was punctured. We are about to return." Hara read this cable and could hardly imagine a worse scenario. But Hagiwara's message continued, saying, "We were attacked by enemy fighters. The pilot was killed. I am replacing him."[24]

Hara went to the flight deck, where he met with Commander Yamaoka, Commander Shimoda, and Lieutenant Commander Mieno. They were appalled by the news. Shimoda particularly remembered Lieutenant Murakami's comments about sending the striking group without a fighter escort. Now Murakami was dead. At 1840 hours Shimazaki's report from 1820 hours was deciphered at the bridge: "Most of the torpedo bombers were destroyed in an air fight, and my engine was hit as well. We are now returning; I don't know if I will have to ditch."[25] Younger staff officers started to whisper and cheer each other up, saying, "Taichō will be fine, he will be fine." The last thing the Japanese needed was to lose Shimazaki.[26]

When the Japanese gave up the striking mission and decided to return before it was too late, the dwindling fuel supplies on the Wildcats forced the Americans to reshuffle CAP. Ramsey's section, minus Baker, was the first to land on the *Lexington*, starting at 1825 hours. Subsequently, four of Bull's and some of Gayler's six F4Fs were back on the carrier. McCormack's section returned to the *Yorktown* and was replaced by a section led by Lieutenant (jg) Leonard. With his section, Flatley soon appeared over TF 17. Landing so many fighters in the dark was a new experience for American pilots, so the air operations took longer than usual. It seemed that the carriers had been successfully defended. However, the following minutes showed that this wasn't the end.

Immediately after receiving the message about abandoning the mission, Captain Yokokawa gave Commander Shimoda detailed instructions on how to prepare for the landing of the striking group. The Japanese knew the gravity of the situation and were particularly worried about Shimazaki's damaged bomber. They didn't have room for any mistakes. The estimated time of arrival was 1930 hours. It was already dark then, so at least a few warships had to turn on their searchlights, which posed an additional risk to the MO Kidō Butai. At 1840 hours Hara transmitted to Takagi his plan for accommodating the planes:[27]

1. The 5th Sentai and one destroyer, separated by five kilometers, will be five kilometers ahead of the 5th Kōkū Sentai.
2. The carriers will be steaming abreast, separated by seven kilometers.
3. From the estimated arrival time of the striking group, the 5th Sentai will turn on the searchlights.

Hara's plan was approved instantly, and the crews received the order to take up their positions so that the planes could land on desks swiftly and defend the task force against any intruders. The stage was set up and the Japanese needed only to wait for the bombers' arrival.

Roughly thirty minutes had passed since the Kates and Vals had disengaged from the fight with the Wildcats and taken the return route. Takahashi spearheaded the mauled striking group, followed by Ema's dive and torpedo bombers at the back. There is no doubt that the *hikōtaichō* was exhausted and dreamed about guiding his colleagues back to the MO Kidō Butai without any additional incidents. He suddenly noticed immediately in front of him two silhouettes of carriers. Their decks flashed with bright lights and looked ready to accommodate the planes. Takahashi didn't doubt that he had found the *Zuikaku* and the *Shōkaku* and felt nothing suspicious about them. "Let's approach for landing," he said to his observer. "Alright," replied Ens. Nozu vigorously. Both were happy to come back from the disastrous mission. They could even see some friendly planes in the air, probably sent by Hara to help them on the last section of the route.

Takahashi and Ema descended from two thousand meters and separated their groups to proceed with the landing. Takahashi turned on his recognition lights and headed toward the carrier to send a flash signal. "Permission for landing," he asked, according to the procedures. He immediately received a flash black, which he understood to mean "permission granted." Next, he waved his wings to inform the other Vals to prepare for landing. Although Ema didn't see those signals clearly see, he trusted Takahashi's judgment and instructed his group to loosen the formation and form a queue prior to landing on the second carrier. Takahashi was already below two hundred meters and was steadily approaching the alleged *Shōkaku*. He would soon discover that he was heading straight toward the *Yorktown*.[28]

We know how the Japanese realized their unique misidentification thanks to Ema's memoires. When his dive bomber was about to land, WO Higashi shouted "Kago masuto!" ("Basket mast!") to him from the back seat. The Nippon Kaigun didn't have warships with this type of construction, which was peculiar to the U.S. Navy at the time. Ema immediately pulled the control stick and flew away. His surprised colleagues behind did the same thing and narrowly avoided a fatal landing on the *Lexington*. The account also says that soon after, the American antiaircraft artillery opened fire, finally waking up from a long stint of lethargy. "So, it was the enemy," Ema thought, and turned off his recognition lights so as not to draw the attention of the American fighters.[29]

The *buntaichō* wasn't the only one who had figured out what was happening. After all, Takahashi had also noticed the unfamiliar superstructure of the carrier and had pulled up at the last moment. At 1845 hours, moving away from the *Yorktown*, he instantly sent a cable to the MO Kidō Butai: "I spotted the enemy. Bearing 160 degrees from Russell Islands, distance 110 miles, course 230 degrees." The message reached the *Zuikaku* at 1900 hours.[30]

The American sources are consistent with Ema's memories. The *Yorktown* report says, regarding three enemy planes, that they "flew by on the starboard side with their lights on and blinking in morse code on an Aldis Light DOT DOT DASH DOT DOT DOT DASH DOT, these planes crossed over the bow to port, where 1 VF opened fire on them."[31] The Wildcat in CAP that attacked the Vals was piloted by Lt. (jg) Macomber. He was the only pilot to find additional aircraft circling over the *Yorktown*, which was suspicious. He started to chase three dive bombers that were withdrawing eastward. But his pursuit soon turned out to be futile, because the Japanese scattered, skillfully dodged the subsequent salvos, and just as the fighter direction distinguished one pilot from the other, the radar screen lost sight of Baker. After more than an hour of trying to reestablish contact, at 2028 hours the *Yorktown* instructed him to fly for 120 miles on a course of 320 degrees. He was to ditch near Tagula Island, assuming his fuel supplies would allow that. Ens. John Baker was never heard from again and his fate remains unknown.[32] He was posthumously awarded the Navy Cross for his distinguished service during the Battle of the Coral Sea, particularly for ensuring the safe return of VF-42 fighters after the ambush on the Japanese bombers.

The American losses during the dusk action amounted to three F4Fs and their pilots—Lt. (jg) Paul Baker of VF-2 and Ens. Leslie Knox and Ens. John Baker of VF-42. Additionally, Lieutenant (jg) Barnes' fighter was severely damaged and was unfit for air operations the following day.

S. Mori points out two reasons why Takahashi nearly made the colossal mistake of landing on the *Yorktown*. First, the report of the *Aoba*'s seaplane, used by the striking group as a navigational marker, was flawed. The actual

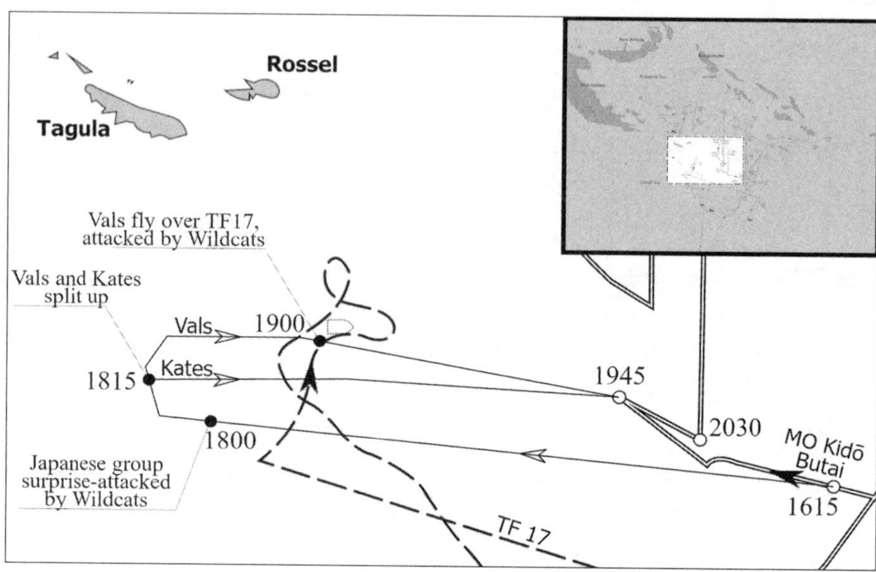

MAP 10 ■ Japanese dusk attack and the encounter of TF 17, evening 7 May

position of the American carriers was 110 miles closer; thus, he had grounds to be confused about the encountered vessels. Unfortunately, when he tried to confirm his readiness for landing, the *Yorktown*'s flash signals happened to be similar to the Japanese Morse code for "friendly aircraft." Notably, the MO Kidō Butai also had extremely bad timing on 7 May. If the Vals hadn't jettisoned their bombs so fast, given that they could have kept them for longer, they would have had a perfect opportunity to secure very clean hits on both enemy carriers. Ema regretted his entire life that he missed this chance, which would never happen again.[33]

All of the confusion about the identification of the carriers did not, however, cause any additional Japanese losses. Still, it didn't mean that the striking group was in a better position than before. Besides Shimazaki's damaged Kate and the pilot in Hagiwara's plane being killed, Ema's *kambaku* and WO Yaegashi's *kankō* had inoperative radio transmitters.[34] The altimeter in WO Yokomakura's torpedo bomber was not working, and the pilot knew he would have to land by the seat of his pants. However, the most critical situation was the one in Hagiwara's aircraft, because his fuel tank was punctured. He didn't have the best skills to pilot the Kate and nervously hung on to the control stick. Just as the *Shōkaku* crew was preparing to take off, his pilot and best junior colleague since the attack on Pearl Harbor, PO1c Ishikawa, woke up from an afternoon nap. Hagiwara scolded him for being drowsy and told him to make sure he was alert for the mission. However, he got the cavalier reply that WO Yonekura would fly instead. Yonekura had more experience in air operations on the carrier than Ishikawa, so there was some logic behind this. But fate had it that a stray bullet killed Yonekura, so the benefit of his superior flying skills didn't last long, unfortunately. Once the cable about his death and Hagiwara being behind the stick reached the *Shōkaku*, Ishikawa and other junior pilots gathered on the deck and impatiently waited for the return of the striking group.[35]

At 1920 hours Shimazaki cabled the following message to the *Zuikaku*: "My radio receiver is damaged. From about 1725 hours, we plan to return from a bearing of 270 degrees. I guess that the reflectors will illuminate the air space." According to Hara's instruction, the MO Kidō Butai had already assumed the required special formation to accommodate the planes. The 5th Sentai was about five kilometers ahead of the carriers, closer to the starboard side, illuminating the port sector in front of them. One destroyer was put five kilometers ahead of the *Shōkaku* and the *Zuikaku*, which steamed next to each other, separated by seven kilometers. The carriers prepared their decks by illuminating them and turning on the reflectors. Additionally, one destroyer followed each carrier two kilometers astern and seven kilometers from the outward quarter part. The rearmost destroyers also turned on their searchlights to light up the biggest areas at the sides of the carriers.

According to the MO Kidō Butai's report, accommodating planes started at 1915 hours. Half an hour before that the carrier observers could hear the hollow sound of aircraft engines, which were getting closer to the group from the west. The beams of light from the 5th Sentai's reflectors illuminated the air space from a long distance away, which the pilots noticed immediately.[36] Since a light wind was blowing from the southeast, the *Shōkaku* sharply turned to starboard to temporarily steam upwind. Finally, the crew could see the planes. Takahashi landed first without any incidents. "Heave-ho, heave-ho," the crew chanted as they gathered in forward corners of the deck and enthusiastically

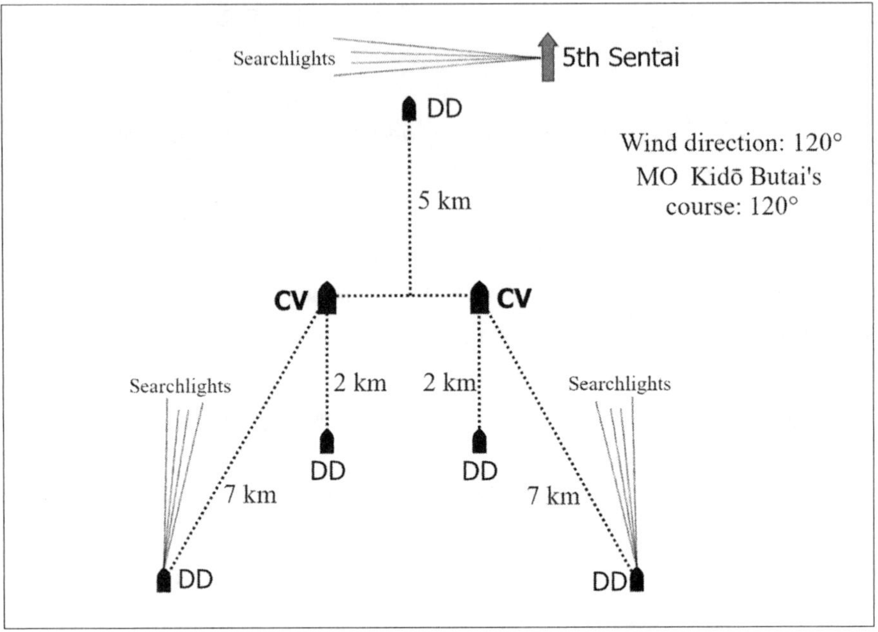

MAP 11 ■ MO Kidō Butai's formation to accommodate the striking group at dark, evening of 7 May JACAR: MO Kidō Butai (2), 12

welcomed the *hikōtaichō*. But they didn't have time for celebration and cleared the deck for the next plane. By 2020 hours the noise of tires screeching had been heard again several times. Eventually, six Vals and three Kates found their way back to the *Shōkaku*. Hagiwara was still missing. Sitting in a corner, Ishikawa stubbornly looked into the air for his plane's silhouette and prayed for its return. But he soon realized that it wasn't going to happen. "They did a great job . . . " he stood up and said brokenheartedly. Ichihara was equally devastated when he learned about Hagiwara not returning from the *Shōkaku*'s flight officer, Lt. Tetsujirō Wada, during the debrief. The *buntaichō* didn't even see him during the last section of the route, meaning he had to ditch too far from the carrier.[37]

Exhausted, Takahashi hastily climbed to the bridge and yelled to the skipper, "Captain, enemy carriers are nearby!" He also explained the fuss about the misidentification of the enemy vessels and expressed his regrets regarding jettisoning the bombs.[38] Because there had been a lot of confusion during the unexpected encounter with TF 17, Captain Jōjima instructed Wada to collect crews' testimonies to get their story straight, particularly regarding the number, type, and class of warships.

The *Zuikaku* started accommodating the striking group a bit later than the *Shōkaku*. At about 2000 hours the observers saw Shimazaki's bomber. It was so damaged that he could not extend the landing gear. But he skidded in on his belly, something many Japanese pilots could only dream of doing. Other bombers arrived after him, including Ema's. The *buntaichō* referred to the great luck of his engine stalling due to the lack of fuel exactly when he touched the deck.[39] Most of the surviving Kates and Vals were scarred but landed safely. Lieutenant Satō was one of the pilots who thought about crashing into the enemy carrier but was scolded on the radio and told to stay alive, so he obediently returned. Everybody's attention was now focused on Yokomakura. The carrier helped to determine his approach angle based on his speed and altitude, estimated from below. Despite one of his eyes bleeding, he made several circles above the *Zuikaku*, descending lower and lower on each turn. When he eventually touched the deck, Shimoda heaved a sigh of relief and approached him. "I am terribly sorry. We sent you all to die, I am so sorry. Please rest now." His apology was extremely sincere. The procedure of accommodating the planes on the flagship was over. Yokomakura was safe but was so exhausted he couldn't swallow a bite of his dinner despite not eating for many hours.[40]

Meanwhile, Ishikawa in the *Shōkaku* was trying to find out news about Hagiwara again. They had received a cable from him saying "I can see the searchlights" when the striking group's engines could be heard a long distance away. Since then he had been missing, and every minute made it less probable that his fuel supplies would be sufficient for him to fly back to the carrier. But suddenly Lt. Iwakichi Mifuku ran toward Wada and said, "Flight Officer, a cable from Hagiwara has arrived." Despite the initial hope, it wasn't a positive one: "I am ditching. I hope that the sea's surface will be illuminated." Mifuku recalled that the message was sent twice in quick succession. However, the vessels had turned off the searchlights since most of the planes had been accommodated on the MO Kidō Butai. The American carrier task force was too close, and Jōjima didn't want to risk exposing his position. Operations Officer Lt. Cdr. Kaneo Fukuchi approached Wada to ask for the reflectors to be put on, at least for a while. He didn't get permission, so he went directly to Jōjima: "Captain, let's illuminate the sea's surface." He even crossed the line and started to beg insistently. Sadly, the *Shōkaku*'s skipper refused and could not be persuaded. No matter how much he pitied Hagiwara deep down inside, he was obsessed with the carrier's safety.[41]

It is worth adding a rumor relating to the story concerning Hagiwara. Ishikawa claimed that he saw a small black silhouette of the aircraft in the distance, half-sunk and drifting on the starboard bow side. He started to shout to turn on the searchlights, but because of his low rank, he didn't get much attention except from a small group of ordinary sailors on the deck. He thought about doing something desperate but could not personally go to the bridge. The Nippon Kaigun would not forgive him for such insolent behavior. Eventually, he gave up and blamed Jōjima for the rest of his life. However, documents and personal statements do not confirm Ishikawa's version. Even K. Fukuchi, the most senior officer advocating turning on the searchlights, admitted that the surface of the sea was investigated as far as possible and nothing like a floating aircraft was seen in the dark.[42]

At 2118 hours the carrier ceased waiting for Hagiwara. The *Zuikaku* got a message about one plane being lost. Although someone picked up a cable two minutes later requesting that the searchlights should be turned on, it remains a mystery when it was sent. As a last resort, at 2133 hours the *Shōkaku* cabled the *Zuikaku* about the circumstances of losing contact with Hagiwara and informed the carrier about sending one destroyer for a rescue mission near the task force.[43] But the crew wasn't found. Hagiwara's death greatly touched the members of the *Shōkaku* air group. Although Jōjima tried to make up for the initial decision not to use the reflectors, his men were outraged that he had deserted one of their most senior officers and started to resent the skipper strongly. Japanese historians, though, are more reticent to criticize Jōjima for making this difficult decision.[44]

However sad Hagiwara's drama was, it happened in the shadow of the more crucial events of the Japanese plan to seize Port Moresby. At 2040 hours the *Shōkaku* transmitted the following report to Hara:[45]

PHOTO 12 ■ *Zuikaku*'s *hikōtaichō*, Lt. Cdr. Shigeru Shimazaki *NDL*

"According to what our crews said, the force at a bearing of 270 degrees and distant by about 100 miles comprises one *Saratoga*-class carrier, one [other] carrier, two heavy cruisers and one light cruiser. Eastern course and unknown speed but not high."

The actual position of the American carriers greatly surprised the command of the 5th Kōkū Sentai. It seemed that all the previous reconnaissance reports sent by the seaplanes were misleading. The MO Kidō Butai and TF 17 were separated by less than thirty minutes of flight. The Japanese saw this as an excellent opportunity to tip the scales back in their favor. The dusk attack mission was the final straw for the luckless day of 7 May. Including Hagiwara's *kankō*, the 5th Kōkū Sentai lost eight Kates and one Val and their respective crews: twenty-six men, all of them considered experienced. But that wasn't all. Many of the surviving planes were beyond the repair capacities of the carriers' maintenance teams, which were assisted voluntarily by some pilots. They did what they could, sweating while they worked for most of the night on the hangar deck. Each hole in the wings and the fuselage had to be correctly patched, because any imperfection could reduce the plane's speed.[46] Despite this, some bombers were not only full of holes but generally unfit for service, at least for the next day.[47]

Hara faced a situation in which the *Zuikaku* and the *Shōkaku* had departed from Truk with 116 aircraft and 112 crews but after the reckless dusk mission he had only 96 aircraft and 97 crews. He became visibly disadvantaged in numbers compared to Fletcher, who had 118 planes with crews at the time.

Since the early afternoon, the Fourth Fleet had been wondering how the 5th Kōkū Sentai would execute the dusk attack. Once Rabaul learned about the destruction of the striking group and the trouble with recovering the planes, there was growing mistrust in Hara and in his men's skills. Although no one openly criticized Hara for sending the striking group without a fighter escort, everybody knew that the responsibility for the failed attack would fall on him. Even though he claimed that he had found two American carriers after sunset, the Fourth Fleet was not stupid. Inoue's staff officers had noticed that among all the reconnaissance dispatches sent on 7 May, the 5th Kōkū Sentai had produced the most erroneous one. There was much less confidence that Hara would resolve the battle the following day, so the Fourth Fleet queried him about TF 17. "Aren't you wrong about their position?"—this embarrassing message was signed by Captain Yano, who was more inclined to believe the *Kamikawa Maru*'s afternoon reconnaissance report.[48]

TABLE 33 **Number of Operational Planes in the 5th Kōkū Sentai, End of 7 May**

	Kates	Vals	Zeros	Total
Zuikaku	12	14	19	45
Shōkaku	14	19	18	51
Planes in total	**26**	**33**	**37**	**96**
Zuikaku	12	15	19	46
Shōkaku	14	19	18	51
Crews in total	**26**	**34**	**37**	**97**

Sources: JACAR: MO Kidō Butai (2), 16, 21; JACAR: Sangokai Shiryō (1).

Notwithstanding the lack of confidence in the 5th Kōkū Sentai, the essential thing for Inoue was to outline the priorities for the upcoming night and 8 May. The carrier's dusk attack had been a disaster, and there was much confusion about TF 17's position. Thus, the early afternoon's bold plan to push the cruisers and the destroyers against the unidentified group seemed highly irrational. At 2040 hours the Fourth Fleet cabled the Secret Operational Order 378:[49]

1. For the upcoming night, the night surface attack is canceled.
2. All forces should continue the operation to seize Port Moresby according to the plan. However, the invasion of Port Moresby is postponed by two days. The 2nd Division of the 6th Sentai [the *Kinugasa* and the *Furutaka*] should join the MO Kidō Butai.
3. Just after dawn on 8 May, the MO Kidō Butai shall destroy the enemy.

Notably, the 5th Kōkū Sentai was in the hot seat. The staff had to figure out how to convince Inoue that despite their mistakes during the day, the late dispatch about the American carriers was correct. Yamaoka pressed to keep a straight and steadfast stance, saying, "Let's write that the enemy's location is right."[50] But they needed something more persuasive. Thus, at 2120 hours the 5th Kōkū Sentai sent the summary report on the action during the day to the Fourth Fleet and all other units involved in Operation MO. Since there was nothing to boast of, Hara and his officers focused on showing that after the long struggle with the bad weather, namely the rain squall, which veiled the enemy moves and thawed the dusk attack mission, they eventually detected TF 17. They believed that the American task force consisted of one *Saratoga*-class and one *Yorktown*-class carrier and several other screening vessels that were hard to identify. At sunset the enemy was about one hundred miles from the MO Kidō Butai. Hara explained that he had to proceed northward at twenty knots to recover the planes in the dark. He also informed Inoue about the number of aircraft left on the *Zuikaku* and the *Shōkaku*. Finally, he said that the MO Kidō Butai was working on a detailed plan to link up with the *Kinugasa* and the *Furutaka* the following day.[51]

On 7 May Hara and his staff officers made, in the author's view, two undeniably bad calls. First, they attacked the secondary target based on an erroneous reconnaissance report produced by their aircraft. Second, they decided to go for the risky dusk attack, which didn't pay off. However, before blaming them for the failures, it is crucial to understand that the 5th Kōkū Sentai was working under the considerable pressure of the Fourth Fleet, not to mention peer pressure. When Hara initially cabled about having no plans to proceed with the afternoon strike, Inoue was disappointed by his passive attitude. The insistence on winning the battle on 7 May, especially after the loss of the *Shōhō*, was one of the reasons why the 5th Kōkū Sentai took too much risk despite the navy's procedures. On the eve of the decisive day in the Coral Sea, Hara and his staff officers had to change their attitude to make the right decisions, but, most importantly, to make independent ones. Indeed, something changed after the late communication with the Fourth Fleet. Inoue suggested conducting morning reconnaissance missions in a 360-degree sector with a center point of latitude 13° S, longitude 155° E. However, Mieno came up with an alternative plan of commencing the search 120 miles farther north and focusing on the southern sector. This would save the 5th Kōkū Sentai a few torpedo bombers for the decisive strike.[52] Theoretically, Hara could also count on the heavy cruisers' and the *Kamikawa Maru*'s seaplanes and the Yokohama Kū's flying boats,[53] especially when the Fourth Fleet instructed him to use the seaplanes in the early morning missions.[54] Still, contrary to his command style, he decided to rely on more flexible Kates to maintain radio contact with them. Eventually, Inoue felt convinced by Mieno's reconnaissance plan and authorized it as one of the last decisions dispatched on 7 May.[55] This was a very long day for the commander of the Fourth Fleet. It was full of ups and downs regarding many critical events and was undeniably emotionally draining. Inoue even admitted that he felt this single day "significantly shortened his life."[56]

When viewed from a neutral position, the biggest victim of the day was the MO Main Force. Once Gotō lost the *Shōhō* and had to hand over two heavy cruisers to the MO Kidō Butai, his group suddenly became of secondary importance. Although the 18th Sentai was supposed to join the 6th Sentai as the reinforcement, the Port Moresby Invasion Force had to wait northward until the battle was resolved in favor of the Japanese. The remaining part of the MO Main Force was supposed to refuel and head north to link up with the Port Moresby Invasion Force the following day at about 1600 hours.[57]

At midnight Takagi finally issued the instructions for the upcoming day. The content of the 5th Kōkū Sentai Secret Order No 862 was as follows:[58]

1. By 8 May, 0200 hours, the MO Kidō Butai will reach the coordinates 11°50'S 156°05'E and from that point will steam at the course of 240 degrees at twenty knots to reach the coordinates 13°S 155°E to destroy the enemy carrier force.
2. The commander of the 5th Kōkū Sentai will conduct reconnaissance missions first thing in the morning, covering the southern and south-western sectors at 200–250 miles and prioritizing air strikes.
3. The link-up with the 6th Sentai, 2nd Division, will be executed on the evening of 8 May.

Forty minutes later the 5th Kōkū Sentai informed the 5th Sentai that due to heavy losses in aircrews on 7 May, the strike against TF 17 would be carried out with all available aircraft. Hara advised that he would therefore also need to engage the 5th Sentai's and the 6th Sentai's seaplanes.[59] Even though the *Kako* and the *Furutaka* were to join the MO Kidō Butai slightly later in the morning, the *Myōkō* and the *Haguro* had three Daves each at their disposal. Having agreed on the details, at 0226 hours Hara cabled Takagi and the *Shōkaku* with the first concrete plan of the morning reconnaissance missions. Three of the *Zuikaku*'s Kates were to search in 80-, 100-, and 120-degree sectors, while four of *Shōkaku*'s would do the same in 120-, 140-, 160-, and 180-degree sectors. All bombers were to cover 250 miles and 40 miles in the outward right leg. Their departure was scheduled for 0600 hours. Takagi agreed with this and notified the MO Kidō Butai that from 0700 hours the group would change the course to 215 degrees at 18 knots while searching for the enemy. However, as it soon turned out at 0348 hours, the bad weather would not allow the *Myōkō* or the *Haguro* to use their floatplanes. Two of them had already been damaged during the landing on the rough sea, so Takagi informed Hara that he couldn't count on the heavy cruisers. Therefore, Mieno had to reconsider the reconnaissance plan rapidly. Finally, at 0420 hours the 5th Kōkū Sentai transmitted the revised version. The *Shōkaku* was to cover 140-, 155-, and 170-degree sectors, while the *Zuikaku* would be responsible for

185-, 200-, 215-, and 230-degree sectors. The distance and the departure time didn't change, but the outward leg was reduced to thirty miles.[60]

Once the accommodation of the planes officially ended at 2300 hours, the Japanese pilots had a few hours to rest before the air operations resumed. Although the night was peaceful and without incidents, many of those who didn't take a hypnotic drug couldn't sleep a wink. Sitting together and having dinner made them realize how many had died during the dusk mission. Some burst into tears and some were visibly angry as they walked around the carrier. Shimoda was equally shaken and had a memorable conversation with Murakami in his head. Overall, it wasn't the easiest night for anyone. The officers started to doubt whether they could win the battle if they had already made several mistakes and lost many experienced crews. Still, the infallible Takahashi lifted their spirits and said, "Indeed, we failed during the reconnaissance mission. However, being flawless in carrier warfare is highly unlikely. Today, we were forestalled, but we will make it for sure tomorrow."[61]

Surprisingly, as Ugaki's diary shows, the Combined Fleet staff was quite aware of the situation in the Coral Sea. His entry for 7 May contains a lot of precise information about the battle, including all the slipups. Ugaki was right to think that the invasion of Port Moresby had to wait until the American carriers had been sunk. Yet he understood that the MO Kidō Butai was at a disadvantage regarding the number of torpedo planes at its disposal. This entry means that it is possible to say that the Fourth Fleet's decision to postpone Operation MO by two days was strongly influenced, if not decided, by the Combined Fleet. The tone of the entry in Japanese suggests much disappointment at the loss of the *Shōhō* and an expectation that the battle would be resolved the following day, this belief being primarily addressed to Admiral Inoue.[62]

On the opposing side, soon after the Japanese bombers had withdrawn and the Wildcats had been recovered, at 2134 hours, Fletcher transmitted his daily report to CINCPAC. He notified it about the sinking of one large carrier and a cruiser near Misima Island. However, he also warned that his plans would change and that he would have to withdraw from the Coral Sea within a few days due to the loss of the *Neosho*. During the night, the *Monaghan* was detached to search for survivors from the destroyed Fueling

TABLE 34 **Number of Operational Planes in TF 17, End of 7 May**

Carrier	F4Fs	SBDs	TBDs	Total
Lexington	17	34	12	63
Yorktown	14	32	9	55
Total	31	66	21	118

Sources: NARA: USS *Lexington*, May 7–8; NARA: USS *Yorktown*, May 8; Bates, 81.

Group.[63] Although at 2200 hours the *Lexington*'s CXAM radar picked up contact with a single aircraft on a single bearing of 90 degrees at 30 miles, just before midnight Fletcher informed Fitch that he was not planning a night surface attack on this target.[64]

Further operations against the Japanese carriers were to resume the following morning. On 8 May the commander of TF 17 intended to find and strike the MO Kidō Butai, refuel the destroyers, and prevent the enemy from seizing Port Moresby. Unlike the Japanese, Fitch proposed conducting reconnaissance missions in all sectors, particularly emphasizing the northern part. It was to be searched up to 200 miles, while the southern sector was to be investigated up to 125 miles.[65] Fletcher agreed to this plan and said TF 17 would steam westward to close the gap between the Crace team and the Port Moresby Invasion Force but would still be able to hit the enemy carriers. As mentioned previously, 7 May brought Fletcher a significant advantage in numbers, which he had an excellent opportunity to capitalize on the following day.

PART 3

8 MAY 1942

Chapter 12

"WE WILL GUIDE YOU"— KANNO'S SELFLESS DECISION

The early morning of 8 May welcomed the MO Kidō Butai with thick clouds and rain squalls. The strong southeastern breeze was creating heavy seas, but the weather wasn't so bad that it would prevent the carrier operations.[1] The Japanese pilots had been up since 0430 hours, especially the Kates' crews, waiting for news about their assignment to the reconnaissance flights. PO3c Yokomakura was one such crew member. He recalled that he hadn't slept much due to the excitement and woke up immediately.[2] Being selected for the morning search could be considered honorable, because Hara had instructed torpedo bombers' *buntaichō* to pick trusted men this time, especially from the *Shōkaku*, to be responsible for the most crucial southwestern sectors. According to the plan, between 0615 and 0620 hours the *Shōkaku* and the *Zuikaku* scrambled seven Kates to find the American carriers in a bearing from 140 to 230 degrees. The crews were to fly 250 miles and 30 miles in the right outward leg. Despite the unknown track of TF 17 since the unexpected meeting the previous evening, the Japanese expected they would find them in about two hours. No one doubted Takahashi's report, nor was there any doubt that the enemy should be located nearby.[3] While waiting for the first news from the torpedo bombers, at 0750 hours the *Kinugasa* and the *Furutaka* joined the MO Kidō Butai.[4]

TABLE 35 ■ **The *Shōkaku's* Reconnaissance Missions, Morning of 8 May 1942**

Aircraft	No.	Pilot	Observer	Radio operator	Notes
Kate/*Shōkaku* 215 degrees	1	PO1c Satō	WO Isono	PO2c Ishihara	Takeoff: 0615 Landing: 1045
Kate/*Shōkaku* 185 degrees	2	PO1c Okimura	WO Ukita	PO2c Tozawa	
Kate/*Shōkaku* 200 degrees	3	PO1c Gotō†	WO Kanno†	PO2c Kishida†	
Kate/*Shōkaku* 230 degrees	4	Sea1c Ōtani	PO1c Yamauchi	Sea1c Gomi	

Source: JACAR: Shōkaku (1), 45.
† *Lost in action*

TABLE 36 ■ **The *Zuikaku's* Reconnaissance Missions, Morning of 8 May 1942**

Aircraft	No.	Pilot	Observer	Radio operator	Notes
Kate/*Zuikaku* ? degrees	1	PO1c Satō	PO1c Kawabata	Sea1c Yoshimura	Takeoff: 0620 Landing: 1026
Kate/*Zuikaku* ? degrees	2	PO3c Yokomakura	PO2c Kishi	PO2c Satō	
Kate/*Zuikaku* ? degrees	3	PO3c Hatanaka	PO1c Ushijima	Sea1c Morishita	

Sources: JACAR: Zuikaku (1), 44; JACAR: Gunkan Zuikaku (2), 42.

At about 0630 hours the Yokohama Kū also began searching for the enemy carriers by sending three flying boats from Tulagi.

Additionally, between 0630 and 0700 hours the *Kamikawa Maru* dispatched one Pete and one Jake. The first seaplane circled near Deboyne to protect the tender against the snoopers, while the second one headed toward the anticipated location of the enemy carriers. As Takagi had advised before sunrise, the 5th and 6th Sentai's floatplanes couldn't conduct any reconnaissance flights due to the bad weather.[5]

A bit later, between 0710 and 0718 hours, the 4th Kū's four Bettys scrambled from Rabaul to investigate the area around the Louisiades.

The Americans also launched an intensive search for the enemy carriers that morning. By 0635 hours VS-2 had sent twelve SBDs on a reconnaissance

TABLE 37 ■ **The Yokohama Kū's Reconnaissance Missions, Morning of 8 May 1942**

Unit	No.	Commander	Notes
Mavises / Yokohama Kū	1	Ens. Ōmori†	Takeoff: 0630 Landing: 1550
	2	WO Miwa	
	3	WO Yamaguchi	

Source: JACAR: Yokohama Kū (2), 27.
† *Lost in action*

TABLE 38 ■ ***Kamikawa Maru* Air Group's Activity, Morning of 8 May 1942**

Unit	No.	Crew members			Notes
Jake / *Kamikawa Maru* air reconnaissance	1	PO1c Asanaga†	PO2c Hirao†	Sea1c Ishida†	Takeoff: 0700
Pete / *Kamikawa Maru* air cover	1	PO2c Kihara	PO3c Aono		Takeoff: 0630 Landing: 0900

Source: JACAR: Kamikawa Maru (2), 7.
† *Lost in action*

TABLE 39 ■ **The 4th Kū's Reconnaissance Missions, Morning of 8 May 1942**

Unit	No.	Commander	Notes
Bettys / 4th Kū	1	WO Takahashi	Takeoff: 0710 Landing: 1700
	2	Ens. Sasaki	Takeoff: 0715–18 Landing: 1640–1700
	3	PO1c Honda	
	4	PO1c Adachi	

Source: JACAR: 4 Kū (1), 17.

mission in the northern semicircle at two hundred miles. In case the enemy had other vessels behind TF 17, VB-2 sent six SBDs took off to investigate the southern semicircle at 150 miles.[6] As the dive bombers rose into the air, Ramsey's four F4Fs also scrambled from the *Lexington* for the first morning CAP. After that, twelve VT-2 planes were brought from the hangar deck and armed with torpedoes. Also, just before 0700 hours Fitch ordered the *Yorktown* to send the first CAP and eight SBDs to an anti-torpedo plane patrol. However, since the message was not copied to the air officer, the takeoff of the aircraft was delayed by about half an hour. After four VF-42s and F4Fs, and eight VS-5 SBDs, were airborne, TF 17 changed course to 125 degrees and headed at 15 knots for Point Option, where Fletcher intended to recover all reconnaissance planes.[7]

The weather in the northern semicircle wasn't in the Americans' favor, especially regarding finding the MO Kidō Butai, whose position could be predicted but was not certain. However, after four days of conducting air operations in conditions in which they were half blind, they finally managed to locate the enemy carriers. At 0815 hours Lt. (jg) Joseph Smith spotted the group of warships in the distance. He observed the enemy vessels from above and saw the carriers going into the wind. Watching their decks closely, Smith noticed the planes being armed and fueled, apparently waiting for the signal to scramble. He reported by voice to the *Lexington*, which received his message immediately: "Contact 2 Carriers 4 Cruisers many DD bearing 006 120 speed 15." One might think that the scouting job was done and that all TF 17 had to do was hit the opponent hard. However, the bad weather caused interference and meant that the message was garbled. It also wasn't apparent whether the reported "120" was the enemy's course or the distance from the reference Point Zed (14° 00' S, 156° 00' E). The radiomen were also unsure whether Smith meant Point Zed or the *Lexington*'s actual position. There were about fifty-five miles of difference between the two possible locations of the enemy carriers. Still, the TF 17 command agreed that the pilot referenced Point Zed; thus, the MO Kidō Butai was 175 miles north-northeast of their actual position. Again, despite the consensus, because the attack was intended to be carried out against the target at the limit of the striking radius, the Americans needed to know the enemy's course to avoid hitting a nonexistent target. In the end, Smith saved them from further deliberations at 0833 hours. Even though they did not expect him to repeat the message, he did so. This was because when he got no acknowledgment from the *Lexington*, he thought his radio was malfunctioning so he transmitted the contact report on key and confirmed the points he had previously referred to.[8]

At 0847 hours the *Lexington* clarified on the radio that the enemy carriers were 175 miles away with a bearing of 28 degrees. Since Fitch was afraid that the MO Kidō Butai could escape out of their striking range, just one minute later he ordered the launch of the attack group.[9] Hitting the Japanese as fast as possible wasn't the only concern in TF 17 at the time. At 0807 hours, before Smith's report came in, the *Lexington*'s CXAM-1 radar had picked up contact with one bogey at twenty-two miles with a bearing of 330 degrees. The intruder was moving relatively low and heading toward them at high speed. Ramsey's section was vectored out but it could not find him.[10] The enemy aircraft was on the screen for a few minutes and then disappeared. At 0831 hours another unidentified plane was picked up. The bogey was at thirty miles and coming in from a bearing of 80 degrees. Again, F4Fs were vectored out but didn't make contact. The plane disappeared off the screen at fifteen miles and was not picked up going away, so the fighter director believed it may have been a friendly aircraft.[11] However, the situation suddenly changed at 0832 hours. The *Lexington* intercepted a Japanese message reporting two carriers on a course of 28 degrees.[12]

The American race against time had begun. Capt. Sherman predicted that the enemy attack would come in at about 1100 hours. At 0900 hours the *Yorktown* scrambled thirty-nine aircraft, which Pederson divided into two smaller groups. VS-5's and VB-5's 24 SBDs, each armed with a 1000-pound bomb, were led by Burch and escorted by Fenton's two F4Fs. They were to proceed at 17,000 feet without waiting for the remaining planes. The second group of nine TBDs, each armed with Mk XIII torpedoes, were led by Taylor and escorted by Leonard's four F4Fs. Once they reached the MO Kidō Butai, Burch and Taylor were supposed to coordinate their attack while Wildcats covered their approach. The *Yorktown* striking group departed at 0915 hours.[13]

The *Lexington* was slightly behind, but she finally started to scramble her thirty-six planes at 0910 hours. In her case, the striking group was divided into three smaller parts. Hamilton's 11 SBDs, each armed with a 1000-pound bomb, were escorted by Vorse's F4Fs. With approximately thirty gallons less than usual in their tanks, the dive bombers were to proceed at about 18,000 feet and immediately return to TF 17 once they had completed the attack. However, Vorse lost one Wildcat from his section even before the takeoff. The fighter piloted by Ens. Edward R. Sellstrom was struck in the tail by another aircraft's propeller. There was no time to fix this minor damage, so he remained on the deck.[14]

Brett's twelve TBDs, each armed with an Mk XIII torpedo, were escorted by Gayler's four F4Fs. They proceeded toward the target at six thousand feet.

TABLE 40 **Composition of the TF-17 Striking Group, Morning of 8 May**

Unit	Carrier	Commander	Planes
VF-42	*Yorktown*	Lt. Cdr. Charles Fenton	6 F4Fs
VS-5		Lt. Cdr. William Burch	7 SBDs
VB-5		Lt. Wallace Short	17 SBDs
VT-5		Lt. Cdr. Joe Taylor	9 TBDs
CLAG/VS-2	*Lexington*	Lt. Cdr. William Ault	4 SBDs
VF-2		Lt. Noel Gayler	9 F4Fs
VB-2		Lt. Cdr. Weldon Hamilton	11 SBDs
VT-2		Lt. Cdr. James Brett	12 TBDs
Total: 15 F4Fs, 39 SBDs, 21 TBDs = 75 planes			

Sources: NARA: USS *Yorktown*, May 8; NARA: USS *Lexington*, May 8; Lundstrom, *First Team*, 225–27.

As there were some concerns about the Wildcats' endurance, the section was instructed to attack Japanese planes it encountered on the way and to try to scatter the enemy's group on the return route to TF 17. Finally, Ault's four SBDs, each armed with a 1000-pound bomb, were escorted by two F4Fs, piloted by Lt. Richard S. Bull Jr. and Ens. John B. Bain. To maintain visual contact with the rest of the planes, Ault took up position at about 15,000 feet.[15] The *Lexington*'s group departed at 0925 hours.[16]

During the striking group's takeoff at 0907 hours, Fletcher handed over the tactical command of TF 17 to Fitch. According to Fletcher, he intended to reduce unnecessary signaling between carriers and let Fitch act faster and more independently.[17] Notably, some American historians have wondered about the timing of the transfer of the tactical command, which also surprised Fitch. They have even presented some theories on Fletcher and his cunning plan to shift the responsibility on the eve of the upcoming Japanese attack. Still, there is no conclusive evidence to presume that he was so calculating.[18]

Notwithstanding the views on this decision, TF 17 commenced preparing to repel the enemy's strike. Between 0910 and 0920 hours the *Lexington* sent four F4Fs led by Borries to CAP, and they replaced Ramsey's section. Soon after, ten SBDs from the morning reconnaissance patrol returned to the carrier. At 0940 hours the *Yorktown* scrambled McCormack's four F4Fs, which took over from Flatley's section. Once in the air, McCormack was tasked with finding an enemy aircraft picked up at thirty-nine miles by the CXAM radar at 0932 hours. Even though the intruder reduced the distance to twenty-five miles within the next quarter of an hour, the fighters failed to intercept it.

Smith's report was not only a puzzle for the TF 17 command. It attracted Dixon's attention, who was also on a search mission in the adjacent sector. On hearing the location of the enemy, the VS-2 commander thought his colleague might be wrong. Thus, at 0830 hours he decided to verify this contact with the MO Kidō Butai. After about an hour he spotted the Japanese main force and sent the warning about two carriers and two destroyers bearing 0 degrees and 160 miles from Point Zed. He soon amplified his cable by indicating a 180-degree course and a speed of 25 knots. Unfortunately, none of his dispatches reached TF 17 on time to confirm the initial reconnaissance report. Dixon followed the enemy group for another hour, taking advantage of clouds and rain squalls. He took the return course at about 1045 hours when his SBD started to run out of fuel.[19]

At 1000 hours, TF 17 sent a radio dispatch to SoPac and gave the MO Kidō Butai's position at 0900 hours, hoping that the Allied land-based aircraft could bomb and track the enemy.[20] The expected attack was to materialize in less than an hour, and the Americans had every reason to believe that the Japanese were desperate to change the battle in their favor.

While awaiting the news from the Kates, the atmosphere in the *Shōkaku* and *Zuikaku* was tense. The expectations concerning winning the battle were even higher than on the previous day, so there was little room for any mistakes. Since torpedo and dive bombers in both air groups were already depleted, a debate about assigning particular crews for the attack mission broke out among the fighter pilots. The 5th Kōkū Sentai had thirty-seven Zeros—at least half needed to be in CAP. Those pilots who had already seen combat action on 7 May were now supposed to give way to their colleagues. Still, some pilots wished to play the system so they asked their *buntaichō* if they could be on "the lucky list" and avoid the less exciting duty of defending the carriers. Lt. Takumi Hoashi, the buntaichō of the *Shōkaku*'s fighter group, was one of those who should have stayed. The previous morning he had played *janken* (rock, paper, scissors) with his friend Lt. Shigehisa

Yamamoto and won; his reward was flying in a combat mission. They had an unwritten agreement that one would always stay to protect the *Shōkaku*. However, Hoashi's victory turned out to be a venture against the *Neosho*. He also felt incredibly guilty for acceding to the plan concerning the dusk mission without the escorts. He had many thoughts, but the most disturbing one was the sense of wanting to redeem himself for this mistake. "Let me go this time," Yamamoto said; he wanted just as fervently to enforce their deal. "But we didn't do anything yesterday, so it doesn't count," Hoashi replied. But Yamamoto was persistent and didn't want to give up. Finally, for the sake of revenge on the enemy, Hoashi agreed, because he had a conciliatory nature and they both had the same emotions. The best two fighter pilots went on the attack mission, and this decision could have significantly affected the defense of the *Shōkaku*.[21]

For more than an hour the Japanese were preparing the striking group for departure. The bombers and fighters were slowly being transferred onto the deck. Hoashi had just finished breakfast at 0825 hours when he heard the order from the *Shōkaku*'s megaphone: "Be ready for the mission." He stood up and went to talk with his colleagues. Suddenly, at 0830 hours, the reconnaissance cable came in—"0822 hours: I spotted the enemy carrier task force." The message was sent by WO Kenzō Kanno, who was flying the 200-degree sector. The *Zuikaku* rapidly copied the news to the MO Kidō Butai.[22] Hara was one of the first officers to see it and commented as follows:[23]

> Although the scouting planes had taken off, there was no news on detecting the enemy. I worried that we would not be able to find them again today. From the beginning of the operation, there were problems with air transport, an air raid hit Tulagi, we missed the target on the 6th, and the attack didn't go as planned on the 7th, so I thought my military luck ran out. The reconnaissance report came in at the last moment. I immediately ordered to send the striking group, but since the distance was long, I could not attack. I was determined to hit the enemy, so the carriers rapidly steamed south.

Indeed, the report came at the last moment, because impatience was growing in the 5th Kōkū Sentai. And now officers and crews were shaken by the exciting news. Theoretically they could agree with the attack. But they didn't know the location of the enemy carriers. However, at 0840 hours reliable Kanno came back with another report. It had been sent right after the first one but took a little longer to reach the carriers: "0822 hours: Position of the carriers: bearing 205 and distance 235 miles from our task force. Course 170 degrees, speed sixteen knots."[24] Hara was impressed by the detailed information he received. He could see that his crews were highly motivated to compensate for the errors they had made the previous day. But this wasn't the end of the matter. In quick succession, Kanno cabled the following messages:[25]

0825 hours	The weather in the area is clear, wind direction 120, speed 7 m, clouds 800 m, view range 15 km. [Received at the *Zuikaku* at 0847 hours.]
0854 hours	The enemy changed the course to 130 degrees. [Received at 0856 hours.]
0855 hours	I am in touch with the enemy from the east, no trouble maintaining the contact. [Received at 0856 hours.]

Although the *Lexington*'s CXAM-1 radar picked up the bogey and CAP fighters rushed to intercept, Kanno knew how to trick Wildcats. He faked his withdrawal into the clouds and planned to approach TF 17 a bit later to provide partial updates on the American movements. He and his two crew members had already done an outstanding job, but he decided to keep track of the enemy carriers to ensure the friendly forces would find them.

Hara now had precise information on the position of TF 17, so at 0845 hours he quickly confirmed that the enemy carriers, about 250 miles away and with a bearing of 200 degrees, would be the primary target. Five minutes later he also informed the MO Kidō Butai that the departure of the striking group was scheduled for 0915 hours. At this stage it was known that the *Zuikaku* and the *Shōkaku* would launch sixty-nine planes. Additionally, in response to Hara's order, the group changed the course to 198 degrees to close the gap between the two opposing task forces. It didn't take long for the Fourth Fleet to ask all units if they knew the precise location of the enemy carriers. The 5th Kōkū Sentai replied in a quarter of an hour by giving the coordinates based on the calculations from less than an hour previously, 14° 47' S, 154° 45' E.[26] At 0858 hours Hara slightly adjusted the course to 196 degrees to facilitate the takeoff of the striking group and to steam toward TF 17 simultaneously.[27]

Captain Yokokawa passed the word to the aircrews to get into the cockpits. At the last briefing before the departure, Shimazaki stood up in front of sixty of his men selected for the striking mission and said, "During yesterday's attack, unfortunately, we lost half of our forces. However, no matter how deficient in numbers we are, I want you to demonstrate the results from the regular training. Do your best." His speech inspired them greatly and showed determination and trust in their skills.[28]

The *Zuikaku* was ahead of schedule and had finished scrambling her thirty-one aircraft by 0910 hours. Twenty minutes later the *Shōkaku* sent her thirty-eight planes into the air.[29] Like the day before, the Kates were armed with Type 91 aerial torpedoes while the Vals departed with 250-kg ordinary bombs. Takahashi was in charge of the attack mission as the most senior *hikōtaichō*. Before the departure, he smiled and told his men, "Kakare!"—"Take off! We gonna make it today!"[30] Although no one could yet know that those would be the last words Takahashi said on the *Shōkaku*, everybody felt that the pivotal moment had finally come. Commander Harada recalled being incredibly moved when the formation disappeared over the southern horizon.[31]

Once the enemy carriers were spotted and the order to proceed with the strike was issued, the Japanese sent additional planes to help Kanno maintain contact with them. At 0845 hours the *Kiyokawa Maru* scrambled two Jakes (commanded by Ensign Kozaki and Petty Officer 1st Class Narita) to proceed to the location indicated in the report. Despite the fine weather, the seaplanes couldn't find TF 17. Due to fuel limitations, they were forced to return to the tender by 1345 hours.[32]

The 5th Kōkū Sentai was in the middle of sending the striking group when Kanno contacted them again:[33]

0910 hours Clouds over the sea, altitude 800 meters, attack possible at less than 200 meters. [Received at the *Zuikaku* at 0919 hours.]

0920 hours The enemy formed the [battle] formation, and I am passing from the front. [Received at 0929 hours.]

0930 hours The group of enemy planes is heading toward our main force, 30 planes. [Received at 0942 hours.]

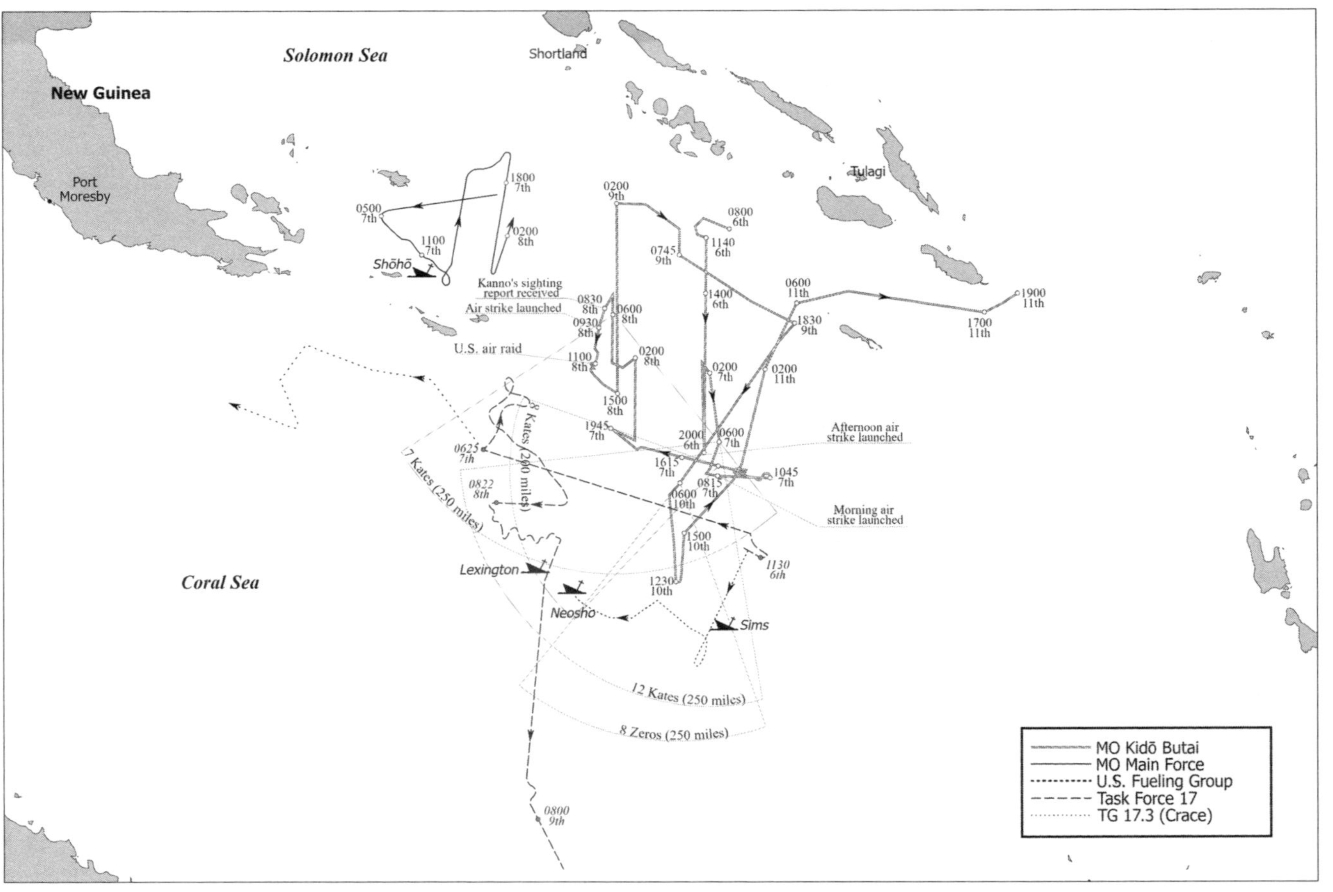

MAP 12 ■ The Battle of the Coral Sea, 8 May

TABLE 41 ■ **MO Kidō Butai Striking Group, 8 May 1942**

<table>
<tr><th>Unit</th><th>No.</th><th colspan="3">Pilot</th><th>Notes</th></tr>
<tr><td rowspan="3">14th shōtai
Zeros/Zuikaku</td><td>1</td><td colspan="3">Lt. Tsukamoto (C)</td><td rowspan="9">Takeoff: 0910
Landing: 1310–1430</td></tr>
<tr><td>2</td><td colspan="3">PO1c Shimizu</td></tr>
<tr><td>3</td><td colspan="3">PO2c Ōkura</td></tr>
<tr><td rowspan="3">15th shōtai
Zeros/Zuikaku</td><td>1</td><td colspan="3">PO1c Makino (S)</td></tr>
<tr><td>2</td><td colspan="3">PO2c Nakata</td></tr>
<tr><td>3</td><td colspan="3">Sea1c Nisugi</td></tr>
<tr><td rowspan="3">16th shōtai
Zeros/Zuikaku</td><td>1</td><td colspan="3">PO1c Kanō (S)</td></tr>
<tr><td>2</td><td colspan="3">PO1c Kamei</td></tr>
<tr><td>3</td><td colspan="3">Sea1c Kurata</td></tr>
<tr><td rowspan="3">11th shōtai
Zeros/Shōkaku</td><td>1</td><td colspan="3">Lt. Takumi Hoashi (B)</td><td rowspan="9">Takeoff: 0900
Landing: 1320</td></tr>
<tr><td>2</td><td colspan="3">PO1c Nishide</td></tr>
<tr><td>3</td><td colspan="3">PO3c Horiguchi</td></tr>
<tr><td rowspan="3">14th shōtai
Zeros/Shōkaku</td><td>1</td><td colspan="3">Lt. Yamamoto (S)</td></tr>
<tr><td>2</td><td colspan="3">PO1c Matsuda</td></tr>
<tr><td>3</td><td colspan="3">PO2c Sasaki</td></tr>
<tr><td rowspan="3">15th shōtai
Zeros/Shōkaku</td><td>1</td><td colspan="3">WO Hanzawa (S)</td></tr>
<tr><td>2</td><td colspan="3">PO2c Yamamoto</td></tr>
<tr><td>3</td><td colspan="3">Sea3c Kōno</td></tr>
<tr><th>Unit</th><th>No.</th><th>Pilot</th><th>Observer</th><th>Radio operator</th><th>Notes</th></tr>
<tr><td rowspan="2">41st shōtai/1st chūtai
Kates/Zuikaku</td><td>1</td><td>Lt. Cdr. Shimazaki (H)</td><td>Ens. Matsunaga</td><td>PO1c Yoshinaga</td><td rowspan="8">Takeoff: 0910
Landing: 1310–1430</td></tr>
<tr><td>2</td><td>WO Yaegashi</td><td>PO1c Himeishi</td><td>Sea1c Ōuchi</td></tr>
<tr><td rowspan="2">42nd shōtai/1st chūtai
Kates/Zuikaku</td><td>1</td><td>PO1c Hori</td><td>WO Kanazawa (S)</td><td>PO2c Ōta</td></tr>
<tr><td>2</td><td>Sea1c Morimitsu†</td><td>PO2c Hiwatashi†</td><td>Sea1c Tani†</td></tr>
<tr><td rowspan="2">43rd shōtai/2nd chūtai
Kates/Zuikaku</td><td>1</td><td>Lt. Satō (C)</td><td>PO1c Ōtani</td><td>PO2c Yoshida</td></tr>
<tr><td>2</td><td>Sea1c Tsubokawa†</td><td>PO1c Yamada†</td><td>PO2c Moriki†</td></tr>
<tr><td rowspan="2">45th shōtai/2nd chūtai
Kates/Zuikaku</td><td>1</td><td>Sea1c Ishihara</td><td>WO Ni'ino (S)†</td><td>PO2c Nishizawa</td></tr>
<tr><td>2</td><td>PO1c Fukutani†</td><td>PO2c Idehara†</td><td>PO2c Ikushima†</td></tr>
</table>

TABLE 41 ■ **MO Kidō Butai Striking Group, 8 May 1942** (*continued*)

Unit	No.	Pilot	Observer	Radio operator	Notes
41st shōtai/1st chūtai Kates/*Shōkaku*	1	Lt. Ichihara (B)	WO Saitō	PO1c Munakata	Takeoff: 0930 Landing: 1320
	2	PO2c Itakura	PO1c Matsuyama	Sea1 Morishita	
	3	PO2c Orikasa	PO1c Shigeta	Sea1c Itō	
42nd shōtai/1st chūtai Kates/*Shōkaku*	1	WO Shindō†	Lt. Yano (S)†	PO2c Ibayashi†	
	2	PO2c Toda	PO1c Kodama	PO2c Abe	
	3	Sea1c Itō†	PO3c Satō†	PO3c Takada†	
45th shōtai/2nd chūtai Kates/*Shōkaku*	1	Lt. Iwamura (C)†	PO1c Nakamura†	PO2c Misumi†	
	2	Sea1c Okafuji†	PO2c Akaishi†	Sea1c Kobayashi†	
46th shōtai/2nd chūtai Kates/*Shōkaku*	1	PO1c Ishikawa (S)	PO1c Mimori	PO2c Fukushima	
	2	PO2c Yoshitomo†	PO2c Tanaka†	PO2c Ōta†	

Unit	No.	Pilot	Observer/navigator	Notes
21st shōtai/1st chūtai Vals/*Zuikaku*	1	Lt. Ema (B)	WO Higashi	Takeoff: 0910 Landing: 1310–1430
	2	PO1c Hatakeyama	PO2c Fujioka	
	3	Sea1c Egusa	PO3c Matsushita	
22nd shōtai/1st chūtai Vals/*Zuikaku*	1	Lt. Kuzuhara (S)†	PO1c Kawase†	
	2	PO1c Hori	PO2c Uetani	
	3	Sea1c Kakuta	Sea1c Miyake	
23rd shōtai/1st chūtai Vals/*Zuikaku*	1	PO1c Nakanishi	WO Izuka (S)	
	2	PO1c Katō	PO2c Fukugaki	
24th shōtai/2nd chūtai Vals/*Zuikaku*	1	PO1c Andō	Lt. Ōtsuka (C)	
	2	PO1c Igata	PO1c Shirakura	
	3	PO2c Sakamaki	PO2c Negishi	
25th shōtai/2nd chūtai Vals/*Zuikaku*	1	WO Fukunaga (S)	PO1c Ishikawa	
	2	PO1c Kamioka†	Sea1c Izumi†	
	3	Sea1c Uenaka	Sea1c Nakane	

TABLE 41 ■ **MO Kidō Butai Striking Group, 8 May 1942** *(continued)*

Unit	No.	Pilot	Observer	Radio operator	Notes
hikōtaichō shōtai Vals/*Shōkaku*	1	Lt. Cdr. Kakuichi Takahashi (H)†	Ens. Nozu†		Takeoff: 0930 Landing: 1320
	2	PO1c Shinohara	PO1c Someno		
	3	Sea1 Fukuhara†	PO2c Suzuki†		
20th shōtai/1st chūtai Vals/*Shōkaku*	1	Lt. Yamaguchi (C)	Ens. Naka		
	2	PO1c Ueshima	PO1c Kōda		
	3	Sea1 Odagiri	Sea1c Yokota		
21st shōtai/1st chūtai Vals/*Shōkaku*	1	PO1c Itō†	Lt. Koizumi (S)†		
	2	PO1c Shirai	PO1c Koitabashi		
	3	PO3c Harashima	PO3c Tanaka		
22nd shōtai/ 1st chūtai Vals/*Shōkaku*	1	PO1c Suzuki	WO Kokubu (S)		
	2	PO2c Katō†	PO2c Kushima†		
	3	Sea1c Ōgawa	PO3c Ōura		
23rd shōtai/2nd chūtai Vals/*Shōkaku*	1	Lt. Mifuku (C)	PO1c Imada		
	2	PO2c Ikeda†	PO1c Nagasawa†		
	3	PO2c Sugimura	PO3c Yoshinaga		
	4	Sea1c Okada	PO2c Kitamura		
24th shōtai/2nd chūtai Vals/*Shōkaku*	1	WO Matsuda (S)†	PO1c Nobe†		
	2	PO1c Nakasho	PO2c Togashi		
	3	PO3c Hanawa†	Sea1c Matsuda†		

Sources: JACAR: Shōkaku (1), 39–44; JACAR: Zuikaku (1), 45–46, 49–50; JACAR: Zuikaku (2), 1–2; JACAR: Gunkan Zuikaku (2), 43, 45–46.
† *Lost in action*

Even without this dispatch, Hara was aware that the Americans had also spotted him and would strike soon. Takagi warned all units to prepare for the enemy's attack. The 5th Kōkū Sentai was instructed to scramble fighters and the screening cruisers and destroyers and assume a defense formation around the carriers, supporting them with their antiaircraft guns.[34] The first CAP, the *Zuikaku*'s three Zeros led by PO1c Tetsuzō Iwamoto, a famous Japanese fighter ace, had already been in the air since 0900 hours.[35] Hara needed at least a dozen more fighters but could not send them too early. However, the

Shōkaku kept six Zeros ready on the deck. In the absence of Hoashi and Yamamoto, WO Yasujirō Abe was responsible for defending the carrier and waited for orders to scramble anytime.[36]

That morning, Kanno was incredibly useful to the 5th Kōkū Sentai. He not only spotted TF 17 and provided precise information about its location and the weather in the area but also cabled Hara all the necessary details to defend the Japanese carriers:[37]

0950 hours	The group of enemy planes is heading toward our main force at about 2000 meters. The enemy has a direct escort. [Received at the *Zuikaku* at 1002 hours.]
0955 hours	From now on, I am coming back. [Received at 1008 hours.]

The 5th Kōkū Sentai steamed southward at twenty-eight knots through moderate wind and frequent rain squalls. The heavy clouds at five hundred to two thousand meters were a double-edged sword. They protected the carriers from early detection by reconnaissance planes but impaired directing the fighters in CAP to defend the ships. The Japanese knew the lack of radar equipment put them at a massive disadvantage because it meant they had to rely on traditional air-monitoring methods. Investigating the horizon carefully through gaps in the clouds, the observers awaited the arrival of the enemy striking group. Unexpectedly, someone in the *Zuikaku* screamed, "I can see the enemy planes!" Shimoda jumped from the back to confirm. "Why are you so silly? Looking at the time, it's way too early," he commented immediately. Yet the observer was sure about what he saw. "Sir, please take a look over there." He pointed his finger at the starboard bow. They could both see tiny black dots coming in at about three thousand meters and flying between the clouds.[38] "Those are friendly planes. They are trying to avoid the rain squalls. Calm down. Can anyone see that?" Shimoda looked for confirmation. "Yes, Sir. They are undeniably the friendly planes," the second observer reassured him, and other men nervously watched the sky. As S. Mori argues, Shimoda could have asked Wada what he saw, but he didn't. However, the *Shōkaku*'s flight officer was more inquisitive. "First of all, let's send one fighter to ascertain," he said to Jōjima. "The distance to the enemy is 250 miles. I believe we still have one hour before they come." The officers were dubious about the spotted aircraft.[39]

At 0955 hours the Japanese sent Abe's six Zeros into the air.[40] "The enemy or the friendly aircraft, if we make a mistake, it will have severe consequences," Mieno deftly pointed out. He told Shimoda to scramble the fighters immediately if the enemy was identified. The antiaircraft gunners were already at their stations and were waiting nervously for updates. Finally, it turned out it was Takahashi with the dive bombers. Since the *hikōtaichō* had flown into a terrible squall, he had been forced to make a long detour and had therefore been noticed by the carriers.[41] After about twenty minutes, all of the Kates from the reconnaissance missions landed on the *Zuikaku*, followed by the *Shōkaku*'s three torpedo bombers.[42] Only Kanno was missing, but as he had advised previously, the carrier could expect him to return a little later. Once the 5th Kōkū Sentai recovered the scouting planes, Hara ordered the carriers to speed up to thirty-one knots.

The Japanese anxiously awaited news from Takahashi, who was supposed to reach the target soon after 1100 hours. However, before that, the *Zuikaku* received another cable from Kanno: "I am joining all friendly planes and will guide them." This message was sent at 1045 hours, meaning the torpedo bomber's crew had already been in the air for four hours and twenty minutes. The officers in the *Shōkaku* began worrying about whether they would make it back to the carrier. "Air Officer, will Kanno have enough fuel to return?" Wada was asked, and he had no other answer than a negative one. Everybody felt uneasy because they knew that Kanno was putting his life and those of his two colleagues on the line to ensure that Takahashi would not lose track of the enemy carriers.[43]

When the striking group proceeded south at three thousand meters, the clouds slowly parted, giving decent visibility of a ten-mile stretch of the area from above. Ema noticed a small black dot coming from the opposite direction. Observing the characteristic canopy shape and *hinomaru* (rising sun) on the wings, he quickly realized it was one of their reconnaissance planes. The aircraft made a U-turn, caught up with the formation and passed by Ichihara's Kate. The *buntaichō* briefly saw the unshaved faces of Kanno, Gotō, and Kishida, who placed their *kankō* at the head of the formation. They messaged the other planes, saying, "We will guide you," and the rest of the bombers figured out that they were very close to the Americans. Many of them understood the consequences of Kanno's decision but did not pity him because they would have done the same in his position. Unfortunately for Kanno, since the enemy was supposed to be within the normal range, they took off without an extra fuel tank, which could have saved them.[44]

Many might wonder why Kanno made a U-turn to guide the striking group at the cost of his and his crew members' lives. Theoretically Takahashi was on a good course and could have found the American carriers without his help. Still, the reality was more complex. On 8 May the Japanese had no more room for mistakes and couldn't afford to miss the target. Since the *Shōkaku*'s *kankō* had made a fatal error during the morning reconnaissance missions the previous day, the carrier's torpedo bomber group had a great sense of collective responsibility. If there was anyone who could wash away the guilt, it was Kanno—he had to prove that the *Shōkaku* got jobs done.

Chapter 13

TF 17 KNOCKS THE *SHŌKAKU* OUT OF ACTION

On the way north, fighter pilots Lt. Cdr. Charles Fenton and Ens. Harry B. Gibbs followed SBDs from VS-5 and VB-5, which had managed to climb faster to 17,000 feet. Fenton tried to catch up with the *Yorktown*'s dive bombers so as not to use too much fuel before reaching the target. Unexpectedly, about halfway, he passed the enemy planes heading south. Some SBDs also spotted the enemy striking group, but they could do nothing except continue their route north. Burch recalled the meeting with the Japanese:[1] "On the way to the attack, I was climbing all the way, and at about 17,500 feet I saw down below me, at about 12,000 or 14,000 feet, a large group of Jap dive bombers going in the opposite direction. I reported them by voice, giving position, course, speed, and altitude. I heard Joe Taylor report a large group of torpedo planes proceeding in that same direction."

At 1032 hours the *Yorktown*'s SBDs sighted in the distance two carriers, one *Ise*-class battleship, three heavy cruisers, and four light cruisers or destroyers proceeding on a course of 190 degrees at 20 knots. The *Zuikaku* and the *Shōkaku* were separated by eight to ten miles, and the latter steamed at the task force's rear. To avoid detection by enemy CAP, Burch led the dive bombers through thick clouds, and by 1049 hours he found himself southeast of the MO Kidō Butai, keeping an altitude of 17,000 feet. He wanted to attack as soon as possible but had to wait for the slower TBDs, which were twenty minutes behind him. VS-5 and VB-5 had the opportunity to surprise the Japanese, but orders called for a coordinated strike with torpedo bombers, so he impatiently circled in the area. Precious time passed, and part of the enemy task force could soon have been lost from sight due to low-level heavy clouds and rain squalls coming over the *Zuikaku* and her screening vessels.[2] Burch recalled that moment in the following words:[3]

> Between 2,000 and 15,000 feet there were intermittent storms, and the Japs were just to the north of one the largest of these storms. Conditions were bad. I called Joe as soon as we got over the fleet. He was still 20 minutes behind us. We were at about 20,000 feet and we could see the fighters circling up towards us. I climbed higher to make them climb higher while we were waiting for Joe. Every five minutes he would check in with me.

Despite the lack of radar, the 5th Kōkū Sentai did everything to take advantage of the warning sent by Kanno. By 1020 hours the *Shōkaku* had scrambled all her nine Zeros, including three led by PO1c Miyazawa, fresh reinforcement. Soon after, Ensign Abe's two Zeros landed on deck to refuel and be ready to set off again. The *Zuikaku* kept in readiness the remaining seven fighters, which were to take off as soon as the enemy was sighted. The American torpedo bombers were still not in the required position, but the *Shōkaku*'s lookouts eventually sighted SBDs at about 0850 hours. Five minutes later, the *Zuikaku* confirmed spotting twenty enemy dive bombers, which looked cleared for the attack. The flagship needed only minutes to scramble four Zeros led by Lieutenant Okajima. With the engines running and pilots sitting in the cockpits, Hara held WO Sumita's *shōtai* as an emergency reserve that could be sent into the air as soon as possible. The summary of the 5th Kōkū Sentai CAP is provided in table 42.

As we know from Burch, he was in touch with Taylor, who informed him of the time remaining until his TBDs arrived. At one point, Burch got a strange message: "Bill, it's Joe. Refrain from attacking for another fifteen minutes." Burch felt from the beginning it wasn't Taylor, who yelled a second later, "Bill, that's not me. Don't listen to that guy!" After a moment of silence, the mysterious voice was heard on Burch's radio again: "Bill, this is Joe . . . hold up for ten or

TABLE 42 **Defense of the *Shōkaku*, 8 May**

Unit	No.	Pilot	Notes	Ammo expended	Claims	Notes
1st CAP shōtai Zeros/ *Shōkaku*	1	PO2 Okabe (S)	takeoff: 0955 landing: —	unknown	4 × fighters 4 × dive bombers	ditched
	2	PO3c Tanaka		unknown	2 × dive bombers 1× torpedo bomber	ditched
2nd CAP shōtai Zeros/ *Shōkaku*	1	PO1c Minami (S)	takeoff: 0955 landing: —	700 × 7.7-mm 20 × 20-mm	2 × fighters	hit by 5 bullets
	1	PO2c Ichinose†		unknown	—	shot down
3rd CAP shōtai Zeros/ *Shōkaku*	1	PO1c Miyazawa (S)†	takeoff: 1020 landing: —	unknown	2 × torpedo bomber	shot down
	2	PO3c Komachi		750 × 7.7-mm 20 × 20-mm	1 × fighter 1 dive bomber	hit by 3 bullets
	3	Sea1c Imamura		unknown	3 × fighters 1 × dive bomber	ditched
4th CAP shōtai Zeros/ *Shōkaku*	1	Ens. Abe (S)	takeoff: 0955/1100 landing: 1025/—	unknown	1 × dive bomber	ditched
	2	PO1c Kawanishi		700 × 7.7-mm 20 × 20-mm	1 × dive bomber	hit by 30 bullets
11th CAP shōtai Zeros/ *Zuikaku*	1	Lt. Okajima (B)	takeoff: 1057 landing: 1650	5150 × 7.7-mm 700 × 20-mm	24 × fighters and dive bombers (2 × unconfirmed)	4 × Zeros damaged
	2	PO1c Komiyama				
	3	PO2c Sakaida				
	4	PO2c Kuroki				
12th CAP shōtai Zeros/ *Zuikaku*	1	WO Sumita (S)	takeoff: 1200 landing: 1650			
	2	PO1c Tsukuda				
	3	Sea1c Fujii				
13th CAP shōtai Zeros/ *Zuikaku*	1	PO1c Iwamoto (S)	takeoff: 0900 landing: 1650			
	2	PO1c Itō				
	3	Sea1c Mae				

Sources: JACAR: Shōkaku (1), 46–47; JACAR: Zuikaku (1), 44–45; JACAR: Gunkan Zuikaku (2), 44.

fifteen more minutes." Upset, Taylor got on and responded again: "Get off the line, you slant-eyed son of a bitch!"[4] Although no Japanese sources confirmed this incident, the Americans were almost ready to hit the enemy carriers. At 1058 hours the torpedo bombers were finally in position and a coordinated attack was commenced.[5] Not all the Japanese fighters in CAP rushed toward the sighted SBDs because of technical problems with radio receivers. At least five pilots noticed the threat and started climbing up, while the rest, circling in the different sectors, were unaware of the enemy's presence. Due to the low heavy clouds and rain squalls, the Type 96 mod. 1 radio mounted on the Zeros was practically useless and did not receive signals when they were too far away from the mothership. Okajima's freshly scrambled *shōtai* wouldn't have noticed the SBDs above if they hadn't been surprised by the *Zuikaku*'s antiaircraft guns, which suddenly opened fire. The *buntaichō* looked around and noticed Iwamoto and his two wingmen climbing up at high speed. Then he realized that radio calls would not work in such terrible weather and that he must fly south to protect the *Shōkaku*. The need to strengthen CAP was also understood in the *Zuikaku*, where the last *shōtai* received the order to scramble. Sumita was already halfway across the deck in his Zero when he suddenly stopped. The maintenance team member ran up to him and had a short conversation. "I can't

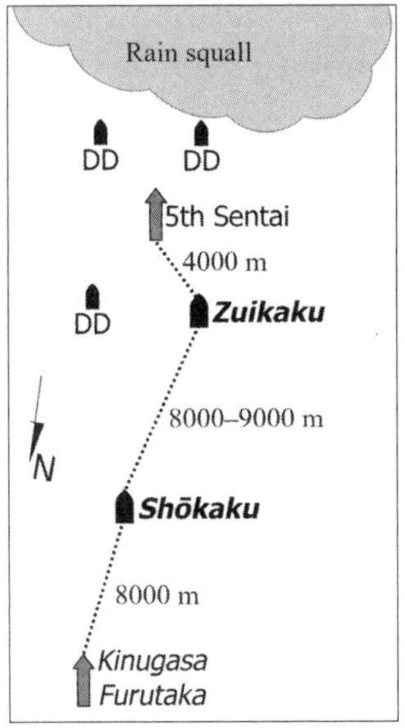

MAP 13 ■ MO Kidō Butai before the American attack, morning of 8 May

fly in the middle of the explosion blasts," the *shōtaichō* said, openly expressing his concern and refusing to risk his life. Shimoda was annoyed when he heard this explanation, but even if the two remaining pilots from *shōtai* decided to take off, Sumita's Zero was blocking the forward deck.[6]

By about 1030 hours the MO Kidō Butai had assumed a defensive formation. The leading *Zuikaku*, steaming southward, increased the distance from the *Shōkaku*. The *Haguro* and the *Myōkō* were positioned about four kilometers ahead of the *Zuikaku*, while the *Furutaka* and *Kinugasa* steamed eight kilometers astern the *Shōkaku*. The destroyers were placed around both carriers to provide antiaircraft support.[7] The rapidly changing weather in the area unexpectedly worked in favor of the *Zuikaku* and left the *Shōkaku* in the spotlight, making her a primary target for the American bombers.

The first to attack were VS-5's SBDs, which decided to approach the carrier from the starboard side. Iwamoto's *shōtai*, the most alert part of the CAP, harassed the dive bombers at 3,350 meters. The famous Japanese ace focused on shooting at Burch from close range with his 20-mm cannons while his two wingmen targeted the plane piloted by Ens. John H. Jorgenson.[8] However, ignoring antiaircraft fire and the Zeros chasing them desperately, seven SBDs got close enough to the *Shōkaku* to make the final move. At 1100 hours, from an altitude of about 450 meters, they released their bombs. But the carrier was in the middle of a sudden turn to the left, so they all missed and only sprayed her deck, creating huge water geysers. The Americans reported as many as three direct hits and four Zeros shot down, but the enemy did not suffer any losses. Instead, while recovering the plane from a dive, Jorgenson was struck by an artillery shell, which almost flipped his bomber onto its back. Then he was attacked by three Zeros and got his wings and cockpit punctured. His leg was wounded and he was lucky to avoid being killed, but Iwamoto suddenly stopped chasing him and returned to the defense of the *Shōkaku*. It seemed that VS-5 was safe, but then it came across Okajima, who appeared out of nowhere. In reality, he was a bit late with his *shōtai*. The *buntaichō* saw that Burch's attack had failed, so during the dash toward VB-5, he only briefly machine-gunned the SBDs withdrawing into the clouds. Jorgenson's plane was a wreck but survived thanks to its self-sealing tanks.[9]

PHOTO 13 ■ A famous Japanese fighter ace, PO1c Tetsuzō Iwamoto *NDL*

Once VS-5 had completed its dive and missed an excellent opportunity to deliver the first blow, Captain Jōjima used the precious seconds available to scramble his last two Zeros, held back on the deck due to the enemy's attack. Shortly after 1100 hours the *Shōkaku* steamed steadily at thirty-one knots and headed into the wind. Abe's *shōtai* lifted into the air and rushed toward the other dive bombers approaching the carrier. The situation was rapidly changing: in the following seconds the *Zuikaku* and her screening vessels hid below the thick rain clouds, becoming invisible to the American planes.[10]

In the meantime, Short completed the circle around the MO Kidō Butai and climbed up to proceed with the dive attack. Okabe, Miyazawa, and Iwamoto's *shōtai*, eight Zeros in total, were already chasing them and hoped to disperse them, or at least slow them down. PO3c Komachi remembered this moment as follows:[11] "Dive bombers appeared one after another, so I did my best to intercept them. There were only a few of our fighters, so we engaged in several chaotic skirmishes. Rather than going for a dogfight with just one plane, I knew I must protect the *Shōkaku*. Thus, I was fixated on deflecting the enemy attacks."

VB-5 had a numerical advantage, however, and went down to two thousand feet through the antiaircraft barrier. At that point they released their bombs. Most of them fell short, but one 1000-pound bomb struck the port side forward, shredding the flight deck and jamming the forward elevator. Some American pilots later complained that fogged windshields and telescopes prevented them from securing more hits. Lt. John "JoJo" J. Powers was beyond that. During the dive, his fuel tank was damaged by a 20-mm shell, which set the bomber on fire and probably also seriously injured both crew members. Determined to deliver the blow, JoJo passed the magical altitude of one thousand feet and pulled out only at two hundred feet. At 1105 hours his bomb slammed the carrier's starboard side abaft the island. This one set afire the flight deck and upper hangar deck. Although the *Shōkaku* had been patched up after the first hit, the second one definitely made her unfit to conduct air operations. JoJo's bravery cost him and his companion their lives, because he didn't pull out of the dive and crashed into the sea. The moment of their death was recalled by Nielsen:[12]

> Just then Harlan Dickson crossed over, and the skipper followed the last man in Scouting Five. It was then that I realized the circle was going all the way around. There just wasn't room enough to turn that many airplanes and get them down on the target; so, to help straighten out the mess, I turned into the target from abeam, and Harlan Dickson came with me. This maneuver subtracted two full intervals from the circle,

and enabled JoJo to make a nice, easy turn and approach the target in line with its flight deck.

As I pulled out, I looked around to see if either Harlan or I had made a hit. It's mighty hard to hit a ship when you're coming at it from the side, but I think we did that day. We could see the explosions.

As I looked at the carrier I could see an airplane directly over the center of the flight deck—about 300 feet—and nosed down at almost 45 degrees. It was headed into an area of smoke and debris which covered the whole after part of the Jap carrier.

It must have been JoJo. It couldn't have been anyone else. In the position he was in, it would have been impossible for him to pull out. I was banking hard to watch when Straub, my back seat man, called and said, "Mr. Nielsen, there are three Zeros back there."

When the *Shōkaku* received the first blow, Lieutenant Commander Fukuchi was the first to be informed about the extent of the damage. He immediately drafted the summary for the skipper: "Forward damage control team report: bomb struck the forward flight deck and set it on fire."[13] Apart from the jammed and collapsed forward elevator, the most critical situation was starboard, where ten thousand liters of aviation gasoline were stored and where the hangar deck would turn into an inferno if the flames weren't put out quickly enough. The damage control team did everything to extinguish the fire, but the mixture of seawater, oil, and incredible heat resulted in thick black smoke coming out of the *Shōkaku*. During the firefighting action, the second bomb slammed the carrier and set afire the life rafts in the afterpart and demolished all the davits. This hit was, however, more deadly to crew members. Many men from the antiaircraft machine gun stations and maintenance team were killed on the spot. Despite the effort to put out the flames in the forward hangar, leaking gasoline was repeatedly flaring in the same spots again, supported by intake air. As an emergency measure, Fukuchi instructed his men to close the after compartments with the fuel in them to avoid spreading the fire inside the vessel. Since he also had to investigate the situation aft, he ran to the flight deck to see the damage from the second hit with his own eyes. He inspected the starboard part, especially the 25-mm gun stations and the stern. This is where he came across several dead bodies ripped apart and more flames. One cannot fully visualize the next shocking scene, but Fukuchi recalled one sailor chopping off his left leg below the knee with a hand axe because some shrapnel had severely mangled it. Once he had finished the self-amputation, he continued to do his best to save the carrier from the flames. His effort perfectly exemplifies the Japanese obsession with protecting the ship. Despite the difficult situation on the flight and hangar decks, the *Shōkaku*'s engine and boiler rooms were untouched. She was steaming at a stable thirty knots, meaning the probability of spreading the fire from the stern to the bow was minimal. Fukuchi saw no critical danger for the carrier there, so he went back to the forward part.[14]

After its attack was completed, VB-5 headed northeast to join VS-5 and return safely. One of the pilots realized that his bomb release mechanism had not worked during the dive, so he jettisoned his payload into the sea. Okajima's *shōtai* was mad about the scored hits on the *Shōkaku* and started chasing the retreating SBDs.[15] The Japanese fighters mainly aimed at the fuel tanks, hoping it would be easier to set the dive bombers on fire than to shoot them down. Although the pursuit of VB-5 ended with a confirmed victory on a plane piloted by Ens. Davis E. Chaffee, most of the Zeros were engaged in combat while the TBDs were proceeding with their attack. Losing two SBDs, VB-5 claimed three hits on the *Shōkaku* and three enemy fighters downed. In reality, Short's group scored only two hits and failed to destroy a single aircraft.[16]

Just before VB-5's dive, nine TBDs finally approached the battlefield. Flying at just above two hundred feet, they spotted both Japanese carriers. They were escorted by two Wildcats from Leonard's section and two from Woollen's section, which remained at two thousand feet to have a better view of the area. VT-5 targeted the wounded *Shōkaku* and approached the enemy in two columns, descending to only fifty feet and increasing speed to 110 knots. After less than a minute, the Devastators formed one line. To the surprise of the American fighters, waiting with their machine guns ready for the defense, no Zeros attacked the TBDs. Leonard therefore headed toward the nearest screening ship and strafed to distract her antiaircraft artillery from targeting the slow torpedo bombers.[17]

PHOTO 14 ■ Damage inflicted on the *Shōkaku* by the first bomb *Fukuchi, Kūbo* Shōkaku *Kaiseki*

Suddenly, McCuskey noticed some Zeros coming from the opposite direction at 2,800 feet. They were PO1c Minami's *shōtai*, which passed over VT-5 and headed toward the F4Fs. McCuskey did not have time to warn Leonard because he had to climb up to stand any chance against the agile enemy fighters. Despite the initial disadvantage, his plan paid off because the Japanese could not hit his Wildcat as it swayed from left to right. Deciding to leave McCuskey alone, both Japanese pilots accidentally ended up on Leonard's right side. He saw them almost at the last moment. By turning as tightly as possible, he avoided the Japanese machine guns and, after making two circles, disappeared safely into the clouds. At the same time, McCuskey didn't give up the fight and regained altitude to head toward a lone Zero. It was piloted by inexperienced PO2c Ichinose, who failed to keep looking in all directions.

He was hit by an accurate salvo and his plane was set ablaze and crashed into the water. Ichinose became the first victim on the CAP side.

Understanding the enemy's numerical advantage, PO1c Miyazawa's *shōtai* got into the dogfight and tried to isolate its opponents to eliminate them individually. PO2c Komachi went straight after McCuskey and, after a short pursuit, lost sight of him as he escaped into the clouds. Sea1c Imamura, the youngest pilot in the *Shōkaku*'s fighter group, was the first to detect the TBDs approaching the carrier. He vigorously waved at Minami and Miyazawa from his cockpit, and they knew they had to hurry up. Desperate to reach the bombers before they dropped their torpedoes, they failed to notice two Wildcats piloted by Woollen and Ens. John P. Adams. The two Americans followed the Zeros and used their altitude advantage to pin down Miyazawa's plane, which they damaged. Apart from that, Minami's fuel tank was punctured in several spots, but he escaped the coup de grâce by climbing up rapidly. At 1108 hours, a moment after VB-5 finished its attack, the Devastators dropped their torpedoes at about three hundred to six hundred meters from the target. Taylor recalled this moment as follows:[18]

> The Zeros spotted us as we fanned for the approach, and they came boiling in after us. Jim Flatley wasn't with us, but we had four good fighters along: Leonard, McCuskey, Adams and Woollen. They were right on the job. I would report that we were being attacked by a Zero. In a voice that was just as calm and matter-of-fact as you can imagine, one of them would say, "Okay, Joe, I'll take care of it." And they didn't miss. Woollen got one going in and Adams got one going home. The others must have knocked off a few, too, because they kept those Zeros off our backs.
>
> We finally closed, and the ship started shooting at us. We were rocked and buffeted by the exploding shells. It was the damnedest shaking and jolting I've ever had in my life. One thing I remember distinctly was the small caliber anti-aircraft stuff. They were "walking" it right down the water at us. It looked like hail on the water, and it was a God-awful sight, I'll tell you. "Any minute now . . . any minute!" I kept telling myself.
>
> My radioman called up and said, "I can hear the five-inch stuff. We're getting close."

> Hear 'em, I can smell 'em, and you could, too. Over the noise of the engine, you could hear the five-inch guns go off, and then you could smell that distinct burnt powder smell. It was time to release.
>
> After dropping my fish, I headed for a rain cloud, the rest of the squadron hot on my tail. So were the Zeros. Our back seat gunners were able to hold them off. Just before we plunged into the cloud, I went on the air and gave the boys a compass course to steer in the clouds so we wouldn't bump into each other.

Although VT-5 believed they had secured three hits, the explosions seen from the torpedo bombers were caused by the near misses of bombs dropped by SBDs. After the attack, Taylor set a return course and disappeared in a rain squall. The TBDs were soon joined by Leonard, Woollen, and Adams. McCuskey was missing, because he had got lost during the dogfight over the *Shōkaku*. Pursued and cornered by two Zeros, he broke free but flew into a storm cloud and could not find his colleagues. Noticing one of the Japanese destroyers below, McCuskey determined his position and headed toward TF 17 alone.[19]

The last to appear in the area were two F4Fs piloted by Fenton and Gibbs, who failed to escort the bombers in time. Once they realized the attack was over, both turned back at 1115. The *Yorktown* striking group reported six bomb hits and three torpedo hits, as well as eight downed and seven damaged Zeros. As we already know, the *Shōkaku* was only hit by two bombs. The Japanese CAP lost two fighters, flown by Miyazawa and Ichinose. While observing the burning carrier, identified as the *Kaga*, Short and Taylor were convinced that she would sink.[20] The losses of the *Yorktown* included two SBDs and one severely damaged SBD and TBD each. The Americans correctly estimated that the enemy CAP comprised fifteen to eighteen Zeros. They also admitted that their losses were minimal due to the proximity of two large clouds into which the group flew on completing the attack.[21]

Thanks to Fukuchi's memoirs, we know what VT-5's attack looked like from the *Shōkaku*'s bridge. The carrier was in the middle of evasive maneuvers to avoid being hit by the dive bombers when the torpedo planes appeared to the port, over the sea's surface. Miyazawa's *shōtai* was closest to the ship and in the best position to protect it, and Fukuchi could see that the *shōtaichō* had managed to down one Devastator just as it released a torpedo.[22] He looked around and noticed that despite the fierce antiaircraft fire, from both 127-mm and 25-mm guns, other torpedo planes were coming in and dropping their fish. Men on the deck started to shout "torpedoes, torpedoes!" and the Navigation Officer, Cdr. Tomoichirō Tsukamoto, immediately ordered "omokaji ippai, isoge!" ("rudder full right!"). The *Shōkaku* made a sharp turn, and after a few seconds all the American torpedoes passed next to the port side. Tsukamoto later admitted that this was the critical moment that saved the carrier. Moreover, the helmsman supposedly made a smooth turn, using his own judgment because he hadn't correctly heard Tsukamoto's order.[23]

The defense of the *Shōkaku* coincided with the MO Kidō Butai's strike against TF 17. At 1109 hours one of the bomber crews informed the group about the weather conditions in the proximity of the enemy. The wind was southwesterly with a speed of eight meters. Soon after, at 1116 hours, Hara received Takahashi's order issued at 1100 hours, which instructed all planes to commence the attack. The 5th Kōkū Sentai officers knew that at the time they were reading this cable, the *hikōtaichō* was already in the midst of the strike. Nine minutes later the *Zuikaku* got an exciting message from Ichihara: "*Saratoga* sunk."[24] Despite the initial damage inflicted by VB-5 on the *Shōkaku*, the Japanese started to believe they could win the battle and that the only thing they had to do now was to protect the carrier from sinking. At 1121 hours the last plane from the *Yorktown* striking group left the vicinity of the Japanese task force and *Shōkaku* had a moment of respite.

As Iwamoto recalled, his *shōtai* was left with only a small amount of fuel due to the continual attacks of the enemy bombers. He couldn't stay in the air any longer and got close to the *Zuikaku* to refuel, but she went straight into the wall of rain. Even worse, the carrier started to zigzag and replied negatively to his request for permission to land. However, Iwamoto was in a desperate situation. He knew he had fuel for a few more minutes, so he decided to land despite the odds. "Ichi ka hachi ka"—"all or nothing"—he thought. His Zero swayed from left to right and up and down in the strong wind, and the deck was probably slippery from the rain. Still, he made it. His two wingmen also landed without any accidents, followed by Okajima's *shōtai*. When they got back on the *Zuikaku*, TBDs were dropping torpedoes at the *Shōkaku*. They soon learned that this attack was unsuccessful. Yokokawa, Shimoda, and other officers praised the pilots for the stout defense. The refueling was completed quickly, and Iwamoto's *shōtai* received the order to scramble again. Suddenly, Iwamoto noticed one American fighter, which had emerged from the rain squall, apparently spotted the *Zuikaku* and strafed her, and then escaped into the clouds. Fortunately for the Japanese, the intruder didn't cause any damage to the eight planes on the deck. Eventually, when the news about the second group of enemy planes arrived, Iwamoto and Okajima's *shōtai* took off in difficult weather conditions but fought its way to blue skies.[25]

The MO Kidō Butai had great luck that day, because the second wave of the attackers did not follow directly after the first one. The *Lexington* striking group's problems began just a few minutes after departing TF 17. At 0945 hours Lt. (jg) Steffenhagen reported a damaged engine in his TBD and received an order from Brett to return to the carrier. In less than fifteen minutes Vorse's three F4Fs also turned back toward the *Lexington* because they could not find VS-2 in the terrible weather. Lacking a homing beacon, Vorse preferred not to take risks by flying into the unknown. This wasn't the end of the troubles, though. While en route north, VB-2's eleven SBDs lost visual contact with VT-2. To find them, Hamilton decided to descend to one thousand feet, but he still could not see Ault or Brett due to thick clouds.[26]

At about 1120 hours the first planes from the *Lexington* strike group appeared over the indicated spot, but no Japanese ships were sighted. Unbeknownst to the Americans, the MO Kidō Butai had been heading south for about two hours. However, Ault did not lose his calm and ordered a search of the area, knowing that the enemy carrier could not be far away.[27] Lost Hamilton, who was worried about the fuel reserves in VB-2, informed Ault about his concerns. But when Ault spotted the Japanese group comprising at least one carrier fifteen miles west of the designated location at 1130 hours, he could not steer Hamilton on the correct course without any common reference points. Those pilots close to the enemy vessels could see smoke in the air, indicating that the *Yorktown* striking group had finished its job. With only four SBDs, six F4Fs, and eleven TBDs, Ault had to commit all the planes against one target. Despite all the efforts to guide VB-2, Hamilton was several miles away and could not get out of the thick clouds at low altitude. His dive bombers would take part in the attack. Thus, Ault planned to throw his dive bombers first, distracting the Japanese antiaircraft defense and fighters from the slower torpedo bombers approaching the *Shōkaku* from the south.[28]

The 5th Kōkū Sentai staff watched the battle from the *Zuikaku*, hidden well under the heavy clouds and in the occasional rain squall. The navigation officer, Cdr. Misao Tsuyuguchi, increased the speed to thirty-one knots to distance them from the American aircraft.[29] Hara restlessly looked through his binoculars and saw the black smoke coming out of the sister ship. She was maintaining a high speed, yet he knew that the situation in the carrier must have been tough. Then small black dots appeared above her and started to dive one by one. Hara noticed a flash and red flames, meaning a bomb must have struck the deck. This was the moment when JoJo secured a hit.

Hara wasn't the only one following the events. Someone shouted, "*Shōkaku* is sinking," but it was more of a panic than a reality. As a major fire broke out in the carrier, her condition looked much more severe from the *Zuikaku*'s perspective. But it seemed the attack was over, and no more enemy planes approached the wounded carrier. Just a few minutes later the officers in the *Zuikaku* were exclaiming their joy. They had received the news from Ichihara about sinking the *Saratoga*.[30] After a while they became serious again and shifted their attention back to the *Shōkaku*. Like on 7 May, they were overwhelmed by extreme emotions. They didn't know then that the initially lost *Lexington* striking group had found their carrier and would deliver the next blow.[31]

Unlike previously, the Japanese noticed the second wave of enemy planes. A warning about the upcoming strike was sent to all Zeros aloft. Flying at about sixty-three hundred meters, Iwamoto's *shōtai* spotted the Americans immediately after receiving information from the carrier. Three Zeros had the altitude advantage and split up to chase Ault's SBD, which was covered by two Wildcats piloted by Bull and Bain. The cautious dive bomber managed to evade the first salvo from the first pass. After passing the Wildcats at full speed, Iwamoto's *shōtai* climbed up to regain altitude and regroup before the next pass. However, they were too slow to prevent the Americans from attacking the *Shōkaku*.

Diving from about six thousand feet, Ault had a straightforward route to the enemy carrier, because no Zeros were waiting for him. Without any intervention, VS-2 released its bombs at two thousand feet. Despite desperate warnings from observers on the deck and its own fierce antiaircraft fire, *Shōkaku* was hit for the third time at 1140 hours. One bomb struck the starboard flight deck abaft the island. According to Fukuchi, it completely demolished 25-mm gun station No. 1 (below the bridge), killing most of its crew, including Sub-lieutenant Sugiyama. One machine gun's trigger had jammed and was firing randomly as it dangled over the outer side of the damaged hull. Some gunners standing nearby were blown into the sea by the blast. Many men on the deck were injured by splinters flying in all directions or with third-degree burns, and they needed immediate medical help. The beds were full of wounded people who were screaming in pain. Fukuchi described it as entering hell, especially when he could smell oil in the sick room.[32]

The *Shōkaku* was in the middle of a sharp turn to the right when the third bomb slammed into her near her bridge. It took the carrier a while to move the hull, which started changing course by 15 degrees. At the time she was struck, the officers on the bridge heard a huge bang and the wardroom was soon filled with black smoke. Tsukamoto summarized the damage to the *Shōkaku* in the following words:[33] "Unfortunately, one bomb dropped by SBD hit the starboard after part near the bridge. As a result, crucial communications and command systems were damaged, the flight deck became wrinkled, making it [even more] impossible to take off and land, and the large-caliber guns couldn't be used. Due to the radio antenna damage, we could not transmit any messages and relied on flag signals."

Despite this description and the fire still not being under control, two essential parts of the *Shōkaku* were fully functional—the boilers and engines were intact. Thus, she could maneuver to evade the threats coming from the air. Also, luckily for her, one Dauntless failed to deliver its intended blow. While pulling out of a dive, Ens. John D. Wingfield realized that he was unable to release the bomb. Once informed about this by his colleagues, he decided to turn around and try his chances again. He didn't achieve any tangible results. Other SBDs, escorted by Bull and Bain, headed back. The Wildcats were soon attacked by two Zeros, piloted by Abe and PO1c Kawanishi. Taking advantage of the altitude and speed, the Japanese closed in from above and from the rear. However, Kawanishi made a severe mistake. He incorrectly estimated the distance to Bain, who suddenly turned. The *Shōkaku*'s pilot failed to hit the rival with the first salvo and had to pull up to fly over Bain. The American pilot saw him and increased his speed until he was on the Zero's tail. Having no doubts about the identity of the plane, he fired a burst of machine guns that hit Kawanishi rapidly going up. His *kansen*, choked with black smoke, lost altitude and disappeared below. Bain, wrongly believing he had shot down an enemy fighter, attempted to find Bull. However, in the chaos of combat, he didn't see him. Bull also didn't respond on the radio. It turned out later that he did not return to the *Lexington*, probably shot down by the Japanese CAP. Gaining altitude, Bain was spotted by two more Zeros from the *Shōkaku*—one above him and the other on his tail. Since he didn't want to start another long dogfight, he fired one machine gun salvo to deter the enemy and escaped into a thick cloud.[34]

Escorted by four Wildcats, the TBDs emerged at about six thousand feet from the clouds and gradually approached the carrier from the south. Okajima's *shōtai* was the closest to them and rushed to disperse the formation of the torpedo bombers. Before doing so, though, they needed to get rid of the escorts. Once the Zeros had jumped out of the clouds, they surprised the F4Fs with their speed. Ens. Dale W. Peterson and Ens. Richard M. Rowell were cornered by these more agile enemy planes and fell victim to them momentarily. Only Gayler boldly challenged one *kansen* and reported shooting it down before hiding in the clouds when two other Zeros started to pursue him. After three minutes the *Lexington*'s pilot came out at about one thousand feet and sighted a carrier, a cruiser, and a destroyer. Gayler stumbled on the *Zuikaku*. Because there were no Zeros above her and the Japanese didn't open antiaircraft fire, he made two complete circles. Gayler thought that VT-2 would show up soon to hit the second carrier, but then he caught a glimpse of the second group of enemy vessels fifteen miles to the east. He could see the burning *Shōkaku* and black smoke coming out of her. Since the torpedo bombers were unlikely to hit the *Zuikaku*, he went to the rendezvous point but couldn't find any Allied planes. His situation was even more complicated, because the section leader called him on the radio but could not get an answer.[35]

Even though Brett was unaware of the *Zuikaku* nearby, he was determined to finish off the *Shōkaku*. The sacrifice of VF-2 lured most of the CAP's attention, and it seemed that the only obstacle was the antiaircraft defense. However, Iwamoto's *shōtai* emerged out of nowhere on the last stretch. The Zeros targeted two TBDs piloted by Ens. Thomas Bash and Ens. Norman Sterrie, who were forced to fan out to the left. Despite Iwamoto's advantage over the torpedo bombers, his *shōtai* couldn't get closer, because if they had done so the bombers' guns might have taken them down.

At 1142 hours Bash was the first to drop a torpedo, six hundred yards from the *Shōkaku*'s port side. Sterrie went even closer and released his fish at four hundred yards from the starboard quarter. The *Shōkaku* had been turning to the right ever since the SBDs had commenced their dive. The rest of VT-2 went for independent pushes on the starboard side, missing the chance to execute a coordinated anvil attack. All of the Devastators had dropped their torpedoes by 1150 hours, but since they were too far from the carrier, she evaded them without any problems. Seeing several explosions near the vessel from a distance, VT-2 reported as many as five direct hits, including by Bash and Sterrie. In reality, they failed to deliver a single one.[36]

The VT-2 attack is also connected with the Japanese myth regarding PO1c Miyazawa's death. The *Shōkaku* crew saw him defending the carrier until the bitter end. According to the carrier's report, the *shōtaichō* deliberately rammed the torpedo plane leading the formation and then crashed into another, falling with it into the sea. At least two observers confirmed this story, demonstrating his bravery and sacrifice. However, as we know from the American report, the *Lexington* did not lose any torpedo bombers during this attack. Thus, the version most likely to be true is that Gayler shot down Miyazawa in the dogfight and on the way down he tried to crash into TBDs but without success.[37]

On completing the attack, the *Lexington* striking group set a return course. VT-2, which was withdrawing, was harassed by Iwamoto's *shōtai*, which focused on Bash. After a few passes, they shifted their attention to the next TBD, believing that one well-aimed salvo would be enough to down the bomber.[38] The American planes scattered and looked for a way to escape into the cloud. In the meantime, Bain appeared and joined the bombers, which made the Japanese more hesitant to continue the pursuit. But when the onslaught was over, the Zeros were eager to take revenge. Okabe's *shōtai* attacked three out of four SBDs from the CLAG section. At this stage of the fight over the *Shōkaku*, the Japanese had the upper hand and went for easy victories. The dive bombers had to scatter, but eventually they were hunted down. Only Ens. Marvin M. Haschke returned to the carrier.

Haschke stumbled on the lost Gayler during his return journey. He informed his colleague about VS-2's two hits scored on the *Shōkaku*. Then they both intercepted a radio message from Ault saying that he and his radioman had been severely wounded and that his Dauntless was all shot up. CLAG informed them about the plan to ditch on the water, but before that, Haschke wanted to be credited for scoring one hit on the enemy carrier.[39]

In the end, VB-2 did not take part in the attack on the *Shōkaku*. Hamilton tried to track down the carrier by listening to VT-2's radio traffic but missed it by several miles. During the fruitless search for the enemy, he was sighted by Iwamoto's *shōtai*. The *Zuikaku* fighters saw their twofold numerical disadvantage, though, even including Okajima's *shōtai*, so they didn't want to try their dogfighting skills.[40] Hamilton finally decided to set a return course. His SBDs dumped the bombs only after twenty minutes, hoping that at the last moment they would find out about the carriers' location on the radio or run across them.[41]

The *Lexington* striking group reported hitting the *Shōkaku* with two bombs and five torpedoes. Its performance was not very impressive and accounted for only one bomb hit, which didn't cause critical damage to the carrier. The *Lexington*'s bombers undoubtedly missed the opportunity to finish the *Yorktown*'s job. In particular, the poor outcome of the torpedo attacks by both VT-2 and VT-5 wasted the remarkable effort of VB-5 and VS-2. Nevertheless, when the Americans left the area, they were convinced that the *Shōkaku* was so severely mauled that she would sink soon. However, future events would show that reality vastly differed from expectations.

The American losses linked to the MO Kidō Butai included VF-2's three F4Fs and VB-5's two SBDs. Some other planes also did not return to TF 17, and their story will be covered in the following part of the book. When the Japanese CAP was defending the *Shōkaku*, it lost two pilots—PO2c Ichinose and PO1 Miyazawa. Three Zeros from the *Shōkaku* and four Zeros from the *Zuikaku* were damaged, particularly PO1c Kawanishi's plane, which was hit by thirty bullets and barely stayed in the air. Additionally, some of the *Shōkaku*'s Zeros soon ran out of fuel and were forced to ditch. Four pilots made an emergency landing: WO Abe, PO2c Okabe, PO3c Tanaka, and Sea1c Imamura. They were all rescued by the *Furutaka* and the *Yūgure*. The remaining three *kansen*, piloted by PO1c Minami, PO1c Kawanishi, and PO3c Komachi respectively, found their way back on the *Zuikaku*.[42]

After verifying the individual claims, the *Shōkaku* air group declared twenty-one victories (eight F4Fs, ten SBDs, and three TBDs), including seventeen confirmed victories (five F4Fs, nine SBDs, and three TBDs). The *Zuikaku* air group claimed twenty-four victories, including twenty-two confirmed F4Fs, SBDs, TBDs added together.[43] Iwamoto recalled that after about one hour of the intense dogfight, his uniform was soaking wet with sweat and his face had turned gray due to physical and mental exhaustion.[44]

As for the *Shōkaku* herself, three 1000-pound bombs were enough to put her out of action for the rest of the battle. Although she maintained her ability to navigate at high speed and the fires on the flight deck and the hangar deck were slowly extinguished, any other hit, especially with a torpedo, could end in a calamity.[45] The explosions, splinters, and flames killed 76 crew members

PHOTO 15 ■ *Shōkaku*'s forward elevator after the first hit *Fukuchi, Kūbo* Shōkaku *Kaiseki*

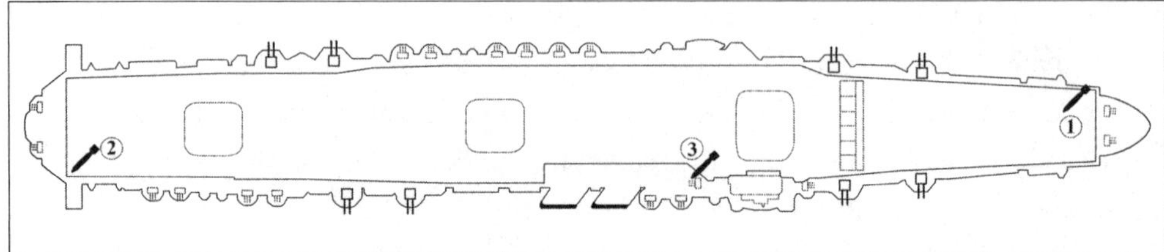

FIGURE 2 ■ Hits scored on the *Shōkaku*

and wounded 114. Thirty-three men were missing, including many blown into the sea without a chance of being rescued. In his memoirs, Fukuchi lists all the people lost on the *Shōkaku* and presents photos showing the extent of the damage dealt by the dive bombers on 8 May.[46] Dr. Naohiro Watanabe, circling tiny provisional rooms with patients, sympathized with the victims. He regretted that the carrier wasn't better prepared to provide emergency medical help to those in critical situations. His conclusion could have been a precious lesson for the Nippon Kaigun.[47]

The *Shōkaku* had to be withdrawn from the battlefield because of its nonoperational deck. At 1150 hours Takagi assigned both cruisers from his squadron to assist and protect her.[48] After the initial setback, at 1200 hours Sumita's *shōtai* also scrambled from the *Zuikaku* and rushed to the sister ship to provide additional help if any enemy planes appeared in the area.[49] The news about the strike on TF 17 had already reached the 5th Kōkū Sentai, but the messages were very chaotic and needed to be confirmed. Hara prepared to accommodate the planes from the attack mission and keep the *Shōkaku* away from any threat. Relying on residual information, he believed they had won the battle and avoided losses. However, the attack on the *Lexington* and the *Yorktown* was even more dramatic than the struggle to defend the *Shōkaku*.

Chapter 14

"TO TO TO, ZENGUN TOTSUGEKI SEYO" ("ALL FORCES ATTACK!")

The *Lexington* Mortally Wounded, the *Yorktown* Hit

Guided by Kanno, the MO Kidō Butai striking group found its way to TF 17 without any delays. Takahashi had been in the air for barely two hours when he spotted two carriers ahead, marked later as appearing at coordinates 15° 10' S, 154° 52' E. Visibility was up to ten miles, with some swirling clouds at eight hundred meters. The *hikōtaichō* was at three thousand meters with his nineteen *kambaku*, while Ema's fourteen bombers remained on his left side. Slightly below this, Shimazaki led all eighteen *kankō*, and their approach was protected by eighteen fighters above. At 1100 hours Takahashi passed the order to "totsugeki jumbi taikei tsukure" ("assume the attack formation").[1] Vals started to climb up to prepare for the dive, and Kates descended to proceed with the torpedo attack. Lt. Yūzō Tsukamoto's Zeros split into two groups—six fighters escorted Ichihara while Kanō's *shōtai* placed themselves above Shimazaki.[2] Hoashi's Zeros were supposed to be used as the cover during the initial approach, because they remained at the same altitude to clash with the Wildcats.[3]

At about 1105 hours Takahashi steered south to windward with the dive bombers, but the torpedo bombers stayed on the same track. Five minutes later Shimazaki finally ordered all forces to attack—"*to to to, zengun totsugeki seyo.*"[4] The *Shōkaku*'s Vals were already able to see the *Lexington*'s impressive

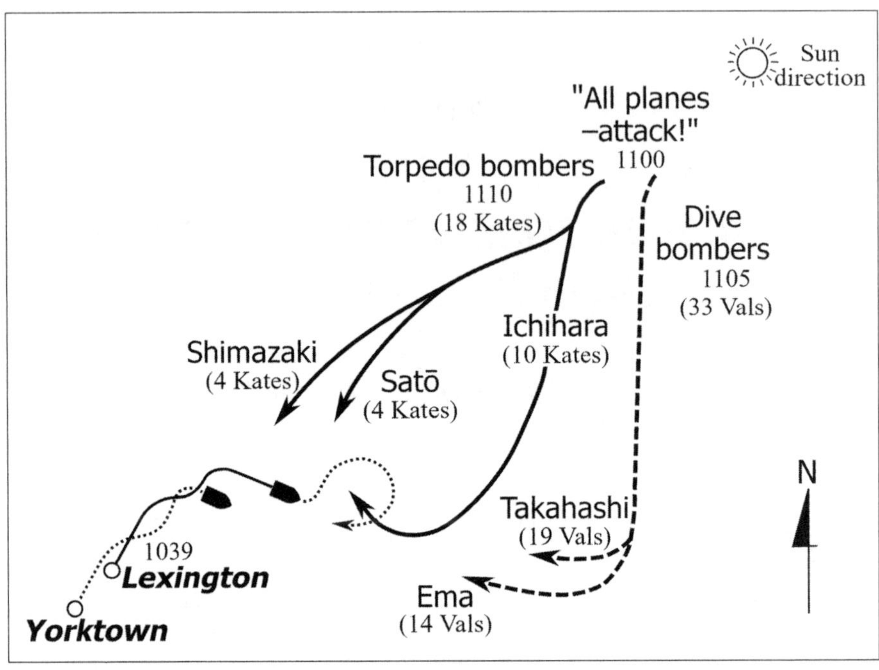

MAP 14 ■ Japanese attack on TF 17, 8 May

silhouette. "The carrier was huge like a cow," recalled Lieutenant Mifuku. He felt that the time to avenge the raid on Tokyo in April had come but wrongly believed that "Lady Lex" had participated. The other Japanese pilots could discern the screening vessels in a defensive formation, waiting for them. PO1c Suzuki, one of the *kambaku*'s pilots from the *Shōkaku*, had a bad hunch. Everything looked different when he was in the Indian Ocean and had participated in the sinking of the British light carrier *Hermes*. Now, the Americans seemed well prepared for the onslaught.[5]

Indeed, TF 17 was aware of the incoming danger for almost an hour. At about 1000 hours SBDs returning from a reconnaissance mission reported the sighting of twelve unidentified aircraft with a bearing of 355 degrees forty-five miles from TF 17. This warning, however, was not confirmed by radars. Gill delegated VF-42's two sections to check the sector. At 1007 hours Fletcher ordered Fitch to send additional fighters to CAP, expecting an imminent

Japanese attack. Just a minute later, observers in the *Yorktown* noticed a single aircraft at fifteen miles bearing 40 degrees. The intruder was one of three flying boats from the Yokohama Kaigun Kōkūtai, which had taken off from Tulagi early that morning. McCormack and Haas started chasing the Mavis, and the latter downed her in a single-sided fight. The base in Tulagi realized that Ensign Ōmori's aircraft and all eight of its crew were lost no sooner than 1130 hours, but believed that she had probably reached a location close to the enemy carrier task force.[6]

TF 17 had much more time to prepare for the defense than had the MO Kidō Butai. At 1011 hours the *Lexington* warned about the incoming Zeros' bearing of 25 degrees. Although it soon turned out that they were SBDs, at 1012 hours the *Yorktown*'s CXAM radar picked up a formation of enemy bombers approaching the group from the west. On hearing the news, ten SBDs took off from the *Lexington* to help the Wildcats in CAP. This unusual use of dive bombers for defense duty was not popular among the crews, who would have preferred to take part in the attack on the Japanese carriers.[7] However, as soon as they were airborne, the observers in the *Lexington* spotted a heavily smoking aircraft at twenty miles bearing 17 degrees. It was Steffenhagen's damaged Devastator and five SBDs that had been sent on the reconnaissance in the morning. Starting at 1023 hours the carrier slowed to fifteen knots and accommodated the bombers. Soon after, she changed course to 28 degrees, and at 1042 hours increased speed to twenty knots. By 1050 hours the last three SBDs from the scouting missions had returned to the deck.[8]

When the *Lexington*'s CXAM-1 radar picked up an incoming large group of enemy planes at sixty-eight miles bearing 20 degrees at 1055 hours, eight F4Fs and eighteen SBDs were already circling over both American carriers.[9] Since four Wildcats had been aloft for more than an hour, Gill feared they would not have enough fuel to defend TF 17. At 1058 hours he got approval to send nine more fighters to CAP. Knowing that the Japanese would be approaching TF 17 at any time, he transmitted "Hey Rube!" to all aircraft in the air, asking them to leave their positions immediately and defend their carriers. Between 1101 and 1106 hours, five F4Fs and five SBDs took off from the *Lexington*, and she increased her speed to twenty-five knots. Gill ordered Ramsey's section to climb to ten thousand feet and fly for thirty miles on the course of twenty degrees as quickly as possible to get more information about the approaching group. The remaining two Wildcats were to descend to the lower altitude and await the arrival of enemy torpedo bombers.[10]

The *Yorktown* was also vigorously preparing to defend TF 17. At 1103 hours she scrambled four more F4Fs, and Gill decided to split the CAP into two groups. The first one, consisting of nine fighters, was to engage the enemy at a distance of approximately fifteen to twenty miles from TF 17, flying at a low altitude and focusing on torpedo bombers. The second group, consisting of eight fighters, was to form the second obstacle against the planes directly attacking the carriers.[11]

Thanks to the early detection, Agnes Red had a chance to attack the enemy striking group before it split into smaller groups. The F4Fs saw fifty to sixty

TABLE 43 **American CAP during the Japanese Attack on TF 17, 8 May 1942**

Unit	Section	Pilot
VF-2	Doris Red	Lt. Fred Borries
		Lt. (jg) Marion Dufilho
	Doris White	Lt. (jg) Clark Rinehart
		Ens. Newton Mason
	Agnes Red	Lt. Cdr. Paul Ramsey
		Ens. George Markham
		Ens. Edward Sellstrom
	Agnes White	Ens. Willard Eder
		Ens. Leon Haynes
VF-42	Wildcat Brown	Lt. Vincent McCormack
		Ens. Walter Haas
	Wildcat Orange	Lt. (jg) Arthur Brassfield
		Lt. (jg) Duran Mattson
	Wildcat Red	Lt. Cdr. James Flatley
		Lt. (jg) Richard Crommelin
	Wildcat Blue	Lt. (jg) Brainard Macomber
		Ens. Edgar Bassett

Sources: NARA: USS *Yorktown*, May 8; Lundstrom, *First Team*, 245.

Japanese aircraft cruising at 10,000 and 13,050 feet, stacked in different layers, about fifteen to twenty miles from TF 17. Ramsey identified them as a mix of fighters and bombers and began climbing to chase them, but going after the enemy at the higher altitude was never the Wildcat's strong point. Thus, the enemy passed by without even noticing him. In reality, he sighted only the dive bombers, which would probably not bother stopping and engaging the fighters.[12]

At 1111 hours Gill warned pilots on CAP to remain vigilant as Agnes Red proceeded with the attack. He tried to find out from Ramsey the altitude at which the enemy planes were pouring in, but the remaining Wildcats were forced to look for the Japanese planes on their own due to communication disruptions. Arriving at the designated location, Wildcat Red found no enemy torpedo bombers, and Flatley was convinced they were still ahead of him. The nearby Agnes White also failed to intercept the foe, who had passed over, covered by thick clouds. After two minutes, the pilots realized they had missed the striking group. They began a hasty retreat. Two SBDs also left the advanced positions, about five miles to the north, and rushed to defend the carrier.[13]

The reason why the Wildcats missed the enemy striking group at the early stage of the approach is explained well by S. Mori. First, the Japanese torpedo planes were moving toward TF 17 at a higher than expected altitude. Second, they were much faster than TBDs, even when armed with torpedoes, which made the calculations about their distance to the carriers inaccurate.[14] Closing in on the formation of the American warships, Shimazaki recognized the silhouette of a *Saratoga*-class carrier and, a few miles away, another one—a *Yorktown*-class. Even without ten Kates, lost during the reconnaissance and dusk attack mission the previous day, Shimazaki was convinced he could sink both carriers. At 1110 hours, soon after he passed the order to attack, Ichihara, with his ten torpedo bombers, steered left toward the *Lexington*, while Shimazaki, with eight torpedo bombers, veered right to develop an attack against the *Yorktown*. However, according to the initial plan, Lieutenant Satō was to lead four *kankō* directly toward the *Yorktown*, and Shimazaki himself, having at hand the last four Kates, intended to strike at the crucial moment, depending on his assessment of the situation. Having the support of fifteen Zeros at five hundred meters, the *Zuikaku*'s *hikōtaichō* believed that the torpedo bombers' crews would prove their skills in a well-developed anvil attack despite the disadvantage in numbers.[15]

The Japanese were surprised by the strength of the screening force, which immediately opened antiaircraft fire from all their guns. WO Kanazawa from the *Shōkaku* remembered this moment as follows:[16] "I was baffled by the large number of the big and smaller guns of the carriers and the other ships. At 0900 hours [Japanese time], we sighted the enemy task force. We immediately launched an assault. The barrage was insane. I was worried that my wings could be blown off, so I sped up as much as I could to head for the torpedo attack."

Pursuing the enemy dive bombers, Agnes Red retreated toward TF 17 and slowly gained altitude. Ramsey wondered whether they could surprise and effectively scatter the Japanese formation. Sellstrom separated from the section without permission and went alone against some Kates, Satō's group, to be exact. The torpedo bombers were surprised, since he appeared out of nowhere from above. They tried to defend themselves, but after two passes Sellstrom downed the *kankō* piloted by PO2c Idehara. PO2c Nishizawa witnessed the death of his colleagues:[17] "Before we could move into the position to begin the torpedo attack, we were caught by the American fighter. We veered to the right and left while holding the heavy torpedo. I also threw aside the radio and grabbed the 7.7mm machine gun. The Grumman fighter passed once, twice, headed forward while shooting and finally turned around to attack again. At first, the plane in my formation was shot down."

PO1c Makino's *shōtai* joined the fight to protect Satō's formation somewhat late. However, after a few passes, they chased away Sellstrom. The first dogfight over TF 17 finished without any victory. At the same time, VS-5's eight alerted SBDs moved against Satō, which focused most of the Americans' attention. Despite the dive bombers' best intentions of contributing to the defense of TF 17, they soon fell victim to Tsukamoto and PO1c Kanō's *shōtai*, which took a position above the Kates. Much slower SBDs, not intended for CAP duty, became easy prey for six Zeros, which shot down aircraft piloted by Lt. (jg) Earl Johnson, Ens. Kendall Campbell, Ens. Samuel Underhill, and Ens. Edward Kinzer. More Japanese fighters were swarming the American dive bombers from minute to minute, preventing VS-5 from successfully chasing after Kates.[18]

The positive aspect of focusing on Satō's group was that Ichihara and Shimazaki now had a much easier approach to their targets. Since the *Shōkaku*'s torpedo planes had made a slightly wider turn, they were a little later than their *Zuikaku* counterparts. They split into two groups to proceed with an anvil attack on the *Lexington*. Lt. Katsuo Iwamura's 2nd *chūtai* aimed for the big carrier's port side with four *kankō*, while Ichihara's 1st *chūtai* and the remaining six planes veered starboard. PO1c Ishikawa from Iwamura's *chūtai* described this memorable act of going for "Lady Lex": "Compared to this one, the other ships were small. When we sighted her, the American carrier steamed southwest, and we approached from port quarter side. Her speed was 25 to 28 knots. Judging from the wake, she couldn't make more than 30 knots. The anti-aircraft fire was tremendous, the sky was full of smoke, the machine gun flashes and the planes were surrounded by fireballs like red and white popsicles. It was terribly noisy."[19]

Despite the initial plan to wait for developments, Shimazaki saw the gravity of the situation and was the first to lead the 1st *chūtai* against the *Yorktown*'s port side. The Japanese bombers could sense the trap they were going into as all the screening vessels were furiously firing at them. The crews had the impression that every gun was pointed at them. Still, Shimazaki's *shōtai* got close enough to drop their torpedoes at 1119 hours. Seeing the wakes, Captain Buckmaster immediately ordered a hard turn to the starboard and to speed up to thirty knots. Two fish were not enough to threaten the *Yorktown*, which smoothly evaded them. Theoretically, WO Kanazawa's *shōtai* now had a chance to pinpoint the carrier, but the reality was different. *Shōtaichō* recalled how the attack failed: "I looked at the second plane in the formation from time to time and considered the best moment to drop my torpedo. However, the American carrier changed course to evade them. The release point was messed up, so I had to make some corrections. Additionally, one Grumman attacked from about 1000 meters to the port. Shortly after dropping the torpedo, the second bomber [in formation] started spewing black smoke from its engine. This plane approached me, and the two of us waved at each other. Then, he fell down and crashed into the sea."[20]

The *kankō* shot down by the Americans was commanded by PO2 Hiwatashi. He didn't make it to the point where he could release his fish. The *Zuikaku*'s report later claimed that he deliberately crashed into one of the heavy cruisers, but that wasn't true.[21] Kanazawa, however, had more luck and avoided destruction. Once he had dropped the torpedo, aiming for the port quarter, he pulled up and set a return course. When the fish was still in the water and going for the target, the *shōtaichō* quickly took a photo of the *Yorktown* for evidence purposes. When they were a few hundred meters away, his radio operator, PO2c Ōta, informed him that he had been shot in his right leg and couldn't move his thigh. There was nothing Kanazawa could do at that time, so he told Ōta to hold on until they withdrew to a safer position. The crew didn't see the effect of their attack and had to leave the area as soon as possible so as not to attract the fighters' attention. Although Shimazaki's group had hoped for success, there is no doubt that its approach ended with no tangible results.

Relying on Shimazaki's testimony,[22] many historians repeated for years that he charged the *Lexington*.[23] However, it was Satō who had to shorten the path because his *kankō* were in grave danger, harassed by Wildcats and antiaircraft artillery. After the loss of one plane at the very beginning, it was more reasonable to attack the *Lexington*'s port bow, passing in front of the *Minneapolis*. The American guns were still all pointed in the direction of Satō's *chūtai*, which descended low enough to proceed with the final approach. Satō led three bombers and dreamed of finishing earnestly what he had commenced. However, when the torpedo bombers were about fourteen hundred meters from the carrier, out of the corner of his eye he saw PO1c Yamada's plane flashing with red light. He had been hit by a 5-inch shell from the *Lexington*, and a few seconds later he splashed into the water. Satō and WO Ni'ino, who was the only one left in the *chūtai*, caught a glimpse of the faces of Yamada's crew as they were going down. They felt terrified but couldn't think about their fate for too long. "One second, two seconds, three seconds"—counting out loud so they knew when to release the torpedoes felt like it took centuries. They finally decided to drop their fish at 1118 hours, aiming for the port bow. But, watching *Lexington*'s reaction and her sharp turn to port, Satō quickly realized that they might not have hit the target. He knew deep down that they had released the torpedoes too early. Still, the barrage incited by seven screening vessels adjacent to the carrier was so extreme that they didn't endure the pressure. The *shōtaichō* was impressed by the steadfast formation of the enemy and how the American cruisers and destroyers massively contributed to the battle, which also demonstrated the beauty of orderly maneuvers seen from above. Once the attack had been completed, he sped up to get out of the ring of death, followed by the last surviving plane in the *chūtai*. Ni'ino's radio operator, PO2c Nishizawa, admitted later that it was an unforgettable moment: "After doing my job, just right after I set the return course to the ship, I suddenly felt the fear. The concentrated fire from the ring formation was so intense that I thought my body curled up. There was a column of water rising in the distance, but I wasn't sure if it was our torpedo. During the withdrawal, our external fuel tank on the right wing was hit. We were safe as we had used up all the fuel from this tank at the very beginning. This must have been extremely lucky."[24]

But they were not all so lucky. One lone bullet from a small-caliber antiaircraft gun penetrated the lower part of the torpedo bomber's fuselage and ripped through Ni'ino's back, going straight into his heart. The *shōtaichō* was mortally wounded, and Nishizawa saw a lot of blood in his seat. He tried to stop the bleeding but Ni'ino was already dead. The death of the plane's commander at the last moment was very unfortunate, but the other two crew members could still save themselves, so Sea1c Ishihara concentrated on withdrawing from the area.

The charge of the *Zuikaku*'s torpedo bombers against both American carriers was costly, because Shimazaki lost three planes and their crews out of eight planes and one senior airman in another bomber. What was worse, he didn't score any hits despite the unit report's claim that it sank the *Saratoga* and the *Lexington*.[25] If the Japanese wished to "scratch one flattop" in the Battle of the Coral Sea, Ichihara had to corner the *Lexington* in the next few minutes.

Benefiting from the enemy's maneuvers in its attempt to evade Satō's torpedoes, the *Shōkaku*'s *kankō* descended to thirty meters and significantly reduced the distance to the carrier. Ichihara, with six planes, went for the port, while Iwamura, with the remaining four planes, closed the pincer movement from the other side. PO1c Matsuyama's Kate from the 1st *chūtai* was the first to drop the torpedo from about six hundred meters. Captain Sherman ordered the rudder to be turned right, but turning the 33,000-ton carrier smoothly was never easy. Matsuyama was followed by Ichihara and PO1c Shigeta, flying slightly behind and closer to the bow, and then by the planes piloted by Lt. Yano, PO1c Kodama, and PO3c Satō.[26] Six torpedoes plummeted into the water and headed straight for the port side. From Sherman's perspective, fish were coming in from both sides, and he maneuvered with a full rudder both ways, which he considered the best option to avoid them.[27]

In the meantime, Iwamura's *chūtai* veered slightly to the right to drop the torpedoes from the starboard quarter. It was still very dangerous to approach the carrier, and PO1c Ishikawa's plane suddenly shuddered due to the close blast from the antiaircraft shell. His aircraft was fine, but he later described his feelings at this point: "Particularly torpedo bombers, if they didn't press hard, they would not score a hit, so the anti-aircraft defense was firing fiercely. It was like in the old times when you put a piece of charcoal in a clay pot with a hole at the bottom and fan it from below; then you could see tremendous sparkles. Also, the noise was much louder than I had imagined, and I think it was good that I returned alive. When I recalled what happened in later years, I quivered."[28]

Ishikawa was more fortunate than Yano, who got hit by a high-caliber shell soon after he released the torpedo. Although the *shōtaichō*'s pilot tried to pull up, the bomber fell like a rock into the sea. The Americans later claimed that VS-2, particularly Lt. (jg) William E. Hall, had an important role in distracting Iwamura's *chūtai*. But none of the Japanese primary sources or testimonies mention that SBDs were on their way then. In reality, it was the TF 17 antiaircraft defense that wreaked havoc among the enemy planes. The *Shōkaku*'s four remaining Kates crossed in front of the two destroyers and the *Minneapolis* to proceed with the attack on the *Lexington*'s starboard side, but this is how they attracted the enemy gunners' attention. About two thousand meters from the target, PO2c Akaishi's plane met its destiny and set ablaze in the air, soon crashing into the water. In the following seconds, Iwamura's *kankō* was torched and finished the run by splashing into the sea. The *chūtai* had been reduced to half of its original numbers yet pushed against the carrier so that it did not seem as if their colleagues had died in vain. They knew the ship's "belly" was the best spot to aim for because a potential hit there could cause severe damage. Finally, they dropped their torpedoes when Ishikawa and PO1c Yoshitomo descended at two hundred meters and got to within nine hundred meters of the carrier. Despite the widely known version, they weren't attacking the *Minneapolis*.[29] The determination to encircle the *Lexington* paid off. The well-coordinated yet very costly approach took its toll on the carrier.

At about 1120 hours the *Lexington*, which used every opportunity to outmaneuver the torpedoes, was struck forward of the port forward gun gallery.[30] As S. Johnston recalled, "the carrier shuddered under our feet, and a heavy blast spouted mingled flame."[31] This hit appeared serious but wasn't dangerous for the survival of the ship. At the place where the torpedo exploded, there were seven layers of steel plate creating between four and six compartments, which prevented water from leaking into the magazine or into any other inhabited compartment. Still, the shock from the explosion disabled the hydraulic system that operated the two elevators, which both dropped onto their safety catches.[32]

At 1121 hours there was another hit. The second torpedo smashed a little farther aft, opposite the bridge. Fire rooms 2, 4, and 6 were flooding, but the water was being controlled by the pumps. The damage control team secured six boilers. The initial report mentioned the saltwater contamination in fuel tanks and an oil leak, which Kinkaid on the *Astoria* could see on the sea's surface and smell in the air.[33] The *Lexington* maintained twenty-five knots despite the significant loss of power. However, the most harmful effect of the torpedo hit was the listing—6 degrees to the port side.[34] She was already not in the best condition, and the second wave of the Japanese bombers was seen from her deck.

When they escaped the enemy formation, Ichihara's *chūtai* saw two enormous explosions and the carrier listing. "Gyorai meichū, banzai!" ("Torpedo hit!") Matsuyama shouted for joy. On the other side of the carrier, the decimated 2nd *chūtai* could also see what was happening and could hear the happy news on the radio. Unexpectedly and strangely, the enemy antiaircraft fire had abated, and thus the surviving Kates could withdraw.[35] The *Shōkaku*'s torpedo bomber group may have felt satisfied, and it reported its amazing performance. The unit's report said that as many as nine hits had been scored out of ten dropped fish: seven against the *Saratoga*-class carrier, which was sunk, and two against the battleship, which was set ablaze and started to leak oil. Compared to the losses of the *Zuikaku*'s group, its losses were slightly

PHOTO 16 ■ *Shōkaku*'s dive bomber a moment before the strike against the *Lexington*
Mori, Akatsuki

lighter and accounted for three *kankō* commanded by Lieutenant Iwamura, Lieutenant Yano, and PO2c Akaishi respectively.[36]

The reason why the American antiaircraft artillery let the Japanese torpedo bombers escape was the appearance of the second wave of invaders. Cutting through the overcast sky, Takahashi saw several wakes from above, which portrayed the struggle of his colleagues to sink both carriers. He stuck to the original plan to deploy the *Shōkaku*'s dive bombers against the *Lexington* while the *Zuikaku*'s group was attacking the *Yorktown*.[37] Lieutenant Mifuku praised the *hikōtaichō* for having perfect navigation sense, because flying to windward helped the Vals fool most American fighters. What's more, the formation was escorted by Hoashi's nine Zeros, which were waiting for any Wildcats to appear at the last stage of the route.

The *Shōkaku*'s nineteen aircraft were cruising at five thousand meters when Takahashi waved his wings at 1121 hours to indicate that they should commence the dive. He led his *shōtai*, followed by Lt. Masao Yamaguchi's nine-plane 1st *chūtai* and Mifuku's seven-plane 2nd *chūtai*. Notwithstanding the uninterrupted approach, they were now faced with the furious American antiaircraft fire and had to find a way to deliver hits. Yamaguchi's *chūtai* commenced the onslaught, coming in threes. When WO Kokubu's *shōtai* was diving, flying valiantly through the exploding shells, the crews noticed that the *Lexington* suddenly listed to the port side. PO1c Suzuki pressed hard, aiming for the after deck. Finally, he released a 250-kg bomb and pulled out of the dive. The crews and the *shōtaichō* looked back. Suddenly, Suzuki shouted to his commander, "It's a hit," and Kokubu replied, "Yes, Suzuki, it's a hit."[38]

Their celebration was interrupted by Doris White and Doris Red, which rushed against some of the Vals from the carrier's port side. Since the American fighters were at about thirty-eight hundred meters, they had to climb up to disrupt the approach of the other bombers. The Wildcats were soon challenged by the *Shōkaku*'s six Zeros, which ripped into them and started a chaotic dogfight.[39] Lieutenant Yamamoto was among them and recalled that moment: "Our unit's mission was to engage the attacking Grumman fighters to ease the charge of the bomber group, so we rushed in determined. We had to be an obstacle in front of them, and I thought I was a little far away, but I started shooting. I could see the pilot in the cockpit in the distance who dodged the bullets, but I resigned from closing the distance and headed for the next target."[40]

Warrant Officer Kokubu's *shōtai* recovered from the dive and one enemy fighter emerged on Petty Officer 2nd Class Ōura's back. The Vals tried to help each other to form a defense against the Wildcats. More of them joined the fight and blindly machine-gunned the F4F, which broke away and disappeared. The Japanese thought that they had downed this aircraft, but the pilot had only given up and escaped.

The next to charge the *Lexington* was Takahashi's *shōtai*. Their dive was directly escorted by Hoashi's three Zeros, which experienced the brutality of American guns of all calibers. Soon after, Mifuku's *chūtai* headed down, and it took them less than a minute to drop from five thousand meters to four hundred meters and release the bombs. The *chūitaichō* recovered from the 50-degree dive only at ten to fifteen meters above the sea's surface and was sprayed by the enemy's 1.1-inch bullets. Although the crew could hear rattling on the fuselage and wings, they were quite safe. The more important thing was that they and Mifuku's observer saw the bomb slamming the carrier's deck. The attack of *Shōkaku*'s dive bombers was over by 1126 hours. The crews claimed to have scored at least ten hits out of nineteen bombs dropped on the *Saratoga*-class carrier, which soon went down due to extensive damage caused by the torpedo and bomb explosions.[41] Since the later clash with the returning American striking group wreaked a little havoc, it is hard to unequivocally state which bombers were lost during the strike on the *Lexington*. The American fighter pilots that were working closely with the antiaircraft defense reported two confirmed victories.[42]

The actual outcome of the Japanese attack on the *Lexington* included two direct hits and five near misses.[43] One bomb slammed into the after end of the port forward 5-inch gun gallery in the ready ammunition locker just outside the admiral's cabin. The other one also exploded on the port side, at the inboard side of the funnel above the flight deck. Two near misses were reported close aboard aft on the port side, although at first they were mistaken for torpedo hits, and one near miss wrecked a gig boat pocket on the port side. There were also two blasts close aboard the starboard side aft. Fragments killed and injured a number of men in the stack machine guns, sky aft, and the after signal station.[44] As R. Stern writes, the first hit inflicted extensive local damage, while the second caused significant casualties on the flight deck. More importantly, both started a brief, intense fire—one at the forward gun gallery and the other in the funnel lining. Viewed from the screening vessels, the carrier made a spectacular plume of flame and dense black smoke, which soon dissipated due to the quick consumption of propellant and the damage control team's effort to extinguish the fire.[45]

Regarding the visual damage to the *Lexington*, the *Shōkaku*'s returning Kates caught a glimpse of their colleagues' performance. Since the effects of the torpedo and bomb attack looked spectacular from above, Ichihara's radio operator started to persuade the *buntaichō* to cable about the sinking of the carrier, because he was convinced that she was having her final moments. Although they could see that she was still floating and Ichihara had doubts, he allowed PO1c Munakata to type by key "Saratoga gekichin" ("*Saratoga* sank"). This premature report, received by the 5th Kōkū Sentai's staff at 1125 hours, aroused huge excitement in the MO Kidō Butai, and it was extremely hard to clarify the report later.[46]

The last chord of the Japanese strike against TF 17 belonged to the *Zuikaku*'s dive bombers. They had the opportunity to change the face of the battle in their favor. Proceeding toward the *Yorktown*, Ema watched from a distance the bombs falling on the *Lexington*. He gave the signal to attack at 1125 hours. Like the other pilots, the *buntaichō* underlined the destructive power of the American antiaircraft defense. When he commenced the dive, he could hear the swish of the small-caliber bullets passing close to his canopy. A moment later he heard a pinging sound, meaning the plane had been hit. His observer and radio operator, WO Nozu, informed him that they had already descended to 1,500 meters. Ema pushed down hard, and in a few seconds he was at 600 meters. He knew he couldn't go below 450 meters, because his altimeter worked with a 50-meter delay in a steep dive. When he reached that level, Nozu notified him they were ready to drop the bomb. The *buntaichō* kept his eye on the bombsight and released the lever. During the pull-up, he could not see the result of the attack, so he relied on his observer. Their plane was about to go into the sea when Nozu shouted, "Atatta!" ("It's a hit!"). To avoid the revenge of the antiaircraft defense, Ema swung right and left unpredictably to mislead the enemy gunners.[47]

Other Vals dived after Ema one by one. Despite the effort of Brown to interrupt the attack in his Wildcat, the enemy was unfazed by such minimal resistance. Petty Officer 1st Class Hatakeyama flew away first, followed by Sea1c Egusa and then the rest. Some even descended to 250 meters. Petty Officer 1st Class Hori flew next to Lieutenant Kuzuhara and noticed his *shōtaichō* being hit by a shell. Initially the fire was small, but it spread along the fuselage during the plunge. Hori could see that Kuzuhara would not be able to finish his run. "No good," he thought, and seconds later the *shōtaichō* splashed into the sea very close to the *Yorktown*'s bridge.[48] One might think he intended to crash into the carrier, but the American sources do not mention this incident. Another Val that fell victim to TF 17's guns was piloted by Petty Officer 2nd Class Kamioka from the 2nd *chūtai*. These were the only losses of the *Zuikaku*'s dive bomber group. Ema believed that there was much less opposition than

Takahashi. However, he didn't translate it into a great result, although the Japanese report claimed that nine direct hits were scored on the *Yorktown*, which was set on fire and sunk afterward.[49]

In reality the carrier was directly hit only by one 250-kg semi-armor-piercing bomb at 1127 hours. It struck the flight deck, near frame 106, twenty-three feet forward of the second elevator and close to the island. The bomb pierced the flight deck and made a 14-inch hole, which was immediately patched up by a metal plate. It went down through the ready room, the hangar deck, and the second deck on an angle toward the starboard side. It then hit a beam and stanchion and angled back to port, piercing the third deck. A fire was reported in one fireroom. All lights were extinguished. Boilers No. 8 and 9 were secured, and then the firerooms were abandoned because the personnel were overcome by gases. Buckmaster asked about available speed and the main control team confirmed it was stable at twenty-four knots.[50]

Much less damage was caused by near misses. The first exploded when it made contact with the sea fifty feet from the starboard bow and caused minor damage to the antiaircraft artillery stations. Another semi-armor-piercing bomb exploded about fifteen feet below the water surface and about twenty feet from the port bow, denting the hull plating by two inches. Despite some leaking and the dense smoke and gases in many compartments, the *Yorktown* kept her ability to handle aircraft. The worst effect of the enemy attack was the killing of thirty-seven men in the Engineering Repair Party.[51]

The Japanese strike against TF 17 was over by 1132 hours. Most of the *Shōkaku*'s and *Zuikaku*'s bombers were already on the return course. Some Wildcats and SBDs continued to engage Zeros for the following few minutes. J. Lundstrom details those clashes and groups them into three melees: low altitude, medium altitude, and Flatley's dogfight. Besides fighters in CAP, several of the *Lexington*'s SBDs had just prematurely returned from the attack mission and encountered the Japanese planes. They started a chaotic engagement with Kates, defended by at least five Zeros. At 1129 hours Lt. (jg) Roy Hale's Dauntless was mistakenly shot down by the *Lexington*'s and other screening vessels' gunners while attempting to land. He crashed into the water near the *New Orleans*, and the crew did not survive. Another SBD, piloted by Ens. Frank McDonald, badly damaged in a duel with one of the Zeros, was

PHOTO 17 ■ Lieutenant Commander Ema, *buntaichō* of the *Zuikaku*'s dive bombers *NDL*

forced to try an emergency landing on the *Lexington*. The carrier, however, had not yet fully positioned herself out of the wind and gave a negative signal. At 1134 hours McDonald tried to make it anyway, and his aircraft slammed into the flight deck, broke an arresting wire, bounced over the corner of the deck, and fell into the sea. Thankfully, both crew members bailed out of the sinking plane and were soon rescued by the *Morris*.[52]

Agnes White, joining the melee between SBDs and Japanese planes in the vicinity of TF 17, claimed to shoot down two torpedo bombers and seriously damage another. Ichihara witnessed this scene, and since the *Shōkaku* lost two *kankō* between the attack and the return to the force, it is possible to say that one of them was Petty Officer 3rd Class Satō's aircraft.[53] The retreating *kambaku* were also attacked at low altitudes by Wildcat Brown and Wildcat Orange, which claimed two confirmed victories and one probable. The dogfight with the Zeros cost Americans several damaged SBDs and F4Fs. Brassfield said he had been incredibly lucky because his self-sealing fuel tank withstood ten enemy bullets.[54]

At mid-altitude, ten F4Fs, mostly from VF-2, engaged the *Shōkaku*'s five Zeros, which climbed up to cover the retreat of the friendly bombers. In the chaotic dogfight, Doris White disappeared in mysterious circumstances. Lt. (jg) Clark Rinehart and Ens. Newton Mason never returned to the *Lexington*. After a few minutes, the clash with the Japanese fighters was joined by three Wildcats, which returned from the attack on the MO Kidō Butai. However, their limited fuel supplies forced them to land on the carrier hastily. This engagement didn't result in any victories. Both sides withdrew with several damaged planes.

Finally, Wildcat Red and Wildcat Blue, led by Flatley, clashed with the *Zuikaku*'s five Zeros southeast of TF 17. At 1123 hours, when the F4Fs were returning from their advanced positions, they spotted six enemy aircraft about five miles from their carriers. Fighting separately and trying to take advantage of their planes' strengths, Flatley, Crommelin, Macomber, and, to a lesser extent, Bassett struggled with the enemy's numerical superiority, which was increased by the arrival of three additional Zeros. Chasing and escaping from the Japanese lasted almost twenty minutes; Crommelin reported downing two Zeros and Flatley one. The defenders claimed that they damaged three more fighters. Their only success was damaging the *Zuikaku*'s Zero, piloted by Petty Officer 2nd Class Ōkura, who was forced to make an emergency landing on Deboyne lagoon.[55] American losses amounted to Crommelin's Wildcat. His engine was damaged, so he made a water landing near the *Yorktown* at 1133 hours. Crommelin was soon picked up by the *Phelps*.[56]

In the battle over TF 17, the Americans lost three F4Fs and six SBDs. CAP comprised twenty fighters and was supported by twenty-four dive bombers from three squadrons. They reported shooting down sixteen fighters, eleven torpedo bombers, and five dive bombers.[57] Not to discount the pilots' effort, but it should be emphasized that the most critical contribution to the defense of both carriers came from antiaircraft artillery. By the time they withdrew, the actual Japanese losses were significantly smaller and accounted for seven Kates and at least five Vals. The next two hours would be a test for many damaged planes, which had to return to the carriers safely.[58] However, as we know from multiple Japanese accounts, the deadliest American asset was the sturdy defense formation with its antiaircraft artillery, which focused on the right targets and destroyed several bombers before they even had a chance to drop their torpedo or bomb.

Although it was located in the shadow of the central events, Warrant Officer Kanno's Kate became another victim of the attack on TF 17. When Kanno successfully guided Takahashi to the enemy, Petty Officer 1st Class Gotō immediately took the return course. At that stage, the bomber already lacked enough fuel to make it back to the *Shōkaku*. Kanno was about halfway between TF 17 and the MO Kidō Butai when Lieutenant (jg) Woollen and Ensign Adams from the *Yorktown* escort noticed him below. Petty Officer 1st Class Gotō also saw the fighters and tried to climb up to escape into the clouds, but the F4Fs were faster and appeared on his tail. After two quick salvos with the machine guns, the torpedo bomber went down in flames and crashed into the sea.[59] It is doubtful whether the Kate would have returned to the carrier, yet there was still a possibility that the crew could have been rescued by a detached destroyer. Their deaths were grieved by many in the *Shōkaku*, because the bravery and dedication they had demonstrated was exceptional even by the standard of the Nippon Kaigun. The proof of this came directly from Admiral Yamamoto, who promoted each crew member by two ranks and announced their sacrifice to the army, navy, and the entire nation on 1 January 1943:[60]

> The *Shōkaku* reconnaissance plane: WO Kanno / PO1c Gotō / PO2c Kishida
>
> On 8 May 1942, they participated in the Battle of the Coral Sea as a reconnaissance plane, spotted an enemy task force, secretly maintained contact, reported the exact data on the enemy regularly, rejoined the friendly striking group and guided it towards the enemy, knowing that their aircraft would run out of fuel and would be unable to return to the ship. Our aircraft gained a significant advantage in the battle thanks to their appropriate decisions. Then, they were engaged by the enemy fighters and were hit by bullets, resulting in a tragic death. Therefore, in recognition of their distinguished service, I hereby declare this to the entire armed forces.
>
> Commander in Chief of the Combined Fleet

Chapter 15

AFTERMATH

Damage Assessments, Recovery of Strike Aircraft, and Postponement of Operation MO Landing

Despite the precarious state of the *Lexington*, her planes on CAP were running out of fuel and needed to land immediately. At 1139 hours the first to appear on the deck were VS-2's two most damaged SBDs, piloted by Lt. (jg) William Hall and Lt. (jg) Chandler Swanson. Both planes were soon jettisoned to the sea. Since the *Yorktown*'s CXAM radar was damaged at the time and the *Lexington* was unable to transmit instructions to F4Fs on CAP, the air direction duty was temporarily assigned to the *Chester*.

At 1142 hours Fletcher and Fitch heard the first positive news about the *Lexington*. Fires in the hangar deck and the compartments on the port side had finally been extinguished. Just three minutes later, the bomb-hit hole was no longer smoking but both elevators were still out of action. Taking advantage of the carrier's semi-operational condition, six F4Fs and eight SBDs landed on the deck, including planes returning from the morning search.[1]

In the meantime, the *Yorktown* began recovering planes, with Sellstrom from Agnes Red landing first followed by Wildcat Brown and Wildcat Orange by 1155 hours. At 1215 hours another eight F4Fs returned to the *Yorktown*, while SBDs that defended TF 17 had to wait for their turn.[2]

By 1220 hours Fitch had passed the summary of the damage to the *Lexington* on to Fletcher, reporting that she had been hit by two torpedoes. The

Yorktown advised that her CXAM radar was being repaired, and that she could still not exceed twenty-five knots due to the three damaged boilers. At 1230 hours, three freshly fueled F4Fs led by Flatley took off for the first afternoon CAP. Immediately after they cleared the *Yorktown*'s deck, its striking group began landing. Jorgenson's SBD was barely flying, so he ditched near the *Aylwin*, which rescued the crew. Another heavily battered Dauntless, piloted by Lt. (jg) Floyd Moan, failed to extend its landing gear and crashed behind the island, fortunately without any crew losses. The plane was a total wreck, so it was later pushed over the side. Still, by 1300 hours the *Yorktown* had recovered twenty-one SBDs, nine TBDs, and five F4Fs from the striking group and had changed course to 60 degrees at 20 knots. In the attack against the MO Kidō Butai, the carrier lost three dive bombers and one fighter. By 1312 hours all the boilers were reported to be back on the main steam line.[3]

The Americans had been optimistic about the *Lexington*'s condition since the damage control team had extinguished almost all the fires by 1233 hours. The list to the port side was stopped, and she was steaming at a stable twenty-five knots. At the same time, personnel refueled the aircraft on the deck. At 1243 hours, five F4Fs joined the CAP and seven SBDs were waiting for the order to take off. However, at 1247 hours, when the last Wildcat scrambled, the carrier was unexpectedly shaken by an internal explosion.[4] A spark from the Motor Generator Room had triggered the accumulated gasoline vapors in the first platform deck. The few survivors from the nearby compartments recalled a "sheet of flame" or a "bright red flash." The first explosion was seen from the hangar deck, which soon became the main battlefield for the fight against the spreading fire. About twenty-five injured men were put there for the time being. The situation was serious—Main Control lost communication with the Central Station, Interior Communication Room, Forward Board, and other rooms. There was some smoke in Main Control accompanied by a sweet-smelling gas.[5] Despite the struggle to save the carrier down below, the crew completed refueling the bombers, which started to take off at 1259 hours, just after McCuskey's F4F landed on the deck.[6]

Awaiting the return of the *Lexington* striking group, Fletcher considered attacking the *Zuikaku* in the following hours. However, on reflecting that none of his carriers was fully suitable for conducting offensive air operations, he gave up this idea. *Yorktown*'s VF-42 was reduced to just seven operational F4Fs, and he knew from Buckmaster that there were not enough torpedoes for the TBDs. Worse, TF 17 received a report about the MO Kidō Butai allegedly regrouping and preparing for a decisive follow-up attack. Having no updates on the *Lexington* air group, which was still waiting for the return of its planes, Fletcher shared his assessment with Fitch: "In view of enemy fighter plane superiority and undamaged carrier, I propose retreating. What do you think?" Fitch acceded to his plan and soon received a further explanation—"Tomorrow may rearm this ship with your planes and renew attack."[7]

During this conversation, the silhouettes of Hamilton's bombers appeared on the horizon. They had landed on the *Lexington* with Haschke's Dauntless and Gayler's Wildcat by 1328 hours.[8] Fitch waited impatiently for the return of the TBDs and the remaining F4Fs and SBDs. At 1334 hours he received a communication from Fletcher instructing him to proceed south at "best practicable speed" once all aircraft had been recovered. In contrast, Fitch proposed a temporary northerly course to reduce the distance to the returning torpedo bombers and provide them with adequate support.[9]

At about 1230 hours Brett's nine TBDs, escorted by Bain, encountered four Zeros, possibly from the *Zuikaku*, approximately fifty miles south of the MO Kidō Butai. The Americans feared the enemy would want to exploit their numerical superiority in fighters. However, after the initial clash they withdrew north, probably lacking fuel and ammunition. Although VT-2's crews reported shooting down two Zeros, the Japanese suffered no losses.[10]

VT-2's remaining two TBDs that had not encountered the enemy returned to TF 17 alone. However, the main part of the squadron was not problem free. Just twenty miles away from the *Lexington*, Thornhill's Devastator began to run out of fuel and his plane started to lose altitude. On learning of this, Fletcher detached the *Dewey* to rescue the crew. The remaining eight torpedo bombers continued to retreat toward TF 17. Finally, at 1400 hours, the observers spotted aircraft silhouettes in the distance. Brett didn't have enough fuel and decided to proceed straight to the *Lexington* without doing any special identification maneuvers. The Americans had trouble recognizing their planes, which were mistakenly considered Japanese. The screening vessels immediately opened antiaircraft fire but, luckily, did not inflict any casualties among the bombers. After four minutes, TF 17 finally recognized the friendly TBDs. The carrier turned into the wind and recovered Brett's eight-plane group, Bain, and the two remaining Devastators. Most of the aircraft from the *Lexington* striking group were now accounted for. There were only four missing planes. Lt. (jg) Howard F. Clark, who got lost after the clash with the Zeros, could not determine the position of the force due to bad weather. He said on the radio that he would ditch, but his F4F was never found. Besides him, Ault's three damaged SBDs, including CLAG himself, struggled to make their way to the carrier.[11]

At 1414 hours the *Lexington* messaged to confirm she could accommodate her planes from the striking group. At the time, it was known that Ault had been wounded in the left arm and leg. As a result of the internal explosion, the carrier's radio and radar went out of commission, and the *Yorktown* was requested to bring the lost planes in. Unfortunately, this attempt also failed.[12] Having no hope of finding the correct course, Ault sent a farewell message at 1454 hours: "From CLAG: OK, so long people. We got a 1000 lb. hit on the flat top."[13] Wingfield's SBD did not return to TF 17 either. Out of four lost planes, the only one that had great luck was piloted by Ens. Harry Wood, who ditched near Rossel Island; the crew was rescued later.[14]

Before Brett's bombers found their way back to the *Lexington*, Fletcher considered a new plan for the afternoon. He had two courses of action in mind: making another air attack or sending in a night surface attack group against the MO Kidō Butai. Fletcher's main objective was to strike the undamaged *Zuikaku*, because he thought the Japanese might attempt to continue their approach toward Port Moresby or pursue TF 17. However, he first needed to transfer the serviceable planes from the *Lexington* to the *Yorktown* to have at least one carrier air group at hand. Fletcher informed CINCPAC about his new instructions for the team at 1352 hours.[15] King, Nimitz, Leary, and MacArthur already knew from him in fairly accurate detail about the damage sustained by both carriers in TF 17. They were glad that neither of them were lost, given that Melbourne and Hypo had intercepted various Japanese communications that mentioned sinking at least one American flattop.[16]

It wasn't long before Fletcher's plan for the afternoon came into question. After 1400 hours he received a report about extensive damage and new fires on the *Lexington*. The situation in the carrier was slowly getting out of control. Also, at 1422 hours Fitch warned him about some unexpected developments. There were strong indications that an additional carrier had joined the Japanese force. Fletcher passed this information to CINCPAC and ComSoWesPac, informing the latter of the location of the damaged Japanese carrier at the time TF 17 had attacked her. The Americans believed the *Kaga* was the carrier that had appeared on the battlefield. Although the friendly reconnaissance planes had sighted the *Shōhō*, not the *Kaga*, near Bougainville the previous day, Fletcher feared that the enemy now had vast numerical superiority. In such circumstances, pushing for another air attack or a night surface attack could result in the detection and sinking of both his carriers even before dark. Fletcher was left with little choice, so he decided to retreat south for further investigation of the damage to ships and to transfer the *Lexington*'s serviceable planes to the *Yorktown* to get the aircraft in the necessary condition to be able to renew the air attack the following day. According to the revised plan, the *Lexington* would be sent back to Pearl Harbor for repairs. Fletcher soon informed CINCPAC about this decision and reassumed tactical command over TF 17 at 1510 hours.[17]

Fletcher warned Crace of two Japanese carriers in the northern part of the Coral Sea. Remembering the attack of the land-based bombers from the previous day, Crace took a northwesterly course toward Port Moresby to withdraw his ships from the range of enemy aircraft. In the early afternoon, CINCPAC also had on its desk the report summarizing the outcome of the battle on 8 May. Fletcher indicated that one Japanese carrier was hit by at least four torpedoes and three 1000-pound bombs. When the American bombers left the area, she was severely damaged and burning badly.[18] However, the early optimistic report on the battle had to wait until the end of the day. Although the Japanese capacities to continue Operation MO were now seriously limited, the following hours would decide the *Lexington*'s fate.

Despite the *Shōkaku*'s impaired capacity to continue the air operations, the 5th Kōkū Sentai's staff felt bolstered by the news of the sinking of the *Saratoga*-class carrier. Once the attack was completed, the *Zuikaku* received multiple cables from the returning planes. At 1138 hours Ichihara informed the carrier that his fuel tank was punctured but that he was coming back. A similar message from another aircraft came in at 1143 hours: "We were hit in the fuel tank but getting back." Shimazaki also confirmed that he had ended the attack and regrouped. A partially received cable said that four bomb hits had been scored on an unknown ship, which could easily have been either the *Saratoga* or the *Yorktown*. At 1205 hours the next pilot confirmed that he was returning.[19]

Since noon the *Kinugasa* and the *Furutaka* had been executing Takagi's order to screen the damaged *Shōkaku* during the emergency damage control duties. The officers on the *Zuikaku* looked at the sister ship and were concerned about her condition. They still did not have any news from Takahashi. At 1217 hours the *hikōtaichō* finally reached out: "Call off the sinking of the *Saratoga*-class carrier."[20] The officers weren't expecting this kind of message, which caused great consternation. Who was wrong? Takahashi or Ichihara? At 1230 hours they learned from one of the Kates that the enemy fighters had attacked the returning planes. And this wasn't the end of the bad news. Two minutes later the *Shōkaku* warned that she would have trouble recovering the planes from the striking group due to her extensive damage. She withdrew north and asked the *Zuikaku* whether she could accommodate all of the aircraft. In the following minutes, one Val reported a punctured fuel tank and one *kankō* advised that she would have to ditch at sea. The Japanese didn't have many alternatives, so the *Shōkaku* instructed the striking group to land on the *Zuikaku*. Her Zeros from CAP were recovered by 1230 hours to avoid cluttering up the only available carrier.[21]

At 1240 hours the 5th Kōkū Sentai was told to withdraw north temporarily to recover the striking group and prepare its available carrier-based force for further operations. The next contact with the unit was scheduled at 1500 hours, when they should have finished accommodating the planes.[22] Initially confident, Hara still couldn't convey the summary report, because he had contradictory information from his crews. The situation, however, was much more tense in the Fourth Fleet's staff. In Rabaul, Inoue and his officers didn't get any news directly from Takagi but followed the cables, sometimes with a little delay. They knew about Kanno's decision to guide the striking group and Takahashi's order to attack. When, at 1125 hours, they read the message about the sinking of the *Saratoga*-class carrier, the people in the Operations Room shouted, "We got it!" Inoue wrote that the air officers felt relieved because they shared responsibility for the carriers' performance after the failures on 7 May. Still, there was something unsettling in the air. The Yokohama Kū's Mavis reported sighting the enemy carriers and four screening vessels. Rabaul couldn't confirm when the flying boat from Tulagi established contact with TF 17 but conveyed the message to the MO Kidō Butai at 1047 hours. Despite this, Inoue's staff hastily sent news to Tokyo about the *Saratoga*-class carrier. They were unaware they had triggered the entire sequence of events because the cable reached the Combined Fleet and the Navy General Staff. Adm. Osami Nagano headed to the emperor's palace to submit a *sōjō* (a report to the throne). The audience with Emperor Hirohito was running a little late but started at 1630 hours. Nagano said that the Nippon Kaigun had sunk a *California*-class battleship and one destroyer, moderately damaged the *Warspite*-class battleship, and seriously damaged the *Canberra*-class heavy cruiser and the tanker on 7 May. The results from 8 May included the sinking of the *Saratoga*-class and the *Yorktown*-class carriers. Nagano also mentioned the Japanese losses, talking about the fate of the *Shōhō* and the damage inflicted on the *Shōkaku*. Finally, he boasted that the 25th Kōkū Sentai lost only four bombers and the 5th Kōkū Sentai nine.[23]

In that particular moment, all eyes in the Nippon Kaigun were on Inoue, the central thinker behind Operation MO. He was admired for achieving an extremely favorable result in the battle. But the unimaginable happened several minutes after the cable was sent to Tokyo. The Fourth Fleet received Takahashi's cable, which cancelled the previous message. The *hikōtaichō* demolished the remaining hope with another report: "*Saratoga*, *Enterprise* . . . wait, wait. Our planes are attacking the enemy's main force." Inoue understood, in a painful way, that the initial joy had been premature. He irreversibly lost face when he later sent Takahashi's update. In his diary, he only noted that the battle situation became uncertain in the afternoon.[24]

The Fourth Fleet was waiting helplessly for the first reports from Takagi. The commander of the MO Kidō Butai had many more problems to deal with than Inoue's accountability at the time. At 1251 hours he disclosed the new plan—he would reorganize his forces and retreat north for the time being. He hoped that if the American carriers hadn't been sunk, he could go for a second

TABLE 44 ■ **Yokohama Kū's Reconnaissance Missions, Afternoon of 8 May 1942**

Unit	No.	Commander	Notes
Mavises / Yokohama Kū	1	Lt. Cdr. Tashiro	Takeoff: 1315 Landing: 2115
	2	WO Hamano	
	3	WO Ueno	

Source: JACAR: Yokohama Kū (2), 28.

strike in the afternoon. All he had to do was recover the planes and maintain contact with TF 17. As for the latter, after the Fourth Fleet's request to the Eleventh Air Fleet and the 25th Kōkū Sentai from 1300 hours, the Yokohama Kū made its move to shed light on the enemy's real situation and to try its chances in a sneak attack.[25] At 1315 hours the base in Tulagi scrambled three flying boats, each armed with a torpedo. They headed the location indicated by the MO Kidō Butai's dispatch issued at 1310 hours, which mentioned the sinking of one carrier and hitting the second one with bombs.[26]

At 1310 hours the *Zuikaku*'s observers noticed the silhouettes of the returning planes on the horizon. These were eight Zeros from the *Zuikaku* air group, followed by slower Vals and Kates. Soon the *Shōkaku*'s fighters and bombers also appeared in the area. The recovery of all the planes by one carrier occupied the Japanese until 1430 hours. They started with the *Shōkaku*'s aircraft. The *Zuikaku* retrieved eight fighters, seven dive bombers, and five torpedo bombers. One Zero and one Val landed on the *Shōkaku* despite the previous warning about her nonoperational deck. This mistake almost cost the pilots their lives and did cost them their planes, because they were shattered during the touchdown. Four Vals ditched near the other vessels and the crews were taken on board. Another *kambaku* crew saved themselves by landing off Tagula Island, where they were found later.[27] Ichihara came back with only five Kates. During the return route, he noticed that although Petty Officer 3rd Class Satō's torpedo bomber had been downed, the crew had bailed out and waved to him from the floating fuselage. At 1237 hours the *buntaichō* sent a radio dispatch informing the task force about them.[28] The *Shiratsuyu* was detached for a rescue mission, but the crew wasn't found. Equally painful was the 2nd *chūtai*'s attempted return. Lieutenant Iwamura, a distinguished *chūtaichō*, was killed, and Petty Officer 1st Class Ishikawa was the only one to land on the carrier. He admitted that he had a moment of overwhelming emotions at the time: "When we were returning in silence, the memories of the others caused me to cry so hard I couldn't withhold it."[29]

As for the *Zuikaku* air group, the carrier eventually recovered eight Zeros, eleven Vals, and four Kates. One *kankō* and one *kambaku* were so damaged that the pilots ditched close to the *Shiratsuyu*. All crews, including Shimazaki himself, were rescued by the destroyer. The ship reported that apart from Shimazaki sustaining minor injuries to his face, he was fine. The fact that even these minor injuries were reported could imply that the Japanese were obsessed with his safety.[30] The *Zuikaku* air group was indeed decimated, and the *Shōkaku*'s looked only slightly better. However, this wasn't the end of the story. Quite a few planes were so mauled that the Japanese decided to push them into the sea to clear the flight and hangar decks. They started with *Shōkaku*'s two Vals, then dumped three Kates. The *Zuikaku* lost two fighters, two dive bombers, and two torpedo bombers in this way.[31] Assessments were done continually. When a plane landed, the mechanics briefly examined it and classified it as "repairable" or "unusable." Some crews begged for machine guns or radio equipment to be spared at least, but the maintenance team was merciless. The 5th Kōkū Sentai's command realized that they had gone too far and had misjudged the situation when Lieutenant Satō got off the canopy and said he was the last one. Someone from the staff commented, "Damn, we dumped too many planes." Hara replied that nothing could be done, but he had the remainder of the two carriers' air groups at his disposal.[32]

Besides the planes, particularly the bombers, the 5th Kōkū Sentai lost far too many experienced crews. The second day of the deathly marathon ended with no clear victory over the enemy. Warrant Officer Ni'ino's corpse, covered in blood, was pulled out of the canopy. However, the most upsetting thing was that no one saw Takahashi return. Mifuku, blinded in the right eye during the attack, sighted his aircraft after the dive, and then he was attacked by the American fighters. Once their bombs had been dropped, the Vals were supposed to rendezvous at the designated point to return together. This plan, however, was upset by Wildcats. Ema recalled that his group was extremely lucky. The *Zuikaku*'s dive bombers withdrew on the left side of the enemy's task force and didn't meet any opposition. On the contrary, the *Shōkaku*'s dive bombers went on the right side and were ambushed by some fighters, which attacked them at a low altitude. Ema wrote that this was probably where the *hikōtaichō* had got cornered right after he sent the dispatch to the MO Kidō Butai.[33] He wanted to avoid a duel with the Wildcat, but he and his observer, Ensign Nozu, were badly wounded and their aircraft was severely damaged. If we accept the American accounts, we can be almost sure that he fell victim to Lt. (jg) Leonard. Leonard was running out of fuel so he didn't continue pursuing to deliver the coup de grâce, but he had done enough to prevent Takahashi and Nozu from returning to the carrier.[34]

Takahashi's death was a significant blow to the Nippon Kaigun, which lost a true leader who was one of the most skilled, brave, and down-to-earth commanders. His legend would be preserved by the younger generation of pilots, who repeated his words: "It's better to fight in silence and die in silence."[35] Admiral Yamamoto acknowledged his service and promoted him by two ranks, sending the commendation to all armed forces. As if that wasn't enough, Adm. Shigetarō Shimada, the navy minister, awarded Takahashi's court rank promotion to him posthumously during a cabinet meeting in November 1943.[36]

> As a striking group commander, [Takahashi] was involved in operations in Hawaii, Port Moresby, and the Indian Ocean. During the Battle of the Coral Sea, he led the striking group to attack the enemy task force at dusk but found the carriers accidentally when he set the return course. He skillfully read the enemy movements and returned at night, cheering up his exhausted subordinates. The next day, he attacked the enemy carrier task force. He was hit by enemy bullets while sinking the *Saratoga*-class carrier, resulting in a tragic death in battle. Therefore, I acknowledge and announce his distinguished service to the armed forces. Commander in Chief of the Combined Fleet.[37]

Ema was one of the pilots who was questioned about the outcome of the attack on TF 17 after he landed on the *Zuikaku*. In the heat of the battle, the Japanese crews were overoptimistic about many of the things they saw. But the *buntaichō* rationally mentioned that the *Saratoga*-class carrier was most likely sunk. As for the *Yorktown*, he had seen flames coming out of her

PHOTO 18 ■ *Shōkaku*'s *hikōtaichō*, Lieutenant Commander Takahashi *NDL*

flight deck but was unsure whether she went down. He believed she was left in a much better condition than the *Saratoga* but could still be assessed as a nonoperational carrier.[38]

Despite the differences in the reported results, Hara had to figure out how to proceed with the second strike. Out of sixty-nine planes participating in the attack mission, the Japanese recovered only forty-six and then dumped twelve into the sea. Including the aircraft not sent against TF 17, the 5th Kōkū Sentai disposed of only thirty-nine operational planes on the *Zuikaku*—twenty-four fighters, nine dive bombers, and six torpedo bombers. Some aircraft were being repaired, but even assuming they would be fixed soon, Hara had no offensive potential to strike TF 17 again in the afternoon.

Shimoda had a conversation with some crews and noticed they were exhausted. He decided he would not send them on another mission that day,

TABLE 45 **Number of Planes on the *Zuikaku*, Afternoon of 8 May**

	Shōkaku air group	*Zuikaku* air group	Total
Zeros	8 operational	16 operational	24 operational
	1 in repairs	—	1 in repairs
Vals	3 operational	6 operational	9 operational
	2 in repairs	6 in repairs	8 in repairs
Kates	1 operational	5 operational	6 operational
	2 in repairs	2 in repairs	4 in repairs

Sources: JACAR: Sangokai Shiryō (1), 9; JACAR: MO Kidō Butai (2), 29.

especially after the blunder on 7 May. Looking at the numbers and other circumstances, Hara became vehemently opposed to the afternoon strike and notified Takagi and the Fourth Fleet of his view. At 1430 hours he released the first report on the clash with TF 17. He briefly described the situation in the morning and said that his force had sunk two carriers—the *Saratoga*-class and the *Yorktown*-class. He mentioned the *Shōkaku* being bombed but assured everyone that she was doing fine, besides some human casualties. Hara also said he had been recovering the planes since 1300 hours. His most crucial point, however, was that he didn't envisage sending the second attack group in the afternoon.[39]

At 1415 hours the *Shōkaku* advised that she was withdrawing north at thirty knots. After forty-five minutes Hara informed the Fourth Fleet about the enemy's estimated position and probable moves. He added that the 5th Kōkū Sentai could reconsider the second strike but it had too few operational planes and needed to refuel soon. In reality, Hara never intended to risk the next round of the battle and felt convinced by his decision with every passing minute. Some of his ships had only 40 percent of fuel supplies, which wasn't enough to continue Operation MO in the following days. What he missed commenting on in his report was the aircrew situation. Several men were scattered among the screening vessels because they had been rescued after ditching. For example, the *Kako* confirmed that she had taken on board crews from three Zeros and three Vals.[40]

Inoue was particularly worried about the condition of the *Shōkaku* and felt that the next strike could end in a disaster. Similarly, he didn't know much about the remaining American air forces in the area. At about 1530 hours several B-17s appeared over the MO Invasion Force and dropped bombs on the convoy. They didn't hit any transport ships, but during the attack an antiaircraft gun on *Tsugaru* jammed and wounded five men. Although the Japanese suffered no losses, the Americans proved they were still committed to defending Port Moresby against the landing operation.[41] Thus, Inoue sought support from the 25th Kōkū Sentai to involve land-based bombers again in the battle. This time, however, he got the response that the weather in the Coral Sea would deteriorate in the following hours so Rear Admiral Yamada could not support the MO Kidō Butai. Additionally, it had been raining all morning in Rabaul and the soggy airstrip at the Vunakanau airfield was judged unsafe for any bomber missions.[42] Undoubtedly, the high losses the previous day strongly influenced Yamada's negative answer. He could be assertive because he enjoyed independence from the Fourth Fleet. His superior was Vice Admiral Tsukahara, not Inoue. Without the helping hand of the ground-based air units, Inoue couldn't risk more. Thus, at 1600 hours he ordered Takagi to withhold the second strike and withdraw north.[43] At 1620 hours Hara assured Takagi that he was retreating with the carriers at twenty-six to thirty knots and waiting for further decisions.[44]

Once Inoue had all the necessary information, especially about the *Shōkaku*'s condition, and no possibility of sending the second striking group, he postponed the invasion of Port Moresby. At 1620 hours he told the MO Kidō Butai to break away from the opponent, steam to refuel northeast of Tulagi, and be ready to support the landing operations on Nauru and Ocean. The army transport ships were to return to Rabaul with the 6th Suirai Sentai. The 6th Sentai was recalled north to participate in the invasion of Nauru. Finally, the forces in the Deboyne area were to hold their position to provide information on the enemy moves.[45]

The decision to withdraw north and recall the second strike is supported by all Japanese historians. At 1700 hours the Yokohama Kū's flying boats arrived at the indicated spot, didn't find a track of the enemy carrier task force, and returned to Tulagi.[46] By then, the 5th Kōkū Sentai staff had collected the testimonies from the *buntaichō* and was ready to release the first official summary of the battle. At 1710 hours Hara informed all units that the

Saratoga had been hit by nine torpedoes and more than ten bombs, while the *Yorktown* had been struck by at least three torpedoes and eight bombs. He said both carriers were left burning heavily and listing, which led to the assumption that they would sink. The Fourth Fleet also learned that about sixty enemy planes had attacked the *Shōkaku* and scored two bomb hits. They had caused a great fire inside the vessel but no negative consequences for her cruising capacity. Since the flames weren't extinguished quickly enough and the carrier had a damaged deck, the *Zuikaku* recovered all the returning planes from the attack mission.[47]

In the following hour Hara cabled a more detailed battle report. He reaffirmed that the 5th Kōkū Sentai had sunk the *Saratoga* and that he was convinced that the *Yorktown* also went down. Mori described the latter part of the message as *kibōteki kansoku* (wishful thinking). The 5th Kōkū Sentai staff concluded that "set afire and severe damage" was a death sentence to the *Yorktown*, so they quickly translated it into a confirmed success.[48] No member of the aircrews had ever said that he saw the *Yorktown* sinking, though, so the aircrews could not be blamed for this incorrect version of events. The 5th Kōkū Sentai staff invented this version during nervous moments of collecting testimonies, and it wasn't their only exaggeration. Hara reported that one battleship had been struck by a torpedo, which set it on fire and caused an oil leak. Interestingly, someone supposedly saw one torpedo bomber armed with a torpedo that deliberately crashed into the heavy cruiser. The enemy vessel was seen ablaze and listing. Hara wrote that during the enemy strike on the MO Kidō Butai, the antiaircraft defense and CAP shot down thirty bombers in the first wave, thirty-five bombers in the second wave, and thirteen Grumman fighters and fifteen Curtiss bombers and Douglas dive bombers in the third wave. In the dogfight over TF 17, his crews downed thirty-two Grumman fighters and seventeen Curtiss bombers. The *Shōkaku* was directly hit by three bombs and suffered eight near misses. However, apart from the nonoperational deck, some fires inside the vessels and human losses, her technical condition was described as not risking her safety. The most critical part of the report contained information about operational planes and those being repaired. The 5th Kōkū Sentai admitted it had only twenty-four Zeros, nine Vals, and six Kates at its disposal. One Zero, eight Vals, and four Kates were being repaired, so the Japanese expected to improve their air offensive potential soon.[49]

At 1830 hours Takagi set up a refueling plan with the *Tōhō Maru*. It was scheduled to take place on 9 May at Point C, described by the coordinates 10° 20' S and 157° 0' E. The MO Kidō Butai planned to replenish the fuel supplies of the destroyers first, then the cruisers. The group had an order to remain vigilant and commence the procedure if the weather allowed them to do so without taking unnecessary risks. At 2000 hours Takagi updated the Fourth Fleet on the aircraft and crew situation in the 5th Kōkū Sentai. He said he would merge both carriers' air groups in the *Zuikaku* the following day. At that time he had twenty-eight fighter pilots, seventeen crews for dive bombers, and fifteen for torpedo bombers. As for the air strength, besides thirty-nine operational planes, he expected that one Zero, eight Vals, and eight Kates could be repaired. The *Shōkaku* was to be withdrawn to Truk and the screening vessels refueled.[50]

When the news about the decision to withdraw north with the MO Kidō Butai reached Hashirajima, the Combined Fleet staff was furious about it. Hara and Inoue were equally blamed for misleading the higher command and for the lack of determination to resolve the battle in the Nippon Kaigun's favor. Many officers didn't understand why the *Zuikaku* had to "reorganize" the air groups by breaking away from the enemy. All of them wondered why landing on Port Moresby had been postponed if the American carriers had been annihilated. In a heated debate, Captain Yoshitake Miwa of the Operation Planning Section suggested that the MO Kidō Butai should press for a night battle. His words gained much support from the others.[51] In general, the dissatisfaction with the Fourth Fleet's leadership was so strong that Admiral Yamamoto decided to step in directly. At 2200 hours he issued Combined Fleet Operational Order No. 140: "From now on, you shall do your utmost to destroy the remaining enemy forces."[52]

Inoue hadn't much choice but to comply with Yamamoto's directive. At 2340 hours he issued his order to all units participating in Operation MO. He told the MO Kidō Butai to resume reconnaissance missions and be prepared to strike the enemy once the refueling was finished. The MO Invasion Force was supposed to keep its position in Deboyne and work with the planes from the

Kamikawa Maru and the *Kiyokawa Maru* to find the enemy's surface forces. The 1st Division of the 6th Sentai and most of the 6th Suirai Sentai would be under Takagi's control and would directly support the MO Kidō Butai after the refueling. Rear Admiral Gotō would determine the MO Invasion Force's moves.[53]

At 0040 hours Takagi replied that the replenishing of the fuel supplies from the *Tōhō Maru* would be prolonged to the evening of 9 May due to rough seas. Thus, he transferred five hundred tons to destroyers from both the *Haguro* and the *Myōkō*. According to estimations made at 2300 hours, the fuel situation in the force was as follows: the *Zuikaku* 60 percent, the *Shōkaku* 54 percent, the *Myōkō* 53 percent, the *Haguro* 38 percent, the Kinugasa 60 percent, the *Furutaka* 60 percent, and the destroyers from 20 to 54 percent. Finally, Takagi confirmed that the *Kinugasa*'s and *Furutaka*'s four seaplanes had been transferred to Deboyne.[54]

Despite the Combined Fleet's resolute order to press for a decisive victory in the Battle of the Coral Sea, the MO Kidō Butai's situation was much more complicated. The upcoming night could give Hara and Takagi a moment of respite to reorganize their carrier-based air force, but another strike against TF 17 was nearly impossible. The Japanese were convinced that nothing more could be done at the moment. Although they had sunk two American carriers, the invasion of Port Moresby had to be postponed. This was unfortunate, but the pure determination could not compensate for the colossal losses in the 5th Kōkū Sentai. There was a widespread feeling that the battle was neither won nor lost.

At the time, the Japanese weren't aware that their consistent reports about the sinking of the two carriers were overstated. The confusion about the *Yorktown* was explained, but the fate of the *Saratoga*-class carrier wasn't as evident as they thought.

In the retreating TF 17, the atmosphere was getting worse by the minute. The fires weren't fully extinguished despite the first positive reports about the *Lexington*'s technical condition. At 1442 hours the carrier was shaken by a second, even more powerful, internal explosion. The tremendous blast raised the forward elevator about six inches and flames came out around the edges. Spilled gasoline set ablaze the entire hangar deck, which was cut out from communications for some time due to the large quantities of smoke. At 1452 hours Sherman informed Fletcher about the dramatic situation in the ship and asked for help. Even the pilots risked their lives and joined in to help the damage control team extinguish the fire slowly consuming the vessel.

At 1505 hours the *Morris*, *Phelps*, and *Anderson* got close to the *Lexington*'s side to assist. The *Yorktown* scrambled four F4Fs and ten SBDs to CAP and conducted an anti-torpedo-plane patrol shortly after. Within a quarter of an hour, ten SBDs and three F4Fs, already aloft for some time, landed on the deck.

The struggle to save the *Lexington* proved futile at 1525 hours when another powerful explosion occurred near the boiler room. Another fire that broke out in the lowest compartments had worse consequences. At 1538 hours the crew reported that the fire was out of control. At 1600 hours the carrier slowed down and then stopped. The fires in the boilers were extinguished and Sherman ordered his men to gather on the deck.[55]

Due to the fear of a Japanese pursuit, at 1601 hours Fletcher detached TG 17.2, which was under Kinkaid's command; it comprised the *Lexington*, two heavy cruisers, and three destroyers. The group's objective was to assist the burning carrier and escort her on the route southward. If it proved impossible to save the *Lexington*, Kinkaid was instructed to rescue the crew members and scuttle her.[56]

When the *Yorktown*'s CXAM radar picked up the enemy approaching TF 17 at about 1700 hours, Pederson scrambled seven more Wildcats. Although it soon turned out to be a false alarm, the Americans realized they could not leave part of their forces at the same spot, exposing them to the Japanese attack. At 1652 hours Sherman transferred all aircrew and flight personnel to the *Morris*. At 1707 hours he ordered all his men to abandon the carrier, which again listed 7 degrees to port. As the sailors were leaving the burning vessel at 1727 hours, two gigantic explosions occurred amidships and aft. This time, the blasts tore off one of the elevators and blew several planes into the sea.

Taking 2,770 men on board three destroyers at sunset was challenging, so Fletcher assigned the *Phelps* and the *Dewey* to assist in the evacuation. By 1818 hours all aircraft from CAP and the anti-torpedo-plane patrol had landed on the *Yorktown*. The area around TG 17.2 was illuminated by the glow of the burning *Lexington*. A few minutes later Fletcher ordered Kinkaid to head on

TABLE 46 ■ **Number of Operational Planes on the *Yorktown*, Evening of 8 May**

Unit	Number of operational planes + planes in repairs
VF-42	7 × F4Fs + 6 × in repairs
VS-5	5 × SBDs + 7 × in repairs
VB-5	10 × SBDs + 5 × in repairs
VT-5	8 × TBDs + 4 × in repairs
VF-2	5 × F4Fs
VS-2	8 × SBDs (one damaged)
VB-2	6 × SBDs (one damaged)

Source: NARA: USS *Yorktown*, May 8.

a course of 225 degrees at 14 knots until 2000 hours and then steam toward the rendezvous point to join up with the rest of TF 17.

Once it was confirmed that no one was left in the ship or in the water, at 1841 hours the *Phelps* received the order to sink the *Lexington*. Between 1915 and 1952 hours the destroyer fired five torpedoes, which caused the carrier to capsize over her port side. She went down at 1952 hours, making her last thud in an underwater explosion. When Kinkaid joined Fletcher at 2037 hours, TF 17 took a southwesterly course. Despite the pursuit ordered by the Japanese the following day, the Americans withdrew from the battlefield in time. Eventually, 2,735 men were rescued from the *Lexington*, and 216 were killed or missing.[57]

On the evening of 8 May, Fletcher was left with one damaged but operational carrier and a significantly reduced air force. Due to taking on board some of the *Lexington*'s planes, TF 17 still had twelve F4Fs, twenty-nine SBDs, and eight TBDs, but this was only a tiny part of what they had disposed of during the first days of May. More than twenty aircraft were being repaired, which didn't change the fact that the Americans were unable to continue the battle and had to withdraw. Table 46 presents the composition of the air units on 8 May evening, including the planes in repair.

PART 4

8 MAY–21 SEPTEMBER 1942

Chapter 16

FINAL MOVEMENTS IN OPERATION MO

On the morning of 9 May Admiral Fletcher sent several SBDs to search the northern sector to find out whether the Japanese intended to pursue him. Although Admiral Halsey was slowly approaching the Coral Sea, the fuel situation in TF 17 was becoming difficult, especially among the destroyers. While considering a new refueling spot after the loss of the *Neosho*, just after 0900 hours Fletcher was suddenly warned by one of his dive bombers that the enemy carrier task force had been sighted. The report was abrupt, and the Americans thought that the plane had been attacked by enemy fighters. Soon after, another SBD completed the message, warning about the Japanese carrier task force 175 miles away with a bearing of 310 degrees and heading 110 degrees at 25 knots. At 0922 hours the *Yorktown* went to general quarters and increased her speed to twenty-seven knots. The carrier was preparing to scramble thirteen operational F4Fs to CAP. Fletcher planned to take advantage of the knowledge about the enemy's location to launch a preemptive strike. He aimed to send most of his SBDs, including the *Lexington*'s four led by Dixon. The dive bombers were to proceed without the escorts since the Wildcats were desperately needed to cover TF 17. Simultaneously, Fletcher assigned one of VS-5's SBDs and his staff gunnery officer, Cdr. Walter G. Schindler, to fly to Rockhampton, Australia. He was to urgently contact MacArthur and organize a massive bomber raid on the located Japanese carriers, ensuring the secrecy of the operation at every stage. Schindler needed to be careful about the secrecy of his mission, because even one message intercepted by the enemy could result in the MO Kidō Butai retreating north.[1]

Dixon's SBDs arrived at the indicated location and found no enemy forces. In reality, there were never any Japanese carriers there, and scouting planes mistook the foamy Lihou Reefs as evidence of ships steaming southward. Before noon the Americans also lost one of VS-2's SBDs, piloted by Ens. Lawrence Traynor, who ditched near the *Yorktown*. The crew was rescued by the *Morris*, and the rest of Dixon's striking group landed safely on the carrier. While the destroyers were transferring the *Lexington*'s survivors to the cruisers, the CXAM radar picked up a group of aircraft coming in. It soon turned out that they were B-17s that had taken off from Noumea and were heading to Townsville to bomb along the way the Japanese carriers detected the day before. Because the MO Kidō Butai was more than two hundred miles north, the bombers passed over TF 17, which continued to retreat southeast.

On the afternoon of 8 May, when the *Lexington* was still functioning, Nimitz ordered Fletcher to withdraw with TF 17 to the West Coast if practicable; otherwise, they would be going to Pearl Harbor. The cruisers and destroyers under Kinkaid's command were to join TF 16 at the earliest opportunity.[2] Nimitz suggested Tongatabu as a rendezvous point where Fletcher could refuel and give his crews a moment of respite. The following day Fletcher acceded to this plan. On the afternoon of 11 May he detached the *Minneapolis*, *New Orleans*, *Astoria*, and three destroyers, which set a course for New Caledonia. TF 17 continued to Tongatabu.[3] The last chord of the American participation in the Battle of the Coral Sea occurred on the same day as, at about 1300 hours, the *Henley* rescued 123 survivors from the *Neosho*.[4] The oiler had been adrift for more than four days and was sunk by the destroyer's guns by 1522 hours.[5]

The Combined Fleet's stepping into Operation MO caused a great stir in the Fourth Fleet's command. Inoue wasn't convinced that the MO Kidō Butai could continue the battle in the Coral Sea with the *Zuikaku* having only the depleted bomber groups at its disposal. However, he didn't have a choice. At 2355 hours on 9 May, when it was already known that the Japanese would chase TF 17, Inoue asked Takagi to inform him about the number of operational planes until refueling began.[6]

The planned refueling of the MO Kidō Butai before the pursuit and the urgent need to screen the damaged *Shōkaku* were probably troublesome for Takagi. At 0530 hours on 10 May the *Yūgure* was detached and ordered to refuel near Shortland and then return to escort the *Shōkaku* on her way to Yokosuka, as decided by Takagi at 0715 hours. In the meantime, the MO Kidō Butai, now reduced to the *Zuikaku* and the screening vessels, was already heading south. At 0600 hours Takagi informed Inoue that he would find and attack the remnants of TF 17. He said that the 5th Kōkū Sentai had only fifteen dive and torpedo bombers at the time. He desperately needed support from the land-based forces to proceed with the successful strike.[7]

The Eleventh Air Fleet didn't remain deaf to these requests and did its share of searching for Fletcher in the Coral Sea, hoping to discover his moves. At 0630 hours the Yokohama Kū sent three flying boats from Tulagi, led by Ensign Kiyomizu. After about an hour the aircraft commanded by Warrant Officer Takahashi reported an engine failure and turned back to the base. At about 1030 hours she was replaced by another plane. On 9 May the Yokohama Kū found only a two hundred-meter-long oil slick forty-eight miles from Tulagi with a bearing of 235 degrees. All of the Mavises had returned to base by 1800 hours.[8]

At about 0800 hours the MO Kidō Butai had a rendezvous with the *Tōhō Maru* and began refueling. The course was changed to the southeast to keep chasing the enemy but maintaining a safe distance. When the Combined Fleet learned more about the *Shōkaku*'s condition during the morning hours,

TABLE 47 **Yokohama Kū's Reconnaissance Missions, Morning of 9 May 1942**

Unit	No.	Commander	Notes
Mavises / Yokohama Kū	1	Ens. Kiyomizu	Takeoff: 0630 Landing: 1800
	2	WO Fujiwara	
	3	WO Takahashi (returned)	
	4	unknown	Takeoff: 1030 Landing: 1800

Source: JACAR: Yokohama Kū (2), 29.

Yamamoto and his staff formally decided to detach her and the *Yūgure* from the Fourth Fleet. The escorted *Shōkaku* was to withdraw to Yokosuka via Saipan supported by the 15th Destroyer Division, which had been temporarily detached from the Fourth Fleet.[9]

Despite the *Shōkaku* being sent back to Japan, the Combined Fleet's pressure to continue the battle was definitely felt in Truk. At 1450 hours Inoue instructed Takagi to resume the reconnaissance missions to attack the enemy's battleships and the cruisers, damaged the previous day, using all his available resources. At 1700 hours Takagi passed the word to complete the refueling and execute the Fourth Fleet's order. The MO Kidō Butai was to dash south at twenty-six knots from 0700 hours on 10 May and send the scouting planes to find and destroy TF 17 or any other surface force. Takagi planned to withdraw north at about 1400 hours if the enemy wasn't located. Although not all the cruisers finished the refueling, particularly the *Haguro*, *Kinugasa*, and *Furutaka*, they were still expected to rejoin the MO Kidō Butai as soon as possible. After the refueling on 9 May the *Tōhō Maru* was to withdraw to Shortland and await further instructions. When this order was issued, the *Zuikaku* had twenty-four Zeros, thirteen Vals, and eight operational Kates at her disposal.[10]

At 1630 hours the MO Kidō Butai finished the refueling that was necessary and headed southwest. The Japanese took seriously the aim of finding and annihilating any enemy ship that didn't escape the Coral Sea on time. The seaplane base at Deboyne continued the air operations throughout the day, dispatching planes for the reconnaissance mission in the area. Between 1230 and 1300 hours the air groups from the *Kamikawa Maru* and the *Kiyokawa Maru* sent two Jakes each, but they failed to locate any enemy vessels in the fifty-mile arc. They had all returned safely by 1715 hours. Additionally, the *Kamikawa Maru*'s two Petes were airborne at 1115 hours to search for the downed crews near Misima Island and southward. Ensign Shimura and Petty Officer 1st Class Ueki encountered one PBY about 120 miles south of Deboyne. Both pilots claimed to have seriously damaged the flying boat in a short skirmish, but it managed to withdraw south.[11]

Since the enemy's activity in the Coral Sea was noticeable, the Japanese thought there was still a chance to cut off Fletcher's line of retreat, especially when he had any damaged ships. The *Zuikaku*'s striking potential was limited,

TABLE 48 ■ ***Zuikaku*'s Reconnaissance Missions, 10 May**

Aircraft	No.	Pilot	Observer	Radio operator	Notes
Kates/*Zuikaku* 160 degrees	1	Lt. Satō (C)	WO Kanazawa	PO2c Yoshida	Takeoff: 0400 Landing: 1120
	2	PO3c Hatanaka	PO1c Ushijima	Sea1c Morishita	
Kates/*Zuikaku* 180 degrees	1	PO1c Hori	Ens. Matsunaga (S)	PO1c Yoshinaga	
	2	PO1c Satō	PO2c Kawabata	Sea1c Yoshimura	
Kates/*Zuikaku* 200 degrees	1	WO Yaegashi (S)	PO1c Himeishi	Sea1c Ōuchi	
	2	Sea1c Nishitani	PO2c Matsuo	Sea1c Ōizumi	
Kates/*Zuikaku* 220 degrees	1	PO1c Ishihara (S)	PO1c Ōtani	PO2c Nishizawa	
	2	PO2c Yokomakura	PO1c Kishi	Sea1c Hara	

Sources: JACAR: Zuikaku (2), 4–5; JACAR: MO Kidō Butai (2), 48.

TABLE 49 ■ **Yokohama Kū's Reconnaissance Missions, 10 May**

Unit	No.	Commander	Notes
Mavises / Yokohama Kū	1	Ens. Yoshida	Takeoff: 0601 Landing: 1625
	2	WO Miwa	
	3	WO Yamaguchi	

Source: JACAR: Yokohama Kū (2), 31.

but the maintenance crew did their best to repair at least a few additional dive and torpedo bombers. The night passed without any incidents. In line with Takagi's order, at 0600 hours the carrier sent eight *kankō* to search the sectors from 160 to 220 degrees at 250 miles and thirty miles in the right outward leg. The aircraft were airborne by 0620 hours.

Just like on the previous day, the Yokohama Kū sent three flying boats from Tulagi to search the area south and southeast of the island. The group led by Ensign Yoshida departed at 0601 hours. At about 1010 hours the aircraft commanded by Warrant Officer Yamaguchi encountered an enemy PBY and clashed with her. Yamaguchi claimed to hit a Catalina several times but said she escaped into the clouds. He was seriously dedicated to downing the enemy, because his Mavis used almost all its ammunition. Apart from this skirmish, the Yokohama Kū's planes didn't find the enemy and had returned to the base by 1625 hours.

Unlike on 9 May the seaplanes from the *Kamikawa Maru* and the *Kiyokawa Maru* didn't participate in reconnaissance missions. Their activity was limited to patrols around Deboyne against the enemy aircraft and submarines.[12]

The Japanese knew Fletcher might be somewhere in the Coral Sea but couldn't guess his withdrawal route. At about 1100 hours the submarine *I-24* was attacked by one carrier-borne bomber about five hundred miles from Townsville at a bearing of 110 degrees. The skipper strongly felt that an enemy carrier could be in the area. *I-24* wasn't damaged and continued the patrol. Unfortunately, the submarine's report didn't reach Takagi until 1820 hours.[13]

All the *kankō* had returned to the *Zuikaku* by 1120 hours. They had found only a burned floating wreck of the oiler about 130 miles from the takeoff point and with a bearing of 205 degrees. The crews identified the object as the tanker, which was assumed to have been sunk by the dive bombers on 7 May. Hara didn't want to waste his planes on attacking an already dead target, so he left it alone.[14]

Despite missing the enemy carriers, the MO Kidō Butai started intercepting Allied radio traffic at about 1230 hours. Hara and Takagi couldn't determine whether the messages were transmitted by Fletcher's planes or from Townsville, though, because they were reducing the distance to the Australian base. Since none of the leaders proposed carrying out an attack that day, Takagi changed the course to the north at 1300 hours. Thirty minutes later, three Zeros led by Lieutenant Sakamoto took off to CAP. The fighters didn't spot any intruders and had landed on the *Zuikaku* by 1630 hours.[15] The enemy radio traffic had been received in the carrier and part of the cruisers until sunset, but the MO Kidō Butai hadn't solved the mystery of its origin.[16]

At 1440 hours Takagi informed Inoue and Yamada that he hadn't found the enemy force and had only intercepted some of its messages. The *Kinugasa* and the *Furutaka* joined the MO Kidō Butai retreating north. Some Japanese vessels still needed fuel, and Takagi planned to send them to Shortland to complete the refueling.[17] Once the chances of reengaging Fletcher were minimal, the Combined Fleet considered that they had come to the end of the Battle of the Coral Sea. At 1530 hours Ugaki informed Inoue that he planned to remove the 5th Kōkū Sentai from the Fourth Fleet's command. One hour later the Combined Fleet also postponed Operation MO to the third stage of the Pacific War, which in practice meant July.[18]

Having tried to intercept the enemy, Inoue gave up at 1730 hours when he sent his final instructions. If Takagi didn't locate the enemy by 2000 hours, the MO Kidō Butai would withdraw northeast of the Solomon Islands to cover the invasions of the Gilbert Islands, Nauru, and Ocean and, finally, would return to Truk. The MO Invasion Force was to leave some of its forces in the Solomon Islands to liquidate the seaplane base in Deboyne. Also, several destroyers and seaplanes were supposed to remain in the Louisiades to search for the lost crews during Operation MO. In general, Inoue told his units to be on guard, especially against the remnants of TF 17, which could try to strike back.[19]

The failure of Operation MO didn't discourage the Fourth Fleet from launching Operation RY. On 11 May Rear Admiral Shima set sail from Rabaul with the *Tatsuta*, *Okinoshima*, *Tsugaru*, *Uzuki*, and *Yūzuki*. The *Myōkō*, the *Haguro*, and four destroyers screened the invasion force. The 6th SNLF and the Kashima SNLF embarked on the transport ships *Kinryū Maru* and *Takahata Maru*.

However, Operation RY didn't go according to the Japanese plans. In the early morning of 12 May, while passing near New Ireland, the *Okinoshima*, already damaged by the *Yorktown*'s planes during the raid on Tulagi, was hit by three torpedoes fired by the submarine *S-42*. The *Mochizuki* took her in tow, but the minelayer capsized and sank in less than two hours. And this wasn't the end of the losses for the Japanese. The repair ship *Shōei Maru* was sent from Rabaul to help the *Okinoshima* but was sunk by the American submarine *S-44* in the afternoon.

Despite losing two ships, Shima continued Operation RY until the Yokohama Kū's flying boat sighted an enemy carrier force about 435 miles away from Tulagi and with a bearing of 100 degrees at 1007 hours on 15 May.[20] TF 16 had finally arrived in the South Pacific and was ready to join the campaign. Fearing that the *Enterprise* and the *Hornet* would annihilate the invasion force, Inoue canceled Operation RY and ordered Shima to return to Truk. The MO Kidō Butai's screening vessels, commanded by Takagi, were to remain about three hundred miles north of Rabaul to await further instructions.[21] TF 16 was also soon withdrawn by Nimitz to begin preparations for the decisive battle in the Central Pacific.

But what happened to the 5th Kōkū Sentai in the meantime? The Combined Fleet focused on the damaged *Shōkaku*, which had to be withdrawn to the mainland immediately. Her condition was terrible but the boilers allowed her to maintain a relatively fast speed. On 9 May the crew learned from the Imperial Headquarters' official announcement about the outcome of the Battle of the Coral Sea. At noon on 10 May the crew sighted one medium bomber overhead. They were initially afraid it was an enemy plane, but it turned out to be the aircraft sent by the Genzan Kū. The *Shōkaku* was already being escorted by the *Yūgure*, and in the afternoon the *Sazanami* appeared on the horizon to give a helping hand. After midnight on 11 May the carrier crossed the equator.[22] During the day the Combined Fleet formally removed the MO Kidō Butai (minus the *Shōkaku*) from the Fourth Fleet's command and assigned it to the Northern Forces. Hara was instructed to return to Japan as soon as possible.[23]

The Combined Fleet's order from 9 May meant that the 15th Destroyer Division, comprising the *Kuroshio*, *Oyashio*, and *Hayashio*, was detached from the Fourth Fleet. It joined the *Shōkaku* and two destroyers in the Philippine Sea on 12 May.[24] In the meantime, it was also decided that the carrier would go to Kure instead of Yokosuka. However, the Japanese didn't know that the U.S. Navy had deciphered their communication about the *Shōkaku* retreating toward the mainland. The Americans passed the word to four submarines, which had set off on a war patrol to hunt down easy prey near her destination.[25] Still, the Combined Fleet was aware that the carrier was in danger, so it ordered extreme precautions. Despite the widespread belief that the *Shōkaku* nearly capsized during her route back to Japan, no sources or testimonies mention this. The most critical moment for the ship was the afternoon of 16 May when she and two destroyers were sighted by the *Triton* about three hundred miles southwest of Shikoku.[26] The American submarine intended to fire torpedoes at the *Shōkaku*, but the prey was steaming too fast to catch. The other submarines unsuccessfully tried to reestablish contact with the carrier in the following hours. In the end, the *Shōkaku* arrived at Kure at 1830 hours on 17 May and was put in reserve while the repairs were

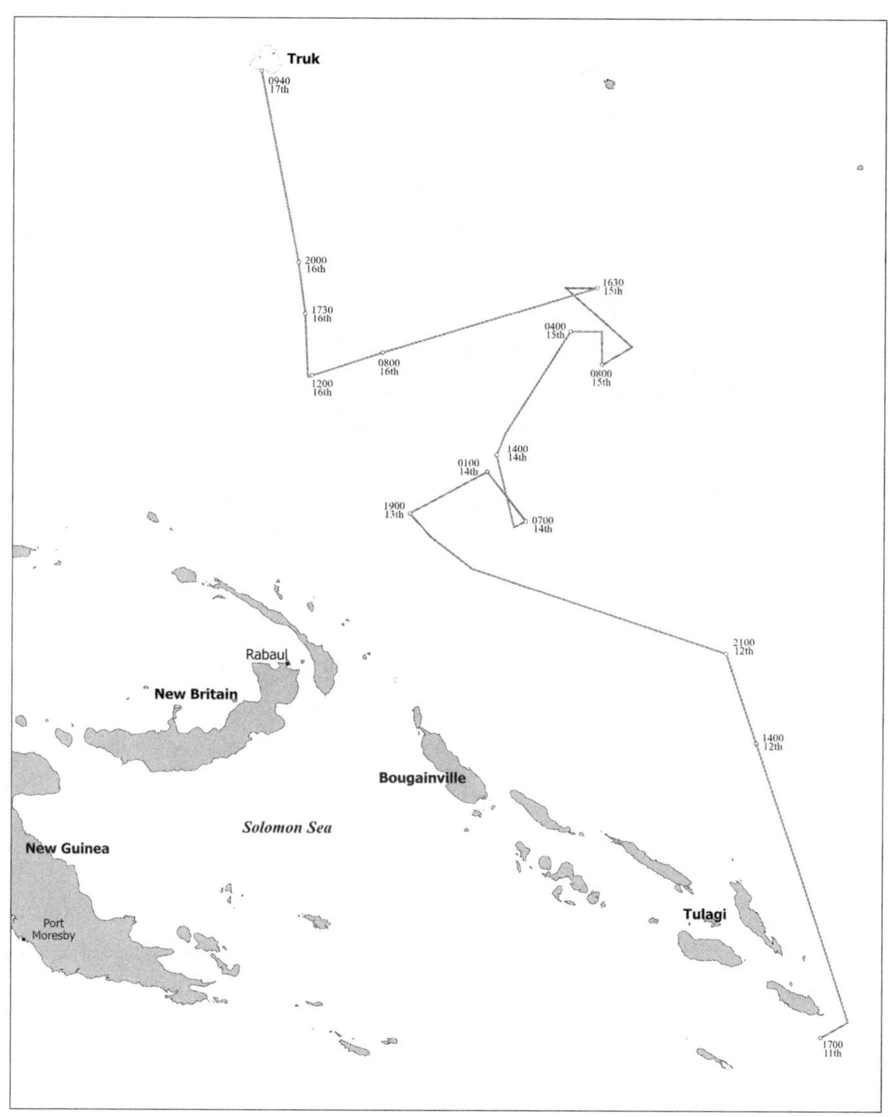

MAP 15 ■ *Zuikaku*'s return route

done.[27] According to Dr. Watanabe, the final number of casualties by the time the carrier returned to Japan was 109 killed or missing crew members and 43 aircrews and 142 wounded.[28]

The story of the *Zuikaku* wasn't much more straightforward. At noon on 12 May, already formally not a part of the Fourth Fleet, she was 150 miles north of Santa Isabel and steaming north to support the invasion of the Gilbert Islands, Nauru, and Ocean on the way to Truk. One day later the carrier completed the task that had been a problem for everybody since Operation MO began. She delivered eight Zeros to Rabaul for the Tainan Kū. The fighter pilots returned to the carrier in six Kates.[29] At 1840 hours the 5th Kōkū Sentai (minus the *Shōkaku*) and the 7th Destroyer Division were detached from the MO Kidō Butai. The *Zuikaku* entered Truk on the morning of 15 May. At the time, the Japanese already knew about the *Enterprise* and the *Hornet* in the South Pacific and Operation RY was canceled. The carrier left sixteen Zeros for the Tainan Kū on the base.[30] She departed for Kure the following evening.[31] In the afternoon she was spotted with four destroyers by the *Greenling* in the Truk Lagoon steaming toward North Pass. The submarine, however, wasn't able to fire its torpedoes. On 17 May the 5th Sentai also arrived at Truk and departed for Yokosuka after a quick refueling. Since Operation MO was over and all Takagi's ships had new assignments, the MO Kidō Butai was disbanded.[32]

The Americans had a unique chance to catch the *Zuikaku* off guard during the night of 21 May when she was on the last leg of the route toward Japan. The *Pollack* sighted her with a destroyer and fired four torpedoes from about two thousand feet, but they all missed the target.[33] The *Zuikaku*, which in Japanese means "the lucky crane," again proved she was a fortunate ship: Lieutenant Commander Fukuchi noticed that she had avoided any damage by hiding in the rain squall during the pivotal moment of the Battle of the Coral Sea, making her sister ship, the *Shōkaku*, take all the hits from the American bombers.[34] Once the *Zuikaku* passed the Bungo Channel, the remnants of her air group (four Zeros, thirteen Vals, and eight Kates) were transferred to the Saeki Kū for reconstruction and training. The carrier had entered Kure by 1645 hours on 21 May.[35]

Chapter 17

CONFLICTING JAPANESE STATEMENTS ON THE OUTCOME OF THE BATTLE OF THE CORAL SEA

When the Combined Fleet decided to allocate the 5th Kōkū Sentai to the Fourth Fleet to proceed with Operation MO, Inoue was told to return the squadron in perfect shape so that both carriers could participate in Operation MI. The reality after the Battle of the Coral Sea was colossally different. According to Captain Miwa's diary, on 14 May Hara submitted a report that said that the *Shōkaku* had lost about 30 percent of her aircrews and the *Zuikaku* about 40 percent. Hara also advised about the deaths of Takahashi and Tsubota, two distinguished figures in the 5th Kōkū Sentai.[1]

Although the 5th Kōkū Sentai's report doesn't include the information mentioned by Miwa, his version is widely quoted by historians, so it's worth looking closely at the numbers. Various Japanese documents show that the aircrew situation in the two carriers was slightly different but equally tricky. Mieno's diary is mostly consistent with the other records in this respect. It says that 35 out of 114 airmen from the *Zuikaku* were killed or went missing and three men were wounded. The total losses as a proportion were 33.3 percent. In comparison, the *Shōkaku* lost 43 out of 113 airmen and three were severely wounded. She lost 40.7 percent of her aircrew. Despite the widespread belief that the Combined Fleet could theoretically replenish the *Zuikaku* air group with the aircrews from the *Shōkaku* and send the undamaged carrier to participate in Operation MI, the entire 5th Kōkū Sentai faced a dramatic shortage of aircrews. Apart from the fact that 78 out of 227 flyers had been killed or were missing, 17 out of 43 seasoned airmen (commissioned officers with a rank of ensign and above) were dead, six men were severely wounded and excluded from service for a long time, and at least 18 other crew members were scattered throughout the different ships or bases that had rescued them after they had ditched at sea. The death toll was particularly dreadful within the torpedo bomber groups, which lost 49.1 percent of their crews and 12 out of 22 experienced officers, which was 54.5 percent in total. And the crews weren't the only problem. On the eve of Operation MI, all spare dive and torpedo bombers had already been allocated to the other carriers. Thus, the *Zuikaku* could not join the Kidō Butai, not because the Combined Fleet didn't want it to but because it lacked aircraft and crews. The Japanese couldn't replenish all the losses in less than one week because Nagumo was scheduled to depart Hashirajima on 27 May.

Keeping the 5th Kōkū Sentai out of Operation MI didn't mean the carriers would wait too long to return to the frontline. On 26 May Hara ordered three weeks of training for the aircrew of the *Shōkaku* and the *Zuikaku*, beginning on 29 May. The first air group would be rebuilt and trained at Tomitaka Kū's base, and the second at the Kanoya Kū's base. The training included, among other things, diving and horizontal bombing, torpedo attacks, fighter escort, reconnaissance, fighter signaling, navigation, and night operations. Thus, the lessons learned from the Coral Sea action were to be taught to the Japanese crews as soon as practicable.[2]

An additional negative consequence of the Battle of the Coral Sea for the Japanese was dealing with the damaged *Shōkaku*. The Combined Fleet knew that she had been hit by three bombs on 8 May, but her exact condition couldn't be assessed until she returned to Japan. The report about her being a nonoperational carrier could mean anything. Since she could steam at thirty knots, some believed her deck would easily be patched up in the following days. However, when the *Shōkaku* arrived in Kure the bitter truth emerged. On 17 May, a Sunday, many shipyard workers, including the executive personnel, were on their day off. The ship could have entered the dry dock immediately, but she was left on anchor outside of the harbor due to the staff shortage and

TABLE 50 **Aircrew Losses in the 5th Kōkū Sentai during Operation MO**

	Zuikaku			Total	*Shōkaku*			Total
	K	V	Z		K	V	Z	
Crew members	59	36	19	114	57	38	18	113
1 May	2	—	—	2	—	—	—	0
7 May (morning attack)	—	2	—	2	—	—	—	0
7 May (dusk attack)	15	2	—	17	9	—	—	9
8 May (recon)	—	—	—	0	3	—	—	3
8 May (attack)	10	4	—	14	15	14	—	29
8 May (defense)	—	—	—	0	—	—	2	2
Killed or missing	27	8	0	35	27	14	2	43
Severely wounded	3	0	0	3	0	3	0	3
Total	**30**	**8**	**0**	**38**	**27**	**17**	**2**	**46**
Percent (incl. wounded)	45.7% (50.8%)	22.2%	0%	30.7% (33.3%)	47.3%	36.8% (44.7%)	11.1%	38% (40.7%)

Sources: JACAR: Sangokai Shiryō (1), 42–48; JACAR: Shōkaku (1); JACAR: Zuikaku (1); JACAR: Zuikaku (2).

considerable damage. According to the official announcement, the Kure shipyard thought its job would involve standard deck repairs, but that wasn't the case. On that day, even Yamamoto came from Hashirajima to see the devastated carrier with his own eyes. He inspected the ship and visited the wounded crew members to express his gratitude for their effort during the first carrier battle in history. Yamamoto probably also hadn't realized that three medium-sized bombs could inflict such massive damage on a 30,000-ton vessel. In the following days, the specialists from the technical departments of the Nippon Kaigun closely examined the *Shōkaku*. Although the carrier's participation in Operation MI was pure fiction and her repairs would take at least six weeks, the Combined Fleet had a chance to learn about a successful damage control experience. At 1000 hours on 26 May, Lieutenant Commander Fukuchi was invited to the *Yamato* to give a two-hour lecture on firefighting in the Battle of the Coral Sea. His observations about better protecting the hangar deck and fuel storage at all costs were precious. However, Nagumo departed Hashirajima for Operation MI the following day, so he didn't have

PHOTO 19 ■ The most heavily damaged section of the *Shōkaku* documented in Kure Naval Dockyard *Fukuchi, Kūbo* Shōkaku *Kaiseki*

time to implement Fukuchi's conclusions. The undue haste to fight the U.S. Navy in the decisive Battle of Midway would backfire on the Japanese quicker than they expected.[3]

The postponement of Operation MO was a significant setback for the Combined Fleet. The Nippon Kaigun had failed to fulfill its initial strategic objective for the first time in the Pacific War. By leaving Port Moresby in Allied hands, the Japanese positions in New Guinea and New Britain remained exposed to the enemy's air raids and continued to suffer from the war of attrition. On 8 May Yamamoto and his staff knew that the Fourth Fleet would not seize Port Moresby according to the plan. Even if the MO Kidō Butai annihilated the remaining part of TF 17 in the following days, which didn't happen, the convoy was unlikely to reach its destination safely by 10 May. The American and Australian land-based bombers remained the most critical threat for the slow transport ships, which were too important to be lost in a risky approach toward Port Moresby. This first Japanese strategic loss had to be presented at least as a spectacular tactical victory, secured at some cost, to boost the morale of the armed forces and the public.

The Imperial Headquarters had been collecting all the unit reports and testimonies about the progress of Operation MO to produce one comprehensive announcement. The higher command had to compare the data produced by the Fourth Fleet and the Eleventh Air Fleet, because some of the claims were duplicated. Additionally, the officers in Tokyo remembered perfectly the confusion about sinking two carriers, which arose after Nagano visited the emperor on 8 May. Some observers may have thought that the Nippon Kaigun would wait for more precise information so it could establish one version. But that wasn't the case. The pressure to disclose positive news as an answer to the gossip and to demonstrate the magnitude of the victory before the negative information about postponing Operation MO came to light was so intense that the Imperial Headquarters released its first official announcement at 1720 hours on 8 May. It summarized the 25th Kōkū Sentai's attack on Crace's group and the main battle on 8 May. Tokyo claimed that it had sunk a *California*-class battleship and heavily damaged a *Warspite*-class battleship and a *Canberra*-class heavy cruiser. The list of the ships sent to the bottom of the sea included two carriers: the *Saratoga*-class and the *Yorktown*-class carriers. According to the Imperial Headquarters, the battle was still in progress. Thus, it was natural to expect updates soon.[4]

Following this announcement, the state-controlled Japanese newspapers started translating the claims into slogans for the masses the following morning. An article in one of the newspapers published in English said, "It's hard to overestimate the meaning of this Japanese victory. It's the final blow to the Allied battleship and carrier forces. The United States will not dare to face Japanese ships." Prime Minister and Army Minister Gen. Hideki Tōjō received congratulations directly from Adolf Hitler, who expressed his admiration for the Nippon Kaigun's achievement against the common enemy.[5]

At 1540 hours the Imperial Headquarters made a second announcement about the "ongoing battle in the Coral Sea." Apart from the hits just mentioned, the Japanese claimed that they had sunk one destroyer and that their torpedo bombers had severely damaged one heavy cruiser. The Americans had allegedly lost eighty-nine planes. Notably, the Imperial Headquarters disclosed the Japanese losses for the first time, which were described as "one light carrier and thirty-one planes."[6]

Once all data was collected and Operation MO was officially postponed, the Imperial Headquarters made the final announcement about the Battle of the Coral Sea at 1600 hours on 12 May. Tokyo confirmed sinking the *Saratoga*-class and the *Yorktown*-class carriers, the *California*-class battleship and one destroyer, and severely damaging the *Warspite*-class battleship, the *Canberra*-class cruiser, another cruiser of unknown class, and the 20,000-ton tanker. Allegedly, the Americans had lost ninety-eight planes. The Japanese losses included one light carrier converted from a tanker and thirty-one planes. On 25 May the Imperial Headquarters added to the assessment the sinking of a *Portland*-class cruiser and damaging a *North Carolina*–class battleship. The previously reported cruiser of unknown class was identified as belonging to the *Louisville* class.[7]

Soon after, the Battle of the Coral Sea became a topic in Japanese magazines that was addressed to the broader public. The *Weekly Bulletin* No. 293 explained the importance of the first carrier clash in history and presented the list of the destroyed Allied ships until 10 May.[8] Additionally, on 3 June, on the eve of the Battle of Midway, the Japanese released the *Weekly Photographic Bulletin*, which revealed the first photographs taken during the Battle of the Coral Sea. The first pages of the magazine showed the *Saratoga* and the *Yorktown* being attacked by the torpedo and dive bombers.[9]

Despite multiple signs and facts suggesting the need to verify the American losses in the Battle of the Coral Sea, the official narrative, boasting of the sinking of two carriers and at least one battleship, was repeated by all Japanese works published during the Pacific War that touched on this topic.[10]

Unlike the Imperial Headquarters, CINCPAC tried not to multiply the enemy's losses in the Coral Sea until confirmation was obtained from intercepted messages. The Americans were sure they had sunk one light carrier and probably also a fleet carrier of an unspecified class and several other smaller vessels. There was a delay in releasing detailed analysis of the battle because CINCPAC insisted on keeping the number of American carriers secret before the upcoming Operation MI. The mysterious silence became suspicious for some skeptics, who believed that the U.S. Navy had covered up a disastrous defeat. They were soon proved wrong because the victory at Midway was also followed by the disclosure of the results of the action in the Coral Sea.

The outcome of the first carrier battle was presented entirely differently in the American press, which celebrated the Nippon Kaigun's defeat. On 9 May the newspapers in Washington informed the public that for the first time since the outbreak of war in the Far East, an Allied fleet had secured a brilliant victory against the Japanese. On 10 May the *New York Times* included a headline about beating the enemy in a long battle in the Pacific. The Japanese supposedly lost seventeen to twenty-two ships and were escaping from the battlefield. Hanson Baldwin, a famous press commentator, also claimed that the course of the Pacific War and World War II was completely reversed and that the Battle of the Coral Sea would surely go down in history as one of the most significant victories of the U.S. Navy.[11]

Regardless of the war propaganda, CINCPAC had little time to celebrate the victory. It was a significant success for the Allies to prevent the Japanese from seizing Port Moresby, especially in terms of securing the shipping lines to Australia. Still, the U.S. Navy's eyes were already turned to the Central Pacific in the second part of May. The Combined Fleet planned to invade Midway by committing at least four carriers. Nimitz decided to take up the gauntlet and use all his advantages. It wasn't hard to predict that the upcoming battle had the potential to overshadow the first carrier clash in history.

Chapter 18

WHAT FAILED ON THE JAPANESE SIDE?

An Analysis

The Battle of the Coral Sea was a Pyrrhic victory for Japan. It resulted in the sinking of the *Lexington* and damaging the *Yorktown* but did not entail the strategic success that Operation MO had envisaged. In several respects, the events in early May 1942 were groundbreaking for both sides. But it was the Nippon Kaigun that experienced something that didn't look promising for the future. It was the first clash between carriers and it also resulted in the first failed campaign, the loss of the first carrier, and the first horrendous losses in the carrier air groups, both material and in personnel. The Japanese confidence in achieving all the objectives of Operation MO backfired at the least expected moment. The underestimated enemy not only defended Port Moresby but also significantly weakened the Kidō Butai's potential on the eve of the Battle of Midway. Putting the *Shōkaku* and the *Zuikaku* in reserve for more than a month during the most critical period of the war probably led to the most significant gain for the U.S. Navy. The Nippon Kaigun, considered invincible in the first phase of the conflict, revealed its weaknesses and gave the enemy little, but it had enough time to learn a precious lesson before the fateful month of June in 1942.

It is no exaggeration to say that the MO Kidō Butai could have won the Battle of the Coral Sea by destroying TF 17 and that Operation MO could have ended with the seizure of Port Moresby. The Fourth Fleet would probably have suffered some losses, such as the sinking of the *Shōhō* or any transport ship. This strategic success wasn't impossible. It was on the horizon, but the Japanese forfeited it because they made multiple blunders. Additionally, even if Port Moresby hadn't been captured, Fletcher could have lost two fleet carriers, significantly changing the stage for Operation MI. Instead, the MO Kidō Butai sank only the *Lexington* and nearly lost the *Shōkaku*. The Japanese exchanged their two carriers for the *Lexington* in the longer term. The result of the Battle of the Coral Sea was something the Nippon Kaigun should have avoided at all costs. So, what went wrong on the Japanese side? The answer might be shocking to the reader: almost everything.

Researching the Japanese primary and secondary sources made it possible to answer the first question in the introduction to this book. Operation MO, developed by the Fourth Fleet, should be assessed as a colossal misunderstanding. Inoue didn't possess enough resources to progress with such a detailed and complicated plan, yet he created various task groups whose roles were interdependent, and the tasks often remained too broad to be executed in a short period. For example, although the idea of securing Tulagi to open up the seaplane base and extend the reconnaissance range in the eastern part of the Solomon Islands before the MO Kidō Butai entered the Coral Sea was good, the MO Main Force covered the landing in the Solomon Islands and then needed to rush westward to screen the Port Moresby Invasion Force. After a short break, the Fourth Fleet intended to conquer distant Nauru and Ocean by 15 May by using some ships from the previous stage of the operation. Still, the final version of Operation MO was much better than the initial one, because the Combined Fleet canceled the 5th Kōkū Sentai's air raids on the Australian bases. One can only imagine what would have happened regarding the original plan of sending two carriers against Townsville and Cooktown if Ugaki hadn't intervened on 29 April. Inoue's obsession with using two precious carriers against the ground targets when the enemy carrier task force was expected to be in the Coral Sea was also criticized by the 5th Kōkū Sentai's staff. And surprisingly, those concerns were shared even by some of the Fourth Fleet staff members, and Yano's support for Hara made Inoue less adamant. Nevertheless, excessive complexity left no room for delays or mistakes, which were regular parts of each war campaign. They had already happened in the first days of Operation MO, when the Japanese hadn't even seen the enemy, and this immediately affected the entire schedule.

Most Japanese historians are critical of Operation MO. One cannot disagree with S. Mori's view that after the Dutch East Indies campaign, the Nippon Kaigun started to believe that the enemy was too beaten up and weak for the time being to stop the advance beyond the Malay barrier. To save time and resources for the decisive battle in the Central Pacific, the Japanese sent their second-rate ships to execute Operation MO, and they stumbled across the unexpectedly solid American opposition.[1]

In other words, the Japanese lost their first gamble in the South Pacific. They failed to secure their objectives by using only two carriers and sticking to the preparations for Operation MI, a top priority for the Combined Fleet since early April.

However, to spare Yamamoto from unfair criticism, it is essential to mention that Inoue never suggested engaging more than two carriers in Operation MO. His preference was the 2nd Kōkū Sentai, which was more experienced than the 5th Kōkū Sentai but was in a similarly tricky position after the Indian Ocean raid. The *Shōkaku* and the *Zuikaku* lost nine planes and the *Hiryū* and the *Sōryū* lost eight.[2] Even assuming that the losses in the 2nd Kōkū Sentai would be replenished in the same way that ended up happening in reality, the unit still needed additional training and some rest. Moreover, although the *Hiryū* and the *Sōryū* might be more efficient against the American carriers, they were very vulnerable to receiving hits. As the Battle of Midway showed, three 1000-pound bombs were enough to sink the *Sōryū*, something that the *Shōkaku* survived in the Coral Sea.[3] It is impossible to state that the course of an "alternative Battle of the Coral Sea" would be the same, but it is vital to say that Japanese damage control was universally very poor at the time, and the older carriers lacked the structural protection that the *Shōkaku* and the *Zuikaku* possessed as the newer constructions. Thus, locating the 2nd Kōkū Sentai in the South Pacific could have resulted in more potent offensive capacities at the cost of the higher risk of losing the first fleet carrier. Notably, no one in the Nippon Kaigun saw the need to assign more than one carrier

PHOTO 20 ■ Sea burial ceremony on the *Zuikaku*'s deck soon after the Battle of the Coral Sea *Mori,* Akatsuki

squadron to support Operation MO. The responsibility for a gamble rested on everyone involved in the planning.

Even with this significant setback in operational planning, the 5th Kōkū Sentai was close to destroying two American carriers or, at least, to sinking the *Lexington* and putting the *Yorktown* out of service for a long time and making her miss the Battle of Midway. The Japanese were correct that the 5th Kōkū Sentai could be enough to win Operation MO. But the unit made too many mistakes to make a strategic victory a realistic outcome. The Combined Fleet and the Fourth Fleet knew about the inexperienced crews in the 5th Kōkū Sentai and sent them for "additional training" but expected an excellent performance. The gamble didn't pay off, and the price for losing this bet was high.

The risk concerning the allocation of the 5th Kōkū Sentai to the demanding operation could have been reduced by using the Fourth Fleet's asset, the *Shōhō*. Hara's staff officers directly recommended combining all carriers into one task force. Their suggestion was rejected due to Inoue's promise made to

Horii. In reality, the *Shōhō* air group was feeble and unsuitable for deterring Allied bombers in two distant locations, particularly after the convoy passed the Jomard Passage. Despite some successful patrols in the first days, her support for the transport ships was illusionary. Her presence near the Port Moresby Invasion Force only attracted the enemy's attention and made the group more vulnerable to air attacks. As the events would show, the *Shōhō*'s presence alongside the MO Kidō Butai, even with her several Zeros and six Kates, could have become critical support on 8 May when the striking group lacked the bombers to develop a full-scale and coordinated attack on the *Yorktown*. Instead, she was pointlessly lost on 7 May and had no real chance to contribute to Operation MO.

Another of Inoue's planning blunders was sticking to the idea of delivering Zeros for the Tainan Kū to Rabaul. Using the carriers heading to the Solomon Islands to transfer several additional fighters wasn't a unique concept. In the same campaign, the Americans also intended to employ TF 16, which was rushing southward, to ferry a squadron of fighters to Efate. Although the idea itself wasn't bad, the first failed execution on 2 May should have resulted in postponing the transfer until the MO Kidō Butai was certain about the enemy's situation. In such a tight schedule, where every Japanese move depended on coordination and air support, delaying Takagi's march southward was leaving everything to chance regarding the hope that the Americans would not intervene.

Some elements of Operation MO revealed Inoue's true nature. He was more of a military politician than a commander committed to helping his subordinates fulfill strategic and tactical objectives. When he was developing a plan for seizing Port Moresby, he focused on conciliating the interests of the Fourth Fleet, the South Seas Detachments, and the Eleventh Air Fleet. He sacrificed the *Shōhō* to give Horii a sense that he had air support and slowed down the MO Kidō Butai to deliver the fighters for Yamada. He put others' interests ahead of his own and that of the men under his command. He acted as if Operation MO was a joint action rather than his sole responsibility and his planning mistakes led to the first strategic loss of the Nippon Kaigun.

The failure of Operation MO was a great surprise to the Combined Fleet, which hadn't expected that the U.S. Navy could halt the Japanese advance in the South Pacific. But after looking at the first report of the Battle of the Coral Sea, Yamamoto still criticized Inoue for his insufficient aggressiveness. In one of the letters, he said, "Inoue is not good at fighting."[4] The emperor also expressed his opinion on the Fourth Fleet commander to the navy minister. Admiral Shimada heard from Hirohito that Inoue was more of a scholar than a commander.[5]

Nonetheless, it would be unfair to blame Inoue for all of the Japanese errors, especially for the tactical command in the battle. He set up the rocky stage but didn't make the decisions regarding the air operation on critical days. This leads us to the second question from the introduction, namely the mistakes committed by the 5th Kōkū Sentai's command. When the MO Kidō Butai departed Truk, Takagi and Hara were in an excellent position to surprise Fletcher. Despite deciphering some Japanese messages about Operation MO, the Americans still lacked substantial knowledge about the moves of the enemy carrier task force. They expected the MO Kidō Butai to enter the Coral Sea west of Bougainville while Takagi passed east of the Solomon Islands and found himself on Fletcher's right flank. Thus, I agree with H. Itō, a Japanese historian of the intelligence in the Pacific War, that regarding four fundamental questions, "3W1H" (where, when, what and how?), the U.S. Navy only knew the answers to the first two and that they weren't enough to give the battle on its ground.[6] Still, the Americans used their knowledge to immediately deploy two carriers to oppose Operation MO in the first phase and another two to join the combat in the following days. Thus, even if MO Kidō Butai destroyed Fletcher's forces, it couldn't continue the fight with Halsey on an equal footing.

In July 1942 Lt. Cdr. Kazuo Dohi from the Combined Fleet's command found the file containing the cables sent to Inoue during the Battle of the Coral Sea, and he was astonished by the annotations at the margins: "Stupid Fourth Fleet" and "What the hell are they doing?" The language of Yamamoto's staff was offensive yet reflected the frustration resulting from the decisions made by Inoue, especially on the afternoon of 8 May.[7]

Interestingly, Inoue also had an unfavorable opinion of the leadership during Operation MO, although he never publicly expressed it. When one of the Japanese newspapers published an article about the great victory in the

Battle of the Coral Sea, he wrote in his diary, "In general, this naval battle was the one in which the admirals failed, and the soldiers won. Their mistakes caused the subordinates to struggle. As a commander in chief, I was not in a celebratory mood."[8]

Inoue was right, but only to some extent. In addition to the Fourth Fleet's errors, the 5th Kōkū Setai command and "ordinary soldiers" committed many critical mistakes that influenced the course of the battle. They had an opportunity to secure a more assured victory, but the clash ended in horrendous losses. Apart from the previously mentioned numbers of the killed, missing, and wounded aircrews, the 5th Kōkū Sentai irreversibly lost 61 out of 116 planes. Those losses could have been significantly lower if a few things had been done differently. Primarily, Hara's decision to send the most experienced crews for the very risky dusk attack on 7 May was a blunder. Despite Mieno's warning, he trusted Yamaoka's overly optimistic assessment. He was indeed pressed by the Fourth Fleet, which expressed disappointment in his initial intention not to send the striking group. However, there was only a vague idea about the enemy's position, and the 5th Kōkū Sentai pointlessly lost nine planes, including eight torpedo bombers. Four dive bombers were also severely damaged, and one dive bomber crew couldn't take part in action the following day. The numbers show that Hara's decision effectively lost ten *kankō* and *kambaku*, which could have changed the outcome of the attack on the *Yorktown*.

Before the decisive clash on 8 May, the casualties in the 5th Kōkū Sentai were excessively high due to wrong calls or mistakes. On the evening of 7 May Hara disposed of 96 out of the 116 planes he had when the MO Kidō Butai set off from Truk. Among twenty lost aircraft, only two of them were lost in the actual attack on the enemy's ships—the *Neosho* and the *Sims*. The other losses resulted from bad decisions or errors of inexperienced crews. For example, Hara lost four torpedo bombers and one dive bomber during the regular reconnaissance or anti-torpedo-plane patrols on 1 and 7 May. Even after the attack on TF 17 on 8 May, the 5th Kōkū Sentai's maintenance officers recklessly jettisoned twelve planes without knowing the actual losses. It is hard to deny that some aircraft were unserviceable, but some were thrown overboard rashly to speed up accommodating the other planes. This resulted

TABLE 51 ■ **Number of Lost Planes (Shot Down, Ditched, Jettisoned, and Damaged beyond Repair) in the MO Kidō Butai during Operation MO**

	Zuikaku			*Shōkaku*			Total
	K	V	Z	K	V	Z	
30 April	19	21	19	19	19	19	116
1 May (patrol)	2	1	—	—	—	—	3
7 May (morning attack)	—	2	—	—	—	—	—
7 May (recon)	—	—	—	2	—	—	2
7 May (dusk attack)	5	*(4)	—	3	—	—	9
7 May (unknown)	—	—	—	—	—	1	1
8 May (recon)	—	—	—	1	—	—	1
8 May (attack)	6	5	1	8	13	1	34
8 May (defense)	—	—	2	—	—	7	9
Lost in total	13	9	3	14	13	9	61
Percent	68.4%	42.9%	15.7%	73.6%	68.4%	47.3%	52.6%

Sources: JACAR: Shōkaku (1); JACAR: Zuikaku (1)(2); JACAR: Sangokai Shiryō (1), 14.

*(4) Represents four Vals that were damaged during the dusk attack on 7 May and didn't participate in the battle on 8 May but were pending repairs in the days following

in only fifteen operational bombers and twelve pending repairs on the evening of 8 May, but a couple more could have been salvaged if the maintenance team had been better organized. Overall, the plane losses and the course of the battle on 8 May proved that the *Shōhō* could have become a critical support for the 5th Kōkū Sentai. Her six Kates could have tipped the balance during the attack on the *Yorktown*, and her thirteen Zeros could have helped the CAP to defend the *Shōkaku*. The outcome of this hypothetical clash will always remain a mystery because the *Shōhō* could have become a target for the enemy like the *Shōkaku*.

Poor decisions made by the 5th Kōkū Sentai's command between 1300 hours on 6 May and 2000 hours on 7 May significantly reduced the Japanese chances of winning the Battle of the Coral Sea decisively. The series of poor choices started when Hara didn't send the reconnaissance planes to follow up on the contact report of the flying boat from the Yokohama Kū. He could easily have found both American carriers and their location in the afternoon.

Even if the envisaged attack didn't materialize on 6 May, the morning scouring missions would have looked different if he had found them, and the probability of attacking the secondary targets, the *Neosho* and the *Sims*, would have been reduced. Instead, Hara, Mieno, and Yamaoka were confident enough on the evening of 6 May that they would find and destroy Fletcher before he hit the Port Moresby Invasion Force. Despite many warnings from the friendly group, they consciously gambled on the convoy's safety, which resulted in the sinking of the *Shōhō*. Ironically, in response to the erroneous reconnaissance report, the first blow was directed against two unimportant ships. Since the Fourth Fleet had lost the *Shōhō* in the morning, it pressed the 5th Kōkū Sentai to attack in the evening. Hara didn't have a strong enough personality to command decisively and yielded to Yamaoka's optimism. He took another risk and ordered the dusk attack despite many alarming indicators. This gamble was lost as well.

When Hara returned to Japan, he talked honestly with Ugaki about the battle. Hara admitted that 7 May was unfortunate for him and that he had thought about leaving the navy that day. Events on 8 May reversed the situation, but the *Shōkaku* was also damaged. He said that he acted according to instructions and retreated north and then rushed south to finish off the enemy, but he didn't have confidence in this plan.[9] This conversation alone demonstrated that Hara was mentally unprepared for being a successful commander, because he tended to collapse after slipups and waited for orders rather using his initiative and acting according to his own judgment. The Combined Fleet was also dissatisfied with his performance during the battle. On 14 July 1942, at the same time as the 5th Kōkū Sentai was disbanded, he was recalled by the Naval General Staff of the carrier command and put in charge of the 8th Sentai, which suited his competencies better.

Much attention has been paid to the blunders of the Japanese commanders, but what about the ordinary pilots who fought the Battle of the Coral Sea? The 5th Kōkū Sentai's aircrews desperately wanted to prove their value to their older colleagues and paid a tremendous price for the tactical victory. The attack on TF 17 on 8 May showed their high skills and spirit. However, it didn't mean they avoided mistakes. The most notable one was made by the *Shōkaku*'s reconnaissance bombers, who reported seeing one carrier south of the MO Kidō Butai. The initial sighting error could have been quickly clarified, but this didn't happen until Takahashi arrived at the spot. This fatal mistake soon turned into another one when the pilots lost their way and didn't return to the *Shōkaku*, weakening the 5th Kōkū Sentai's striking potential.

It's important to mention that the crews of two of the *Shōkaku* torpedo bombers weren't the only ones who made an error during the reconnaissance mission that significantly influenced the course of the battle. On 6 May the Yokohama Kū's flying boat made a crucial sighting that could have been used in Japan's favor, but WO Yamaguchi reported an incorrect course for TF 17. Fletcher was heading northeast, not south, so another Mavis sent from Tulagi couldn't reestablish contact with the American carriers and confirm their distance, bearing, and course. Unfortunately for the Japanese, Yamaguchi informed the base about only one carrier rather than two, which led the 5th Kōkū Sentai to the conclusion that the *Shōkaku*'s *kankō* had found the same carrier task force on the morning of 7 May.[10]

On 8 May some crews made a mistake by releasing torpedoes from an altitude too high and too far away from the target. According to the navy's "attack method no. 1," a torpedo should be released from 20 meters and about 1,000 meters while flying at 160 knots and keeping the bomber horizontally over the sea's surface. The observer checked the victim's speed and course changes to adjust the aim.[11] Due to heavy American antiaircraft fire and insufficient experience of the Japanese crews, several Kates didn't get as close as one thousand meters. Thus, the *Yorktown* wasn't even threatened and the *Lexington* wasn't sunk as fast as she could have been.

As for the dive bombers, their attack ended in scoring only three direct hits and a couple of near misses. The hit ratio was lower than 10 percent, but the Japanese expected a performance of at least two times higher than this, based on past actions. Notably, Ema's *buntai* had a unique chance to put the *Yorktown* out of service for longer but failed to take advantage of the situation on the battlefield.

Although the Japanese fighter pilots proved their skills and reported low losses, their performance left a lot to be desired, especially considering the defense of the *Shōkaku*. The lack of radar and the faulty fighter direction caused the planes to await the enemy's arrival in the wrong sectors, while the

American bombers outmaneuvered CAP and weren't harassed by antiaircraft fire as much as their Japanese counterparts.

Both *hikōtaichō* remained lucid during the entire battle and were the brightest points of the 5th Kōkū Sentai. Even when Ichihara sent the first overly optimistic report about sinking two American carriers, Takahashi tried to correct him while withdrawing from the battlefield. Soon after, he and his observer were mortally wounded by the enemy fighters and didn't return to the *Shōkaku*. The shooting down of Takahashi was the most devastating blow to the 5th Kōkū Sentai after the death toll within the aircrews.

Even considering every mistake and setback, the Japanese aircrews demonstrated that they were well trained and highly motivated. The sacrifice of Kanno's crew and the reaction of other crews going to strike TF 17 spoke for themselves.

Surprisingly, the Japanese failed to use their trump card in Operation MO, the 25th Kōkū Sentai, which could have attacked TF 17 at a critical moment and helped the MO Kidō Butai to achieve a more sound battle result. Land-based bombers weren't as efficient as in the first weeks of the Pacific War, but their arrival on the battlefield at the correct time, especially after the 5th Kōkū Sentai strike, could have become a deathly threat for the American carriers. Instead, Yamada eliminated his only opportunity to change anything to favor the Japanese. His haste resulted in huge losses being suffered in the 4th Kū. If the 5th and the 25th Kōkū Sentai had worked out how to coordinate, Fletcher could have faced severe trouble trying to save the *Yorktown* from additional hits or near misses.

In May 1942 the Japanese repeatedly underlined that they had just fought the first carrier battle in history. This consciousness was visible at each level of the naval hierarchy.[12] The experiences from the clash with the Americans could have become essential to preparing a better plan for Operation MI. Observations made by the 5th Kōkū Sentai command and the aircrews, which had experienced their first chance to cross swords with the U.S. Navy carriers, could have been precious for the Kidō Butai and the entire navy. Apart from the lecture given by Lieutenant Commander Fukuchi on 26 May, mentioned previously, the Combined Fleet didn't try to study the battle to make necessary improvements, even at the last moment before Operation MI began. Many historians explain this phenomenon by referring to the famous *senshōbyō* (a victory disease), but the Japanese knew there was much room for improvement. The decision to proceed with a new offensive in the Central Pacific without two of the six carriers and a profound discussion about the 5th Kōkū Sentai's experience was dictated by a desperate race against time. Having received the reports about the sinking of two American carriers in the Coral Sea, the Combined Fleet believed that early June was the last time the Kidō Butai could use its visible numerical advantage. The estimations proved wrong, and the decisive carrier battle turned into a disastrous defeat.

Despite the Combined Fleet's arrogance, the Japanese conclusions from the Battle of the Coral Sea are worth mentioning. Although they were not reflected in the action taken on the eve of the Battle of Midway, this doesn't mean that private observations could not be valuable in the longer term.

For example, Inoue made seventeen comments in his diary about Hara's battle report. He started with remarks about the attack on the *Neosho* and the *Sims* and the unfortunate timing of the reconnaissance cables sent by the torpedo bombers and the seaplanes. Inoue wrote that Hara didn't sufficiently search the spotted enemy task force in the western direction during the unfortunate morning strike and lost almost two hours. Also, he didn't understand why Hara changed his mind about sending the dusk attack despite being 350 miles from the enemy and initially informing the Fourth Fleet about having no plans to strike. Inoue felt that the weather on that day wasn't in Japan's favor. It prevented the MO Kidō Butai from spotting TF 17 and led to high losses among the crews who participated in the risky dusk attack. According to Inoue, the pilots were extremely unfortunate because they dumped their bombs and torpedoes and soon stumbled on the enemy carriers on which they almost landed. When discussing 8 May, Inoue wrote that he was concerned about the confusion related to the sinking of the *Saratoga* and the *Yorktown*. He tried to find reports that unanimously confirmed the battle results. For him, the 80 to 90 percent accuracy of the torpedo and dive bombers was marvelous. However, it seems reasonable to wonder whether he believed these figures. He noted that the *Yorktown* was hit by three torpedoes and nine bombs and that she sank, like the *Hermes*. He assessed that the fighter escort was good enough and that the losses among the bombers were low during the approach. However, the antiaircraft fire forced some torpedo bombers to drop their torpedoes from above fifty meters. The American torpedo planes' attack on the *Shōkaku* was summarized as illustrating a very poor performance, although the planes managed to slowly descend close to the sea's surface.[13]

Yamaoka also had his own conclusions. In the last pages of his diary, he disclosed a private opinion. He had a strong awareness that he had participated in the first carrier battle in history, but he felt that many things could have gone better. He divided the battle into two parts. The first, from 1 to 7 May, was extremely bad for the Japanese. The second, on 8 May, turned the tables. He noted the high losses in the 5th Kōkū Sentai from when the unit departed from Truk. He complained about its insufficient knowledge of the enemy task force and its movements. Yamaoka felt that submarines and air reconnaissance from land bases (flying boats) could have contributed more to the battle. However, he also criticized the 5th Kōkū Sentai for weak scouting that led to many negative consequences. Finally, he noticed the problems with planes refueling, especially regarding carriers in the frontal positions, which needed reconsideration. He understood that the clash had a special value for the Nippon Kaigun, because it could finally learn American carrier tactics. But the reality was different. Yamaoka knew that the Japanese had underestimated the lessons it could learn from the Coral Sea in the crucial moment of the Pacific War.[14]

On 21 September 1942 the Yokosuka Kū released a secret report on the Battle of the Coral Sea, which was part of a bigger project on lessons learned from the war. It comprised ninety-eight pages and mostly reflected the conclusions covered in this chapter. It confirmed, among other things, the mistakes made in air reconnaissance, in the defense of the *Shōkaku*, in communication, in coordination, and in several bad decisions. According to the authors, Hara didn't use the 5th Kōkū Sentai's full offensive potential and thus he didn't secure the objectives. The report also noted that the American defense of the carrier task force was much more effective than the Japanese defense and that the bombers couldn't feel safe even after completing the attack. In comparison, the American dive bombers, described as "Curtiss" aircraft, were considered very dangerous. Since the report was produced in the middle of the Guadalcanal campaign, the Japanese had already tasted the destructive power of SBDs and could not revert the course of the Battle of Midway. Despite sharing many critical reflections, the report had a limited effect on the war situation.[15]

I believe, the Nippon Kaigun could have learned one essential lesson from the Battle of the Coral Sea, even without a detailed analysis, based on firsthand observations. This lesson could have been communicated to officers and aircrews without delay, especially considering the tight schedule before Operation MI commenced.

What was this lesson?

When Hara returned to Japan and headed to the Ministry of the Navy to attend a hearing about the battle, he met officers he was acquainted with in the corridor. They asked him, "How was it?"

Hara replied, "Amerika wa tsuyoi desu yo."[16]

What he meant was straightforward: "America is strong."

The Japanese could have learned not to gamble by underestimating the enemy.

Appendix 1

Order of Battle, Japanese Forces

Source: JACAR: MO Kidō Butai (1), 3; JACAR: MO Sakusen: Tsuragi, 3–6; NDL: Yamaoka Shuki, 18; NDL: Senkun: Sangokai Kaisen; *Senshi Sōsho*, 49:267–68.

Nanyō Butai—South Seas Force

Commander: Vice Adm. Shigeyoshi Inoue, commander in chief of the Fourth Fleet

1. MO Kidō Butai
   Commander: Vice Adm. (since 1 May) Takeo Takagi, commander of the 5th Sentai
   1.1. Main Force
      5th Sentai (heavy cruisers): *Myōkō* (F), *Haguro*
      7th Destroyer Division: *Akebono, Ushio*
   1.2 Carrier Force
      Commander: Rear Adm. Chūichi Hara, commander of the 5th Kōkū Sentai
      5th Kōkū Senta: *Zuikaku* (F) (19 fighters, 21 dive bombers, 19 torpedo bombers), *Shōkaku* (19 fighters, 19 dive bombers, 19 torpedo bombers)
      27th Destroyer Division: *Ariake, Yūgura, Shirayuki, Shigure*
   1.3 Supply Force
      Oiler: *Tōhō Maru*
2. MO Invasion Force
   Commander: Rear Adm. Aritomo Gotō, commander of the 6th Sentai
   2.1 MO Main Force
      6th Sentai (heavy cruisers): *Aoba* (F), *Kako, Kinugasa, Furutaka*
      Light carrier: *Shōhō* (16 fighters, 6 torpedo bombers)
      Destroyer: *Sazanami*
   2.2 Covering Force
      Commander: Rear Adm. Kuninori Marumo, commander of the 18th Sentai
      18th Sentai (light cruisers): *Tenryū* (F), *Tatsuta*
      Seaplane tenders: *Kamikawa Maru, Kiyokawa Maru*
      Gunboats: *Keijō Maru, Seikai Maru, Nikkai Maru*
      Two auxiliary minesweepers
   2.3 Port Moresby (RZP) Invasion Force
      Commander: Rear Adm. Sadamichi Kajioka, commander of the 6th Suirai Sentai

6th Suirai Sentai: *Yūbari* (F) (light cruiser); *Oite, Asanagi, Mutsuki, Yayoi, Mochizuki* (destroyers)
Minelayer: *Tsugaru*
Minesweeper No. 20
Six navy transport ships: *Mogamigawa Maru, Chōwa Maru, Goyō Maru, Akiba Maru, Shōka Maru, Azumasan Maru*
Six army transport ships: *Asakasan Maru, China Maru, Mito Maru, Matsue Maru, Taifuku Maru, Hibi Maru*
Oiler: *Irō*

2.4 Tulagi (RXB) Invasion Force
Commander: Rear Adm. Kiyohide Shima, commander of the 19th Sentai
19th Sentai (minelayer): *Okinoshima* (F)
Destroyers: *Kikuzuki* and *Yūzuki*
Transport ships: *Kōei Maru, Azumasan Maru*
Auxiliary minesweepers: *Wa-1, Wa-2, Tama Maru, Hagoromo Maru, Noshiro Maru No. 2*, subchaser *Tama Maru No. 8*

Submarines

Commander: Capt. Noboru Ishizaki
I-21, I-22, I-24, I-28, I-29, Ro-33, Ro-34

Land-Based Air Forces

(participated in the battle)
Commander: Vice Adm. Nishizō Tsukahara, commander in chief of the Eleventh Air Fleet

1. 25th Kōkū Sentai (5th Kūshū Butai)
Commander: Rear Adm. Sadayoshi Yamada, commander of the 25th Kōkū Sentai

1.1 4th Kaigun Kōkūtai
12 land-based bombers (Betty)

1.2 Tainan Kaigun Kōkūtai
11 land-based fighters (Zero)

1.3 Genzan Kaigun Kōkūtai
20 land-based bombers (Nell)w

1.4 Yokohama Kaigun Kōkūtai
7 flying boats (Mavis)

Appendix 2

Order of Battle, Allied Forces

Task Force 17

Commander: Rear Adm. Frank J. Fletcher

1. Carrier Air Group (Task Group 17.5)
   Commander: Rear Adm. Aubrey W. Fitch
      Carriers: *Yorktown* (F) (17 fighters, 35 dive bombers, 13 torpedo bombers)
      Lexington (21 fighters, 35 dive bombers, 12 torpedo bombers)
      Destroyers: *Morris, Anderson, Hammann, Russell*
2. Attack Group (Task Group 17.2)
   Commander: Rear Adm. Thomas C. Kinkaid
      Cruisers: *New Orleans, Astoria, Minneapolis, Portland, Chester*
      Destroyers: *Phelps, Farragut, Dewey, Monaghan, Aylwin*
3. Support Group (Task Group 17.3)
   Commander: Rear Adm. John G. Crace
      Heavy cruisers: *Chicago, Australia*
      Light cruiser: *Hobart*
      Destroyers: *Perkins, Walke* (since 7 May)
4. Fueling Group (Task Group 17.6)
   Commander: Capt. John S. Phillips
      Oilers: *Neosho, Tippecanoe*
      Destroyers: *Sims, Worden*
      Search Group (Task Group 17.9)
5. Seaplane Tender Group
   Commander: Cdr. Clifton A. F. Sprague
   Seaplane tender: *Tangier* (12 flying boats [Catalina])

South West Pacific Area

Command: Gen. Douglas MacArthur

1. Allied Naval Forces
   Commander: Vice Adm. Herbert F. Leary
2. Allied Air Forces
   Commander: Lt. Gen. George Brett
   1.1 USAAF
   1.2 RAAF
3. Port Moresby Garrison
   Commander: Maj. Gen. Basil M. Morris

Appendix 3

Zuikaku and *Shōkaku* Air Group Rosters

瑞鶴飛行機隊 ***Zuikaku* hikōkitai** ***Zuikaku* Air Group** Planes marked as スカ (SU-KA); tail code EII.			
No.	**戦闘機隊 (Sentōkitai) (Fighter Group)**	**艦上爆撃機隊 (Kanjō bakugekikitai) (Dive Bomber Group)**	
	Pilot	**Pilot**	**Observer/navigator**
1	Lt. Kiyokuma Okajima (B)	Lt. Tamotsu Ema (B)	WO Higashi
2	Lt. Yūzō Tsukamoto	Lt. Kuzuhara[d†]	PO1c Kawase[d†]
3	WO Sumita	PO1c Andō	Lt. Ōtsuka
4	PO1c Makino	WO Fukunaga	PO1c Ishikawa
5	PO1c Tsukuda	PO1c Nakanishi	WO Izuka
6	PO1c Iwamoto	PO1c Fukugaki[c†]	WO Koyama[c†]
7	PO1c Itō	PO1c Igata	PO1c Shirakura
8	PO1c Komiyama	PO1c Katō	PO2c Fukugaki
9	PO1c Shimizu	PO1c Hatakeyama	PO2c Fujioka
10	PO1c Kanō	PO1c Hori	PO2c Uetani
11	PO1c Kamei	PO2c Sakamaki	PO2c Negishi
12	PO2c Sakaida	PO2c Ishizuka[b†]	PO3c Kawazoe[b†]
13	PO2c Ōkura	PO1c Kamioka[d†]	Sea1c Izumi[d†]
14	PO2c Nakata	PO1c Yamanaka	Sea1c Nakane
15	PO2c Kuroki	Sea1c Matsumoto	Sea1c Tsuji
16	Sea1c Mae	Sea1c Egusa	PO3c Matsushita
17	Sea1c Kurata	Sea1c Kakuta	Sea1c Miyake
18	Sea1c Nisugi	PO2c Sugazaki[a]	Sea1c Sei'ichi[a]
19	Sea1c Fujii	(no crew)	(no crew)

(*continued*)

	艦上攻撃機隊 **(Kanjō kōgekikitai) (Torpedo Bomber Group)**		
	Pilot	**Observer**	**Radio operator**
1	Lt. Cdr. Shigekazu Shimazaki (H)	Lt. Iwami[#]	PO1c Yoshinaga
2	Lt. Tsubota (B)[c†]	PO1c Kosakada[c†]	PO1c Endō[c†]
3	Lt. Murakami[c†]	WO Baba[c†]	PO1c Miyada[c†]
4	Lt. Satō	PO1c Ōtani	PO2c Yoshida
5	PO3c Yokomakura	PO2c Kishi	PO2c Satō
6	Sea1c Nishitani	PO2c Matsuo	Sea1c Ōizumi
7	WO Yaegashi	PO1c Himeishi	Sea1c Ōuchi
8	PO1c Sugimoto[c†]	WO Ni'ino[d†]	Sea1c Hasegawa[c†]
9	Sea1c Tsubokawa[d†]	PO1c Yamada[d†]	PO2c Moriki[d†]
10	PO1c Ishihara	WO Kanazawa	PO2c Nishizawa
11	PO3c Hatanaka	PO1c Ushijima	Sea1c Morishita
12	PO3c Nozawa[c†]	PO1c Kawahara[c†]	Sea1c Honda[c†]
13	PO2c Fukutani[d†]	PO2c Kojima[c†]	Sea1c Hara
14	PO1c Hori	Ens. Matsunaga	PO2c Ōta[#]
15	Sea1c Morimitsu[d†]	PO2c Hiwatashi[d†]	Sea1c Tani[d†]
16	PO1c Satō	PO1c Kawabata	Sea1c Yoshimura
17	PO1c Tahara[c†]	PO2c Ōnishi[c†]	PO3c Kanetō[c†]
18	PO1c Koyama[a†]	Ens. Kaneda[a#]	PO1c Fujita[a]
19	(unknown)[a]	(unknown)[a]	(unknown)[a]
20	(no crew)	PO2c Idehara[d†]	PO2c Ikushima[d†]

[a] Forced to return to Truk or ditched nearby on 1 May
[b] Died on 7 May during the attack on the *Neosho* and the *Sims*
[c] Died on 7 May during the dusk attack
[d] Died on 8 May during the attack on TF 1
[†] Killed in action

翔鶴飛行機隊 ***Shōkaku* hikōkitai** ***Shōkaku* Air Group** Planes marked as シカ (SHI-KA); tail code EI.			
No.	**戦闘機隊 (Sentōkitai)** **(Fighter Group)**	**艦上爆撃機隊 (Kanjō bakugekikitai)** **(Dive Bomber Group)**	
	Pilot	**Pilot**	**Observer/navigator**
1	Lt. Takumi Hoashi (B)	Lt. Cdr. Kakuichi Takahashi (H)[dt]	Ens. Nozu[dt]
2	Lt. Yamamoto	PO1c Shinohara	PO1c Someno
3	Ens. Abe	Sea1 Fukuhara[dt]	PO2c Suzuki[dt]
4	WO Hanzawa	Lt. Yamaguchi	Ens. Naka
5	PO1c Nishide	PO1c Ueshima[#]	PO1c Kōda
6	PO1c Matsuda	Sea1 Odagiri	Sea1c Yokota
7	PO1c Minami	PO1c Itō[dt]	Lt. Koizumi[dt]
8	PO1c Miyazawa[et]	PO1c Shirai	PO1c Koitabashi
9	PO1c Kawanishi	PO3c Harashima	PO3c Tanaka[#]
10	PO2c Sasaki	PO1c Suzuki	WO Kokubu
11	PO2c Yamamoto	PO2c Katō[dt]	PO2c Kushima[dt]
12	PO2 Okabe	Sea1c Ōgawa	PO3c Ōura
13	PO2c Ichinose[et]	Lt. Mifuku[#]	PO1c Imada
14	PO3c Tanaka	PO2c Ikeda[dt]	PO1c Nagasawa[dt]
15	PO3c Horiguchi	PO2c Sugimura	PO3c Yoshinaga
16	PO3c Komachi	Sea1c Okada	PO2c Kitamura
17	Sea1c Imamura	WO Matsuda[dt]	PO1c Nobe[dt]
18	Sea3c Kōno	PO1c Nakasho	PO2c Togashi
19	(no crew)	PO3c Hanawa[dt]	Sea1c Matsuda[dt]

(*continued*)

	艦上攻撃機隊 (Kanjō kōgekikitai) (Torpedo Bomber Group)		
	Pilot	**Observer**	**Radio operator**
1	Lt. Tatsuo Ichihara (B)	WO Saitō	PO1c Munakata
2	WO Shindō[dt]	Lt. Yano[dt]	PO2c Ibayashi[dt]
3	PO1c Ishikawa	Lt. Hagiwara[bt]	PO2c Sagara[bt]
4	Lt. Iwamura[dt]	PO1c Shirai[bt]	PO2c Misumi[dt]
5	PO1c Satō	WO Isono	PO2c Ishihara
6	PO1c Gotō[ct]	WO Kanno[ct]	PO2c Kishida[ct]
7	PO1c Okimura	WO Ukita	PO2c Tozawa
8	PO1c Saitō[a]	WO Shibata[a]	PO3c Dōmae[a]
9	WO Yonekura[bt]	PO1c Nakamura[dt]	PO2c Fukushima
10	PO1c Akao[a]	PO1c Ōtake[a]	Sea1c Sakashita[a]
11	PO3c Irimi[bt]	PO2c Akaishi[dt]	PO2c Shimomichi[bt]
12	Sea1c Murakami[bt]	PO1c Takahashi[bt]	Sea1c Kodama[bt]
13	PO2c Yoshitomo[dt]	PO2c Tanaka[dt]	PO2c Ōta[dt]
14	PO2c Toda	PO1c Kodama	PO2c Abe
15	PO2c Orikasa	PO2c Shigeta	Sea1c Itō
16	Sea1c Itō[dt]	PO3c Satō[dt]	PO3c Takada[dt]
17	Sea1c Okafuji[dt]	PO1c Mimori	Sea1c Kobayashi[dt]
18	Sea1c Ōtani	PO1c Yamauchi	Sea1c Gomi
19	PO2c Itakura	PO1c Matsuyama	Sea1 Morishita

[a] Ditched at Indispensable Reefs on 7 May, rescued on 8 May by the *Ariake.*
[b] Died on 7 May during the dusk attack
[c] Died on 8 May during the reconnaissance mission
[d] Died on 8 May during the attack on TF 17
[e] Died on 8 May during the defense of the MO Kidō Butai
[†] Killed in action.
Wounded

Appendix 4

Shōhō Air Group Roster

The author finds presenting the undisputed number of planes (*jissū*), their types, and the details about the *Shōhō* air group members challenging. Many years of research conducted on multiple Japanese sources, including primary and secondary ones, that are often contradictory, mean that it is possible to say that the *Shōhō* participated in the Battle of the Coral Sea below her combat potential. The carrier's fixed number of planes (*teisū*) included twelve *kansen* (plus four spares) and nine *kankō* (plus three spares), bringing her group to twenty-one operational planes (plus seven spares). In a perfect scenario, she should have been furnished with Type 0 fighters and Type 97 torpedo bombers. However, due to the shortages of aircraft and crews in late April 1942, the *Shōhō* set off from Yokosuka to the South Pacific with the following:

- 10 × Type 0 fighters (no spares)
- 6 × Type 96 fighters (including 2 × spares)
- 6 × Type 97 torpedo bombers (no spares)

There is no information about allocating any additional planes in Truk.

According to PO3c Nakayama, a pilot wounded during the evacuation of the *Shōhō* who survived the Battle of the Coral Sea, the Zero fighters always had priority in combat action. Claudes were used by four flyers from the same *kō hi 5-ki* (5th pilot class of January 1942), that is, PO2c Aoki, PO2c Inoue, PO2c Tamura, and PO3 Ishikawa.

Surprisingly, the *Shōhō* took part in Operation MO with only six Kates despite having more crews qualified for service in the carrier. The reason for this was the lack of torpedo bombers at the time. The spare aircraft were used to replenish the air groups of fleet carriers as a matter of priority.

Source: JACAR: Gunkan Shōhō (8); JACAR: Shōhō (2); JACAR: MO Kidō Butai (1); Ishikawa, 143–44; Kudo, 132; Kawasaki, 142; Maru, 158; Mori, *Akatsuki*; Hata, Izawa, and Shores, 387.

祥鳳飛行機隊 ***Shōhō* hikōkitai** ***Shōhō* Air Group** Planes marked as シホ (SHI-HO); tail code DII.				
	戦闘機隊 (Sentōkitai) (Fighter Group)	**艦上攻撃機隊 (Kanjō kōgekitai) (Torpedo Bomber Group)**		
No.	Pilot	Pilot	Observer	Radio operator
1	Lt. Nōtomi (B)[a]	Lt. Nakamoto (B)	WO Suzuki	PO1c Hino[b†]
2	PO1c Imamura[b†]	PO2c Ōtsuka	WO Matsumoto	Sea1c Etō
3	PO1c Okugawa[d]	PO3c Seguchi	Sea1c Nishimura	Sea1c Saza[b†]
4	PO2c Aoki[b†]	PO3c Komazaki	Sea1c Mitani[b†]	Sea1c Kanei
5	PO2c Inoue[b†]	Sea1c Takahashi	PO3c Shigetomi	Sea1c Ishiya[b†]
6	PO2c Okazaki[d]	Sea1c Suzuki	PO3c Masuda	Sea1c Nemoto[b†]
7	PO2c Tamura[c†]	(no plane)	(no plane)	(no plane)
8	PO2c Hayashida[d]	(no plane)	(no plane)	(no plane)
9	PO2c Kuwabara[b†]	(no plane)	(no plane)	(no plane)
10	PO3c Ishikawa[a]	(no plane)	(no plane)	(no plane)
11	PO3c Nakayama[d]	—	—	—
12	PO3c Hayakawa[b†]	—	—	—
13	Sea1c Ban'no[a]	—	—	—

[a] Landed at Deboyne on 7 May 1942
[b] Died on 7 May 194.
[c] Died on 2 May 1942
[d] Rescued on 7 May 1942
† Killed in action

Appendix 5

List of Japanese Aircraft

Allied code name	Japanese operational / abbreviated name	Technical name
Alf	Type 94 reconnaissance seaplane (94 *teisatsuki*)	Kawanishi E7K
Betty	Type 1 land-based bomber (1 *rikkō*)	Mitsubishi G4M
Claude	Type 96 carrier fighter (96 *kansen*)	Mitsubishi A5M
Dave	Type 95 reconnaissance seaplane (95 *teisatsuki*)	Nakajima E8N
Jake	Type 0 reconnaissance seaplane (*reisui*)	Aichi E13A
Kate	Type 97 carrier attack plane (97 *kankō*)	Nakajima B5N
Mavis	Type 97 flying boat (*daitei*)	Kawanishi H6K
Nell	Type 96 land-based bomber (96 *rikkō/chūkō*)	Mitsubishi G3M
Pete	Type 0 scouting seaplane (*reikan*)	Mitsubishi F1M
Val	Type 99 carrier dive bomber (99 *kambaku*)	Aichi D3A
Zero	Type 0 carrier fighter (*zerosen*)	Mitsubishi A6M

Appendix 6

Japanese Terminology Relating to the Battle of the Coral Sea

English name	Japanese name	Transcript
Battle of the Coral Sea	珊瑚海海戦	Sangokai Kaisen
Operation MO	MO 作戦	MO Sakusen
Port Moresby Invasion Operation	ポートモレスビー(RZP) 攻略作戦	Pōto Moresubii (RZP) Kōryaku Sakusen
Tulagi Invasion Operation	ツラギ (RXB) 攻略作戦	Tsuragi (RXB) Kōryaku Sakusen
Deboyne	デボイネ諸島	Deboine Shotō
New Guinea	ニューギニア島	Nyū Ginia-tō
Port Moresby	ポートモレスビー	Pōto Moresubii
Rabaul	ラバウル	Rabauru
Tulagi	ツラギ島	Tsuragi-tō
Fourth Fleet	第四艦隊	Dai Yon Kantai
Southern Seas Force	南洋部隊	Nanyō Butai
MO Striking Force	MO 機動部隊	MO Kidō Butai
5th Carrier Squadron	第五航空戦隊	Dai 5 Kōkū Sentai
MO Invasion Force	MO 攻略部隊	MO Kōryaku Butai
MO Main Force	MO 主隊	MO Shutai
Cover Force	掩護部隊	Engo Butai
Port Moresby Invasion Force	ポートモレスビー攻略部隊	Pōto Moresubii Kōryaku Butai
Tulagi Invasion Force	ツラギ攻略部隊	Tsuragi Kōryaku Butai
25th Air Flotilla	第二十五航空戦隊	Dai 25 Kōku Sentai
Tainan Air Group	台南航空隊	Tainan (Kaigun) (Kō)kū(tai)
South Seas Detachment	南海支隊	Nankai Shitai
Task Force 17	第 17 任務部隊	Dai 17 Nim'mu Butai
Lexington	レキシントン	*Rekishinton*
Yorktown	ヨークタウン	*Yōkutaun*

Notes

List of Abbreviations in the Notes

AWM54	Australian War Memorial
JACAR	Japan Center for Asian Historical Records (Kokuritsu Kōbunshokan: Ajia Rekishi Shiryō Sentaa)
KKS	National Archives of Japan (Kokuritsu Kōbunshokan)
NAA	National Australian Archives
NARA	U.S. National Archives and Records Administration
NDL	National Diet Library (Kokuritsu Kokkai Toshokan)
NIDS	National Institute for Defense Studies (Bōei Kenkyūsho)
Senshi Sōsho, vol. 49	Japan's official history of the Battle of the Coral Sea, edited by National Institute for Defense Studies (Bōei Kenkyūsho)

Chapter 1. Japanese Navy Planning for Operation MO

1. *Senshi Sōsho*, 38:94.
2. Mori, *Akatsuki*, 13.
3. Inoue Shigeyoshi Denki Kankōkai, 7.
4. Inoue Shigeyoshi Denki Kankōkai, 267.
5. Inoue Shigeyoshi Denki Kankōkai, 291.
6. Agawa, 221.
7. Chihaya, *Nippon Kaigun Shippai*, 160.
8. *Senshi Sōsho*, 49:103.
9. *Senshi Sōsho*, 49:103.
10. *Senshi Sōsho*, 80:174.
11. NIDS: S16.11.5: Kimitsu GF, 2.
12. *Senshi Sōsho*, 80:174.
13. NDL: Inoue Teichō, 3.
14. NIDS: Chūō, Meirei, 116: Daihon'ei, 3.
15. NDL: Inoue Teichō, 3; *Senshi Sōsho*, 49:104–5.
16. *Senshi Sōsho*, 80:384.
17. Itō, 283–84.
18. JACAR: 6 Suirai Sentai (1) (Ref. C08030122800), 38; *Senshi Sōsho*, 49:109.
19. NIDS: Chūō, Meirei, 116: Daihon'ei, 3; NDL: Inoue Teichō, 5–6; *Senshi Sōsho*, 80:369.

20. Units' reports provide only partial data, which are sometimes contradictory. Most of the losses were suffered by the 6th Suirai Sentai. JACAR: 6 Suirai Sentai (3); JACAR: 6 Suirai Sentai (4); *Senshi Sōsho*, 49:124.
21. *Senshi Sōsho*, 49:130–31.
22. Mori, 29–30.
23. JACAR: Gunkan Shōhō (3), 3; JACAR: Shōhō (1), 11–12.
24. *Senshi Sōsho*, 80:344. However, planning the advance into the Aleutian Islands was more complex. It is essential to mention that the Combined Fleet and the Navy General Staff had held the same opinion since the outbreak of the war. Piegzik, *Into the Endless Mist*, 2–6.
25. *Senshi Sōsho*, 80:341–42.
26. *Senshi Sōsho*, 80:384.
27. Itō, 748.
28. *Senshi Sōsho*, 49:167.
29. JACAR: 5 Sentai (3), 18.
30. Piegzik, *Darkest Hour*, 1:30.
31. Mori, 40.
32. JACAR: 5 Kōkū Sentai Nisshi, S17.05, 1–2.
33. JACAR: 5 Sentai (3), 18–19.
34. *Senshi Sōsho*, 49:188.
35. JACAR: Jirei Kōhō, 1.
36. Piegzik, *Darkest Hour*, 2:61. The table on p. 61 also includes the list of the lost crew members.
37. JACAR: 5 Kōkū Sentai S17.04/3. Reitatsu, 23–24.
38. JACAR: 5 Kōkū Sentai S17.04/5. Sakusen Keika, 3.
39. *Senshi Sōsho*, 49:170.
40. Lundstrom, *First South Pacific*, 66.
41. NDL: Nankai Shitai Kimitsu, 5–8; *Senshi Sōsho*, 49:171–72.
42. NDL: Inoue Teichō, 6; (Sangokai Kaisen Gaiyō, Inoue Dai 4 Kantai Shireichōkan Teichō) *Senshi Sōsho*, 49:176.
43. KKS: Beikokunai Hōsō, 1–2.
44. Yamaoka wrote about one or two expected carriers. NDL: Yamaoka Shuki, 4.
45. *Senshi Sōsho*, 49:176–77.
46. JACAR: MO Kidō Butai (1), 4–5.
47. Itō, 749.
48. JACAR: MO Kidō Butai (1), 13.
49. Mori, 42–43.
50. Mori, 44–46.
51. *Senshi Sōsho*, 49:189–91.

52. JACAR: MO Kidō Butai (1), 5–6.
53. JACAR: MO Kidō Butai (1), 8.
54. Mori, 47–48.
55. JACAR: MO Kidō Butai (1), 8–11.
56. JACAR: 25 Kōkū Sentai/1. Keika, 1.
57. JACAR: 25 Kōkū Sentai/1. Keika, 3.
58. JACAR: Genzan Kū (3), 29; *Senshi Sōshō*, 14:94.
59. JACAR: 25 Kōkū Sentai/3. Reitatsu, 16–21.
60. Mori, 52–55.

Chapter 2. Intercepting Japanese Naval Messages and Responses to Operation MO

1. MacArthur, *Reports of General MacArthur*, 1:23.
2. Lundstrom, *First South Pacific*, 78.
3. *Graybook*, 1:196, 241.
4. Carlson, 251.
5. Lundstrom, *First South Pacific*, 75.
6. K. Hara, 129.
7. Carlson, 270.
8. Lundstrom, *First South Pacific*, 76–77.
9. Hone, 61.
10. *Graybook*, 1:341.
11. Lundstrom, *Black Shoe*, 113.
12. Holmes, 70.
13. *Graybook*, 1:351.
14. Carlson, 271–72.
15. *Graybook*, 1:365.
16. The *Kasuga Maru* was in reality the *Taiyō*.
17. *Graybook*, 1:371–77.
18. Lundstrom, *Black Shoe*, 126.
19. Lundstrom, *First South Pacific*, 85.
20. Carlson, 277–78.
21. Until 22 April the group was called ANZAC Squadron; thus, the unit didn't have a U.S. Navy commander.
22. Lundstrom, *First South Pacific*, 87.
23. Buell, 197.
24. Potter, 68.
25. Carlson, 280.
26. Lundstrom, *First South Pacific*, 88–89.
27. Lundstrom, *First South Pacific*, 89.

28. Carlson, 280.
29. *Graybook*, 1:432.
30. Lundstrom, *Black Shoe*, 134.
31. Lundstrom, *Black Shoe*, 135.
32. NARA: ComTaskFor17, "Battle of the Coral Sea," May 4–8, 1–2; U.S. Navy, 3.
33. Lundstrom, *Black Shoe*, 144.
34. NARA: ComTaskFor17, "Battle of the Coral Sea," May 4–8, 2; Sugawara, 47–50.
35. Lundstrom, *Black Shoe*, 144.

Chapter 3. The Invasion of Tulagi

1. JACAR: 18 Sentai (3), 37; *Senshi Sōshō*, 49:227.
2. JACAR: Kamikawa Maru (1), 3.
3. *Senshi Sōshō*,49:227.
4. Jersey, 58.
5. JACAR: Yokohama Kū (2), 1–2.
6. *Senshi Sōshō*, 49:227–28.
7. JACAR: Yokohama Kū (2), 3.
8. ADF-Serials, Australian & New Zealand Military Aircraft Serials & History, RAAF A24 Consolidated Catalina, www.adf-serials.com.au/2as24/htm (accessed 12 March 2024). Information on the Catalinas and crew can be found on Australian webpages about the missing crews.
9. JACAR: Yokohama Kū (2), 4.
10. JACAR: Kiyokawa Maru (4), 10–11.
11. JACAR: Kamikawa Maru (1), 3.
12. JACAR: MO Sakusen: Tsuragi . . . , 3–4.
13. JACAR: Gunkan Shōhō (8), 2.
14. JACAR: 6 Sentai (4), 12.
15. JACAR: MO Kidō Butai (1), 10, 14, 25; Mori, *Akatsuki*, 57.
16. JACAR: MO Kidō Butai (1), 25.
17. JACAR: Yokohama Kū (2), 5.
18. NDL: Inoue Teichō, 7; JACAR: 4 Kantai (2), 12; Agawa, 255.
19. JACAR: Nantō Hōmen, 5.
20. JACAR: MO Kidō Butai (1), 25–26.
21. JACAR: MO Kidō Butai (1), 25.
22. JACAR: Yokohama Kū (2), 10, 12.
23. JACAR: Shōhō (2) (Ref. C08051586300), 26; JACAR: Gunkan Shōhō (8), 2; Kudo, 132–33. The Japanese report didn't mention the pilot's name, but it is possible to deduct this by examining the crew list.
24. JACAR: Kamikawa Maru (1), 3–4.

25. NDL: Yamaoka Shuki, 5.
26. JACAR: MO Kidō Butai (1), 28–31; NDL: Yamaoka Taisa Shuki, 4.
27. Jersey, 48–49.
28. Jersey, 48.
29. Jersey, 49.
30. Moore, 394.
31. *Senshi Sōshō*, 49:228. The Kokosuka was a landing craft initially designed as a gunboat to protect Chinese rivers. One Kokosuka could transport about one hundred people or fifteen tons of supplies.
32. Mori, 77.
33. Jersey, 60.
34. JACAR: Shōhō (2), 27.
35. JACAR: Kamikawa Maru (3), 5.
36. JACAR: Kiyokawa Maru (4), 10–11.
37. *Senshi Sōshō*, 49:228.
38. JACAR: Yokohama Kū (2), 14, 16; *Senshi Sōshō*, 49:228.
39. JACAR: 6 Sentai (4), 13.
40. JACAR: Kamikawa Maru (1), 5.
41. JACAR: MO Kidō Butai (4), 4.
42. *Senshi Sōshō*, 49:229.

Chapter 4. The *Yorktown* Strikes on Tulagi and Gavutu

1. NARA: ComTaskFor17, "Battle of the Coral Sea," May 4–8, 3.
2. Bates, 34.
3. NARA: USS *Yorktown*, Attack Made by *Yorktown* Air Group, 3.
4. JACAR: Yokohama Kū (2), 17.
5. JACAR: Kamikawa Maru (1), 5–6.
6. JACAR: Kiyokawa Maru (4), 15.
7. NARA: USS *Yorktown*, Attack Made by *Yorktown* Air Group, 5; Lundstrom, *First Team*, 171.
8. JACAR: 19 Sentai (3), 41.
9. NARA: USS *Yorktown*, Attack Made by *Yorktown* Air Group, 4.
10. Mori, *Akatsuki*, 97.
11. Bates, 53.
12. JACAR: Kiyokawa Maru (3), 24.; JACAR: Kiyokawa Maru (4), 15.
13. NARA: USS *Yorktown*, Attack Made by *Yorktown* Air Group, 6; Bates, 56.
14. NDL: Inoue Teichō, 7.
15. JACAR: Gunkan Zuikaku (1), 21.
16. JACAR: 19 Sentai (3), 30.

17. JACAR: MO Kidō Butai (1), 32–33.
18. NDL: Yamaoka Shuki, 4.
19. JACAR: MO Kidō Butai (1), 33.
20. JACAR: 19th Sentai (3), 32; JACAR: MO Sakusen: Tsuragi, 19.
21. NARA: USS *Yorktown*, Attack Made by *Yorktown* Air Group, 6.
22. JACAR: Kiyokawa Maru (4), 16.
23. JACAR: 19 Sentai (3), 42.
24. JACAR: Kiyokawa Maru (4), 16.
25. Lundstrom, *First Team*, 172.
26. NARA: USS *Yorktown*, Attack Made by *Yorktown* Air Group, 8–9.
27. Mori, 100.
28. NDL: Yamaoka Shuki, 4.
29. JACAR: Gunkan Zuikaku (1), 22.
30. JACAR: Kamikawa Maru (2), 4.
31. JACAR: MO Sakusen: Tsuragi, 19.
32. JACAR: 19 Sentai (3), 42; JACAR: MO Sakusen: Tsuragi, 21.
33. Mori, 101.
34. JACAR: Zuikaku (1), 30.
35. JACAR: MO Kidō Butai (1), 34.
36. Tilman, 58.
37. NARA: USS *Yorktown*, Attack Made by *Yorktown* Air Group, 6.
38. Lundstrom, *First Team*, 174.
39. JACAR: 19 Sentai (3), 42.
40. JACAR: 19 Sentai (3), 41.
41. NARA: USS *Yorktown*, Attack Made by *Yorktown* Air Group, 9–10.
42. Lundstrom, *First Team*, 177.
43. U.S. Navy, 41.
44. Bates, 38.
45. Potter, 70.
46. JACAR: Kiyokawa Maru (4), 15.
47. JACAR: Kamikawa Maru (2), 4.
48. JACAR: Gunkan Zuikaku (1), 27; NDL: Inoue Teichō, 13.
49. JACAR: Gunkan Tsugaru (1), 8; JACAR: MO Sakusen: Tsuragi, 23.

Chapter 5. May 5 and 6 Searches by Each Side for Opposing Carrier Forces

1. JACAR: MO Kidō Butai (1), 37.
2. JACAR: 6 Sentai (4), 16.
3. Takahashi, *Tettei Kaibatsu*, 65.

4. JACAR: Gunkan Shōhō (8), 11.
5. JACAR: Shōhō (2), 28; JACAR: 6 Sentai (4), 16.
6. JACAR: Kamikawa Maru (2), 5; JACAR: Kiyokawa Maru (4), 17.
7. Mori, *Akatsuki*, 110.
8. JACAR: Gunkan Zuikaku (1), 30–31.
9. NARA: ComTaskFor17, "Battle of the Coral Sea," May 4–8, 4.
10. Ludlum, 111.
11. JACAR: Yokohama (2), 18.
12. Lundstrom, *Black Shoe*, 151.
13. JACAR: 5 Sentai (4), 26.
14. Mori, 109.
15. JACAR: Gunkan Zuikaku (1), 32.
16. JACAR: MO Kidō Butai (1), 39.
17. JACAR: Gunkan Zuikaku (1), 32.
18. JACAR: Gunkan Shōhō (8), 12.
19. JACAR: Kamikawa Maru (2), 5; JACAR: Kiyokawa Maru (4), 17–18.
20. JACAR: MO Sakusen: Tsuragi, 23–24.
21. "Squadron Leader Godfrey Ellard Hemsworth," Australian War Memorial, https://www.awm.gov.au/collection/P10322900, accessed 12 April 2024. The entire crew was presumed dead on 6 May 1942 by the Australians.
22. JACAR: Gunkan Zuikaku (1), 33–34; JACAR: MO Kidō Butai (1), 39–40.
23. Since the *Tippecanoe* had run out of fuel, she was sent back to Efate on 3 May, escorted by the *Warden*. Both vessels arrived there a day later.
24. Lundstrom, *First Team*, 181.
25. JACAR: Yokohama Kū (2), 22.
26. JACAR: MO Kidō Butai (1), 42.
27. JACAR: Yokohama Kū (2), 20, 23.
28. Mori, 115.
29. JACAR: 6 Sentai (4), 17.
30. JACAR: Gunkan Zuikaku (1), 5, 33.
31. JACAR: Gunkan Zuikaku (1), 33.
32. JACAR: MO Kidō Butai (1), 41.
33. NDL: Inoue Teichō, 15.
34. JACAR: MO Kidō Butai (1), 42.
35. JACAR: MO Kidō Butai (1), 42–43.
36. JACAR: Kamikawa Maru (1), 5; JACAR: Kiyokawa Maru (4), 19.
37. JACAR: Yokohama Kū (2), 23.
38. JACAR: MO Kidō Butai (1), 42–43.

39. JACAR: Gunkan Zuikaku (1), 36.
40. JACAR: MO Kidō Butai (1), 44–46.
41. Mori, 119–28.

Chapter 6. Morning Search Missions for American Carriers and Movements of Mo Kidō Butai in Response

1. JACAR: MO Kidō Butai (1), 45; *Senshi Sōsho*, 49: appendix 3.
2. Mori, *Akatsuki*, 169–70.
3. The *Zuikaku*'s report does not provide detailed data on the sectors covered by Kates—this information is based on JACAR: MO Kidō Butai (1), 46; *Senshi Sōsho*, 49:276 and Mori, 134.
4. Both carriers also replenished their fuel and ammunition supplies. Fukuchi, *Kūbo Shōkaku Kaiseki*, 60.
5. Mori, 133–34. The story about the gastric problems of one senior *Shōkaku* airman on the morning of May 7 is based on K. Fukuchi's memories, confirmed later by the *Shōkaku*'s doctor, Naohiro Watanabe. Fukuchi, *Kūbo Shōkaku Kaiseki*, 62; Kimata, 224; Watanabe, 147; Hara, *Sangokai Kaisen*, par. 1125–29.
6. Mori, 135–36.
7. JACAR: 6 Sentai (4), 19–20.
8. JACAR: Kamikawa Maru (1), 10.
9. *Kamikawa Maru*'s report indicates two different hours of departure: 0630 and 0700.
10. JACAR: Kamikawa Maru (1), 10.
11. JACAR: Kamikawa Maru (2), 6–7, 27.
12. *Senshi Sōsho*, 49:274.
13. JACAR: Gunkan Zuikaku (1), 37.
14. JACAR: MO Kidō Butai (1), 46; JACAR: Sangokai Shiryō (2) (Mieno's diary), 17; JACAR: Shōkaku (1), 30.
15. Mori, 140.
16. JACAR: MO Kidō Butai (1), 47.
17. The report was also copied to the *Zuikaku* after these ten minutes had passed. JACAR: MO Kidō Butai (1), 46; JACAR: Gunkan Zuikaku (1), 37.
18. Mori, 141.
19. JACAR: MO Kidō Butai (1), 46–47; JACAR: Sangokai Shiryō (2), 18.
20. Watanabe, 146.
21. JACAR: MO Kidō Butai (1), 47; JACAR: Gunkan Zuikaku (1), 38; JACAR: Shōkaku (1), 30. There are some discrepancies in Japanese sources regarding this contact. The *Shōkaku*'s air group action report indicates that the bomber spotted a tanker accompanied by a destroyer at 0720 hours. The reports of the MO Kidō Butai

and the *Zuikaku*, which are generally more precise about the content and times of cables received from all scouting planes, only mention the "transport ship" (*yūsōsen*) regarding receiving/forwarding the message from 0830 hours. It is unlikely that the *Shōkaku*'s report is wrong about the encountered ship, so the Nanyō Butai must have shortened the cable sent by the torpedo bomber.

22. JACAR: 6 Sentai (4), 21; JACAR: MO Kidō Butai (1), 47. There is a ten-minute difference between the first and the second dispatch in the Japanese documents. The author assumes the 6th Sentai's version is more precise.
23. JACAR: Sangokai Shiryō (2), 19.
24. JACAR: 6 Sentai (4), 21.
25. JACAR: MO Kidō Butai (1), 48.
26. JACAR: MO Kidō Butai (1), 47.
27. JACAR: MO Kidō Butai (1), 49.
28. Mori, 155.
29. JACAR: MO Kidō Butai (1), 50; JACAR: Sangokai Shiryō (2), 22.
30. *Senshi Sōsho*, 49:277.

Chapter 7. Morning Reconnaissance Missions and Movements of Task Force 17

1. NARA: USS *Yorktown*, Air Operations of *Yorktown* Air Group, May 7, 1942, Serial: CV5/A16–3/(OP-10-Rd), 2.
2. NARA: ComTaskGroup17.5, Action Report—Coral Sea—May 7–8, 1942, 1.
3. NARA: ComTaskFor17, Battle of the Coral Sea, May 4–8, 5.
4. Stern, 201.
5. Mori, *Akatsuki*, 151–52.
6. NARA: USS *Yorktown*, May 7, 3; NARA: USS *Lexington*, Report of Action, May 7 and 8, 1.
7. The American primary and secondary sources provide different data on the number of scrambled dive bombers, but the most compelling version is presented by Stern, 200, 265.
8. Cressman, 91.
9. NARA: USS *Yorktown*, May 7, 3.
10. Many American historians mention two destroyed floatplanes (possibly the 6th Sentai's), but the unit's report does not cite any losses on 7 May. Only the *Kamikawa Maru* reported losing one Jake, which was piloted by Sub-lieutenant Ogata, that morning. See Bates, 43; Cressman, 91; JACAR: Kamikawa Maru (2), 6.
11. NARA: USS *Yorktown*, May 7, 3.
12. NARA: USS *Lexington*, May 7 and 8, 1.
13. NARA: ComTaskGroup 17.5, May 7–8, 1.

14. Lundstrom, *First Team*, 193.
15. NARA: USS *Yorktown*, May 7, 6; Bates, 55.
16. Lundstrom, *First Team*, 193.
17. NARA: USS *Lexington*, May 7 and 8, 1. Once the VB-5's dive bombers had returned from the scouting mission, Fletcher had eighteen SBDs (VS-2's two, VB-2's six, and VB-5's ten) at his disposal again during the TF 17 strike on the Japanese.
18. Lundstrom, *First Team*, 196–97.
19. Bates, 55.
20. Lundstrom, *First Team*, 196.
21. NARA: USS *Yorktown*, May 7, 3.
22. Lundstrom, *First Team*, 196.
23. NARA: USS *Yorktown*, May 7, 2.
24. NARA: ComTaskFor17, May 4–8, 7.
25. NARA: USS *Neosho*, May 7, 2; Bates, 56.
26. NARA: USS *Yorktown*, May 7, 3; NAA: A11083, 5.
27. Bates, 56.
28. NARA: Pacific and Indian Ocean Naval Activity, 43–44.
29. NARA: USS *Yorktown*, May 7, 3.
30. Lundstrom, 165.
31. Ludlum, 114–15.
32. Ludlum, 116.
33. NARA: USS *Yorktown*, May 7, 6.
34. Lundstrom, *Black Shoe*, 167.
35. JACAR: Yokohama Kū (2), 24.
36. Lundstrom, *Black Shoe*, 169.
37. NARA: USS *Yorktown*, May 7, 4.

Chapter 8. Sinking of the *Neosho* and the *Sims*

1. JACAR: MO Kidō Butai (2), 1–2.
2. JACAR: Gunkan Zuikaku (1), 38–39.
3. JACAR: MO Kidō Butai (2), 2.
4. JACAR: Gunkan Zuikaku (1), 39.
5. Mori, *Akatsuki*, 157.
6. Ema, 219.
7. JACAR: MO Kidō Butai (2), 2.
8. JACAR: Gunkan Zuikaku (1), 41.
9. JACAR: Gunkan Zuikaku (1), 40; JACAR: MO Kidō Butai (2), 2–3.
10. *Senshi Sōsho*, 49:278.

11. JACAR: Shōkaku (1), 30; JACAR: MO Kidō Butai (2), 7–8.
12. JACAR: MO Kidō Butai (2), 3.
13. JACAR: Gunkan Zuikaku (1), 42; *Senshi Sōsho, 49*: 277.
14. JACAR: Shōkaku (1), 31.
15. JACAR: Zuikaku (1), 35.
16. NARA: USS *Sims*, May 7, 3–4.
17. Unlike the *Zuikaku*'s report, the report produced by the *Shōkaku* mentions the "bombing and sinking of the one enemy destroyer of bigger class." Additionally, Tagaya claims that Takahashi "led several of *Shōkaku*'s Type 99s against the *Sims*." Kimata says there were about nine of *Shōkaku*'s bombers. JACAR: Shōkaku (1), 32; Tagaya, 66; Kimata, 225.
18. NARA: USS *Sims*, Personal observation of Sims #409 disaster, 1–4.
19. Various American and Japanese sources indicate that the *Neosho* was hit directly by seven or eight bombs. The ship's report mentions the former number, while some historians refer to the latter number. Kimata, 225.
20. Ema, 220.
21. NARA: USS *Neosho*, May 7.
22. NARA: USS *Neosho*, May 7.
23. Kimata, 226.
24. JACAR: MO Kidō Butai (1), 17.

Chapter 9. Sinking of the *Shōhō*

1. Lundstrom, *First Team*, 197.
2. Mori, *Akatsuki*, 178.
3. Ishikawa, 143.
4. Kuno, 133.
5. Kimata, 218.
6. JACAR: Shōhō (2), 30.
7. JACAR: 6 Sentai (4), 22.
8. Apart from the general information about three fighters, the author hasn't found any Japanese primary sources mentioning the pilots from this *shōtai* and the type of their fighters (Zeros or Claudes). There are only two testimonies of the Japanese pilots, PO3c Ishikawa and PO3c Nakayama. The former stated that he was sent in his Claude on a routine patrol just after 1000 hours. The latter said that the Japanese ships were covered by three Claudes and three Zeros, but we know that three Zeros scrambled later. Various secondary sources are only persuasive enough to confirm that the first *shōtai* consisted of three Claudes piloted by PO2c Tadao Aoki, PO2c Takeo Inoue, and PO3c Ishikawa respectively. S. Mori also confirms that three Claudes scrambled at 1030 hours. See JACAR:

Gunkan Shōhō (9), 12; Ishikawa, 143; Kudo, 133; Mori, 210. For other versions, see Lundstrom, *First Team*, 197; Hata, Izawa, and Shores, 387.

9. JACAR: 6 Sentai (4), 23.
10. JACAR: Gunkan Shōhō (8), 12; *Senshi Sōsho*, 49:283; Mori, 210.
11. JACAR: Gunkan Shōhō (8), 12; JACAR: Gunkan Shōhō (9), 4.
12. Takahashi, 67.
13. Ishikawa, 143.
14. Kudo, 133.
15. Lundstrom, *First Team*, 198.
16. The 6th Sentai's report outlines the American attack on the *Shōhō* but doesn't mention any seaplane being lost at the time. JACAR: 6 Sentai (4), 23–24.
17. NDL: Inoue Teichō, 15–17.
18. Lundstrom, *First Team*, 198.
19. NARA: USS *Lexington*, May 7 and 8.
20. JACAR: Gunkan Shōhō (9), 4–5.
21. NARA: USS *Lexington*, May 7 and 8.
22. Lundstrom, *First Team*, 199.
23. The Japanese primary sources only mention "three fighters" that scrambled at 0917 hours. However, in view of the interviews of surviving pilots, it is possible that the *Shōhō* sent three Zeros, piloted by Lt. Nōtomi, PO1c Shigeshi Imamura, and Sea1c Takao Ban'no respectively. Some secondary sources claim that Imamura was a WO and Ban'no was a PO2c, but the *Shōhō* documents are consistent regarding their ranks. JACAR: Gunkan Shōhō (8), 13; JACAR: Shōhō (2), 30; Ishikawa, 143.
24. NARA: USS *Yorktown*, May 7, Air Operations of *Yorktown* Air Group, May 7, Serial: CV5/A16–3/(OP-10-Rd), 4.
25. JACAR: Gunkan Shōhō (9), 5.
26. Ishikawa, 2010, 144.
27. JACAR: Gunkan Shōhō (9), 5.
28. Lundstrom, *First Team*, 200.
29. NARA: USS *Lexington*, May 7 and 8, 2.
30. Ludlum, 119.
31. NARA: USS *Lexington*, May 7 and 8, 2; Lundstrom, *First Team*, 200.
32. JACAR: Gunkan Shōhō (9), 5.
33. The *Yorktown* report says that he picked up a large CL for his target and scored a hit, causing the immediate sinking of the vessel. NARA: USS *Yorktown*, May 7, 4; JACAR: Gunkan Shōhō (9), 12.
34. Johnston, 82–83.
35. NARA: USS *Yorktown*, May 7, 4–5.

36. JACAR: Gunkan Shōhō (9), 12.
37. Lundstrom, *First Team*, 202.
38. JACAR: Gunkan Shōhō (9), 6.
39. Kudo, 133.
40. Kudo, 133.
41. JACAR: Gunkan Shōhō (9), 6.
42. *Senshi Sōsho*, 49:284.
43. JACAR: Gunkan Shōhō (9), 12.
44. Lundstrom, *First Team*, 203–4.
45. Ewing, 89.
46. The list of 839 crew members included 3 civilian employees: a hairdresser, a cook, and a laundry worker, who all died on 7 May. The official report also contains a minor mathematical error. JACAR: Gunkan Shōhō (8), 18; Tendō, 145–46.
47. JACAR: 6 Sentai (4), 24.
48. Kimata, 222.
49. JACAR: 6 Sentai (4), 28.
50. JACAR: 6 Suirai (7), 17.
51. *Senshi Sōshō*, 49:285.
52. Kudo, 133.
53. JACAR: 5 Sentai (3), 26.
54. JACAR: 6 Sentai (4), 24; JACAR: Shōhō (2), 30.
55. JACAR: Gunkan Shōhō (8), 15.
56. Ishikawa, 144.
57. Stern, 233; Interrogation Nav No. 8, USSBS No. 46, Coral Sea Battle, 7–8 May 1942, Battle of Eastern Solomons.

Chapter 10. The 25th Kōkū Sentai Enters the Fray

1. Agawa, 256; Inoue Shigeyoshi Denki Kankōkai, 333–34.
2. NDL: Inoue Teichō, 17–18.
3. JACAR: 6 Sentai (4), 24.
4. JACAR: MO Kidō Butai (1), 49.
5. JACAR: MO Kidō Butai (2), 6–7.
6. Mori, *Akatsuki*, 226.
7. JACAR: Shōkaku (1), 31–36; JACAR: Zuikaku (1), 34.
8. *Senshi Sōshō*, 49:290.
9. The Australians later rescued him and his gunner/radio operator, ARM3c Robert E. Wheelhouse. U.S. Navy, 15–16.
10. Cressman, 95.
11. NARA: USS *Lexington*, Report of Action, May 7 and 8.

12. NARA: USS *Lexington*, May 7 and 8; NARA: USS *Yorktown*, Air Operations of Yorktown Air Group, May 7, Serial: CV5/A16–3/(OP-10-Rd).
13. Lundstrom, *Black Shoe*, 171.
14. Mori, 171.
15. Mori, 174.
16. JACAR: 4 Kū (1), 13.
17. Mori, 175.
18. JACAR: 4 Kū (1), 16.
19. The report says that the bombers departed with thirty-three bombs (8,250 tons). JACAR: Genzan Kū (4), 8.
20. JACAR: Tainan Kū (3), 22.
21. JACAR: 4 Kū (1), 16.
22. JACAR: Kamikawa Maru (1), 10.
23. JACAR: 6 Sentai (4), 25.
24. JACAR: Tainan Kū (3), 22.
25. JACAR: Genzan Kū (4), 8.
26. Onishi, 196; Mori, 245–46.
27. NARA: USS *Chicago*, May 7, 2; Bates, 62.
28. Onishi, 197.
29. NARA: USS *Chicago*, May 7, 3–4.
30. Mori, 254.
31. Murakami, 76.
32. JACAR: Genzan Kū (4), 8.
33. NARA: USS *Chicago*, May 7, 4.
34. JACAR: 4 Kū (1), 15; Onishi, 196.
35. Kōri, 116.
36. JACAR: Genzan Kū (4), 8; Ōno, 119.
37. JACAR: Tainan Kū (3), 22; Kōri, 116.
38. This claim was recorded in the 4th Kū's report. JACAR: 4 Kū (1), 15; JACAR: Sangokai Shiryō (1), 50.
39. Mori, 255–58.
40. NARA: USS *Chicago*, May 7, 7.
41. Salecker, 181.
42. Lundstrom, *Black Shoe*, 173.
43. Lundstrom, *Black Shoe*, 174.

Chapter 11. "Let's Go for It!"—Dusk Attack by the 5th Kōkū Sentai on TF 17 Carriers

1. Mori, *Akatsuki*, 237.
2. JACAR: Ref. MO Kidō Butai (2), 7–8.

3. JACAR: Sangokai Shiryō (1), 14, 22.
4. JACAR: Gunkan Zuikaku (1), 44; JACAR: Sangokai Shiryō (1), 84.
5. Mori, 260–66.
6. JACAR: MO Kidō Butai (2), 10.
7. Iwamoto, 97.
8. Fukuchi, 64.
9. JACAR: MO Kidō Butai (2), 9.
10. NDL: Inoue Teichō, 19.
11. JACAR: 6 Sentai (4), 26–27.
12. JACAR: MO Kidō Butai (2), 9.
13. NARA: USS *Yorktown*, May 7, 6.
14. Stern, 256.
15. Mori, 287–88.
16. JACAR: Sangokai Shiryō (1), 53.
17. *Senshi Sōsho*, 49:292.
18. Lundstrom, *First Team*, 212.
19. The Japanese secondary sources, based on PO2c Yoshida's testimony, claim that Ensign Knox was shot down by Lieutenant Satō's torpedo bomber when he went too low. Mori, 295.
20. Lundstrom, *First Team*, 213.
21. JACAR: Gunkan Zuikaku (1), 45.
22. Mori, 298.
23. Mori, 298.
24. JACAR: Gunkan Zuikaku (1), 45.
25. JACAR: Gunkan Zuikaku (1), 45.
26. Mori, 300.
27. JACAR: Gunkan Zuikaku (1), 45–46.
28. Ema, 224.
29. Ema, 224–25.
30. JACAR: Gunkan Zuikaku (1), 46.
31. NARA: *Yorktown*, May 7 and 8, 6–7.
32. Lundstrom, *First Team*, 217; Cressman, 96.
33. Mori, 309–10.
34. Ema, 226.
35. Mori, 311–12.
36. JACAR: MO Kidō Butai (2), 10; JACAR: Gunkan Zuikaku (1), 46.
37. Mori, 314.
38. Fukuchi, 65.
39. Ema, 227.

40. Mori, 317, 334.
41. Fukuchi, 66–67.
42. Fukuchi, 67.
43. JACAR: Gunkan Zuikaku (1), 47.
44. Mori, 319–21.
45. JACAR: Gunkan Zuikaku (1), 46.
46. Fukuchi, 68.
47. The Japanese bombers fired at least 6,695 rounds (7.7 mm) during the action, demonstrating a fierce defense against the American fighters. JACAR: Shōkaku (1), 38; JACAR: Zuikaku (1), 39, 41.
48. *Senshi Sōsho*, 49:297.
49. JACAR: MO Kidō Butai (2), 13–14.
50. Mori, 327.
51. JACAR: MO Kidō Butai (2), 14–17.
52. Mori, 327.
53. According to the report submitted at 1920 hours, the *Kamikawa Maru* air group had six Jakes, three Petes (plus one spare), and three Daves at her disposal. The Yokohama Kū had five Mavises in Tulagi. JACAR: Kamikawa Maru (2), 31.
54. JACAR: Gunkan Zuikaku (1), 47.
55. NDL: Inoue Teichō, 21.
56. Mori, 333.
57. JACAR: 6 Sentai (4), 29; JACAR: 18 Sentai (1), 24; *Senshi Sōsho*, 49:296.
58. JACAR: MO Kidō Butai (2), 17.
59. JACAR: MO Kidō Butai (2), 18.
60. JACAR: Gunkan Zuikaku (1), 48–49.
61. Mori, 335–37.
62. Ugaki, 7 May entry.
63. NARA: ComTaskFor17, "Battle of the Coral Sea," May 4–8, 7.
64. Lundstrom, *First Team*, 219.
65. Lundstrom, *First Team*, 219.

Chapter 12. "We Will Guide You"—Kanno's Selfless Decision

1. Miyao, 48.
2. Mori, *Akatsuki*, 342.
3. Fukuchi, 68.
4. JACAR: MO Kidō Butai (2), 20.
5. Neither units' reports mention sending the seaplanes for the reconnaissance missions. JACAR: 5 Sentai (4), 6; JACAR: 6 Sentai (4), 29.
6. NARA: USS *Lexington*, May 7 and 8.

7. Lundstrom, *First Team*, 222.
8. Notably, there is much confusion about Smith's report. Bates, Morison, Lundstrom, Cressman, and Stern present many different pieces of information regarding the initial report and its contents received by the *Lexington*. Stern's version is the most consistent with the carrier's air officer report (known by the author) and is supplemented by other primary documents (unfamiliar to the author). Thus, the book accedes to Stern's research. Stern, 276.
9. NARA: USS *Yorktown*, May 8.
10. NARA: USS *Lexington*, May 7 and 8.
11. NARA: USS *Yorktown*, May 8.
12. NARA: USS *Lexington*, May 7 and 8.
13. NARA: USS *Yorktown*, May 8.
14. Lundstrom, *First Team*, 226.
15. Lundstrom, *First Team*, 226–27.
16. NARA: USS *Lexington*, May 8.
17. NARA: ComTaskFor17, May 4–8, 8.
18. Stern, 276.
19. Lundstrom, *First Team*, 227.
20. NARA: ComTakFor17, May 4–8, 8.
21. Mori, 347–49.
22. JACAR: Gunkan Zuikaku (1), 50.
23. *Senshi Sōsho*, 49:307.
24. JACAR: Gunkan Zuikaku (1), 50.
25. JACAR: Gunkan Zuikaku (1), 50–51; JACAR: MO Kidō Butai (2), 20.
26. JACAR: MO Kidō Butai (2), 21.
27. JACAR: Gunkan Zuikaku (1), 50–52.
28. Mori, 361.
29. JACAR: Gunkan Zuikaku (1), 52.
30. Fukuchi, 69.
31. Mori, 363.
32. JACAR: Kiyowaka Maru (4), 21.
33. JACAR: Gunkan Zuikaku (1), 52.
34. JACAR: MO Kidō Butai (2), 22.
35. JACAR: Zuikaku (1), 47–48.
36. JACAR: Shōkaku (1), 47.
37. JACAR: Gunkan Zuikaku (1), 53.
38. The *Zuikaku*'s report mentions the enemy plane(s) spotted bearing 240 degrees at 0953. It is not clear whether it was the same contact. JACAR: Gunkan Zuikaku (1), 52.

39. Mori, 372–73.
40. JACAR: Shōkaku (1), 46.
41. Mori, 373.
42. JACAR: Zuikaku (1), 44; JACAR: Shōkaku (1), 45.
43. Fukuchi, 73–74.
44. Mori, 376.

Chapter 13. TF 17 Knocks the *Shōkaku* Out of Action

1. Ludlum, 133.
2. NARA: USS *Yorktown*, May 8, 2; *Senshi Sōsho*, 49:312.
3. Ludlum, 133.
4. Ludlum, 134.
5. NARA: USS *Yorktown*, May 8, 2.
6. Mori, *Akatsuki*, 381–82.
7. *Senshi Shōshō*, 49:314.
8. Iwamoto, 102.
9. Lundstrom, *First Team*, 230–31.
10. Mori, 384.
11. Mori, 417.
12. Ludlum, 137.
13. Fukuchi, *Kūbo Shōkaku Kaiseki*, 77.
14. Fukuchi, 77–78; Akemura, 134–35.
15. Lundstrom, *First Team*, 232.
16. NARA: USS *Yorktown*, May 8, 2.
17. Lundstrom, *First Team*, 232.
18. Ludlum, 139.
19. Lundstrom, 235.
20. Cressman, 101.
21. NARA: *Yorktown*, May 8, 3.
22. In reality, it was PO3c Tanaka, who solely damaged the torpedo bomber.
23. Fukuchi, 76.
24. JACAR: Gunkan Zuikaku (1), 53.
25. Iwamoto, 105–6.
26. Lundstrom, *First Team*, 236.
27. Keith, 167.
28. Lundstrom, *First Team*, 237.
29. According to the MO Kidō Butai's report, "the 4th speed" ordered by Tsuyuguchi equaled thirty-one knots in the 5th Kōkū Sentai. JACAR: MO Kidō Butai (4), 26.

30. Miyao, 49.
31. Mori, 446–47.
32. Fukuchi, 83.
33. Mori, 448.
34. Lundstrom, *First Team*, 238–39.
35. NARA: Interview of Gayler, June 17, 3–4.
36. NARA: USS *Lexington*, May 7 and 8, 7.
37. Mori, 449–50.
38. Iwamoto, 109–10.
39. NARA: Interview of Gayler, June 17, 4.
40. Iwamoto, 110.
41. Lundstrom, *First Team*, 242.
42. JACAR: Sangokai Shiryō (1), 15.
43. JACAR: Shōkaku (1), 46–47; JACAR: Zuikaku (1), 47; JACAR: Sangokai Shiryō (1), 15.
44. Iwamoto, 113.
45. Watanabe, 150–51.
46. Fukuchi, 77–89, 95–97.
47. Watanabe, 152–53.
48. JACAR: Gunkan Zuikaku (1), 54.
49. JACAR: Zuikaku (1), 47.

Chapter 14. *"To To To, Zengun Totsugeki Seyo"* ("All Forces Attack!")

1. JACAR: Gunkan Zuikaku (1), 53.
2. JACAR: Zuikaku (1), 46.
3. Mori, *Akatsuki*, 386.
4. JACAR: Gunkan Zuikaku (1), 53.
5. Mori, 387–88.
6. JACAR: Yokohama (2), 27.
7. Lundstrom, *First Team*, 244.
8. NARA: USS *Lexington* Deck Log, May 8.
9. NARA: ComTaskFor17, May 4–8, 8. Relying on other American documents, R. Stern wrote that at 1059 hours the *Lexington*'s radar picked up a bearing of 20 degrees and a range of fifty-two miles and, a minute later, 15 degrees and forty-eight miles. Finally, at 1101 hours, it had elongated into a larger blip that stretched from forty-eight to sixty-five miles away. Stern, 281.
10. NARA: USS *Lexington* Deck Log, May 8.
11. Lundstrom, *First Team*, 245.
12. Stern, 283.

13. Lundstrom, *First Team*, 248.
14. Mori, 392–93.
15. *Senshi Sōsho*, 49:308.
16. Mori, 394.
17. Mori, 395.
18. Lundstrom, *First Team*, 250.
19. Mori, 397.
20. Mori, 398.
21. JACAR: *Zuikaku* (1), 50.
22. Okumiya and Hirokoshi, 139. There are some serious concerns about whether this testimony was produced by Shimazaki himself.
23. It should be noted that Kanazawa's account is consistent with the *Yorktown*'s report, which mentioned the single VT plane approaching parallel to the starboard side from the stern and escaping in a violent left chandelle. NARA: USS Yorktown, May 8, 6.
24. Mori, 405.
25. JACAR: Zuikaku (1), 50.
26. Mori, 409.
27. NARA: USS *Lexington*, May 8, 5–6.
28. Mori, 2009, 410.
29. This version can be found in some American primary sources and all descriptions of the Battle of the Coral Sea published in the West. It was also supported later by *Senshi Sōsho*'s narrative that relied on the *Shōkaku* air group's report and notes from the battle. However, the author claims that it is wrong. The carrier unit's report is unreliable in some parts, because it mentions that the *kankō* scored nine hits out of ten dropped torpedoes. However, we know from the testimonies quoted in the book that the Kates released no more than eight torpedoes. Additionally, crews from both *chūtai*, including PO1c Ishikawa, confirmed that they had aimed only for the *Lexington* and official notes from the battle support that. It might have been the chaos of the battle that made the Americans think that two torpedo bombers were going for the heavy cruiser. Also, the *Shōkaku* air group's report relied on the statement made by Ichihara, who didn't fully see the attack on Iwamura's *chūtai* and was only able to see its approach near the *Minneapolis*. Notably, many years ago, the author also believed that two torpedo bombers attacked the cruiser, as reflected in his Polish version of the book. JACAR: Shōkaku (1), 42; JACAR: Sangokai Shiryō (1), 6; *Senshi Sōshō*, 49:310. The correct version can be found in JACAR: Sangokai Shiryō (1), 65; Mori, 411.

30. NARA: USS *Lexington*, May 8, 6.
31. Johnston, 102.
32. Stern, 291.
33. Stern, 291.
34. NARA: USS *Lexington*, May 8, 6.
35. Mori, 413.
36. JACAR: Shōkaku (1), 42.
37. Fukuchi, *Kūbo Shōkaku Kaiseki*, 90.
38. Mori, 427.
39. Lundstrom, *First Team*, 255.
40. Mori, 428.
41. JACAR: Shōkaku (1), 40.
42. Lundstrom, *First Team*, 256–57; Stern, 292.
43. Bates, 95.
44. NARA: USS *Lexington*, May 8, 6.
45. Stern, 292.
46. JACAR: Zuikaku (1), 53. Some Japanese authors claim that the message was sent at 1122 hours and received instantly by the *Zuikaku*, which is not shown in primary sources.
47. Ema, 230–31.
48. Mori, 437.
49. JACAR: Zuikaku (2), 2.
50. NARA: USS *Yorktown*, May 8, 7.
51. Stern, 295.
52. Lundstrom, *First Team*, 260.
53. JACAR: Sangokai Shiryō (1), 44; Mori, 470–71.
54. NARA: USS *Lexington*, May 8; Lundstrom, *First Team*, 261.
55. JACAR: Zuikaku (1), 42; JACAR: Sangokai Shiryō (1), 15.
56. Stern, 295.
57. Lundstrom, *First Team*, 269.
58. During the attack the *Zuikaku* lost three *kankō* and two *kambaku*, while the *Shōkaku* lost three *kankō* and three *kambaku*. According to Japanese records, the striking group lost eight *kankō* and nine *kambaku*. This means that F4Fs and SBDs must have shot down some of the returning planes and that some did not return to the carriers due to excessive damage. JACAR: Shōkaku (1), 39–42; JACAR: Zuikaku (1), 49–50; JACAR: Zuikaku (2), 1–2.
59. Lundstrom, *First Team*, 270.
60. Fukuchi, 74–75.

Chapter 15. Aftermath

1. NARA: *Lexington*, May 8.
2. NARA: *Yorktown*, May 7–8.
3. NARA: USS *Yorktown*, May 7–8.
4. NARA: *Lexington*, May 8.
5. Stern, 313.
6. NARA: *Lexington*, May 8.
7. Lundstrom, *First Team*, 274.
8. NARA: *Lexington*, May 8.
9. Lundstrom, *First Team*, 274.
10. JACAR: Zuikaku (1), 45–46. The *Zuikaku*'s air group report doesn't mention this encounter. However, when the attack on TF 17 and the dogfight with F4Fs and SBDs was over, all fighters, excluding PO2c Ōkura, had used 7,100 7.7-mm and 990 20-mm rounds.
11. Lundstrom, *First Team*, 274–75.
12. NARA: *Lexington*, May 8.
13. Lundstrom, *First Team*, 275.
14. NARA: *Lexington*, May 8.
15. Lundstrom, *First Team*, 276.
16. Parker, 29.
17. Bates, 101; NARA: ComTaskFor17, May 4–8, 9.
18. Lundstrom, *First Team*, 277.
19. JACAR: Gunkan Zuikaku (1), 54.
20. JACAR: Gunkan Zuikaku (1), 54.
21. JACAR: Gunkan Zuikaku (1), 9, 55.
22. JACAR: MO Kidō Butai (2), 24.
23. Jō and Nomura, 156.
24. NDL: Inoue Teichō, 22–23; JACAR: Zuikaku (1), 55; Mori, 458–59.
25. JACAR: Gunkan Zuikaku (1), 55–56.
26. JACAR: MO Kidō Butai (2), 25–26.
27. JACAR: Sagokai Kaisen Shiryō (1), 11.
28. JACAR: Gunkan Zuikaku (1), 55.
29. Mori, 472.
30. JACAR: Gunkan Zuikaku (1), 57.
31. JACAR: Sagokai Kaisen Shiryō (1), 11.
32. Mori, 488.
33. Ema, 232–33.
34. Lundstrom, *First Team*, 271.
35. Mori, 479–80.

36. JACAR: Takahashi Kakuichi, 5.
37. Fukuchi, 90–91.
38. Ema, 233–34.
39. JACAR: MO Kidō Butai (2), 24–25.
40. JACAR: Gunkan Zuikaku (1), 57–58.
41. JACAR: Tsugaru 23–27, 21–23, 29.
42. NDL: Inoue Teichō, 24.
43. JACAR: MO Kidō Butai (2), 30–31.
44. JACAR: Gunkan Zuikaku (1), 57–58.
45. NDL: Inoue Teichō, 25; JACAR: MO Kidō Butai (2), 33–34.
46. JACAR: Yokohama Kū (2), 28.
47. JACAR: MO Kidō Butai (2), 26–27.
48. Mori, 489.
49. JACAR: MO Kidō Butai (2), 27–30.
50. JACAR: MO Kidō Butai (2), 32.
51. Mori, 511.
52. NDL: Inoue Teichō, 27; JACAR: MO Kidō Butai (2), 34.
53. JACAR: MO Kidō Butai (2), 35–36.
54. JACAR: MO Kidō Butai (2), 41–42.
55. NARA: USS *Lexington*, May 8, 9–10.
56. Lundstrom, *First Team*, 280.
57. NARA: USS *Lexington*, May 8, 9.

Chapter 16. Final Movements in Operation MO

1. Lundstrom, *First Team*, 283–84.
2. *Graybook*, 1:452.
3. Lundstrom, *First Team*, 284.
4. *Graybook*, 1:475.
5. NARA: USS *Neosho*, May 7, 6.
6. JACAR: MO Kidō Butai (2), 40.
7. JACAR: MO Kidō Butai (2), 43.
8. JACAR: Yokohama (2), 29.
9. JACAR: MO Kidō Butai (2), 44–45.
10. JACAR: MO Kidō Butai (2), 46.
11. JACAR: Kamikawa Maru (2), 8–9; JACAR: Kiyokawa Maru (3), 22.
12. JACAR: Kamikawa Maru (2), 9; JACAR: Kiyokawa Maru (3), 22–24.
13. JACAR: MO Kidō Butai (2), 48.
14. JACAR: MO Kidō Butai (2), 48.
15. JACAR: Zuikaku (2), 3.

16. JACAR: MO Kidō Butai (2), 48–49.
17. JACAR: MO Kidō Butai (2), 49.
18. JACAR: MO Kidō Butai (3), 1–3.
19. JACAR: MO Kidō Butai (3), 2–3.
20. JACAR: Yokohama Kū (2), 35; JACAR: MO Kidō Butai (3), 14.
21. JACAR: MO Kidō Butai (3), 17–18.
22. Watanabe, 157.
23. JACAR: MO Kidō Butai (3), 7.
24. JACAR: MO Kidō Butai (2), 44.
25. Kimata, 243.
26. Watanabe, 162.
27. JACAR: 5 Kōkū Sentai/1. Keika, 6.
28. Watanabe, 164–65.
29. JACAR: 5 Kōkū Sentai/3. Reitatsu (2), 21.
30. JACAR: 5 Kōkū Sentai/1. Keika, 6–7.
31. JACAR: 5th Kōkū Sentai/5. Sakusen Keika (Ref. C13120039100), 3
32. JACAR: MO Kidō Butai (1), 23.
33. Kimata, 244.
34. Fukuchi, *Kūbo Shōkaku Kaiseki*, 101–2.
35. JACAR: 5 Kōkū Sentai /1. Keika, 7.

Chapter 17. Conflicting Japanese Statements on the Outcome of the Battle of the Coral Sea

1. *Senshi Sōshō*, 49:114.
2. JACAR: 5 Kōkū Sentai / Besshi Kimitsu Dai 7 (Ref. C13120039400).
3. Fukuchi, *Kūbo Shōkaku Kaiseki*, 93–103.
4. Tominaga, 111.
5. Chihaya, *Nippon Kaigun no Hokori*, 283.
6. Tominaga, 111.
7. Tominaga, 112.
8. KKS: Shūhō 293, 13–17.
9. KKS: Shashin Shūhō 223, 3–5.
10. For example: Nakajima, 190–91; Kaigun Kōkū Hombu, 230; Hiraide, 16–17; Uematsu, 149.
11. Millot, 109.

Chapter 18. What Failed on the Japanese Side?

1. Mori, *Akatsuki*, 34–38.
2. Piegzik, *Darkest Hour*, 2: 61.
3. The *Sōryū* was hit in different circumstances when her hangars were full of refueled and rearmed aircraft. But it is doubtful whether her damage control

team could have extinguished a fire similar to that in the *Shōkaku* during the Battle of Coral Sea, because the team consisted of fewer men and less firefighting equipment. In addition, the *Sōryū* was an older construction with less potent antiaircraft artillery, so her survivability could be assessed as lower than that of the *Shōkaku*-class of carrier.

4. Agawa, 258.
5. Mori, 513.
6. Itō, 287–98.
7. Mori, 514.
8. Agawa, 258.
9. Ugaki, May 24.
10. For more about the Japanese reconnaissance mistakes on 6 and 7 May, see Yokoya, 112–29.
11. Nohara, loc. 459.
12. Fukuchi, *Kūbo Shōkaku Kaiseki*, 100; Miyao, 51.
13. NDL: Inoue Teichō, 51–53.
14. NDL: Yamaoka Shuki, 28–30.
15. NDL: Senkun, Sangokai Kaisen.
16. Agawa, 259.

Bibliography

Archival Sources

The order of archival source entries presented here follows the hierarchy found in the Japanese repositories: (A) public release sources; (B) diplomatic sources (not in this volume); and (C) military sources. Within the military records, the order is: (1) fleet; (2) personal diaries submitted to fleet records; (3) operational diaries; (4) squadron and above-size unit diaries; (5) carriers/land-based air units; (7) surface squadrons (Sentai); (8) surface torpedo squadrons (Suirai Sentai); and (9) individual ships logs (Gunkan). A parenthetical number at the end of an entry indicates part division within the source.

Kokuritsu Kōbunshokan (National Archives of Japan):
Ajia Rekishi Shiryō Sentaa (Japan Center for Asian Historical Records) (JACAR)

Note: Some of the 25th Kōkū Sentai's reports are of very poor quality and were used in a limited scope.

Ref. A12090368500: Ko Kaigun Taisa Takahashi Kakuichi Ichi'i Kaiōshō no Ken.
Ref. C13072085300: Kaigun Jirei Kōhō, 5 (1).
Ref. C08030018300: S16.12.01–S19.08.31, Dai 4 Kantai Senji Nisshi (2).
Ref. C19010320500: Sangokai Kaisen Shiryō (1) [Mieno's diary].
Ref. C19010320600: Sangokai Kaisen Shiryō (2) [Mieno's diary].
Ref. C19010330300: S17.05.01–S17.05.11, Nantō Hōmen Kōkū Sakusen Keika no Gaiyō, Sono 1.
Ref. C19010316400: MO Sakusen: Tsuragi, Pōto Moresubi, Nauru, Ōshan Kōryaku Sakusen.
Ref. C08030728400: S17.05.01–S17.05.17, Nanyō Butai MO Kidō Butai Sentō Shōhō (1).
Ref. C08030728500: S17.05.01–S17.05.17, Nanyō Butai MO Kidō Butai Sentō Shōhō (2).
Ref. C08030728600: S17.05.01–S17.05.17, Nanyō Butai MO Kidō Butai Sentō Shōhō (3).
Ref. C08030728700: S17.05.01–S17.05.17, Nanyō Butai MO Kidō Butai Sentō Shōhō (4).
Ref. C13120037900: Dai 5 Kōkū Sentai Senji Nisshi (Sakusen oyobi Ippan no Bu) S17.04 / Besshi Kimitsu MO Kidō Butai Kōkū Butai Meirei Saku Dai 1 Gō.
Ref. C13120038000: Dai 5 Kōkū Sentai Senji Nisshi (Sakusen oyobi Ippan no Bu) S17.04 / Besshi Kimitsu MO Kidō Butai Kōkū Butai Meirei Saku Dai 2 Gō.

Ref. C13120037400: Dai 5 Kōkū Sentai Senji Nisshi (Sakusen oyobi Ippan no Bu) S17.04 / 3. Reitatsu Hōkoku Nado (1).
Ref. C13120037600: Dai 5 Kōkū Sentai Senji Nisshi (Sakusen oyobi Ippan no Bu) S17.04 / 5. Sakusen Keika Gaiyō.
Ref. C13120038500: Dai 5 Kōkū Sentai Senji Nisshi (Sakusen oyobi Ippan no Bu) S17.05 / 1. Keika.
Ref. C13120038600: Dai 5 Kōkū Sentai Senji Nisshi (Sakusen oyobi Ippan no Bu) S17.05 / 2. Jin'in no Genjō.
Ref. C13120038700: Dai 5 Kōkū Sentai Senji Nisshi (Sakusen oyobi Ippan no Bu) S17.05 / 3. Reitatsu Hōkoku nado (1).
Ref. C13120038800: Dai 5 Kōkū Sentai Senji Nisshi (Sakusen oyobi Ippan no Bu) S17.05 / 3. Reitatsu Hōkoku nado (2).
Ref. C13120038900: Dai 5 Kōkū Sentai Senji Nisshi (Sakusen oyobi Ippan no Bu) S17.05/3. Reitatsu Hōkoku nado (3).
Ref. C13120039000: Dai 5 Kōkū Sentai Senji Nisshi (Sakusen oyobi Ippan no Bu) S17.05 / 4. Sankō.
Ref. C13120039100: Dai 5 Kōkū Sentai Senji Nisshi (Sakusen oyobi Ippan no Bu) S17.05 / 5. Sakusen Keika Gaiyō.
Ref. C13120039200: Dai 5 Kōkū Sentai Senji Nisshi (Sakusen oyobi Ippan no Bu) S17.05 / Betsuzu Dai 5 Kōkū Sentai Kōdōzu.
Ref. C13120039300: Dai 5 Kōkū Sentai Senji Nisshi (Sakusen oyobi Ippan no Bu) S17.05 / Besshi Kimitsu 5 Kōsen Hi Dai 4 Gō.
Ref. C13120039400: Dai 5 Kōkū Sentai Senji Nisshi (Sakusen oyobi Ippan no Bu) S17.05 / Besshi Kimitsu 5 Kōsen Hi Dai 7 Gō.
Ref. C13120073100: Dai 25 Kōkū Sentai Senji Nishhi, S17.03.20–S17.04.30 / 1. Keika.
Ref. C13120073500: Dai 25 Kōkū Sentai Senji Nishhi, S17.03.20–S17.04.30 / 3. Reitatsu.
Ref. C13120073900: Dai 25 Kōkū Sentai Senji Nishhi, S17.05.01–S17.05.31 / 1. Keika.
Ref. C13120073900: Dai 25 Kōkū Sentai Senji Nishhi, S17.05.01–S17.05.31 / 1. Keika.
Ref. C13120074000: Dai 25 Kōkū Sentai Senji Nishhi, S17.05.01–S17.05.31 / 2. Jinin no Genjō.
Ref. C13120074100: Dai 25 Kōkū Sentai Senji Nishhi, S17.05.01–S17.05.31 / 3. Reitatsu Hōhoku no nado (1).
Ref. C13120074200: Dai 25 Kōkū Sentai Senji Nishhi, S17.05.01–S17.05.31 / 3. Reitatsu Hōhoku no nado (2).
Ref. C13120074300: Dai 25 Kōkū Sentai Senji Nishhi, S17.05.01–S17.05.31 / 3. Reitatsu Hōhoku no nado (3).
Ref. C13120074400: Dai 25 Kōkū Sentai Senji Nishhi, S17.05.01–S17.05.31 / 3. Reitatsu Hōhoku no nado (4).

Ref. C13120074500: Dai 25 Kōkū Sentai Senji Nishhi, S17.05.01–S17.05.31 / 4. Sakusen Keika Gaiyō.

Ref. C13120078600: Kichi Kōkū Butai Dai 5 Kūshū Butai Sentō Shōhō, S17.05.04–S17.05.11 / Sangokai Kaisen Sentō Shōhō, Dai 25 Kōkū Sentai Shireibu, 1. Keisei.

Ref. C13120078700: Kichi Kōkū Butai Dai 5 Kūshū Butai Sentō Shōhō, S17.05.04–S17.05.11 / Sangokai Kaisen Sentō Shōhō, Dai 25 Kōkū Sentai Shireibu, 2. Keikaku.

Ref. C13120078800: Kichi Kōkū Butai Dai 5 Kūshū Butai Sentō Shōhō, S17.05.04–S17.05.11 / Sangokai Kaisen Sentō Shōhō, Dai 25 Kōkū Sentai Shireibu, 3. Keika.

Ref. C13120078900: Kichi Kōkū Butai Dai 5 Kūshū Butai Sentō Shōhō, S17.05.04–S17.05.11 / Sangokai Kaisen Sentō Shōhō, Dai 25 Kōkū Sentai Shireibu, 4. Reitatsu Hōkoku.

Ref. C13120079000: Kichi Kōkū Butai Dai 5 Kūshū Butai Sentō Shōhō, S17.05.04–S17.05.11 / Sangokai Kaisen Sentō Shōhō, Dai 25 Kōkū Sentai Shireibu, 5. Kekka.

Ref. C13120079100: Kichi Kōkū Butai Dai 5 Kūshū Butai Sentō Shōhō, S17.05.04–S17.05.11 / Sangokai Kaisen Sentō Shōhō, Dai 25 Kōkū Sentai Shireibu, 6. Kōseki.

Ref. C13120079200: Kichi Kōkū Butai Dai 5 Kūshū Butai Sentō Shōhō, S17.05.04–S17.05.11 / Sangokai Kaisen Sentō Shōhō, Dai 25 Kōkū Sentai Shireibu, 7. Sankō.

Ref. C13120006600: Kichi Kōkū Butai Dai 5 Kūshū Butai Dai 3 Butai Sentō Shōhō, Dai 2 Dan Sakusen ni okeru S17.05.07–S17.05.09 / Sangokai Kaisen, Genzan Kaigun Kōkūtai.

Ref. C08051577600: S16.12–S18.04 / Zuikaku Hikōkitai Sentō Kōdō Chōsho (1).

Ref. C08051577700: S16.12–S18.04 / Zuikaku Hikōkitai Sentō Kōdō Chōsho (2).

Ref. C08051577100: S16.12–S18.11 / Shōkaku Hikōkitai Sentō Kōdō Chōsho (1).

Ref. C08051586200: S17.02–S17.05 / Shōhō Hikōkitai Sentō Kōdō Chōsho (1).

Ref. C08051586300: S17.02–S17.05 / Shōhō Hikōkitai Sentō Kōdō Chōsho (2).

Ref. C08030641100: S17.04.28–S17.07.09 / Kamikawa Maru Sentō Shōhō, MO Sakusen, MI, AL Sakusen (1).

Ref. C08030641200: S17.04.28–S17.07.09 / Kamikawa Maru Sentō Shōhō MO Sakusen MI, AL Sakusen (2).

Ref. C08030646400: S17.03.17–S17.06.03 / Kiyokawa Maru Sentō Shōhō Bōgainwiru-tō Kōryaku Sakusen Adomiraruti-tō Kōryaku Sakusen Nyū Buriten-tō Seibokubu Sōtōsen (3).

Ref. C08030646500: S17.03.17–S17.06.03 / Kiyokawa Maru Sentō Shōhō Bōgainwiru-tō Kōryaku Sakusen Adomiraruti-tō Kōryaku Sakusen Nyū Buriten-tō Seibokubu Sōtōsen (4).

Ref. C08051627400: S17.05–S17.07 / 4 Kū Hikōkitai Sentō Kōdō Chōsho (1).

Ref. C08051612300: S16.12–S17.05 / Genzan Kū, Hikōkitai Sentō Kōdō Chōsho (3).

Ref. C08051612400: S16.12–S17.05 / Genzan Kū, Hikōkitai Sentō Kōdō Chōsho (4).

Ref. C08051602700: S17.04–S17.05 / Tainan Kū, Hikōkitai Sentō Kōdō Chōsho (3).

Ref. C08051608900: S17.04–S17.05 / Yokohama Kū Hikōkitai Sentō Kōdō Chōsho (2).
Ref. C08030043200: S17.03.11–S17.05.15 / Dai 5 Sentai Senji Nisshi Sentō Shōhō (3).
Ref. C08030043300: S17.03.11–S17.05.15 / Dai 5 Sentai Senji Nisshi Sentō Shōhō (4).
Ref. C08030043400: S17.03.11–S17.05.15 / Dai 5 Sentai Senji Nisshi Sentō Shōhō (5).
Ref. C08030043500: S17.03.11–S17.05.15 / Dai 5 Sentai Senji Nisshi Sentō Shōhō (6).
Ref. C08030045500: S16.12.01–S17.10.12 / Dai 6 Sentai Senji Nisshi Sentō Shōhō (3).
Ref. C08030045600: S16.12.01–S17.10.12 / Dai 6 Sentai Senji Nisshi Sentō Shōhō (4).
Ref. C08030060000: S17.04.01–S17.05.31 / Dai 18 Sentai Senji Nisshi Sentō Shōhō (3).
Ref. C08030060100: S17.04.01–S17.05.31 / Dai 18 Sentai Senji Nisshi Sentō Shōhō (4).
Ref. C08030060400: S17.05.01–S17.07.31 / Dai 18 Sentai Senji Nisshi (1).
Ref. C08030060500: S17.05.01–S17.07.31 / Dai 18 Sentai Senji Nisshi (2).
Ref. C08030068300: S17.02.01–S17.04.17 / Dai 19 Sentai Senji Nisshi Sentō Shōhō (3).
Ref. C08030122800: S17.03.01–S17.03.17 / Dai 6 Suirai Sentai Senji Nisshi Sentō Shōhō (1).
Ref. C08030122900: S17.03.01–S17.03.17 / Dai 6 Suirai Sentai Senji Nisshi Sentō Shōhō (2).
Ref. C08030123000: S17.03.01–S17.03.17 / Dai 6 Suirai Sentai Senji Nisshi Sentō Shōhō (3).
Ref. C08030123100: S17.03.01–S17.03.17 / Dai 6 Suirai Sentai Senji Nisshi Sentō Shōhō (4).
Ref. C08030125200: S17.05.01–S17.07.10 / Dai 6 Suirai Sentai Senji Nisshi Sentō Shōhō (1).
Ref. C08030125300: S17.05.01–S17.07.10 / Dai 6 Suirai Sentai Senji Nisshi Sentō Shōhō (2).
Ref. C08030727700: S17.05.08 / Dai 7 Kuchitai Sentō Shōhō, Sangokai Kaisen.
Ref. C16120689600: Sangokai Kaisen, Sono Hoka, 05.07 (Shōkaku).
Ref. C08030742700: S17.05.04–S17.05.10 / Gunkan Zuikaku Sentō Shōhō (Sangokai Kaisen ni okeru Sakusen) (1).
Ref. C08030742800: S17.05.04–S17.05.10 / Gunkan Zuikaku Sentō Shōhō (Sangokai Kaisen ni okeru Sakusen) (2).
Ref. C08030580700: S16.12.01–S17.05.07 / Gunkan Shōhō Senji Nisshi Sentō Shōhō (3).
Ref. C08030580800: S16.12.01–S17.05.07 / Gunkan Shōhō Senji Nisshi Sentō Shōhō (4).
Ref. C08030580900: S16.12.01–S17.05.07 / Gunkan Shōhō Senji Nisshi Sentō Shōhō (5).
Ref. C08030581000: S16.12.01–S17.05.07 / Gunkan Shōhō Senji Nisshi Sentō Shōhō (6).
Ref. C08030581100: S16.12.01–S17.05.07 / Gunkan Shōhō Senji Nisshi Sentō Shōhō (7).
Ref. C08030581200: S16.12.01–S17.05.07 / Gunkan Shōhō Senji Nisshi Sentō Shōhō (8).
Ref. C08030581300: S16.12.01–S17.05.07 / Gunkan Shōhō Senji Nisshi Sentō Shōhō (9).
Ref. C08030750800: S16.11.26–S19.09.14 / Gunkan Yūbari Kōdō Kiroku.
Ref. C08030759000: S17.04.23–S17.05.11 / Gunkan Tsugaru Sentō Shōhō, Dai 22-Gō (MO Sakusen, Sangokai Kaisen ni okeru Sakusen (1).
Ref. C08030759100: S17.04.23–S17.05.11 / Gunkan Tsugaru Sentō Shōhō, Dai 22-Gō (MO Sakusen, Sangokai Kaisen ni okeru Sakusen (2).
Ref. C08030759200: S17.04.23–S17.05.11 / Gunkan Tsugaru Sentō Shōhō, Dai 22-Gō (MO Sakusen, Sangokai Kaisen ni okeru Sakusen (3).
Ref. C08030759500: S17.05.06–S17.05.12 / Gunkan Tsugaru Sentō Shōhō, Dai 23, 24, 25, 26, 27-Gō (MO Sakusen ni okeru tai Kūsentō, RY Sakusen ni okeru Sakusen (1).

Kokuritsu Kokkai Toshokan (National Diet Library) (NDL)

Daitōa Sensō Senkun (Kōkū) Dai 3-hen: Sangokai Kaisen no Bu.

S17: Nyū Ginia Shuyō Sakusen.

Sangokai Kaisen Gaiyō, Inoue Dai 4 Kantai Shireichōkan Teichō. [Inoue's Diary]

Sangokai Kaisen ni kansuru Yamaoka Taisa Shuki. [Yamaoka's Diary]

S17.05–S17.09: Kimitsu Sakusen Nikki, Dai 17 Gun Shireibu.

S17: Nankai Shitai Sakurei Tsutsuri, Dai 2-ka.

S17: Nyū Ginia Shuyō Sakusen.

S17.04.01–S17.05.10: Kimitsu Sakusen Nikki, Dai 4-gō, Pōto Moresubi Koryaku Sakusen. Jumbi made ni Sangokai Kaisen Sanka no Bu, Nankai Shitai.

Kokuritsu Kōbunshokan (National Archives of Japan) (KKS)

Ref. 情00057100: Kakushu Jōhō Shiryō, Beikokunai Hōsō Bōju Jōhō.

Ref. ヨ310—0109: Shūhō 293.

Ref. ヨ310—0116: Sashin Shūhō 223.

Bōei Kenkyūsho (National Institute for Defense Studies) (NIDS)

Chūō, Meirei, 33: S16.11.5, Kimitsu GF Meirei Saku Dai 1-gō.

Chūō, Meirei, 116: S16.11.05–S20.08.24: Daihon'ei Kaigunbu Shiji Tsutsuri Mokuji.

National Australian Archives

NAA: SP551/1: HMAS Australia—Ship's Log—1 May 1942—31 May 1942.

NAA: A9695/487: The Coral Sea battle—7–8 May 1942—Interrogation of Commander H Sekino, Communications Officer, Staff, 6th Cruiser Squadron at Coral Sea.

NAA: A11083/7/113/AIR: North Eastern Area Headquarters—Report on Coral Sea battle.

Australian War Memorial

AWM54 253/5/1: Diary of Member of Kure No 3 Special Landing Party (. . .) Coral Sea Battle.

AWM54 253/5/7: Diaries of Members of Kure No 3 Special Landing Party (. . .) Coral Sea Battle.

National Archives and Records Administration (NARA)

Ally Appreciation—Pacific and Indian Ocean Naval Activity, 1–31 May 1942.

USS *Astoria*. Action Report, Coral Sea. 8 May 1942. May 16, 1942. Serial: CA34/A16–3/(034).

USS *Chester*. Report of Action, Coral Sea. May 15, 1942. Serial: A16–3(031).

USS *Chicago*. Action against Enemy Aircraft, May 7, 1942—Report of May 11, 1942. Serial: CA29/A16/(057).

COMDESSQDN2. Action in Coral Sea Area on May 8, 1942, report of May 18, 1942. Serial: A16/FF12–4(2).

Command Summary of Fleet Admiral Chester W. Nimitz, USN Nimitz, *Graybook*. 7 December 1941–31 August 1945.

ComTaskFor17. The Battle of the Coral Sea, May 4–8, 1942. May 27, 1942. Serial: 0010N.

ComTaskGroup17.5, NARA: Action Report—Coral Sea—May 7–8, 1942. May 18, 1942. Serial: A16–3/FB2–1/(0251).

Gayler, Lieutenant N. A., USN. Interview. USS *Lexington*, 17 June 1942.

Task Unit 17.2.2. (USS *Astoria*, Flagship.) Action Report. May 17, 1942. Serial: A16–3(010).

USS *Lexington*. Preliminary Report. Lost in Action, May 8, 1942.

USS *Lexington*. Report of Action—The Battle of the Coral Sea, 7 and 8 May 1942. May 15, 1942. Serial: CV-2/A16–3/(0100).

USS *Neosho*. Engagement of USS *Neosho* with Japanese Aircraft on May 7, 1942; Subsequent loss of USS *Neosho*; Search for Survivors. May 25, 1942. Serial: AO23/A16–3/P15.

USS *New Orleans*. Report of Action in Coral Sea on May 8, 1942. May 25, 1942. Serial: CA32/A9–3/(036)

US Pacific Fleet, Flagship of the COMINCH, Naval Action in Coral Sea Area, 4–8 May 1942. Jun 17 1942. Serial: A16(4)/Coral Sea (01704).

USS *Portland*. Engagement with Enemy (Japanese) Carrier Aircraft on May 8, 1942, in Coral Sea—report of May 12, 1942. Serial: CA33/A16–3/(030).

USS *Sims*. Personal observation of Sims #409 disaster. May 13, 1942.

USS *Yorktown*. Air Defense Doctrine.

USS *Yorktown*. Air Operations of Yorktown Air Group against Japanese Forces in the vicinity of the Louisade Archipelago on May 7, 1942. May 16, 1942. Serial: CV5/A16–3/(OP-10-Rd).

USS *Yorktown*. Air Operations of Yorktown Air Group against Japanese Forces in the vicinity of the Louisade Archipelago on May 8, 1942. May 16, 1942. Serial: CYAG/A16–3/(02).

USS *Yorktown*. Attack made by Yorktown Air Group on Enemy Forces in Tulagi and Gavutu Harbors. Serial: CV5/A16–3(OP-10-Rd).

USS *Yorktown*. Diagram of approximate disposition and movements of forces during attack of 8 May.

USS *Yorktown*. Direct Hit by Bomb.

USS *Yorktown*. Information on Damage Control. May 30, 1942. Serial: CV5/S88/(CEA-50-swg).

USS *Yorktown*. List of Dispatches and Signals Sent Received and Intercepted on May 8, 1942.

USS *Yorktown*. Noteworthy Incident Occurring during Engagement on May 8, 1942, and in the Operations Leading up Thereto Involving Individual Instances of Personnel Deserving of Praise—Report of May 19, 1942. Serial: C75/A9–8/A18–3.

USS *Yorktown*. Operation Order No. 2–42, May 1, 1942. Serial: A16–3/(007N).
USS *Yorktown*. Report of Action of Yorktown and Yorktown Air Group on May 8, 1942. May 25, 1942. Serial: CV5/A18–3/(CCR-10-hjs).
USS *Yorktown*. Transverse Sectional View Showing Path of Bomb and Damaged Compartments at Frame 107 Looking Forward.
USS *Yorktown*. Underwater Explosions.
USS *Yorktown*. USS *Yorktown* Track during Battle of the Coral Sea May 8, 1942. (Enclosure E.)
USS *Yorktown*. War Damage Report. May 20, 1942. Serial: CV5/S88/A9(CEA-50-swg).

Other Reports

Interrogation Nav No. 8, USSBS No. 46, Coral Sea Battle, 7–8 May 1942, Battle of Eastern Solomons.

Books, Articles, and Dissertations

Agawa, H. *Inoue Shigeyoshi*. Tokyo: Shichōsha, 1994.
Akemura, K. *Kaigun Damēji Kontorōru Monogatari*. Tokyo: Ushioshobō Kōjinsha, 2015.
Armstrong, M. J., and M. B. Powell. "A Stochastic Salvo Model Analysis of the Battle of the Coral Sea." *Military Operations Research* 10(4) (2005): 27–38.
Bates, R. *Battle of the Coral Sea: Strategical and Tactical Analysis*. Newport, RI: US Naval War College, 1947.
Bōei Kenshūsho Senshishitsu, ed. *Senshi Sōsho*, vol. 14: *Minami Taiheiyō Rikugun Sakusen (1) Pōto Moresubi * Ga-tō Shoki Sakusen*. Tokyo: Asagumo Shimbunsha, 1968.
Bōei Kenshūsho Senshishitsu, ed. *Senshi Sōsho*, vol. 38: *Chūbu Taiheiyō Hōmen Kaigun Sakusen (1) Shōwa 17-nen 6-gatsu made*. Tokyo: Asagumo Shimbunsha, 1970.
Bōei Kenshūsho Senshishitsu, ed. *Senshi Sōsho*, vol. 43: *Middowee Kaiasen*. Tokyo: Asagumo Shimbunsha, 1971.
Bōei Kenshūsho Senshishitsu, ed. *Senshi Sōsho*, vol. 49: *Nantō Hōmen Kaigun Sakusen (1) Gashima Dakkai Sakusen Kaishi made*. Tokyo: Asagumo Shimbunsha, 1971.
Bōei Kenshūsho Senshishitsu, ed. *Senshi Sōsho*, vol. 80: *Daihon'ei Kaigunbu * Rengō Kantai (2) Shōwa 17-nen 6-gatsu made*. Tokyo: Asagumo Shimbunsha, 1975.
Bōei Kenshūsho Senshishitsu, ed. *Senshi Sōsho*, vol. 97: *Sensuikanshi*. Tokyo: Asagumo Shimbunsha, 1979.
Buell, T. B. *Master of Sea Power: A Biography of Fleet Admiral Ernest J. King*. Annapolis, MD: Naval Institute Press, 2012.
Carlson, E. *Joe Rochefort's War: The Odyssey of the Codebreaker Who Outwitted Yamamoto at Midway*. Annapolis, MD: Naval Institute Press, 2013.
Chihaya, M. *Nippon Kaigun no Hokori Shōkōgun*. Tokyo: Purejidentosha, 1990.

Chihaya, M. *Nippon Kaigun no Senryaku Hassō*: Haisen Chokugo no Tsūkon no Hansei. Tokyo: Purejidentosha, 1982.

Chihaya, M. *Nippon Kaigun Shippai no Honshitsu*. Tokyo: PHP Kenkyūsho, 2008.

Costello, J. *The Pacific War: 1941–1945*. New York: Harper Perennial, 1982.

Cressman, R. *That Gallant Ship: USS Yorktown (CV-5)*. Missoula, MT: 1993.

Dai Ni Fukuinkyoku Zam'mu Shōribu, ed. *Kaigun Nanyō Butai Sakusen no Kōgai narabi ni Butai Shisetsu no Ippan Jōkyō* (*Japanese Monograph No. 139*). Tokyo: Dai Ni Fukuinkyoku Zam'mu Shōribu, 1949.

Ema, T. *99 Kambaku to tomo ni*. In *Kaigun Kyūkōka Bakugekitai—99 Kambaku, Suisei, Ginga Senkishū*, by M. Nakamura, 217–64. Tokyo: Kyō no Wadaisha, 1986.

Evans, D. C., and M. R. Peattie. *Kaigun: Strategy, Tactics, and Technology in the Imperial Japanese Navy, 1887–1941*. Annapolis: Naval Institute Press, 2012.

Ewing, S. *Reaper Leader: The Life of Jimmy Flatley*. Annapolis, MD: Naval Institute Press, 2002.

Fukuchi, K. "5 Kōsen Shōkaku to Shijō Hatsu no Kūbosen: Sangokai Kaisen." In *Kūbo Kidō Butai*, edited by Maru, 32–41. Toyko: Ushioshobō Kōjinsha, 2010.

Fukuchi, K. *Kūbo Shōkaku Kaiseki*. Tokyo: Shuppan Kyōdōsha, 1962.

Fukuchi, K. *Zoku * Kaigun Kuroshio Monogatari*. Tokyo: Ushioshobō Kōjinsha, 1982.

Fukui, S. *Nihon Kūbo Monogatari*. Tokyo: Ushioshobō Kōjinsha, 2009.

Gill, G. H. *Royal Australian Navy, 1942–1945*. Volume 2, *Australia in the War of 1939–1945, Series 2: Navy*. Canberra: Australian War Memorial, 1968.

Gillison, D. N. *Royal Australian Air Force, 1939–1942*. Volume 1, *Australia in the War of 1939–1945, Series 3: Air*. Canberra: Australian War Memorial, 1962.

Hara, K. *Interijensu Kara Mita Taiheiyō Sensō*. Tokyo: Ushioshobō Kōjinsha, 2021.

Hara, S. "*Sangokai Kaisen to Nichibei no Senkun, Kūbo Shōkaku*." In *Takeki Mōdō: Taiheiyō Sensō Gunkan Senshi*. Toyko: Bungeishunjū, 2000. Ebook edition.

Hata, I., Y. Izawa, and C. Shores. *Japanese Naval Air Force Fighter Units and Their Aces 1932–1945*. London: Grub Street, 2011.

Hoehling, A. A. *The Lexington Goes Down*. Englewood Cliffs, NJ: Prentice-Hall, 1971.

Hiraide, H. *Sakusen Ichiman Kairi*. Tokyo: Gōa Nipponsha, 1942.

Holmes, W. J. *Double Edged Secrets: U.S. Naval Intelligence Operations in the Pacific during World War II*. Annapolis, MD: Naval Institute Press, 1998.

Hone, T. *Mastering the Art of Command: Adm. Chester W. Nimitz and Victory in the Pacific*. Annapolis, MD: Naval Institute Press, 2022.

Hoyt, E. *Blue Skies and Blood: The Battle of the Coral Sea*. New York: Paul S. Eriksson 1975.

Inoue Shigeyoshi Denki Kankōkai, ed. *Inoue Shigeyoshi*. Tokyo: Inoue Shigeyoshi Denki Kankōkai, 1982.

Ishikawa, S. "Kodoku na Kūbo Shōhō Sangokai ni Shisu tomo." In *Zerosen no Eikō—Ōzora no Hasha/Uijin, Nampō Sakusen, Shinjuwan Kōgeki, Sangokai Kaisen*, edited by M. Akimoto, 141–44. Tokyo: Ushioshobō Kōjinsha, 2010.

Itō, H. *Nippon Kaigun Angō no Haiboku, D Angō wa ika ni Yaburaretaka*. Tokyo: Shihō Shuppan, 2018.

Iwamoto, T. *Zerosen Gekitsui Ō: Kūsen Hachinen no Kiroku*. Tokyo: Ushioshobō Kōjinsha, 2004.

Jastrzębski, J. *Bitwa na Morzu Koralowym 2–8 V 1942*. Zabrze: Inforteditions, 2012.

Jersey, S. C. *Hell's Island: The Untold Story of Guadalcanal*. College Station: Texas A&M University Pres, 2008.

Jō, E., and M. Nomura, eds. *Jijūbukan Jō Eiichirō Nikki*. Tokyo: Kashiwa Shobō, 1982.

Johnston, S. *Queen of the Flattops: Abroad the Aircraft Carrier Lexington in the Famous Battle of the Coral Sea*. New York: Ballantine Books, 1972.

Kaigun Kōkū Hombu, ed. *Kaigun Kōkū Senki: Dai Ichi Sōkan*. Tokyo: Kaigun Kōkū Hombu, 1944.

Kanazawa, H. *Kūbo Raigekitai: Kankō Tōjōin Kūtō no Kiroku*. Tokyo: Kyō no Wadaisha, 1988.

Kawasaki, M. *Nippon Kaigun no Kōkūbokan, Sono Oitachi to Senreki*. Tokyo: Dai Nippon Kaiga, 2009.

Keith, D. *The Ship that Wouldn't Die: The Saga of the USS Neosho—A World War II Story of Courage and Survival at Sea*. New York: New Amer Library, 2015.

Kimata, J. *Nihon Kūbo Senshi*. Tokyo: Tosho Shuppansha, 1977.

Kōri, Y. *Tainan Kū Sentō Nisshi*. Tokyo: Ushioshobō Kōjinsha, 2013.

Kudo, J. "Intabyū—Sangokai Kaisen de Kūbo Shōhō no Shoki o Taiken shita Sentōki Tōjōin: Nakayama Mitsuo." *Rekishi Gunzō* 2017, no. 4 (42/2): 130–35.

Ludlum, S. D. *They Turned the War around at Coral Sea and Midway: Going to War with Yorktown's Air Group Five*. Bennington: Lulu Press, 2011.

Lundstrom, J. B. *The Black Shoe Carrier Admiral: Frank Jack Fletcher at Coral Sea, Midway, and Guadalcanal*. Annapolis, MD: Naval Institute Press, 2013.

Lundstrom, J. B. *The First South Pacific Campaign: Pacific Fleet Strategy, December 1941–June 1942*. Annapolis, MD: Naval Institute Press, 2014.

Lundstrom, J. B. *The First Team: Pacific Naval Air Combat from Pearl Harbor to Midway*. Annapolis, MD: Naval Institute Press, 2005.

MacArthur, Douglas. *Reports of General MacArthur: The Campaigns of MacArthur in the Pacific, Volume I*. Washington, DC: United States Army Center of Military History, 1994.

MacArthur, Douglas. *Reports of General MacArthur: The Campaigns of MacArthur in the Pacific, Volume II—Part I*. Washington, DC: United States Army Center of Military History, 1994.

Maru, ed. *Gunkan Meka: Nihon no Kūbo*. Tokyo: Kōjinsha, 2012.

Millot, B. *The Battle of the Coral Sea*. London: Ian Allan, 1974.

Miyao, N. *Kūbo Zuikaku kara Shinkō Maru made—Kaigun Guni Nikkishō*. Tokyo: Kindai Bungeisha, 1992.

Mombushō, ed. *Shotōka Kokugo*. Dai 8. Tokyo: Mombushō, 1942–43.

Moore, C. *Tulagi: Pacific Outpost of British Empire*. Canberra: ANU Press, 2019.

Mori, S. *Akatsuki no Sangokai*. Tokyo: Bungeishunjū, 2009.

Mori, S. *Kaigun Sentōkitai, Vol. 4, Nichibei Taiketsu*. Tokyo: R Shuppan, 1979.

Morison, S. E. *History of United States Naval Operations in World War II, Vol. 4, Coral Sea, Midway and Submarine Actions, May 1942—August 1942*. Annapolis, MD: Naval Institute Press, 2012.

Murakami, M. *Shitō no Ōzora*, Tokyo: Asahi Sonorama, 1984.

Nakajima, T. *Amerika no Senryaku to Sono Zenbō*. Tokyo: Marugen Shoten, 2015.

Nohara, S. Kūbo Tōsaiki no Dagekiryoku: *Kankō, Kambaku no Unyō to Mekanizumu*. Tokyo:⊠ Ushioshobō Kōjinsha, 2024. Kindle edition.

Okumiya, M., and J. Hirokoshi. *Zero: The Story of Japan's Air War in the Pacific—As Seen by the Enemy*. New York: Milk and Cookies Press, 2014.

Ōno, N. "Ichi-shiki Rikkō Hyōryūki." In *Kaigun Rikujō Kōgekikitai: 96 Rikkō, Ichi-shiki Rikkōtai Senkishū*, edited by K. Takahashi, 101–60. Tokyo: Kyō no Wadaisha, 1976.

Onishi, R. "Chūkōtai no Samuraitachi." In *Kaigun Rikujō Kōgekikitai: 96 Rikkō, Ichi-shiki Rikkōtai Senkishū*, edited by K. Takahashi, 161–228. Tokyo: Kyō no Wadaisha, 1976.

Parker, F. C. *A Priceless Advantage: U.S. Navy Communications Intelligence and the Battles of Coral Sea, Midway and the Aleutians*. Washington, DC: NSA, 1993.

Parshall, J., and A. Tully. *Shattered Sword: The Untold Story of the Battle of Midway*. Dulles, VA: Potomac Books, 2005.

Peattie, M. R. *Sunburst: The Rise of Japanese Naval Air Power 1909–1941*. Annapolis, MD: Naval Institute Press, 1999.

Piegzik, M. A. *The Darkest Hour, Volume 1: The Japanese Offensive in the Indian Ocean 1942—The Japanese Naval Offensive in the Indian Ocean 1942—The Opening Moves*. Warwick: Helion, 2022.

Piegzik, M. A. *The Darkest Hour, Volume 2: The Japanese Offensive in the Indian Ocean 1942—The Attack against Ceylon and the Eastern Fleet*. Warwick: Helion and Co., 2022.

Piegzik, M. A. *Into the Endless Mist, Volume 1: The Aleutian Islands Campaign, June–August 1942*. Warwick: Helion and Co., 2023.

Piegzik, M. A. *Morze Koralowe 1942*. Warsaw: Bellona, 2016

Pike, F. *Hirohito's War: The Pacific War, 1941–1945*. London: Bloomsbury Academic, 2015.

Potter, E. B. *Nimitz*. Annapolis, MD: Naval Institute Press, 2008.

Prados, J. *Combined Fleet Decoded: The Secret History of American Intelligence and the Japanese Navy in World War II*. New York: Random House, 1995.

Salecker, G. *Fortress against the Sun: The B-17 Flying Fortress in the Pacific*. Conshohocken, PA: Combined Publishing, 2001.

Spectator, R. H. *Eagle against the Sun: The American War with Japan*. New York: Random House USA, 1985.

Stern, R. C. *Scratch One Flattop: The First Carrier Air Campaign and the Battle of the Coral Sea*. Bloomington: Indiana University Press, 2019.

Stille, S. *Coral Sea 1942: The First Carrier Battle*. Oxford: Osprey, 2009.

Sugawara, K. *I-21 Sen Funsen no Kiroku*. Tokyo: Shuppan Kyōdōsha, 1969.

Tagaya, O. *Aichi 99 Kanbaku "Val" Units 1937–42*. Oxford: Osprey, 2011.

Tagaya, O. *Mitsubishi Type 1 Rikko "Betty" Units of World War 2*. Oxford: Osprey, 2001.

Takahashi, K. "Chōken Senki: Shinjuwan Kōgeki no Kambaku Taichō ga Tsutsuru Wakakihi no Sentōroku, Takahashi Kakuichi (Chū, Nanshi Jinchū Nikki)." *Maru* 2004 (57/11): 231–57.

Takahashi, T. *Tettei Kaibatsu: Jūjun Kako Kanchō Kaisōki*. Tokyo: Kōjinsha, 1994.

Tendō, A. *Sangokai Daikaisen*. Tokyo: Masushobō, 1956.

Tilman, B. *TBD Devastator Units of the US Navy*. Oxford, UK: Osprey, 2000.

Toland, J. *The Rising Sun: The Decline and Fall of the Japanese Empire: The Decline and Fall of the Japanese Empire, 1936–1945*. New York: Modern Library, 2003.

Tominaga, K. *Daihon'ei Happyō Kaigunhen*. Tokyo: Seichōcha, 1952.

U.S. Navy. *The Battle of the Coral Sea: Combat Narratives*. Washington, DC: Office of Naval Intelligence, 1943.

Uematsu, S. *Nihon Kaigun Kōkūtai*. Tokyo: Arusu, 1944.

Ugaki, M. *Sensōroku*, vol. 1, edited by K. Handō. Tokyo: PHP Kenkyūsho, 2019.

Watanabe, N. *Minamijūjisei wa Mite Ita—Shōkaku Gunikan Nikki*. Tokyo: Self-Publishing, 1984.

Werneth, R. *Beyond Pearl Harbor: The Untold Stories of Japan's Naval Aviation*. Atglen, PA: Schiffer, 2008.

Willmott, H. P. *The Barrier and the Javelin: Japanese and Allied Pacific Strategies February to June 1942*. Annapolis, MD: Naval Institute Press, 1983.

Willmott, H. P. *Empires in the Balance: Japanese and Allied Pacific Strategies to April 1942*. Annapolis, MD: Naval Institute Press, 1982.

Willmott, H. P. *The War with Japan: The Period of Balance, May 1942–October 1943*. Wilmington, DE: Rowman and Littlefield, 2002.

Yokoya, H. "Sangokai Kaisen ni okeru Nihongawa no Sakuteki ni tsuite—Gogatsu Nanoka o Chūshin ni." *Gunji Shigaku* 48(2) (2012): 112–29.

Index

ABOUT THE AUTHOR

Michał A. Piegzik is a lecturer at Edinburgh Napier University with a PhD in Japanese private law. He was awarded the Japanese Ministry of Education scholarship for exceptional research results. The Pacific War is his life's passion. He has published in Poland, Japan, the UK, and the Netherlands. *Gamble in the Coral Sea* is his debut book in the United States.

The Naval Institute Press is the book-publishing arm of the U.S. Naval Institute, a private, nonprofit, membership society for sea service professionals and others who share an interest in naval and maritime affairs. Established in 1873 at the U.S. Naval Academy in Annapolis, Maryland, where its offices remain today, the Naval Institute has members worldwide.

Members of the Naval Institute support the education programs of the society and receive the influential monthly magazine *Proceedings* or the colorful bimonthly magazine *Naval History* and discounts on fine nautical prints and on ship and aircraft photos. They also have access to the transcripts of the Institute's Oral History Program and get discounted admission to any of the Institute-sponsored seminars offered around the country.

The Naval Institute's book-publishing program, begun in 1898 with basic guides to naval practices, has broadened its scope to include books of more general interest. Now the Naval Institute Press publishes about seventy titles each year, ranging from how-to books on boating and navigation to battle histories, biographies, ship and aircraft guides, and novels. Institute members receive significant discounts on the Press' more than eight hundred books in print.

Full-time students are eligible for special half-price membership rates. Life memberships are also available.

For more information about Naval Institute Press books that are currently available, visit www.usni.org/press/books. To learn about joining the U.S. Naval Institute, please write to:

Member Services
U.S. Naval Institute
291 Wood Road
Annapolis, MD 21402-5034
Telephone: (800) 233-8764
Fax: (410) 571-1703
Web address: www.usni.org